RAILROADIN' SOME

RAILROADIN' SOME

Railroads in the Early Blues

MAX HAYMES

MUSIC MENTOR BOOKS
York, England

© 2006 Max Haymes. All rights reserved. First edition.

The right of Max Haymes to be identified as Author of this Work has been asserted in accordance with the UK *Copyright, Designs and Patents Act 1988*.

Every effort has been made to trace the copyright holders of material used in this volume. Should there be any omissions in this respect, we apologise and shall be pleased to make the appropriate acknowledgments in future printings.

A full list of illustrations and photo credits appears on page 386. The trade marks Bluebird, Brunswick, Columbia, Decca, OKeh, Paramount, Victor and Vocalion appear by kind permission of the owners.

All rights reserved. No part of this publication may be reproduced, stored in a retrieval system or transmitted in any form by any means, electronic, mechanical, reprographic, recording or otherwise without prior written permission from the publisher.

This book is sold subject to the conditions that it shall not, by way of trade or otherwise, be lent, resold, hired out or otherwise circulated without the publisher's prior consent in any form of binding or cover other than that in which it is published and without a similar condition including this condition being imposed on the subsequent purchaser.

Whilst every effort has been made to ensure the correctness of information included in this book, the publisher makes no representation — either express or implied — as to its accuracy and cannot accept any legal responsibility for any errors or omissions or consequences arising therefrom.

British Library Cataloguing-in-Publication Data
A catalogue record for this book is available from the British Library.

ISBN: 0-9547068-3-8
ISBN-13: 978-0-9547068-3-8

Published worldwide by Music Mentor Books *(Proprietor: G.R. Groom-White)*
69 Station Road, Upper Poppleton, York YO26 6PZ, North Yorkshire, England.
Telephone/Fax: +44 (0)1904 330308   *Email:* music.mentor@lineone.net

Cover by It's Great To Be Rich, York and Max Haymes.

Printed and bound by CPI Antony Rowe, Eastbourne

Front cover photo: The *Sunset* on the T&NO running through sugar fields just east of New Iberia, La., c.late 1930s.

Back cover photo: Tail-end of the *Flying Crow* on the KCS, c.late 1920s or early 30s.

For Zena, Celia, and Rex.

All the African American blues & gospel singers
who have made my life so rich in its quality.

Acknowledgments

First off, despite drawing on over four decades of research and listening to early blues and gospel recordings, there are bound to be some errors and of course these are down to me as the author. I would also like to apologize, in advance, for any inadvertent omissions of photo and text source credits.

I couldn't possibly have completed this book (over the last six years) without the unstinting support of many people within the world of the blues — particularly from Dai Thomas, one of the world's most authentic-sounding rural blues singer/guitarists. Not only did he supply equipment, recordings and invaluable books and other material, especially concerning the 'comic' song, *Billy Barlow*, but also intelligent and on-the-ball criticism when reading parts of the manuscript. Not forgetting the camaraderie of the 'all-dayer' blues and booze sessions! Also, our website master (**www.earlyblues.com**), Alan White. His superior technological know-how has resulted in over 70,000 'hits' to date. He also supplied much material without which *Railroadin' Some* would have been much the poorer. Like Alan, Mike Winstanley is a former student of mine, and he too (as with Dai) has become a close friend who has often furnished me with details of obscure US book titles which I have always found essential references, as well as books themselves and many recordings. I must also offer truly heartfelt thanks to Paul Swinton who shared some of his large 78s collection and memorabilia from the 1920s and '30s, including many excellent label shots which feature throughout this book. Ken Smith of Red Lick Records fame is another long-standing colleague who wrote a report on part of the manuscript which gave me the shot-in-the-arm that I didn't realize I needed! Ta, Ken. Robin Andrews, another regular 'all-dayer' attendee, for not only supplying recording material but in-depth and challenging discussions on the early blues (Hey! It's not *all* booze!) and yet another warmly valued friendship. Apart from being a great and sensitive harp blower, he is also pretty nifty on guitar and washboard. Keep playing and singing those old 'Rising River Blues', Robin!

Although I have listed all my sources (hopefully) in the Chapter Notes and the Bibliography, I would like to take this opportunity to thank all the great research efforts and writings that have gone before me; on which I have drawn so freely. Many of these sources go back seventy years or more, some to the early Eighteenth Century, and others to nearly yesterday. Much of this

Acknowledgments

material was originally from the British Lending Library and the British Library in St. Pancras, London. Ain't learnin' fun? It's just too much! I would also like to give thanks to the excellent team at Lancashire C.C. Library in Lancaster, who over the years have obtained some of the most obscure books/microfilms about the Deep South from the Nineteenth Century onwards. I mean, how many subscribers in the North-West of England are going to ask for (and get!) a book on Nineteenth Century black labour in the coal mines of southern Alabama! And an equally brilliant bunch at the Lancaster branch of Waterstone's for getting me all books I ordered (or very nearly) – and then some. And having the never-ending patience to put up with my many visits and endless enquiries. Especially Nina, Chrissie, Laura, and Phil.

I would also add my undying gratitude to the blues writer I deem, as do many thousands of others, to be the Dean of Bluesology. Back in 1960, along with American Sam Charters, Paul Oliver was 'the frontiersman' of the history concerning early blues and gospel. He wrote in his still classic and essential book, *Blues Fell This Morning*: '…in order to understand the blues singers it is necessary to explore the background of their themes, and try to enter their world through them, distant and unapproachable though it may be.' I have tried to follow that maxim for the last forty-odd years, Paul, and it has enriched my life immeasurably in the way I view the world at large; and helped me put some further understanding of the Blues genre into *Railroadin' Some* — at least I hope so. Thank you.

I count the weekly acoustic blues jam sessions at the Golden Lion, and then the Korner's Bar at the Farmer's Arms in Lancaster as an invaluable event. Not only as a place to hear some very fine live blues, but also an excellent social contact point which has also furthered interest in the early blues itself. Thanks to Martin, Dave, Dan, Judy and Brendan, Adrian and Victoria, Sabina and Andrew, the two Mikes, and all the other blues cats who make the atmosphere so 'cool', don't you know.

I would like to extend my greatest heartfelt thanks to my publisher George Groom-White at Music Mentor Books, for having faith in this project. But also for being great to work with and for his several pointers and suggestions (some of which I agreed with!). Cheers, George!

Also my brotherly thanks to Sylvia, who has always supported my efforts, even if she does live some 250 miles down the line. Cheers, Sis. Have one on me! Also my kid brother Rex, who cut his teeth on my 1950s rock'n'roll collection and has travelled on down that Big Road of the Blues with me ever since. A great guitar player and singer, he perpetuates the artistry and feel of our blues heroes from the 1920s, '30s, and '40s. Apart from the odd drink (what?!?!), he has also created some fabulous meals at the 'all dayer' sessions; as well as many, many in-depth (and challenging!) discussions on the blues and just about everything else to put the world to rights. Thanks, Little Bro.

Acknowledgments

Finally, I would like to give my loving thanks, firstly to Celia (that precious, significant other in my life), who even though she is not into early blues to the same level as me, has always been there for me and given moral support and good advice, and understands more lyrics of early blues recordings than most people! Some more malt whisky and 'Reemy Martin' — IF YOU PLEASE!

And lastly, I want to thank my daughter, Zena — herself a pianist/guitarist composer and music therapist. She is also one mean blues singer. She has given me support always — even sometimes when her Dad could be wrong! Her love for music in general matches mine for the blues and, as the great Memphis Minnie once sang, she is going to 'keep the good work on'. Margs, you can be justly proud — thank you.

Ultimately, I thank the early blues singers, most of whom have hoboed their way to that great barrelhouse in the sky. Your art lives! And, as the King of the Delta Blues, Charlie Patton, sang in 1929: *'How can I lose, Lord, with the help I got?'* *

Max Haymes
Lancaster, March 2006

---

* 'Banty Rooster Blues' [Paramount 12792], recorded 14 June 1929 in Grafton, Wis..

Acknowledgments

Contents

Introduction 15

1 Smokestack is black, an' the bell it shine like gold 25
Brief background of railroads in the antebellum era and slaves' involvement — role of Pullman and Red Cap porters — the *Panama Limited* — origins of 'smokestack lightning' and Charley Patton — 'ticket as long as my right arm', 'ballin' the jack' — the 'other' *Midnight Special* — Texas & New Orleans RR and Lucille Bogan.

2 Skippin' 'round from log to log 49
Evolution of logging camps in the South — origins of piano blues, boogie woogie and the barrelhouse — oral transmission of early blues via logging roads — more on the T&NO.

3 Ah! When I leave here, gonna catch that M&O 85
The story of the Mobile & Ohio and the blues from 1852 to 1940; a 'journey' from Mobile to St. Louis — background of the floating bridge of Sleepy John Estes fame — Cairo, Ill. — the real facts of Casey Jones' train wreck in 1900 — river bottoms — the Union Stockyard in Meridian, Miss. — oral transmission and (a) way freight trains on the M&O, (b) stevedores at Mobile Bay.

4 She's givin' it away 121
Short history of the refrigerator car or 'reefer' from 1858 to 1910 — introduction of the banana to the 'masses' in the black community — fast freights: the 'redball' and the 'hotshot' — hoboing on a reefer with T-Bone Walker and David 'Honeyboy' Edwards — sexual symbolism and street market blues — English music hall link with some early vaudeville-blues singers.

5 Goin' where the Southern cross the Yellow Dog 143
Origins of the 'yellow dog' — short history of the Yazoo & Mississippi Valley RR — pea vine railroads — brief survey of labour history and anti-union railroad companies — yellow dog contracts — recordings of the Yellow Dog from 1923 to 1961, by Sam Collins, Bessie Smith *et al*.

6 An' that thing don't keep-a ringing so soon 161
Brief study of early Southern prison/correction systems — convict lease and railroads' involvement — source of the 'longest train' motif in the blues — origin of 'In The Pines' — Joseph E. Brown and Peg Leg Howell — brief survey of the Tennessee Coal, Iron & Railroad Co. or 'TCI', and singers — Railroad Bill and the L&N — short history of Gulfport & Ship Island RR and Robert Johnson link — the 'ding dong' and Frank Stokes.

7 Runnin' down to the station 199
Resumé of beginnings of the *Fast Mail* in 1875 — importance to rural South — source of John Byrd's 'Billy Goat Blues' in the 1850s — fast mail trains such as the *Big 80* and the *Sunnyland* — lineage of Robert Johnson's 'fastest train I see' verse — streamline trains — blues singers' knowledge of railroad operations — the railroad depot: the seamier side and the 'leaving scene' in the blues. As related by Robert Wilkins, Roosevelt Sykes, Ma Rainey and Robert Johnson.

8 I carried water for the elephant 239
Short history of development of circus and carnival in the South — beginnings of medicine shows — circuses in Natchez, Miss. during antebellum era and the early minstrel song, 'Billy Barlow' — excursion trains — blues singers' role in circus and origin of 'ballyhoo' — circus and carnival slang used in the blues — role of steam calliope — short survey of origin of 'hokum' and hokum blues — the railroad crossing — vaudeville-blues singers and travelling shows including Clara Smith — oral transmission process.

9 Gonna leave a Pullman an' ride the L&N 273
Vaudeville blues lyrics and influence on rural singers like Blind Lemon Jefferson by Sippie Wallace, Ida Cox and others — oral transmission and the blues record — passenger train women, platform vendors and Blind Boy Fuller — survey and ancestry of 'Careless Love' — Mae Glover, John Byrd, Bobby Grant and Buddy Boy Hawkins — roots of 'Statesboro Blues' by Blind Willie McTell.

10 Lined out smokin', look like it takin' to scat 301
Short survey of early tramps and hobos on the rails — women hobos and Memphis Minnie — Chicago, the railroad hobo's Mecca — hobo jungles and 'Hoovervilles' — symbolism of the railroad and ultimate freedom for the hobo — 'The Atlanta Special', Bukka White and Blind Willie McTell — riding the blinds and riding the rods — railroad police and Sleepy John Estes — origins of 'hobo'.

Epilogue 337

Contents

Appendix I 343

Appendix II 345

Appendix III 349

Bibliography 351

Glossary of Railroad Abbreviations & Nicknames 363

Index of Artists' Names 365

Index of Song Titles 370

General Index 376

Photo Credits 386

Contents

Introduction

This book sets out to illustrate the world of the blues singers as it appeared to them in the earliest decades of the Twentieth Century; via the lyrics of their songs and contemporary reportage, both written and pictorial. The latter is especially concerned with the major industries in which the African American was involved during this era: the railroads, lumber, mining, turpentine and also in the world of the Southern prison systems in particular. Also, the blues singer's world of entertainment such as the travelling shows, barrelhouses, brothels, etc. Another major objective is to emphasize the central role and importance of the railroad/train/depot to the blues genre itself in that world. Its potential as a form of free transportation, influence on lyrics and symbolism used, playing styles, and its acceleration of the oral transmission process whereby the music 'travelled' much faster from town to town and state to state than had previously been possible.

As the lives of countless working-class blacks depended so much on the railroad and its subsequent development of Southern (and indeed the whole of the US) urban society, it will be necessary to delve into the background of some of the icons of the twin steel rails which were either featured in, or at least influenced so many of the blues sung and recorded in the pre-war era: 1890-1943.

Even before the first business corporations existed, 'land companies issued shares and created many of the financial and legal structures that the Nineteenth Century stock-dealing capitalist economy used to finance the railroads and industrialisation of the United States.'[1] From 1832 onwards, the smallest plot of land that a farmer could bid for at a government land auction was 'the quarter-quarter section, or forty acres, a parcel that has entered American rural mythology... It was the minimum area that was needed to support the average family. Railroads sold land by the forty-acre lot *[and]* after the Civil War, freed slaves were reckoned to be self-sufficient with 'forty acres and a mule'.[2]

This quarter-quarter section or 'forty' appears in one of the earliest songs recalled by contemporaries of the archetypal bluesman Charley Patton, and they claimed he performed 'Mississippi Boweavil Blues' [Paramount 12805] in 1929 in much the same way he would have done around 1910, way down in Mississippi:

Introduction

Boll weevil's lil' wife went [and] sat down on the hill, Lordy.
Boll weevil told 'is wife: 'Let's take this forty here', Lordy. [3]

Although most of the land was sold off to farmers, 'the real money lay in towns'. Railroad companies were given the incentive to build by the Federal Government, who awarded them 'blocks of land, usually a township but sometimes more, alternating on either side of the track.' Many railroads, such as the Illinois Central and the Chicago, Burlington & Quincy 'designed a standard town that could be laid out and sold off wherever they decided to site a passenger and freight depot.' [4] The real attraction was the simple or 'basic model' on which each lot could be measured out. Consisting of 'three 160-acre sections on each side of the track, each section being split four ways into those forty acre — twenty by twenty chains — lots that a surveyor could measure with his eyes closed.' Linklater quotes an earlier Twentieth Century surveyor who claimed that 'with a T-square and a triangle... the municipal engineer, without the slightest training as either an architect or a sociologist, could "plan" a metropolis.' [5]

What made this basic measuring model most attractive to railroad companies was its cheapness to use. Apparently, the most that the CB&Q was prepared to pay to have a town planned was $7. 'Sometimes, the companies built only on one side of the tracks, in which case they simply cut the plan in half, but the depot always remained the focal point.' [6] In these cases, the undeveloped side would later acquire shacks and shanties for the poorest section of the community. In the South, this was often the African American. So, even before a town was built, the large majority of blacks — including the blues singers — were destined to live on the 'wrong side of the tracks'. Of course, fraud and corruption often ran alongside a company's intention to build a railroad through a particular locality, and they often deserved the label 'robber barons'. With the collusion of such a railroad, some of the most powerful and influential citizens in one town would ensure they got a line that avoided a rival town.

This was also true of plantations. Many of the larger ones made sure of securing a railroad's services by fair means or foul — usually the latter. A slave, 'Solomon Bradley... 27... in South Carolina in 1863' tells of an horrific attack on a female slave by a plantation owner, and refers to the incident as 'the most shocking thing that I have seen was on the plantation of Mr. Farrarby, on the line of the railroad.' [7]

Prison farms too were often served by the railroad. Indeed, by the Twentieth Century, Mississippi's infamous State Penitentiary at Parchman Farm had 'in fact, all the establishments that one would typically find in any Delta town, including, of course, a railroad depot with a gin[*] and adjacent

---

[*] A gin was a building where cotton was processed ready for the commercial market, most importantly separating the seeds from the cotton bloom.

warehouses.'[8] And, 'as early as 1905, rail spurs had begun to reach into the plantation; now they reached farther, accelerating clearing operations, bringing the wilderness to heel.'[9] In fact, by 1917, these clearing operations at Parchman 'were virtually complete... Outside the front gate were warehouses, a larger gin, and a railroad depot. One crossed the tracks to approach the gate.'[10]

The railroad was part of virtually every facet of black life in the predominantly rural South during the closing years of the Nineteenth Century and the first few decades of the Twentieth. The region's rail system was built by mostly black labour — slave and freedman — and maintained by blacks after the Civil War. The railroad was also the largest employer of African Americans in the earlier part of the Twentieth Century, usually as trackside labourers, porters or 'grease monkeys' working in the engine sheds or roundhouse. On rarer occasions, they worked as firemen on the locomotives.

At that time, the railroad was the fastest form of transport, as highways were often in a bad condition and did not exist in the South as a joined-up system until well into the 1930s, for a variety of reasons. In 1936, Thomas Clark, an Illinois Central chronicler, stated that 'muddy roads were the bane of rural life in Mississippi, and the Illinois Central's southern lines in reality pulled the state out of the mud, for the highways were nothing more than disfiguring muddy "traces" across the landscape.'[11] Things had only really started to improve for highways a few years prior to Clark writing these words. The situation was fairly similar across the South, and even in the Northern state of Maryland during the same year Hyatt noted 'there were still few cars* in 1936 — roads could be muddy and sometimes sandy towards the water.'[12]

This era from the 1890s to the early 1940s covers the approximate period when the blues were generally deemed to have evolved and flourished, helped to some extent by the recording of the music from 1920 onwards. Bluesman 'Honeyboy' Edwards recalled a medicine show in 1934: 'We'd set up and play on flatcars on the railroad tracks. We'd set up there on the platforms and play different things, tell jokes and lies... I'd play a few Lemon Jefferson songs like *'Blues come to Texas lopin' like a mule / Brownskin woman hard to fool.'* I used to play that pretty good. *'Lay me down a pallet on the floor / Make it down by your door.'* I used to play all that old stuff like that.'[13] Indeed, the railroad figures in 'Crazy Blues' by Mamie Smith [OKeh 4169] — the first blues ever committed to record — in August 1920; these recordings, as I have said, making a large contribution to this book as part of its central theme.

Not only did the railroad help spread the blues to the farthest corners of the map, it also contributed to the sounds that players adopted — especially

---

* This is the only time in this work that 'car' refers to an automobile rather than a railroad vehicle, and 'road' means a highway.

Introduction

in the driving boogie rhythms *(Chapter 2)* of pianists like Joe Dean or George Noble. This is admirably demonstrated by the Chicago-based Noble's thundering left hand, interspersed with flashes of brilliance in his right on such titles as 'If You Lose Your Good Gal, Don't Mess With Mine' *b/w* 'The Seminole Blues' (named after an IC train) [A.R.C. 7-06-75], both recorded in 1935. Or the 'screaming howl' of the harp (harmonica) solo from the unique George 'Bullet' Williams on 'Frisco Leaving Birmingham' [Paramount 12651] in 1928, and the moaning, droning fiddle of Andrew Baxter on 'The Moore Girl' [Victor 21475] and 'KC Railroad Blues' [Victor 20962] from 1927. All of these artists and many more besides must have been inspired by the sound of the trains as they whistled for the crossing and rumbled through the Southern countryside.

The 'Moore Girl', as Wyatt states, 'is most likely a misnomer for 'mogul', a type of freight locomotive.'[14] Or, more correctly, a misheard pronunciation. In black Southern parlance this title would come across as 'Mo'gul', as indeed would 'Moore Girl'. They were a particular type of freight locomotive used in both south and north Georgia, as well as other states such as Tennessee and North Carolina. Characterised by a 2-6-0 wheel formation, they were supplanted by more modern and powerful locos by the turn of the Twentieth Century. The Nashville, Chattanooga & St. Louis Railway sold the last of their quota of Moguls in 1919. These engines 'dated back to 1872-73'.[15] The NC&St.L served Calhoun, Georgia in Gordon County *en route* from Atlanta via Nashville to Chattanooga, Tenn..

In the absence of any written word left by the early blues singers at the time[*] and as the main theme of this book, I am using the content of their songs, coupled with relevant facts about Southern railroads and some Northern ones too — which are obviously linked — to hopefully present a more detailed picture of the environs of the early blues singer.[**] Although the vast majority of books on US railroads (and there are lots of them) don't mention the African American[***], much less the blues, some of these works do throw a light on the scene as it was in the South and in Chicago, New York and elsewhere at the time. They also contain some fascinating pictures.

Some of these railroad books contain written descriptions and

---

[*] Some essential books on both early blues and gospel have been written since 1959 into the Twenty-First Century. See the Bibliography for details of some of them.

[**] Some blues featured in the text could be open to different interpretations, because, generally, these songs come from a different ethnic group, culture and time period and are therefore sometimes difficult to comprehend. While I respect any alternatives to my own interpretations, I reserve the right to use the latter. This is based on over forty years listening to and researching early blues and gospel recordings. By digging much deeper into the socio-economic and industrial background of the blues singer, I am proud to feel I have an understanding far beyond that of the average reader. My quote from Paul Oliver, with my added comments in the *Acknowledgements* at the beginning of this book, refers.

[***] For the sake of brevity, I shall generally use the terms 'blacks' and 'whites' throughout the book, and 'African American' only occasionally.

illustrations — several of which are included here — such as the (railroad) car ferry/float bridge operations made famous by Sleepy John Estes in his 'Floating Bridge' [Decca 7442] in 1937; the sources of *'highball'* and the *'longest train I seen'*, featured by singers such as Barbecue Bob, Henry Thomas and Peg Leg Howell; together with views of how the Union Station in Chicago looked to singers arriving from the South during the second and third decades of the Twentieth Century.

These descriptions add something concrete to the lyrics, which remain indisputable and give us, here in the Twenty-First Century, much more of a sense of what was being sung about. Or, put another way, they fill in some of the gaps in our perception of the world that the blues singers lived in. Too often in the past, certain writers have warned against accepting a singer's words as being true. While there is some wisdom in this, it has also had the effect — quite accidentally, I'm sure — of deterring much serious research into what the blues was *actually* referring to on many occasions. This included numerous references to particular railroads and their ways of operating from the main source of a description of the blues world — the singers themselves. A rare exception to this seems to be Scrapper Blackwell's song about the Yellow Dog, 'Goin' Where The Monon Crosses The Yellow Dog' [LP **Blues Before Sunrise** (77 LA-12-4) 1960], composed and recorded in his later years *(see Chapter 5)*. Several railroads which figure prominently in the blues started life in the antebellum period during the 1850s. These include the Illinois Central, the Frisco and the Mobile & Ohio. Within the three decades following the end of the Civil War, other roads popular with the blues singer were up and running — the Southern, Santa Fe and Texas & Pacific among them. By the time that blues records were being produced in the 1920s, these and a host of other roads were serving all the Southern states from whence the blues sprang into life: Mississippi, Texas, Georgia, Alabama, Tennessee, Louisiana and the Carolinas.

As the blues is based on an oral tradition and was sung, in this earlier period, by working-class blacks for working-class blacks, there is not a great deal of literature that historians can turn to for information and guidance. Fortunately, it is *primarily* a vocal music, and the importance of the lyrics in the blues cannot be overstressed. What singers said in their songs — and they sang the same way they spoke — was the main message in any given blues. If an experience related by a bluesman/woman had not been theirs, they knew full well it had happened to many of thousands in their audience. Because of this knowledge, a two-way traffic existed between the listeners and the artists, and created a solidarity within the black community which continues to this day.

One of the few black writers on blues, Daphne Duval Harrison, gives an example of Texas singer Sippie Wallace, who 'sang for her living, that was her job; and she believed that when she provided her listeners with information about her life that might help them come to grips with their own lives.' [16] The philosophical and psychological knowledge that 'I ain't the only one' when concerned with everyday problems and situations gives the blues an unassailable strength. As Blind Willie McTell sang in 1931 on 'Broke Down Engine Blues' [Columbia 14632-D] to his own phenomenal guitar accompaniment:

> Feel like a broke down engine, ain't got no drivin' wheel.
> Feel like a broke down engine, mama, ain't got no drivin' wheel.
> You ever been down an' lonesome, you know how a poor man feel.
>
> Feel like a broke down engine, ain't got no whistle or bell. *(x2)*
> If you'se a real hot mama, drive away daddy's weepin' spell.
> *(Spoken)* I won't be back no more, baby.[17]

That is why artists who recorded prolifically — such as Walter Davis, Peetie Wheatstraw, Kokomo Arnold and Barbecue Bob — were so popular, even though they used a favourite accompaniment for much of their output. The same could be said of highly successful post-war singers such as Lightnin' Hopkins, Elmore James and John Lee Hooker. This does not detract from the often superlative and very moving music that these performers produced. Indeed, it obviously added to the popularity of their records.

Early blues singers would quite freely use verses from other performers or their records, but they would normally adapt them to their own situation and singing/playing style. For example, on 'Cow Cow Blues' [OKeh 8250] from 1925, Dora Carr sings that, from hearsay, her lover left town on a train running either on the Seaboard Air Line (SAL) or the Western & Atlantic *(see Chapter 9)*. Given that she was based in Alabama for a while, this sounds logical, as both railroads served the state. However, when Charlie McCoy from Jackson, Miss. used the same verse for his 'I've Been Blue Ever Since You Went Away' [OKeh 8881] in 1930, he substituted the Southern and the Chicago & Alton. One main line on the Southern Railway ran from Meridian, Miss. to St. Louis, Mo., where the C&A continued on to Chicago (where McCoy was recording this song). On the way home, he would have had to change at Meridian and catch the Illinois Central back to Jackson.

It is also important to consider the popular — and personal — concept of the blues singer of his/her surroundings. Some would refer to the Baltimore & Ohio line from Cincinnati to Chicago as the 'Monon', which in fact only had trackage rights granted by the B&O. But the blues singer saw Monon rolling stock (freight and passenger) on this stretch of the B&O and assumed it was the Monon; or the Chicago, Indianapolis & Louisville RR. Similarly, Lee Brown could leave Dyersburg, Tenn. (his home town) on a Mobile & Ohio freight and make a detour to Kokomo, Miss. (via the Fernwood, Columbia & Gulf RR) before joining the New Orleans, Jackson & Great Northern going on down to New Orleans. As far as Brown was concerned, he was riding in an M&O box car, so it was still the Mobile & Ohio RR *(Chapter 3)*. He was therefore quite happy to sing on his version of 'Sweet Home Chicago', 'Down By The M&O' [Decca 7587]:

> She cried, 'Oh, baby, don't you want to go
> To that eleven-light city, down by that M&O?' [18]

when referring to Kokomo, which was on the FC&G.

Not only did the trackage rights of different railroads put 'foreign' rolling stock on the tracks — there was also the 'interchange system'. This was an agreement made between all US roads just after the end of the Civil War. 'The interchange of cars among the nation's railways… in effect took a fragmented collection of several hundred independent rail lines and turned it into one unified system so far as the movement of through freight was concerned. A single car could go from one end of the system over a dozen railroads and never be unloaded or turned back.' All companies agreed to any repairs needed *en route* and would be reimbursed. In the event of a box car being destroyed — in a crash, for example — the owner would be compensated. This system worked, because 'everyone benefited'. White adds that 'it was figured as a general rule that 40 percent of the cars on any given railroad were foreign or borrowed cars. Full and empty, hundreds of thousands of lookalike cars rattled around the countryside or stood idle in yards often thousands of miles from home.' [19]

An illustration of this personal (albeit not always factually correct) view by the blues singer is given by Joe Dean. This pianist recorded just two sides in 1930 for the Vocalion label and, in addition to the brilliant boogie-based 'I'm So Glad I'm Twenty-One Years Old Today' [Vocalion 1544], he cut the slower 'Mexico Bound Blues'. Dean said later that he got inspiration for this title after seeing a freight train passing in Newton, Kan. with *'Mexico'* on the side of the box cars. They probably belonged to the Texas Mexican Railway Company, which was ultimately controlled by the National Railways of Mexico. He told his interviewer that, before doing a gig in Newton, he went and sat by the railroad tracks where the Santa Fe crossed the Missouri Pacific as 'I always liked trains.' [20] The Mexican box cars were part of a Santa Fe freight that went chugging by and 'I knew that the Santa Fe road ran into Mexico, so I said to myself: "This train must be going to Mexico, or it's Mexico-bound." And right then and there I conceived the idea for that song, 'Mexico Bound' — because that train must have been bound for Mexico.' [17] In truth, the box cars in question could have been headed for Memphis, New Orleans or any number of destinations within the US border, only finally becoming 'Mexico Bound' weeks or months later.

Although hailing from St. Louis, he was billed as 'Joe Dean (From Bowling Green)' for his recording — apparently just because it rhymed! Bowling Green is actually in Kentucky, and this thwarted researchers for years before he was finally rediscovered. As with many of his surviving contemporaries, he was now a man of the church but quite happy to talk about earlier days and the blues.

Although Dean liked trains, they embodied a whole range of emotions in the minds of blacks — from the sheer joy of freedom when travelling aimlessly *(Chapter 10)* or with a circus or show *(Chapter 8)*, to the heartbreak and despair of a lover's final farewell at the station *(Chapter 7)*, to the horror and fear of forced work on the railroad in the brutal convict-lease system *(Chapter 6)* to the hope that railroads represented when they took on black workers in the thousands — even if the majority of the jobs were the lowest paid in the industry by the 1900s. These would include Pullman porters and Red Caps *(Chapter 1)* and trackside labourers. Compared to the dangerous and often very unhealthy conditions in the logging and turpentine camps 'reserved' for black workers *(Chapter 2)*, the railroad was king in more ways than one.

On a more general note concerning the text, the following points should be observed. Unless otherwise indicated, all the singers and musicians are/were black and all the writers are/were white. A discography has been included at the end of every chapter, listing details of CDs (and a handful of vinyl releases) which feature all the blues I have quoted either in part or completely. Many of these are from the Document label, which is easily available and generally offers good sound quality. Until recently, their catalogue contained over 800 CDs[*] for collectors who, like me, 'just have to have' all of an artist's output, and are also essential tools of research. For those who want only a representative selection — often in even better sound — there are the Yazoo, Catfish, J.S.P., Old Hat and Frog labels, although again some items have been deleted from their catalogues over the last few years. Nevertheless, the interested reader can rest assured that these labels are the best in the pre-war blues and gospel field and, like me, will inevitably find CDs from all of them appearing in his/her collection. Complete details of the 'Notes' at the end of each chapter are listed in the *Bibliography*.

Whilst I have attempted a form of chronology in the text in regard to the development of the blues, as well as to continuity, there are obviously going to be overlaps, as with life in general. One of several examples occurs in *Chapter 4*, where the experiences of hoboing and riding refrigerator cars related by David 'Honeyboy' Edwards and T-Bone Walker could just as easily have been slotted into *Chapter 10*. Some railroad legends such as Railroad Bill and Casey Jones are covered, but I have omitted John Henry. The reason for this is that so much has already been written about the 'steel-driving man', and an entire book devoted to him — *John Henry: An American Legend* by Ezra Jack Keats (Sagebrush, 1999 (reprinted from 1987)) — has

---

[*] Sadly, within the last few years, Document have inexplicably withdrawn around 60% of this total!

reappeared within the last few years.

It should also be noted that, in the world of the blues, there are two artists who went by the name of 'Sonny Boy Williamson'. The older man, Rice Miller from Mississippi, did not make any discs until the early 1950s, as far as we know; only John Lee Williamson recorded in the pre-war era. Commencing in 1937, the latter had a successful career with recordings and live performances until his untimely death in Chicago in 1948. Originally from Jackson, Tenn., this artist is the one referred to throughout in the text.

Also in this blues world, the word 'Delta' refers to a specific area of land in north-western Mississippi, rather than the mouth of the river. This land mass — variously described by writers as 'D-shaped' or even 'triangular' — stretches from the state line just south of Memphis down to Vicksburg, Miss.. It is bordered on the west by the Mississippi River and on the eastern side by the Yazoo, the 'river of death'. Repeatedly inundated by flood waters every year, this vast flat landscape has a rich, fertile soil as a result, akin to that of the Nile delta in Egypt.

When quoting a blues I will generally write '*(x2)*' if the second line is identical to the first.

Finally, on general topics, I have used the abbreviations for US states as they were recognised in the era being covered by this book — so that Mississippi and Alabama, for example, read as 'Miss.' and 'Ala.' rather than the more usual present-day 'MS' or 'AL'.

Railroadin' Some is the outcome of an original intention I had several years ago to write what would have been the first book on the Mobile & Ohio Railroad and the blues. As is often the case, my idea mushroomed to add the M&O's 'sister' road, the Illinois Central, and finally all Southern roads to become the present volume. Even as I write, *Chapter 3* (featuring the M&O) remains the only literature on this subject.

The railroad (along with sex, alcohol and hoodoo) is one of the central themes running through the early blues of the African American — including pre-blues and religious songs, such as the spirituals from before the Civil War which later evolved into black gospel music in the 1920s and '30s. My original plan was to include a chapter on preachers and 'gospel train' blues, but due to the large amount of relevant material on earlier US railroads and the blues which I have collected, I have had to put this on the famous 'back burner'. This was also the case with the feature on roads in St. Louis, and the interurbans' role in the blues — mainly in Indiana, the 'crossroads of America'. These and much else will hopefully make up a second volume in the not-too-distant future (*Railroadin' Some Mo'* ?).

Notes to Introduction

1	Linklater, A.	p.164
2	Ibid.	p.181
3	'Mississippi Boweavil Blues'	Charley Patton - vocal, guitar, speech (14 June 1929, Richmond, Ind.)
4	Linklater	Ibid, p.199
5	Mumford, L.	Quoted in Linklater, ibid.
6	Ibid.	
7	Catton, B.	p.17
8	Banks Taylor W.	p.ix
9	Ibid.	p.39
10	Ibid.	p.41.
11	Clark, T.D.	p.21
12	Hyatt, H.M.	p.xxi
13	Edwards, D.	p.53
14	Wyatt, M.	Notes to CD *Violin Sing The Blues For Me*
15	Prince, R.E.	p.143 ('NC&St.L Railway')
16	Harrison, D.D.	p.145
17	'Broke Down Engine Blues'	Blind Willie McTell - vocal, guitar, speech (23 October 1931, Atlanta, Ga.)
18	'Down By The M&O'	Lee Brown - vocal; acc. Sam Price's Fly Cats: Sammy Price - piano; unk. guitar; unk. drums (24 March 1939, New York City)
19	White Jr, J.H.	*The American Railroad Freight Car*, p.55
20	Rowe, M.	*Joe Dean From Bowling Green* (interview with Joe Dean) p.7 *Blues Unlimited* No. 127

Discography

'Broke Down Engine Blues' (Blind Willie McTell)
5-CD: *Blind Willie McTell – The Classic Years (1927-40)* [J.S.P. JSP-7711] 2003

'Down By The M&O' (Lee Brown)
CD: *Lee Brown (1937-40)* [Document DOCD-5344] 1995

'Mississippi Boweavil Blues' (Charley Patton)
5-CD: *Charley Patton – Complete Recordings (1929-34)* [J.S.P. JSP-7702] 2002

Smokestack is black, an' the bell it shine like gold

'Moon Going Down' – Charley Patton (1930)

CHAPTER 1

RAILROADS IN THE BLUES

Ever since the blues evolved or were 'born' sometime in the late Nineteenth Century, whether in the Mississippi Delta or the East Texas piney woods, they have featured the railroad as one of the major themes. One alternative theory claims that the blues is much older, and some earlier singers interviewed in the 1960s and '70s said that they had been going for 'centuries an' centuries'. However, no written evidence has survived to support this.

If the origins of the blues are hazy, the opposite is true of US railroads. Beginning in 1827 when the Baltimore & Ohio RR was first chartered, the 'iron horse' (as the steam locomotive was known in earlier days), reached a peak of popularity by the 1880s. If the more popular belief is true that the blues sprang into life during this decade, then an entire generation of Southern blacks had grown up hearing the sound of a train whistle blow at the same time as the blues 'arrived'.

Railroads (an old English term, incidentally) and trains were a central part of the lives of the earliest blues singers — as well as the lyrics of their songs — into the 1940s. Indeed, the railroad was a powerful influence in the social and the economic world of the African American. The vast majority of the Southern roads had been built by blacks before and after the Civil War. Both as slaves and lower-paid 'free' workers, they represented cheap labour, which was eagerly exploited by white railroad employers. In the South, it was mainly blacks who were hired to maintain the tracks and permanent way. Railroads were not only a major factor in slaves' employment off the plantations, but also became the inspiration for a way of escape to the North. Even when they were not actually used, railroads became a source of symbolism for runaway slaves. Some of the most daring would return South to free their families and friends. One notable example was Harriet Tubman, who organised escape routes to the North and Canada dotted along the way by the homes of freedmen/women and occasionally sympathetic whites. These were known as 'stations' and the routes became the 'Underground Railroad'. Of course, countless other slaves also used the real railroads, as they 'found ways of sampling the excitement of the rails with or without authorization.' [1]

Not surprisingly, symbolism drawn from the railroad and the 'excitement of the rails' soon entered the rich language of the blues. For example, Hubbard lists one definition of a 'scoop' as a 'fireman's shovel'.[2] In 1932, Blind Willie McTell used this term as part of a sexual advance to Ruby Glaze on his fine and raggy 'Mama, Let Me Scoop For You' [Victor 23328] (no doubt also inspired by a new dance introduced in 1926 on 'Scoop It' [Paramount 12379] by Leola B. & Wesley Wilson):

> Oh! I ain't scooped none since way last fall.
> Can't you shake it like a cannonball?
>
> *Refrain:* Come on baby, can I scoop for you?
> *(Spoken – Ruby Glaze)* Come on, let's go see.[3]

A 'cannonball' often referred to any fast or non-stop passenger train running on Southern lines *(Chapter 9)*.

In 'TP Window Blues' [OKeh 8795] Texan Jack Ranger describes a scene at the depot *(Chapter 7)* in poetic imagery when alluding to the Texas & Pacific ('TP'). The locomotive all fired up to go or is otherwise 'running', ready to take the train and his lover out of the station and out of his life. One minute, he sees a huge billowing cloud of white smoke and steam which envelops both the passenger cars and his 'easy rider', then the smoke clears to reveal an empty space and the gleaming railroad tracks.

> Say, the TP runnin', smoke standin' on the ground. *(x2)*
> After the train was gone, couldn't find my easy rider around.[4]

After the Civil War, the railroads became the largest employer of Southern blacks, who were generally hired as trackside labourers or station hands, rather than for more skilled and better-paid positions such as engineer or conductor. These were usually 'reserved' for whites. The highest grade an African American could normally hope to achieve on the railroads was that of fireman — and even then more rarely by the 1920s. So, it is not too surprising to find that black employees 'were the most transient of all railwaymen'.[5]

Most of the black section of any Southern town lived right next to the railroad tracks, and Jack Ranger's words *'the TP passed my window'* could be taken as literal. From the 1880s until well into the 1930s the railroad was king and, for the first quarter of the Twentieth Century, Sullivan was able to claim for the USA: 'The parts of this country were bound together for the purposes of trade and mutual intercourse by almost 200,000 miles of railroad, more than 200,000 miles of telegraph lines, and more than a million miles of telephone wire in service.' [6]

Not surprisingly, it is from this period — starting with the first blues record in 1920 until World War II — that most of the blues reflecting the railroad's all-powerful influence, both musically and lyrically, can be found. Digging into the background of the blues will develop a deeper understanding and appreciation of the genre, and hopefully the blues singers and their original audience — working-class blacks. Today's listener can sometimes pick up clues that give an insight to a particular singer who is sometimes little more than a name on a record label.

For instance, a fiddler in Memphis, Tenn. called Tom Nelson used the pseudonym 'Blue Coat' on his 1928 recordings for OKeh. Apart from the probability that he was originally from Vicksburg in the southern tip of the Mississippi Delta, virtually nothing is known of Nelson or his guitar-playing partner, T.C. Johnson, under whose name the recordings are listed in Dixon, Godrich & Rye's *Blues & Gospel Records*. The Jackson, Miss. guitarist Ishmon Bracey told Wardlow in 1963 that Tom Nelson 'played over there for picnics in Vicksburg. He had a little string band. He always wore a blue coat... that's how he got his name.' [7] Fellow Mississippian David 'Honeyboy' Edwards not only confirmed that Nelson often played in Vicksburg in the 1930s, but also added the snippet that he 'last saw him in Helena, Ark. in 1941' [8], where he was hustling a living as a policy writer*.

Four of the five sides made by Nelson and Johnson on 16 and 17 February 1928 have been reissued on vinyl and CD. On the second session (listed under 'Johnson–Nelson–Porkchop'), it is readily apparent that the rich timbre of Tom Nelson's vocal — akin to Joe Calicott and Frank Stokes — is the main back-up to another singer known only as 'Porkchop' on 'G. Burns Is Gonna Rise Again' [OKeh 8577]. This is a parody of a religious song, 'These Bones Are Gonna Rise Again'. And, despite the comment in *Blues & Gospel Records* that 'it is not known what role Tom Nelson plays in these recordings' [9], it is only Nelson who provides the secondary vocal on the reverse of OKeh 8577, 'In The Mornin' '. Porkchop even addresses his opening comments on 'G. Burns' to 'Tom'.

Leading bluesologist Paul Oliver speculated that the term 'blue coat' may have links going back to minstrelsy days in the early part of the

---

* 'Policy' or 'the numbers racket' was a kind of semi-legal form of gambling or lottery. See *Screening The Blues* by Paul Oliver for an in-depth survey on policy in the blues.

Nineteenth Century.[10] Indeed, the songs on OKeh 8577 would have fitted admirably into a minstrel or travelling show. However, the generally topical nature of the blues suggests a connection closer to 'Blue Coat' Tom Nelson's own time in the 1920s.

In railroad slang, 'blue coat' referred to the conductor on many roads, who insisted on their employees wearing a smart, long-tailed coat, invariably in blue. This ultimately derived from the roustabouts' 'uniform' in the Nineteenth Century — the 'long-tailed blue' jacket or coat which they wore while working the steamboats up and down the Mississippi and Ohio Rivers. In 1944, Mary Wheeler interviewed some of the old roustabouts (who were black) and collected some snatches of the songs they remembered using in their earlier days on the river. One verse* runs:

> I went on down to Cairo,
> Callin' fo' Sue.
> Police got after me,
> Tore my long-tailed blue.[11]

Adams gives the definition 'blue-tail coat as 'the dress of a passenger conductor' [12], while Holbrook tells us that the Pennsylvania RR (known as the 'Pennsy') 'gave some thoughts to esthetics. Even before the Civil War, its conductors were ordered to dress in fine cutaway coats of blue broadcloth, with shining brass buttons, buff vests and black trousers.' [13] But it was not only conductors (who were nearly always white on Southern trains) who wore blue coats. Describing the departure of the Pennsy's crack express, the *Broadway Limited*, from New York's Grand Central Station circa 1932, Stevers notes the Pullman porters boarding the train: 'Here they come in ones and twos from the Pullman office, in outdoor uniform with blue coats.' [14]

Nearly every Pullman porter in the US was black. An American writer claimed in 1931 that, apart from the farm, the blacks had found no place in industry since Emancipation 'outside the Cotton Belt'. The writer (Kelly Miller) continued: 'There is no other industry in which the colored man is deemed indispensable unless he considers the comparatively small field of Pullman porter. In these two fields the black man is irreplaceable.' [15] In the same year Sterling Spero noted that 'of about 12,000 porters in Pullman service, all are Negroes except some 400 Mexicans employed on cars running into Mexico and a few dozen Filipinos, Japanese and Chinese recently placed on club cars. To the general public, the Pullman porter is above all else a Negro.' [16] In addition, there were in 1919 'over 7,000 train porters,

---

* From a song called 'Beefsteak When I'm Hongry'. Wheeler gives the preceding verse in musical notation. The text runs: *'Beefsteak when I'm hon-gry / Whiskey when I'm dry / Green-backs when I'm hard-up / Sweet heaven when I die.'* This was later adapted in the blues, often as a floating verse: *'Give me water when I'm thirsty / Whiskey when I'm dry / A good woman to love me / An' heaven when I come to die.'*

practically all Negroes, in the railway service.' Although they did similar jobs, these employees were 'not to be confused with Pullman porters'.[17] The main difference was that train porters could become 'porter-brakemen' when required by a specific company. So, we might assume with some certainty that Tom 'Blue Coat' Nelson was a railroad man — probably a porter — for part of his life at least. He would be in good company, along with Big Bill Broonzy and another Memphis-based bluesman, Robert Wilkins, who 'also worked as a Pullman porter'[18], amongst many others.

Pullman porter, c.1880.

Staying with railway porters for a while, Hubbard writes that 'sometime between 1890 and 1900, an unnamed luggage-carrying porter in Grand Central Station… tied a red flannel band around his black uniform cap for quick identification in the crowd. This strategy paid off. Other porters copied it. George H. Daniels, New York Central's publicist, observed the practice, coined the term 'Red Cap' and ordered red uniform caps for all Grand Central's porters. That style soon became universal.'[19] Ramon Adams puts the date of origin for 'Red Cap' at 1900, but an advertisement from 1896 for the New York Central pinpoints the year exactly. Risher states that 'as a general practice, only Negroes were employed as redcaps, although a few white employees worked as redcaps in Midwestern cities.'[20]

The Red Cap porter crops up in many blues, including some by the (predominantly female) vaudeville-blues artists *(Chapter 9)*. The following verse from Edward Thompson's 1929 recording, 'Florida Bound' [Paramount 12873] has a reference to heavy suitcases or trunks used on long train journeys:

> Say, Mr. Red Cap porter, help me with my load.
> Red Cap porter, help me with my load.
> Red Cap porter, help me with my load.
> [Carry it] for your steamboat captain, let me get on board.[21]

On the original version of this song, Bessie Smith's 'Florida Bound Blues' [Columbia 14109-D], written by pianist Clarence Williams, who accompanied Smith here, the singer likewise adopted the much-respected persona (in black society) of a steamboat captain:

Hey! Hey! Red Cap help me with this load.
Red Cap porter, help me with this load.
(Spoken) Step aside!
Oh! As [I'm a] steamboat Mr. Captain, let me get on board.[22]

This recording originates from 1925, and ultimately the Red Cap verse — if Williams did not originate it — can be traced back no further than 1896. Other black performers adopted the terms 'Red Cap' and 'Pullman Porter' as pseudonyms on their recordings, as well as incorporating them into their repertoire. One group, who recorded as 'Henry Johnson & His Boys' for Gennett in 1927, went out as 'Watson's Pullman Porters' on Champion and 'Bud Warner & His Red Caps' on Bell, while another group cut at least four acappella sides for Paramount the same year as the 'Pullman Porters Quartette'. They included 'Pullman Passenger Train' as one of their two secular titles. Also in 1927, guitarist Sylvester Weaver cut a 'Railroad Porter Blues' [OKeh 8608], while Elnora Johnson sang 'Red Cap Porter Blues' [Black Patti 8039] to Benton Overstreet's piano accompaniment. Two years later, Elzadie Robinson made 'My Pullman Porter Man' [Paramount 12795] at her last session in 1929. Against a backdrop of Will Ezell's fine archaic barrelhouse piano, she declares:

> My man's a Pullman porter over on the IC line. *(x2)*
> He can put you to sleep, wake you up on time.

In earlier sleeping cars, the usual accommodation was bunk beds or 'berths', and Ms. Robinson's Pullman porter knows all the tricks of the trade to make an attractive female passenger enjoy her journey!

> He rides first on top, then from side to side. *(x2)*
> If he moves your baggage, you'll sure be satisfied.[23]

In 1931, the Grand Central Red Cap Quartet (also using a piano for their backing) waxed three sides for the Columbia label, while in 1937

Georgia White recorded a 'Red Cap Porter' [Decca 7389], transposing the Bessie Smith verse quoted earlier into an entirely different song.

Rural bluesman George Torey was also in a recording studio in 1937, playing fine guitar on a steel National. The results (which sadly only yielded two issued sides) were a throwback to the 1920s, with some magnificent singing. On 'Lonesome Man Blues' [A.R.C. 7-08-57] Torey coins an apparently unique verse as he arrives at the 'Union Station' — possibly in Birmingham, Alabama — searching for his woman who has caught the train and gone, appealing to the Red Cap porter with a hopelessly inadequate description of his beloved:

> Hey! Red Cap porter, did my best woman ever get on board?
> Sayin', I don't know what clothes she had on.[24]

A decade earlier, Bertha Ross (who aurally is almost certainly Lucille Bogan) also went to the Union Station in Birmingham to ask a Red Cap about her *'lost man'* before heading on down to New Orleans. The singer's concentration on the railroad for the first four verses of 'Lost Man Blues' [Gennett 6243] also brings Bogan to mind. The latter was married to a railroad man — who was probably a fireman — for a time:

> How long, how long is that Frisco train been gone?
> How long, how long, Lord, is that Frisco train been gone?
> 'Mr. Red Cap porter, did you help my man on board?
> When 'e gets to Memphis, help my man with his heavy load.'
>
> I went to New Orleans, asked the ticket agent there:
> 'How long, how long, Lord, is that train been gone?'
> It's been gone so long, Lord, can't even hear that engine moan.
> It's been gone so long, Lord, I can't even hear that engine moan.[25]

As well as cropping up in blues lyrics, Pullman porters were responsible for the distribution (or at least a significant part of it) of blues records in the 1920s: 'It has been estimated that blacks were buying 10,000 race records a year by 1927, and that 10-20% of black families had phonographs. More had records, many of which they purchased from pullman *[sic]* porters who purchased them in larger cities farther north and who sold them farther south.'[26] Calt & Wardlow give some details of a specific label, Paramount, the major pre-war blues record company: 'In the early 1920s, Paramount records were so scarce in many southern localities that Pullman porters did a profitable business in selling Paramounts they obtained at Mayo Williams' office.'[27]

Williams was that rare species, a black executive in a pre-war company. In an interview many years later, he recalled: 'They'd come *[the*

Pullman porters] to Chicago — see, Chicago was a railroad headquarters then... They had orders for 'em and would pay for 'em the wholesale price... Then they'd sell 'em both to dealers and private persons.' [27] Lomax concurs: 'Paramount at first had no distribution system — it didn't need one. Pullman porters running out of Chicago bought stacks of records for a dollar a copy and sold them at bootleg prices on runs from Texas to Florida!' [28] Williams' description of Chicago was an accurate one, as some forty railroads served the Windy City in the 1920s.

Not only did porters act as record salesmen/distributors, but they were also early disc jockeys — as the famous rock'n'roll bandleader, Johnny Otis recalled when reminiscing about his earlier years out on the West Coast in the 1930s: 'I can remember hearing Peetie Wheatstraw, Big Bill, Doctor Clayton. I heard Robert Johnson's 'Terraplane Blues' recently *[1973]* and, although I didn't know the artist or the title then, it was something I remembered from my childhood. The porters who worked on the trains used to bring in records from Chicago and places, and they would play them on Saturdays or Sundays in the neighborhood.' [29] This spreading of the sounds of the blues via records was potentially nationwide, as 'aside from the major portion of the two Canadian railway systems and a few lines in the United States... the sleeping and parlor car service of the entire continent' was 'in the hands of the Pullman Company'.[30] Or, more precisely, in the hands of the Pullman porter.

Of course, the major reason why Pullman porters got involved with these outside interests was simply because of their appallingly poor wages. As one writer has observed, their 'pay was low and based almost entirely on tips'.[31] To help ease the porters' financial struggle, many blues singers (generally women) would, in an act of solidarity, run a party in a good-time flat, often referred to as a 'buffet' or 'barrelhouse' flat. This was generally in the Northern cities like Chicago, New York, and Detroit. Living in run-down and overcrowded tenements themselves, these singers would set up a table of cold food (the buffet), get in some cheap moonshine liquor and provide an evening's entertainment by either supplying it themselves or hiring a musician or two. For all this, a moderate charge would be made at the door. Some of the proceeds would be donated to the Pullman and Red Cap porters.

Several blues invoke this scenario, such as Maggie Jones' 'Good Time Flat Blues' [Columbia 14055-D] from 1924 and Mary Johnson's 'Barrel House Flat Blues' [Paramount 12996], made some five years later. A similar operation was run to pay a landlord when times got 'tight' — these were the 'house rent parties'. More tangible support for these railroad employees was forthcoming when A. Philip Randolph, who ran a Marxist newspaper called *The Messenger* and became the *enfant terrible* of black journalism, organised 'the Brotherhood of Sleeping Car Porters in the mid-1920s.' [32] However, even this most successful of the early black unions was severely restricted in what it could achieve for its members, largely due to the racially-motivated 'unholy alliance' between employers and powerful white craft unions within the industry.

Nevertheless, despite these setbacks, the railroad porter continued to be an important part of the black community. As well as acting as deejays and as part-time distributors of blues records, the Pullman porters were also cast in the role of human 'fanzines' for the more popular singers such as Leroy Carr, Ma Rainey and Bessie Smith. News of their latest exploits and recordings would travel by word-of-mouth from rural communities and black sections of Southern cities 'to Chicago's South Side to Harlem by way of touring entertainers and Pullman porters.' [33] The latter would also relate the 'goings-on' and latest scandal of the idle rich and famous whites who sunbathed on the beaches of southern Florida. This news and gossip would often reach the ghettos of Chicago, New York, Detroit or Atlanta, etc. via the Pullman porters on the Seaboard Air Line or the Atlantic Coast Line before they appeared in the leading daily tabloids in these cities.

Racialist attitudes decreed a white porter in this 1896 ad.

As can be seen, the influence on the blues stemming from the Pullman porters and Red Caps has been considerable, in more ways than one. For instance, Charley Patton's reference to a railroad strike in Chicago on his 'Mean Black Moan' [Paramount 12953] with Henry Sims' jagged fiddle, may allude to the Pullman employees' strike of 1894. In the typically heavy-handed fashion of many employers of the time, George Pullman imposed wage cuts on his workers in an attempt to counteract the 'panic' (economic depression) of 1893. First, the Pullman workers went on strike, and then other railroad workers joined in. The latter refused to work on Pullman trains, and soon major cities across the country were in a state of semi-paralysis. Chicago itself was the hardest hit, being the railroad hub of the USA. Also, the company town of Pullman, Ill. was situated some 'fourteen miles south of Chicago'. Founded in 1880 by the railroad magnate and deemed 'the most extensive car-works in the world' [34], its 14,000 residents had to endure the tyrannical rule of their employer even outside the workplace. The strike was only 'resolved' with the aid of Federal troops.

Alternatively (and closer to Patton's adult life), 'Mean Black Moan'

Chapter 1 — Smokestack is black, an' the bell it shine like gold

Passengers stranded on the C&A at Bloomington, Ill. – 1894 strike.

most probably refers to the devastating strike on the Illinois Central in 1911. Large numbers of blacks were brought into the IC repair and maintenance shops in an effort by the company to 'break a strike which affected the entire system from Chicago to New Orleans' and 'lasted officially for about three years'.[35] Certainly its impact made itself felt in McComb, Miss., not too far south of Patton's usual haunts in the Delta. The strike at the large IC repair shops in McComb City — named after its founder Colonel Henry S. McComb in 1870 — lasted for two months, and the ensuing violence was particularly horrendous after strike-breakers had been brought in: 'A number of men were killed, martial law was declared, machine guns were placed on tops of buildings; barbed wire surrounded the shops.'[36]

Colonel McComb was president of the New Orleans, Jackson & Great Northern RR when he decided on the southern Mississippi location for an important railway and maintenance shop centre. The NOJ&GN was absorbed into the IC in 1872, and McComb became 'the most populous industrial and commercial center between Jackson and New Orleans.'[37]

The city was also an active blues centre for pianists and guitarists in the 1920s and '30s. One of the latter, Sam Collins, frequented McComb with King Solomon Hill (*aka* Joe Holmes), a younger man who played slide in a similar style to Collins. The 1911 strike would certainly have been remembered by the likes of Collins and his contemporary, Charley Patton, who at that time would reputedly have been 24 and 20 years old respectively.

Another singer from the Mississippi Delta who played with Patton, Son House, disappeared from the blues scene in 1943 and was 'rediscovered' by white researchers in 1964. House claimed that his contemporary had never visited Chicago. Bradley Sweet duly reported: 'Son House suggests that Patton may have hallucinated the affair.'[38] But House, who was only a boy in 1911 (he was born in 1902), did not know Patton before 1930 and certainly would not have had a detailed account of the latter's wanderings from the two previous decades. In any case, Patton himself claimed to have visited several cities in the 1920s — including Chicago — according to fellow bluesman and 'road buddy', Booker 'Mr. Pink' Miller from Greenwood, Miss.. As well as visiting Grafton, Wis. for recording purposes, and Detroit, Patton also travelled to New Orleans and paid at least two visits to St. Louis. He told Miller that he 'went to Chicago, a city he was to use as a backdrop of 'Mean Black Moan'.[39] This blues, recorded in 1929, could well indicate an earlier visit to Chicago (and McComb) by Patton in the 1910s, and his subsequent experience during the Illinois Central strike of 1911.

Certainly, a more detailed study of railroads and blues recordings gives an insight as to the meaning of what might otherwise be dismissed as nonsensical lyrics. A verse which appears from time to time concerns the singer buying *'a ticket as long as my right arm'*. Not long after cutting the first-ever blues record by a black artist in 1920, vaudeville-blues singer Mamie Smith included the phrase in her 'Fare Thee Honey Blues' [OKeh 4194], made in September that same year. One of Ms. Smith's contemporaries, Ethel Ridley, retained it in her 1923 reworking of the theme, 'Alabama Bound Blues' [Columbia A-3965] and it also cropped up in 'Goodbye Rider' [Victor V-8030], recorded by Ida May Mack, a tough rural singer from Texas, in 1928. A variation of it also appeared in the more urban blues of pianist Walter Davis' first record, 'M&O Blues' [Victor V-38618] from 1930. And one year earlier, Lynchburg, Va.'s premier bluesman, Luke Jordan, was at the station pleading with his woman not to leave him on 'My Gal's Done Quit Me' [Victor V-38564]. But her mind is obviously made up, as she replies:

'I done bought my ticket, daddy, I'm compelled to ride.' *(x2)*
Say: 'You know when you had me, man, you couldn't be satisfied.'
(Spoken) Tell the truth, mama, tell it.

Jordan continues:

Then she showed me a ticket that was long as my right arm.
Then she showed me a ticket, long as my right arm.
I said: 'You are ridin' so long, I think you are dead an' gone.'[40]

Chapter 1 — Smokestack is black, an' the bell it shine like gold

On the face of it, these lines seem to consign Jordan's departing lover to some sort of eternal journey on the 'steel highway', whilst employing some obscure symbolism related to the length of her ticket along the way! But this reference in Jordan's blues is much less surreal. In the late 1940s, railroad entrepreneur Robert Young (with an eye on controlling both the New York Central and Pennsylvania RRs) attacked the old-fashioned ideas of 'traditional railroad men'. Said Young: 'A hog can travel through Chicago without changing trains, but you can't!' This referred to the fact that transcontinental passengers had to leave their 'comfortable Pullmans' when they arrived in Chicago, and 'dragging their hand luggage along, scramble for a taxi or stand in line for the Parmalee Transfer limousine that hauled the never-ending flood of travelers from their arrival station to their departure station.' Apparently, the limousine was available to any Pullman passenger who had bought a ticket going through Chicago, who had to change from one railroad to another (and therefore change stations). Martin notes that: 'The Parmalee coupon was right in the ticket, which sometimes reached hilarious lengths.' [41] This service went back nearly a hundred years at the time of Young's attack. As Stover reports: 'In 1853, Frank Parmalee (1816-1904) established a transfer service long noted for its handsome rigs, excellent horseflesh, and genial and distinctively dressed drivers.' [42] Luke Jordan's 'ticket' verse suddenly becomes clearer: his partner is going on a transcontinental rail journey via Chicago, to Alabama:

Illustration of a 'highball' signal.

> One of my gals have quit me, talk's all over town.
> Mama, my gal have quit me, the talk's all over town.
> She left a note on the kitchen table, saying 'Dad[dy], I'm Alabama-bound.' [43]

Moreover, it is quite likely the singer was recalling an actual incident. As it was impossible to make such a rail trip from Lynchburg, he must have been referring to a scenario set somewhere in the North — possibly New York City, where he recorded 'My Gal's Done Quit Me'. Jordan may have spent some time living in New York — long enough to strike up a relationship with a woman that was apparently far from casual. As Kent observes 'he did travel some in the 20s'.[44]

One of the most familiar phrases in the early blues is 'balling the jack'. It has come to refer to a black dance, but has its origins in railroad slang. The 'jack' was a steam locomotive which ultimately replaced the mule in the South as the major means of hauling agricultural goods to the marketplace. The female mule is known as a 'jenny' and the male as a 'jack'. Originally, 'balling the jack' meant to run a train at high speed. This derived from the term 'highball', a name used for early US signals which consisted of little more than a ball attached to a line on a tall wooden post. When the ball was in a raised position at the top of the post, it indicated that the track was clear for the train to proceed: thus, 'highball'. This term soon became identified with the trains that had top priority on the right of way, usually the 'express' or the fast mail *(Chapter 7)*. It is not surprising therefore, that the aforementioned dance is partly described by Paul Oliver as including 'vigorous revolving or twisting' [45] — otherwise, a fast-moving dance.

Another trackside icon were the large advertising hoardings used to sell Uneeda Biscuits. The seminal Texas bluesman Blind Lemon Jefferson included this product in the sardonic and superbly-sung 'Rabbit Foot Blues' [Paramount 128454] — essentially a song about starvation, his complex guitar giving the number a rather jaunty air that belied its protest content:

> Ah! Uneeda Biscuits, gal, an' a half-a-pint of gin.
> Uneeda Biscuits, gal, an' a half-a-pint of gin.
> The gin is mighty fine, but the biscuits a little too thin.[46]

A couple of years later, in 1928, Alec Johnson (who sounded straight off the minstrelsy stage) injected some punning humour into his song, 'Miss Meal Cramp Blues' [Columbia 14446-D], also about starvation, drawing on a Uneeda sign by the side of the highway — possibly like the one in Knoxville, Tenn., next to the tracks of the Southern Railway *(see overleaf)*:

> Standin' on the road-side, a great big sign, it read, *(x2)*
> Say, 'Uneeda Biscuit', because I was, I near drop-dead.

Inspired by the symbolism of a box car full of hobos *(Chapter 10)*, Johnson continues:

> My body feels so weary, 'cos I've got the miss meal cramps. *(x2)*
> Right now, I could eat more than a whole carload of tramps.[47]

Of course, with such a powerful image and such a central role on the railroads, it is no surprise that the steam locomotive itself inspired many a blues singer. A striking piece of blues poetry in the shape of 'Moon Going

Chapter 1 — *Smokestack is black, an' the bell it shine like gold*

The Uneeda Biscuit sign, Knoxville, Tenn., c.1900.

Down' [Paramount 13014] eloquently describes the utility-black engine with its brass bell hauling its load through the humid Mississippi countryside, as the heavy twin guitars of Charley Patton and Willie Brown emulate the pulsating rhythm of the loco's driving wheels:

> Lord, the smokestack is black an' the bell it shine like gold,
> Bell it shine like, bell it shine like gold.
> Aw, the smokestack is black an' the bell it shine like gold.
> *(Spoken)* Shuck 'em boy, you know it looks good to me.
> Lord, I ain't gonna walk here, baby, round no more.[48]

The combination of Patton's ferocious vocal with the vision of near-white hot sparks spewing forth against a background of billowing black smoke as the train pounds through the Delta landscape, makes it easy to recognize the origins of the graphic phrase 'smokestack lightning'. Indeed, Frank Howard, who knew Patton for at least a three-year period from 1921 to 1924, told Wardlow in 1967 that a song which Charley Patton 'sang right smart' (ie frequently) began with the phrase *'Smokestack lightnin', bell just like gold.'*[49] This, of course, was later immortalised by one of Patton's most prominent disciples, Chester Burnett, better known as Chess recording artist Howlin' Wolf, who made this title one of the most popular in post-war Chicago blues in the mid-1950s.

II

As stated earlier in this chapter, the railroad symbolised freedom for the slaves before and during the Civil War and continued to do so for blacks after 1865. Here in the Twenty-First Century, we can only have a shadowy sense of what this new status meant to the freedmen and women after nearly 250 years of bondage. Reflecting back to that traumatic point in time some fifteen years later, in 1880, Park Johnstone (or Parke Johnston/Uncle Parke), formerly a Virginian slave, described the feelings of being free: 'It became so sudden on 'em they wasn't prepared for it. Just think of whole droves of people, that had always been kept close, and hardly ever left the plantation before, turned loose all at once, with nothing in the world but what they had on their backs, and often little enough of that; men, women and children that left their homes when they found out they were free, walking along the road with nowhere to go.'[50]

Of course, they also took to the railroads in the South, once the latter had recovered from the devastation caused by both warring factions. This state of 'nowhere to go' was soon extended to become the very basis of black freedom: travelling the railroads, and not knowing or caring where they were headed. This theme crops up in many blues *(see Chapters 9 and 10)*.

Understandably, not just the locomotive (as in Patton's case), but also the entire train became almost a living thing to the blues singer and blacks generally. With the advent of the *Empire State Express* in 1891 on the New York Central and the *Nancy Hanks* (also the name of a successful racehorse and Abraham Lincoln's mother) in 1893 on the Central of Georgia, railroads began to apply names to crack express trains.* The concept of the express train soon evolved into the *'Limited'* by the 1900s, which were more akin to the contemporary idea of a fast train with only a few limited stops. Inevitably, some of these also passed into blues lore.

One of the earliest to be celebrated was the *Panama Limited* on the Illinois Central, which was named as a salute to the monumental engineering feat, the Panama Canal, which opened in 1914. This train ran from Chicago down through St. Louis and Memphis via Jackson, Miss. to New Orleans. Although it didn't serve either Panama or Panama City, Fla., it was popular with construction workers 'who traveled from Chicago to New Orleans to board ships for Panama'.[51] The *Limited*'s 921-mile journey took twenty-five hours in total.[52]

The first recordings to feature this IC train were sung by vaudeville-blues singers. In 1923, Esther Bigeou cut 'Panama Limited Blues' [OKeh

---

* In the earlier days of US railroading, 'express' denoted a train that only stopped at itemised or 'express' stations, thereby eliminating flag and whistle stops, rather than simply a fast train *(Chapter 8)*.

Chapter 1 — Smokestack is black, an' the bell it shine like gold

The Panama Limited, c.1916.

8125], and other versions by Ada Brown and Bertha 'Chippie' Hill appeared three years later. Between 1929 and 1930, a male vocal group called the IC Glee Club, who were probably employees of this railroad, included three titles about named IC passenger trains. One of these was 'Panama To Chi' [OKeh 8929], which described the route from Memphis to Chicago. Some five months earlier, another major Charley Patton disciple, the intense Mississippi singer, Bukka White (as 'Washington White') recorded the definitive version as 'The Panama Limited' [Victor 23295], his scintillating guitar evoking the sounds of the train with uncanny accuracy as it wove in and around his alternating monologue and dark, 'trembling' vocal. Here, Aunt Hagar, an 'old soul', is trying to leave Memphis, and probably her man as well. In her emotional state, she has no idea of the train times:

> *(Spoken)* So the old soul, you know, went on down to the Union Station, you know. She ax the depot man what time it was. She heard th' eight-thirty freight blowin', but she was gon' catch that fast Panama Limited, you know. They kinda blow a little different, you know.
>
> *(Guitar solo)*
>
> *(Spoken)* After she heard this freight, you know, she ax the man again, what time it was. He told 'er, go lay her head on the railroad line, until the rail poppin': train-time wasn't long. Old soul, sittin' down, she heard the rail poppin', you know. She got up singin', you know.
>
> *(Vocal)* I'm a motherless child, I'm a long ways from my home.
> Mmmmmmm-mmmmm, mmmmmm-mmmmm.

> *(Spoken)* Don't moan it so loud, Aunt Hagar. So when th' old soul, you know, begin to moan, you know, she heard this 'ere train comin' in there, hollerin', you know. After hollerin', you know, she heard the bell blowin'. After the bell blowin', she heard it when she cut out.
>
> *(Guitar solo)*
>
> *(Spoken)* Air brakes! When I heard, you know, heard the train cut out, you know. The old soul got happy, you know, comin' up singin', you know.
>
> *(Vocal)* The train I ride, it don't burn no coal.*
> Mmmmmmm-mmmmmm, mmmmmm-mmmmm.
> Mmmmmmm-mmmmmm, mmmmmm-mmmmm.
> Mmmmmmm-mmmmmm, mmmmmm-mmmmm.[53]

Although other named trains also featured in the blues, they are surprisingly — or perhaps not — in the minority. There was the *Sunshine Special* on the T&P, the *Dixie Flyer* on the Central of Georgia, the Katy had the *Texas Special*, and the IC boasted both the *Chickasaw* and *Seminole Limited*. But, generally speaking, these were too expensive for the blues singers' audience to use, and they also travelled too fast to jump a free ride. As Bukka White commented on another railroad blues, 'Special Stream Line' [Vocalion 05526]: *'The hobos don't fool with this train / They stand on the track with they hat in they hand'*.[54] In fact, blacks usually found travel on any passenger train in the South a less-than-pleasant experience. Because of segregation laws they were forced to ride in the 'combination car'. This was an old converted box car which also acted as a baggage carrier. Dilapidated and often filthy, these 'Jim Crow cars' were coupled right behind the locomotive. In the event of a train wreck, the worst damage would be inflicted on these flimsier vehicles and their black occupants would sustain the most serious injuries. On top of this, they were expected to pay the same fare as the whites travelling in modern, comfortable steel cars on the same train!

A few trains were also given unofficial nicknames — the most famous being the *Midnight Special*. In addition to the well-known Texas train on the Southern Pacific whose locomotive's headlight shone nightly through the bars of the state penitentiary, cruelly reminding the inmates of a freedom which never seemed to be theirs, another *'Special'* existed in Mississippi. This was the special train on the Yazoo & Mississippi Valley RR that served

---

* This refers to the experimental conversion from coal to oil-fired locomotives in the 1920s and '30s.

Parchman Farm, where the married prisoners were allowed conjugal rights in every month that included five Sundays. On the fifth Sunday, wives (and prostitutes posing as such), visited the Mississippi state pen for a spell, the train arriving at dawn and leaving at dusk. One of the most famous — or infamous — of these 'wives' was Rosie, who is celebrated in many prison worksongs.

III

But most of the time, blues singers praised, appealed to, or abused the train via the railroad company itself. So, there are many blues which refer to the IC, L&N, Santa Fe, M&O, M-K-T (or Katy), Southern and so on. Many of these and others will appear in subsequent chapters.

One of the Texas roads which was later to be absorbed by the Southern Pacific was the Texas & New Orleans RR. This railroad started life (as did many in East Texas) as a log-hauling line *(Chapter 2)* called the Sabine & Galveston Railroad & Lumber Company and was chartered in 1856. With an obvious eye on the rich lumber pickings from the East Texas piney woods[*], the plan was to build 'from a point on the Sabine River at or near Madison in Orange County to tidewater on Galveston Bay, not north of Liberty or south of Smith's Point.' [55] By 1869, the name had been changed to 'Texas & New Orleans'.[56] The T&NO ran principally via Houston and Beaumont in Texas through Shreveport, La. and down to New Orleans. It also ran trains to Dallas, Fort Worth, San Antonio and Port Arthur. As has been mentioned, this railroad was later absorbed by the SP, but retained its name. By 1940, it had become simply the 'Texas & New Orleans Railroad Company'.[57]

In 1933, the T&NO became the subject of one of the finest blues ever made by Lucille Bogan and Walter Roland, 'T&NO Blues' [Banner 32845], which appeared as by 'Bessie Jackson'. Although Bogan recorded very few covers (another was Bessie Smith's 'Midnight Blues'), she generally equalled or surpassed the original when she did so. In this instance, however, no comparison is possible, as the earlier recording remains untraced. First cut by Hattie Hyde in 1930, it is listed in *Blues & Gospel Records* as 'TN&O *[sic]* Blues' [Victor 23374]. Nonetheless, with Ms. Bogan's raw and yet majestic vocal, cunningly interspersed with Walter Roland's moaning boogie piano, their 'T&NO Blues' must surely rank as the definitive rendition, as the singer describes in graphic terms just how much the railroad and the train mean both to herself and her man:

---

[*] These and most of the other quotes on railroads in Texas are taken from the definitive work, *A History Of Texas Railroads* by S.G. Reed *(see Bibliography)*.

Lucille Bogan, c. early 1930s.   Walter Roland, 1933.

The train I ride, is eighteen coaches long.
Train I ride [is] eighteen coaches long.
An' the man that I love done bin here an' gone.

I hate to hear that T&NO blow.
I hate to hear [that] T&NO blow.
Puts my mind on a wander, makes me want to go.

Gonna beat the train to the crossing, goin' to burn the trestle down.
Beat the train to the crossin', goin' to burn that trestle down.
That's the onliest way I can keep my man in town.

He's a railroad man an' he sure do love to ride.
He's a railroad man, sure do love to ride.
If he don't ride that T&NO, he sure ain't satisfied.

Gon' fall down on my knees, pray to the Lord above.
Fall on my knees, pray to the Lord above.
Please send me back the only man that I love.[58]

In 1971, English writer Mike Leadbitter referred to 'the Englewood marshalling yards of the T&NO (South Pacific Railroad *[sic]*)', when discussing Duke/Peacock Records and the location of owner Don Robey's offices 'deep in the North-Eastern suburbia, away from Houston's city centre, on the corner of Liberty and Erastus Streets.'[59] These marshalling yards were referred to much earlier by S.G. Reed *[ibid]* as the centre for the whole of the Southern Pacific lines in Louisiana and Texas. It is as likely that Lucille

Bogan picked up 'T&NO Blues' from a live performance by Hattie Hyde as from hearing her elusive (and only) record. Or maybe another singer transmitted the song via one of the many 'rollin' rattlers' (ie freight trains) that were made up daily in the Houston yards, which Bogan occasionally rode.

Apart from East Texas guitarist 'Funny Paper' Smith's reference to the *'TNO'* in 1931 on his 'Honey Blues' [Vocalion 1633], the only other allusion to this railroad that I have come across in nearly forty years appears on a side by another fine and earthy female singer, 'Blanche Johnson' (thought to be a pseudonym for Elzadie Robinson), 'Galveston Blues' [Herwin 92016]:

A Mo-Pac freight approaches the T&NO crossing at Houston, Tex. in 1938.

> I've got the blues for Galveston, Texas. I can't be satisfied. *(x2)*
> Every time I hear a train, it makes me want to ride.
>
> Oh! Mal[vern] is on the SP, Galves[ton] on the Santa Fe. *(x2)*
> I've got a man way down in Texas sure do worry me.[60]

If Elzadie does sing 'Mal', then Malvern, Tex. in Leon County might have been a flag stop on the Southern Pacific or its T&NO section from Houston to Dallas. This could indicate a possible home base for Ms. Robinson, who is generally attributed a Shreveport background by blues writers. The Southern Pacific also ran a direct line through Nacogdoches, Tex. to Shreveport, La..

For earlier blues singers such as Charley Patton, Blind Lemon Jefferson, Lucille Bogan and Elzadie Robinson, the railroad was as much a part of their environment as the air they breathed. Another superb singer, Sleepy John Estes from Tennessee, captured the feeling admirably on his 'Whatcha Doin'?' [Victor V-38628]:

> When I hear that Illinois Central blow.
> My feet get tickled, makes me want to go.[61]

Notes to Chapter 1

1. Reidy, J.P. — p.103
2. Hubbard, F. — p.194
3. 'Mama Let Me Scoop For You' — Blind Willie McTell - vocal, guitar; Ruby Glaze - speech (22 February 1932, Atlanta, Ga.)
4. 'TP Window Blues' — Jack Ranger - vocal; unk. piano; unk. guitar (28 June 1929, Dallas, Tex.)
5. Licht, W. — p.76
6. Sullivan, M. — p.34
7. Wardlow, G.D. — p.58
8. Edwards, D. — p.232
9. Dixon, R.M.W., W.J. Godrich & H. Rye — p.480
10. Oliver, P. — *Songsters & Saints*, p.134
11. Wheeler, M. — p.10 ('Appendix')
12. Adams, R.F. — p.16
13. Holbrook, S.H. — p.83
14. Stevers, M.D. — p.190
15. Miller, K. — p.74
16. Spero, S.D., & A.L. Harris — p.430
17. Ibid. — p.302
18. Spottswood, D. — Notes to Piedmont PLP-13162 (LP)
19. Hubbard — Ibid, p.41
20. Risher, H.W. — p.52
21. 'Florida Bound' — Edward Thompson - vocal, guitar (c.23 October 1929, New York City)
22. 'Florida Bound Blues' — Bessie Smith - vocal, speech; Clarence Williams - piano (17 November 1925, New York City)
23. 'My Pullman Porter Man' — Elzadie Robinson - vocal; Will Ezell - piano (c.March 1929, Chicago, Ill.)
24. 'Lonesome Man Blues' — George Torey - vocal, guitar (2 April 1937, Birmingham, Ala.)
25. 'Lost Man Blues' — Bertha Ross (prob. Lucille Bogan) - vocal; Vance Patterson - piano (5 August 1927, Birmingham, Ala.)
26. Garon, P.& B. — p.247
27. Calt, S., & G.D. Wardlow — p.11
28. Lomax, A. — p.441
29. Broven, J. — p.14
30. Spero & Harris — Ibid, p.431
31. Martin, A. — p.87
32. Meier, A., & E. Rudwick — p.246
33. Albertson, C. — p.48

34	Porter, H.	p.?
35	Spero & Harris	Ibid, p.308
36	Mosley, D.C.	p.254
37	Corliss, C.J.	p.203
38	Sweet, B.	Notes to Belzona L-1001 (LP)
39	Calt, S., & G.D. Wardlow	*King Of The Delta Blues*, p.173
40	'My Gal's Done Quit Me'	Luke Jordan - vocal, guitar (18 November 1929, New York City)
41	Martin	Ibid, p.117
42	Stover, J.F.	p.44
43	Jordan	Ibid.
44	Kent, D.	*78 Quarterly* No. 7, p.76
45	Oliver	Ibid, p.38
46	'Rabbit Foot Blues'	Blind Lemon Jefferson - vocal, guitar (c.December 1926, Chicago, Ill.)
47	'Miss Meal Cramp Blues'	Alec Johnson - vocal; Bo Carter - violin; Charlie McCoy - mandolin; Kansas Joe - guitar; unk. piano (2 November 1928, Atlanta, Ga.)
48	'Moon Going Down'	Charley Patton - vocal, guitar, speech; Willie Brown - guitar (c.28 May 1930, Grafton, Wis.)
49	Calt & Wardlow	*King Of The Delta Blues*, ibid, p.146
50	Litwack, L.F.	p.215
51	Wheaton, M.	p.44
52	Dubin, A.D.	p.141
53	'The Panama Limited'	Bukka White (as 'Washington White') - vocal, guitar, speech (26 May 1930, Memphis, Tenn.)
54	'Special Stream Line'	Bukka White - vocal, guitar, speech; Washboard Sam - washboard (8 March 1940, Chicago, Ill.)
55	Reed, S.G.	p.84
56	Ibid.	p.149
57	Ibid.	p.87
58	'T&NO Blues'	Lucille Bogan (as 'Bessie Jackson') - vocal; Walter Roland - piano (17 July 1933, New York City)
59	Leadbitter, M.	p.181
60	'Galveston Blues'	Blanche Johnson (prob. Elzadie Robinson) - vocal; Will Ezell - piano (c.January 1927, Chicago, Ill.)
61	'Whatcha Doin'?' *[sic]*	Sleepy John Estes - vocal, guitar; Yank Rachell - mandolin; Jab Jones - piano (21 May 1930, Memphis, Tenn.)

Discography – Chapter 1

'Florida Bound'
(Edward Thompson)

CD: *Alabama: Black Secular & Religious Music (1927-34)*
[Document DOCD-5165] 1993

'Florida Bound Blues'
(Bessie Smith)

8-CD: *Bessie Smith: The Complete Recordings – Volume 3* [Frog DGF-42] 2002

'Galveston Blues'
(Blanche Johnson [Elzadie Robinson])

CD: *Elzadie Robinson – Volume 1 (1926-28)*
[Document DOCD-5248] 1994

'Lonesome Man Blues'
(George Torey)

CD: *Memphis Blues (1927-38)*
[Document DOCD-5159] 1993

'Lost Man Blues'
(Bertha Ross)

CD: *Barrelhouse Women (1925-30)*
[Document DOCD-5378] 1995

'Mama, Let Me Scoop For You'
(Hot Shot Willie [Blind Willie McTell])

4-CD: *Blind Willie McTell – The Classic Years (1927-40)* [J.S.P. JSP-7711] 2003

'Miss Meal Cramp Blues'
(Alec Johnson)

CD: *Mississippi String Bands & Associates (1928-31)* [Blues Document BDCD-6013] 1992

'Moon Going Down'
(Charley Patton)

5-CD: *Charley Patton – Complete Recordings (1929-34)* [J.S.P. JSP-7702] 2002

'My Gal's Done Quit Me'
(Luke Jordan)

3-CD: *Never Let The Same Bee Sting You Twice (1927-38)*
[Document DOCD-5678] 2005

'My Pullman Porter Man'
(Elzadie Robinson)

CD: *Elzadie Robinson – Volume 2 (1928-29)*
[Document DOCD-5249] 1994

'The Panama Limited'
(Washington White [Bukka White])

5-CD: *Legends Of Country Blues – The Complete Pre-War Recordings of Son House, Skip James, Bukka White, Tommy Johnson, Ishmon Bracey* [J.S.P. JSP-7715] 2003

'Rabbit Foot Blues'
(Blind Lemon Jefferson)

4-CD: *Blind Lemon Jefferson – The Complete* [J.S.P. JSP-7706] 2002

'Special Stream Line'
(Bukka White)

5-CD: *Legends Of Country Blues – The Complete Pre-War Recordings of Son House, Skip James, Bukka White, Tommy Johnson, Ishmon Bracey* [J.S.P. JSP-7715] 2003

'T&NO Blues'
(Bessie Jackson [Lucille Bogan])

CD: *Lucille Bogan – Volume 2 (March 1930-20 July 1933)*
[Blues Document BDCD-6037] 1993

'T.P. Window Blues'
(Jack Ranger)

CD: *Dallas Alley Drag (1929-34)*
[Yazoo YAZCD-2054] 2002
One of the early piano blues series.

'Whatcha Doin'?'
(Sleepy John Estes)

2-CD: *Sleepy John Estes – Gus Cannon (1928-30)* [J.S.P. JSP-3406] 2002

Skippin' round from log to log

'Log Camp Blues' – Ma Rainey (1928)

CHAPTER 2

LOGGING CAMPS, RAILROADS AND ORAL TRANSMISSION

If it was true of most railroads in East Texas, including the T&NO, that they had their origins as logging concerns, this was also the case for many railroads in other Southern states including Mississippi, Louisiana, Alabama and Georgia. All were fertile breeding grounds for the blues. Because the Southern lumber industry employed a large majority of black workers — certainly in the late Nineteenth and early Twentieth Centuries — the oral transmission process of the blues was given an 'accelerated boost', especially after the railroad arrived, basically because transient black workers/singers could travel from one logging camp to a town and on to another logging camp much more rapidly. But black workers (usually slaves) were prevalent in logging camps even before the Civil War, at least as early as the 1820s. This included women, as Hickman observed: 'Employment of women sawmill workers was not unusual in the late antebellum period.' [1] But, before plunging into the world of lumber, 'dummy roads' and arguably the earliest barrelhouses, etc, I will consider some of the other means of oral transmission in the Southern states at the end of the Nineteenth Century.

There were other black labour-intensive settings in the South, such as mining and levee camps, which also contributed to the spread of the early blues, although it would appear that these phenomena came into existence at a slightly later date than the logging camp. One of the reasons for this is that — certainly in the case of the mining or 'coal camps' — they would be located nearer to a town, or, more often than not, constitute a 'town' in themselves. So, mining camps were always to be found in a more urban setting, rather than a completely rural one. Trotter comments that the shift from farming to mining was not all that radical for black workers, 'since coal mining evolved in a semirural area.' [2] However, not all miners were drawn from the farms; some were railroad workers, whom he describes as 'nonagricultural laborers'.[3]

In the earlier Twentieth Century, black as well as white coal miners in southern West Virginia lived in coal towns, though they were usually segregated. Blacks' houses were of the worst kind 'located close to coal tipples and railroad tracks.' [4] (A 'tipple' was situated over the rail lines in order to fill up the coal trains waiting underneath.) Obviously, the coal towns contributed to the oral transmission process of the blues — via the railroads particularly — but I would suggest not as early as in the totally rural logging camps. Titles such as 'Mining Camp Blues' [Paramount 12256] by Trixie Smith in 1925, 'Coal Camp Blues' [Victor 23309] by Walter Taylor in 1931 and 'Poor Coal Loader' [Champion 50076] by Frank 'Springback' James in 1935, amongst others, reflect experiences — personal or otherwise — involving time spent in the coal industry in the first decades of the Twentieth Century.

The levee camps too, featured singers and musicians like Mississippi's nine-string guitarist Big Joe Williams. But the appalling conditions of these camps (sometimes known as 'line camps'), including the ever-present danger of potential drowning, as well as the often shoestring budgets of the white levee camp bosses, were factors not conducive to a thriving music scene in the early days. Pioneering blues author Sam Charters gave a typically graphic account in 1959: 'The levee camps and the line camps were squalid, filthy collections of tents or shacks. The work was exhausting and the living wasn't much easier... In the levee camps they'd work twelve to sixteen hours a day, then crawl onto rotten mattresses laid out under big tents.' [5] Although there was a commissary in the levee camp ('Everyone of um had a commissary' [6]), it only provided the very basics for survival such as food and protective clothing — all of which the workers either paid for in company script (outlawed by 1935), or their debt went into a 'doodling book', which they had to settle whenever the levee camp boss decided to pay their wages.

An old river man, Walter Brown (not the singer with the Jay McShann band), told the celebrated white researcher Alan Lomax in the 1970s: 'You could go there *[the commissary]* and get anything you wanted to wear. You could charge something to that doodling book an *[sic]* carry it to the kitchen... and your cook could get anything that she wanted to cook with.' [7] Since there was generally no provision for a social life, apart from congregating outside the commissary to either tell tall tales ('lies') or shoot craps, the levee camp workers would 'have to go find people who were living "backwater" in the ground between the levee and the river to get a meal or a woman.' [8]

Charters' main informant at this point was Big Joe Williams, who was born into a large family in Crawford, Miss. on the edge of the Knoxford Swamp, in 1903. Like many other blues singers, he rejected life on the farm with its unending drudgery at a very early age and became a wanderer, hoboing his way across the South and back again. At the earliest, it would seem that Williams' recollections stretched back to circa 1915.

Part of the reason for the lack of resources at this time was the very haphazard approach to levee construction and maintenance, which included not only the state authorities, but plantation owners as well. As there was no truly cohesive programme until the US Federal Government accepted the concept of a national approach to the wayward Mississippi River after the horrendous 1927 flood in Greenville, Miss., riparian landowners relied on their own ideas as to how a levee should be built and how it should be maintained. Many resented having to pay out for such work when instructed by the state legislature, and some questioned why they should have to build a levee at all! This situation was even worse back in the late Nineteenth Century, when individual state support was negligible or non-existent. Octogenarian Phineas McClean told Alan Lomax in 1942: 'I come in here *[the Mississippi Delta]* in '79, young fellow... Them times we didn't have no levees holdin' *[sic]* back the waters. The river could come in and replenish the land every year. Didn't have to put on no fertilizer.' [9] But, certainly from the 1880s onwards, levee-building increased and, more to the point, became more efficient at stopping the river overflowing; or, at least, less frequently.

So, levee camps presumably only became commonplace from this point onwards. Unfortunately, very little information about the period from the 1880s to the 1910s has so far come to light. Like their mining counterparts, the levee camps also clearly contributed to the oral transmission of the blues. But, in the earlier period from the 1880s to 1900, the music heard there would have been worksongs rather than blues *per se*, often very similar in construction to the prison songs that Alan Lomax and his father, John, recorded from the early 1930s onwards for the Library of Congress archives in Washington, DC. These songs — often 'hollers' — lay at the very roots of the blues.

The latter style is very much in evidence on many of Texas Alexander's recordings, and in particular the superbly archaic 'Levee Camp Moan Blues' [OKeh 8498] from 1927. Significantly, Alexander played no instrument on his records (although he reputedly carried a guitar when travelling around, for others to back him), though he was occasionally accompanied by the brilliant guitarist, Lonnie Johnson, as on this occasion. Johnson, a multi-instrumentalist and a very sophisticated musician, was the complete antithesis of Alexander, but he stayed with the erratic singer all the way. Without directly mentioning the levee camp, the Texan conveys the dark, brooding and violent atmosphere which prevailed in these places where 'there was no law. The law wouldn't even come up on top of the levee' [10]; the white levee camp foremen, who carried a pistol like all the workers, 'were the law and everything in those camps' [11]:

> Mmmmmmmmmmmm-mmmmm-mmmmmmmmm.
> Mmmmmmmmmmmm-mmmmm-mmmmmmmm.
> Mmmmmmmmmmmm-mmmmmmmmmm.
> Lord, they accuse me of murder, murder, murder. I haven't harmed a man.
> Lord, accuse me of murder-mmmmmm, I haven't harmed a man.
> Ohhhhhhh-errrr, they accuse me of murder an' I haven't harmed a man.

The singer invokes the East Texas equivalent of the 'mercy man'[*], who was based in Memphis and visited a particularly mean and cruel levee contractor in the Delta by the name of Charley Silas about his bad treatment of his mules. The mercy man 'came out to Silas's camp and protested against him working mules with sore necks and shoulders.' [12] Silas apparently shot him dead for his trouble and concern:

> I went all around that whole corral,
>   I couldn't find a mule with his shoulder well.
> Lord, I couldn't find a mule with his shoulder well.
> Oh! Worked all morn, an' I worked all bare (?)
> I couldn't find a mule, like, with his shoulder well.[13]

This story came from an interview which the folklorist, Alan Lomax conducted in 1940 with 'Black Hat' F.M. McCoy, an old, one-legged Irish *'hopper'* or barrow-man who had worked on levee building as long ago as the 1880s. Now reduced to 'push*[ing]* my pencils on the construction-gang circuit' in Greenville, Miss., McCoy told Lomax about 'Charley Silas — the big contractor who made a million and, when he went broke, walked off in the river. All the niggers heard about him when he shot the 'Mercy Man', which was the humane officer out of Memphis'[**].[15]

Lomax adds: 'The Delta levee world was the American frontier, even more lawless than the Far West in its palmiest days — partly because there was, so to speak, open season on blacks, considered less valuable than the

---

[*] A 'mercy man' in the South during the early decades of the Twentieth Century was a white man who 'adopted' a particular black citizen (generally male). If the latter was a good worker and also 'knew his place', then the mercy man promised to get 'his boy/nigger' out of any local bad situations, such as being thrown in jail.
[**] On the origins of the more polite 'Mr. Charlie' (or alternatively 'Mr. Cholly') form of address by blacks to the white man, Lomax notes that 'Black Hat McCoy opined that Mister Cholly was the big-time operator Charley Silas, who shot down the mercy man... Silas's victim was also named Charley. Both men became legends. Some singers addressed their plaints to Mister Cholly the Mercy Man, who cared about the mules — most others to his ruthless killer.' [14]

mules they drove: "Kill a nigger, hire another; kill a mule, you got to buy another one." ' [16] It can therefore be reasonably concluded that the wicked Silas probably treated his black workers worse than he did his mules.

Given the brutality of the conditions, it comes as no great surprise that there was apparently no provision in earlier levee camps in the Nineteenth Century for a 'dance floor' or any place of entertainment where the workers could sing and play at their leisure, and so give the blues a chance to evolve from the type of work-related holler so admirably portrayed by Texas Alexander. Some old roustabouts interviewed in the early 1940s remembered a later camp — presumably from the 1890s to 1900s — colloquially known as the 'Blue Goose Saloon' (described as a 'river town... on the levee'), and recalled how they used to dance there: 'The dancing was accompanied by singing, hand-clapping and stamping, one Negro at a time being in the center of a ring, doing a sort of solo dance, except when he would suddenly catch a nearby companion for a violent whirl or turn.' [17] But, clearly, no piano or any other instrument was present.

II

Unlike mining and levee camps, the logging camp was always on the move via a railroad which was often a 'dummy' (temporary) line. We will return to dummy lines later on. Moreover, this type of camp was often

Chapter 2 — Skippin' 'round from log to log

HANCOCK COUNTY.

This county is rather sparsely populated, it being principally a stock growing county, together with timber, pitch, tar and turpentine, which are the principal exports. There are but four towns in this county of any note, viz: Gainesville, (the county seat) Shieldsborough, Pearlington and Napoleon. Shieldsborough is a very flourishing place, lying immediately upon the Bay of St. Louis and the Gulf of Mexico, much visited in the summer. The other three towns lie on Pearl River, which is navigable at all seasons at either point. In Gainsville there are two Schools, and a Masonic Lodge; the lower part of its hall is set apart for preaching and a School. One Steam Saw Mill, at which is cut an immense amount of lumber. One Cooper Shop. A steamboat runs regularly between this place and New Orleans, making her average trips in about seven hours, stopping at Napoleon and Pearlington. In Pearlington is one store and two Steam Saw Mills; the prospect of the New Orleans and Mobile Railroad running through it, has given a spur to its improvements. Sail vessels do a good business there. There is a flourishing School in Pearlington. Napoleon is on the decline. No physician resides in Gainsville, nor is there a lawyer, which speaks well for health and pocket.

Total population of the county, 3,672.

The following are the Merchants at Shieldsborough:

DRY GOODS AND GROCERIES.—Carr, R. W., Combell, ——, Muniz, M., Rosetto; J., Touline & Carver, Wilson, S. C. & Co.

DRY GOODS.—Bremind, S.

GROCERIES.—Mazilly, John, Robira, J., Savinovich, L., Soler, P., Spotona, ——.

DRUGGIST.—Sales, F.

TAILOR.—Clenk, G.

SHOES AND BOOTS.—Hoffman, C., Wineberger, G.

SADDLES AND HARNESS.—Wagner, D.

STEAM SAW MILL.—Toulme & Walker.

An 1854 glimpse of the scene in Hancock County shows how the lumber industry is already taking hold, even though it is still sparsely inhabited. Note the ironic closing sentence – some things never seem to change! The NO&M became part of the Southern by 1900.

located in a totally rural setting deep in the forest, far from 'civilisation'. These logging camps, sometimes referred to as 'villages', should not be confused with the sawmill towns which grew up near rivers and later on the regular (ie permanent) railroads. These were a more-or-less direct counterpart of the coal towns discussed earlier. But there is no apparent equivalent of the log camp within the mining industry, be it coal, phosphate, or whatever. The mobility of the logging camps is reflected in the accommodation of the (predominantly black) workers. This generally consisted of box cars complete with wheels, so that, when the immediate surrounding trees had been stripped, the whole camp could move on by railway lines built by the lumber company — also usually with black labour of course. Where the railroad was involved with the coal mine — and often they belonged to the same company — the reliance on the twin rails was even more evident in the lumber industry from the 1880s onwards.

Way out among the long-leaf and loblolly pines and literally 'in the sticks' is where I surmise that the barrelhouse was born, and where vocal blues piano and boogie woogie evolved from the earlier 'barrelhouse-style' singers — inspired by the ever-present railroad. But first of all, it seems relevant to delve into some of the earlier history of lumber and its importance to the working-class black community from whence the blues sprang into life.

One unidentified source reports that the timber industry showed up for the first time in the US Census for 1840. But there appear to have been scattered sawmills, certainly in south Mississippi along the Pearl and Pascagoula Rivers, before this date. A diarist, Miss Adeline Russ, wrote of a visit to this region in the piney woods at the end of March 1829: 'We spent the 29th and 30th at Uncle Wingate's.' Thigpen tells us that Judge Wingate 'for a long time had a sawmill at Logtown'.[18] Certainly, by 1840 there were a total of twenty-two sawmills in the Mississippi coast counties of Hancock, Jackson and Lawrence, which included Logtown, located on the Pearl River.[19] Indeed, in association with one of the earliest of the Pearl River lumbermen, W.J. Poitevent, Hickman notes that, in 1844, 'D.R. Wingate... was operating a sawmill'.[20] Most of these mills would have been situated on the riverside before the coming of the railroads.

These early sawmills would have employed slave labour almost exclusively in the antebellum period and the new freedmen after the Civil War. After 1865, the once-plentiful forests of white pine around the Great Lakes in Wisconsin, Michigan, etc. were seriously depleted and Northern lumbermen started looking to the great stands of yellow pine in the South, which by comparison were still largely untouched. One E.J. Stockstill (known as 'Uncle Van'), who was born in 1870 'two miles northeast of Picayune', recollected in 1964 that, when his father decided to move to Gainesville, Miss. in 1875, 'we went down through what is now the west part of Picayune, following generally the present route of the Pearl River Valley Railroad. There was big, fine pine timber everywhere, hardly a log ever having been cut.'[21]

Before the 1880s and the spreading of the railroads, most of the sawmills were on or near a river, and had to employ high-wheeled carts with a team of oxen to haul the lumber to the nearest point where it could be floated down to the mill. Uncle Van gives a description of an early logging camp in 1885 along the Pearl River, when his father was offered a contract by an agent from the large Poitevent sawmill to cut timber there and ship it down to Pearlington, Miss.. After his father accepted the logging contract, he 'got together three four-yoke ox teams of good, well-trained oxen, bought some old-time, high-wheel log carts and set out with about twelve men to start the logging operations... No one lived near where we were logging. The wild turkeys were almost like tame ones... My dad bought two more four-yoke teams of oxen and hired more men. We were bauling about 100 logs a day to the river bank. Now, that was real work, as the logs were all cut with axes back then. Two smart Negro women did the cooking. My dad had a small commissary and would sell the men provisions to carry home to their families. He bought five sows to raise meat, and to eat the left-overs from the camp.'[22] The labour at the camp was all black, as 'the negro slaves had stayed with my folks... the men were for farming, logging, and other things.'[23]

A somewhat earlier account of a logging camp is recounted by

Rafting on the Mississippi, c.1920s.

industrial historian and economist Albert S. Bolles in his classic *Industrial History Of The United States*. Writing in 1878, Bolles (who was born in Connecticut) describes a camp in the late 1870s, which was set up at an unknown location every fall 'for a winter's campaign in the woods'. In his excellent book — despite its slight bias against the South-- he presents a rose-tinted, romanticist's-eye view of a hard, manual operation that could also be very dangerous and monotonous: 'An eligible neighborhood, where there are plenty of trees, and a stream of water near by with perhaps a more or less sloping bank, is selected; and thither a gang of able-bodied woodsmen are despatched ere snow flies. Rude log-huts called 'camps' are erected, with wooden chimneys, and beds of hemlock-boughs; and here they stay for the season. The staple of their diet is salt pork and rum. At night, cards, story-telling and general hilarity, beside a blazing fire, form a marked contrast to the hard toil of the day and the loneliness and cheerlessness of a forest-winter.' [24] The 'season' starts in December and 'generally ends in March'.

He goes on to give a graphic account of the whole logging operation: 'The trees are cut, stripped of their branches, sawed with great cross-cut two-handed saws into logs of the desirable size, and hauled into convenient localities for drawing to the water-side. Then, by means of a chain, a skid, and an ox-team, the logs are loaded upon huge sleds... and are hauled down to the river and emptied in the ice-crust, serving to keep them from floating off... When spring comes, the logs are floated down stream in an immense mass called a "drive". Generally this branch of work is carried on by a

Chapter 2 — Skippin' 'round from log to log

different set of men from those who cut the logs.' Bolles describes the millions of accumulated logs hurtling down swollen rivers full of spring waters: 'The scene resembles an immense herd of furious cattle, such is the confusion, and leaping of logs upon one another.' [25]

In 1928, Gertrude 'Ma' Rainey — the 'Mother of the Blues' — recorded her 'Log Camp Blues' [Paramount 12804], which recalls this scene still in evidence in parts of the South as late as 1930:

> Down in Mississippi, where the air is low an' damp. *(x2)*
> Low down on the Delta is a great big loggin' camp.
>
> I can see my daddy, skippin' round from log to log. *(x2)*
> [All the] hands(?) is standin' on the cargo, everybody's on the hog.

In Southern black parlance being 'on the hog' means to be broke or 'cold in hand'. This indicates that the black workers had yet to be paid — and this didn't always happen when it was due!

Gertrude 'Ma' Rainey* (*née* Pridgett) was born in 1886 in Columbus, Ga. and started into travelling shows at an early age, meeting up with Will 'Pa' Rainey and becoming his wife in 1904. They proceeded to tour all over the South as 'The Raineys – Assassinators of the Blues' in minstrel shows such as the famous Rabbit Foot Minstrels and Silas Green From New Orleans as well as other companies *(see Chapter 8)*. Ma Rainey's voice was powerful, and (unlike Bessie Smith) she was often accompanied by 'down home' instruments like kazoo, jug or washboard, as on 'Log Camp Blues'. She was, on balance, the favourite of all vaudeville-blues singers among black audiences throughout the South, although she didn't start her recording career until December 1923, when she was already a seasoned

Ma Rainey, 'Mother of the Blues', c.1928

---

* See the essential book on this singer, *Mother Of The Blues: A Study Of Ma Rainey* by Sandra Leib (University of Massachusetts Press, 1981).

57

performer of some 37 years of age.

Although there was a healthy lumber industry in her home state of Georgia, the singer acknowledges the prime importance of the scene in southern Mississippi — even if she does refer to the 'Delta' as being in the northern part of that state! She may, of course, have been referring to the actual delta of the 'Father of Rivers'. Her truly awesome vocal and the 'dirty' accompaniment with its booting jug eloquently conjures up the smell and feel of the piney woods as she apparently advocates better-paid employment in a logging camp:

> Meal is in my meat-box, chickens runnin' around my yard.
> Meal is in my meat-box, chickens runs around my yard.
> Yearlin's in my cow-pen, I never know the time was hard.

Yet, everything has its down-side, and when her man is away for months at a time, she misses him more and more. Finally, she can't stand him being gone and checks to see if she has enough money to catch a train to south Mississippi — although she is determined to go whatever:

> If I can't get no ticket, put on my walkin' shoes. *(x2)*
> I'm goin' to Mississippi, singin' those 'Loggin' Camp Blues'.[26]

The operation described by Bolles and referred to implicitly by Ma Rainey in her opening verse was known as 'rafting'[*], and it could take several days (or weeks!) to get the logs down to the dam, where they were sorted according to the various contractors' marks. The gang of workers was accompanied by a cook on the raft 'with their clothing and provisions' who 'ministers to them as in the logging camp'. The sawmills were located at the site of the dam, and through 'the summer and fall, the logs are forced through the mills, and converted into lumber.' [27]

However, rafting began to decline — especially after 1910, when railroads penetrated the interior of the forests far from the river. Although companies such as the IC and M&O had started this process as early as the 1850s, it was not until the 1870s that Northern demand for yellow pine grew to such an extent that lumber companies required more employees to go deeper into the forests of Mississippi, Georgia, Alabama, etc. In 1870, three railroads, 'the Illinois Central, the Chicago, Burlington & Quincy and the Chicago & Alton each carried over 120 million board feet of lumber.' This was into Chicago alone, and Cronon adds that 'only the city's grain shipments could compare in total volume.' These three railroads all ran south out of Chicago. By 1880, the Windy City's shipments had swelled to 'over a billion

---

[*] Interested readers are referred to Chapter 8 - 'Logging And Rafting (1840-1910)' in *Mississippi Harvest* by Nollie Hickman (see *Bibliography*).

Chapter 2 — Skippin' 'round from log to log

Some black logging workers pose on the running board of an IC locomotive on an early pole road in southern Mississippi, c.1887.

board feet — of which the railroads' share had grown to 95 percent.' [28] This included trainloads of yellow pine which first 'arrived in Chicago in 1877.' [29]

It was around this time that the railroads started to go further into the virgin stands of longleaf or 'yellow pine' and built dummy lines for this purpose. These were of a temporary nature to start with, and were often called 'tramroads'. In 1867, Henry Leinhard, a millman in the Southern lumber industry, had 'built what may have been the first crude tramroad for transporting logs in Mississippi. It bore little resemblance to the heavy steel rails that were to be used for later logging operations, for it was constructed of wooden scantlings placed end to end to form the tracks upon which trucks containing only a few hundred feet of logs were pulled by mules and oxen.' [30] As time passed and Leinhard's mills became more successful, 'a pole road was constructed by laying poles end-to-end to form rails, and a steam locomotive weighing from five to ten tons was used to pull the log cars.' [31]

Later still, these dummy lines would use 'the heavy steel rails' and would reach as far as thirty miles deep into the piney woods. There, the lumber company would set up a log camp and, to keep their largely black workforce from melting into the forest, they also provided reasons for staying. This was often in the form of a makeshift shack or perhaps an old box car which featured music, liquor and women! At some point, these shacks became known as 'barrelhouses'. The women were generally prostitutes, who often made their own way to these camps via the dummy lines strewn not just across southern

Chapter 2 — Skippin' 'round from log to log

Laying rails through the piney woods in East Texas, c.late 1890s.

Mississippi, but also East Texas, Alabama, Georgia and other Southern states. Many of these lines were built to standard gauge (ie 4'8½", which became the norm on British railways) and connected with main line railroads. Some of the dummy lines or roads became common carriers and ran passenger as well as freight trains. But, for an unemployed black worker or blues singer, the price of a ticket could often be out of reach, as Ma Rainey intimated.

A young and near-white looking singer from Dallas, Texas called Bessie Tucker presented her blues one step back and nearer to the roots than even Ma Rainey. Tucker's hollered and moaning vocals on 'The Dummy' [Victor 21708] portray a young prostitute jumping on a freight train (or perhaps a mixed train of freight and passenger cars) to get to the log camp and hopefully ply her trade. But the railroads were well aware of the 'freeloaders' or hobos *(see Chapter 10)* and employed railroad police — generally poor whites, who sometimes acted more like thugs in their ways of dealing with this problem. In the song, Tucker is hoboing to Alabama to look for *'a man I love, named Sam'*, when she runs into trouble with the railroad police:

> Now, when I got on the dummy[*], didn't have no fare,
> The police asked me what I was doin' on there.
> I got on the dummy, mama, didn't have no fare,
> An' the police asked me, asked me what I was doin' on there.

---

[*] Not only were the tramroads called 'dummy', but sometimes also the trains that ran on them.

Unfortunately, her 'Sam' story falls on deaf ears, and she is dealt with swiftly and brutally before being thrown out of the box car:

> Well, he caught me by the hand, he led me to the door,
> He hit me 'cross the head with a two-by-four.
> Caught me by the hand, led me to the door,
> An' he hit me 'cross the head with a two-by-four.

But, despite her reportedly small stature, she is one 'tough cookie' (as Texas pianist Whistlin' Alex Moore once told Paul Oliver in an interview), and she makes it to the logging camp to advertise her 'wares' in poetic terms:

> Well, I ain't no pullet, I'm a real young hen.
> If you come by here once, you'll come back again.
> I ain't no pullet, boys, I'm a real young hen.
> If you come by once, you'll come back again.[32]

Pitifully few facts are known about this superb singer, who may have been a prostitute at one time[30], other than she was recorded on two occasions by Victor records in 1928 down in Memphis, and three times in 1929 in what was presumably her home town of Dallas, Texas. Her recorded legacy of twenty-two sides — including a few alternate takes — has been issued/reissued, apart from 'Pick On Me Blues' [Victor, unissued]. Her style is close to the field holler as employed by fellow Texan, Alger 'Texas' Alexander, and her CD is an essential acquisition for the serious blues historian *(see Discography)*.

III

But the barrelhouse where Bessie Tucker was looking for 'tricks' had a precedent, I believe, back in the late 1870s, when logging camps were no longer near the river but deep in the longleaf pines. This was the time when railroad companies had started to take over the entire operation, thereby eliminating rafting. As one US author put it, the railroad rescued the lumber industry 'from the tyranny of the river and made the industry a year-round enterprise.'[34] (This referred to the fact that some rivers or 'streams' often froze over for part of the year, or were simply unnavigable because of unpredictable currents, sandbanks and snags (part-tree trunks, which had become embedded just under the surface of the water). Also, of course, the major rivers such as the Mississippi would change course on occasion, due to extreme climatic conditions, resulting in heavy flooding.)

It is my theory that the first barrelhouses started in the logging camps, and that vocal blues/piano and boogie woogie was born or evolved from these

'End-of-line' logging camp in southern Arkansas, c.early 1900s.

places. But, like the source of the blues 'river', the beginnings of the barrelhouse are shrouded in historical fog. If we follow the 'golden rule' of economics of supply and demand, then this begs the question as to when and where the barrelhouse was first required. I maintain that the barrelhouse first appeared in a logging camp, maybe a decade or so before they were to be found in the levee camps along the Mississippi River, or dotted around the Southern countryside. Between 1870 and 1880, something in the region of one hundred sawmills were operating in the longleaf pines across southern Mississippi. Additionally, forty or fifty were 'erected in the region tributary to Augusta, Ga.; and a number of large mills... were built in northern Florida. In 1870, nine mills in the vicinity of Pensacola sawed 420,000 feet daily. Mobile... (in 1869) shipped nearly 4,000,000 feet from its wharves.' [35]

As Hickman points out, this expansion could, to some extent, be attributed to 'the construction of a railroad from Mobile to New Orleans.' [36] This road, the New Orleans, Mobile & Texas RR, was later to become part of the L&N, which by 1880 had also acquired a link down to Pensacola, Fla.. A large majority of these sawmills would also have had logging camps served by dummy lines connecting to the IC, M&O, L&N and other lumber carriers. 'In 1905, there were reported to be in Mississippi 527 logging camps containing 8,185 workers. An unnamed writer stated in 1913 that two-thirds of all the mills possessed logging camps. Almost one-half of these had semi-permanent houses, while in the other half the workers were quartered in camp cars. The Finkbine Lumber Company, Edward Hines, the Westons, Eastman–Gardiner and other firms built logging villages out in the forest... After the timber was cut in their vicinity, the villages were moved to new locations.' [37]

As with the earlier accounts by Uncle Van and Albert Bolles, Hickman makes no allusion to any music or the barrelhouse. Apart from bootlegging liquor, the workers amused themselves by swapping tall tales on rainy days at the commissary.

Nevertheless, with the advent of the dummy lines travelling farther into the forest, the size of logging camps increased and the number of workers grew to an extent where some sort of more 'focused' entertainment was warranted to 'keep the workers happy'. Hickman notes that 'large log camps composed of fifty workers or more were virtually unknown before the construction of tramroads.' [38] Since earlier logging operations were on a small scale, many of their camps would not have consisted of many more than twenty workers, and often less than this number. As with Uncle Van's recollections, all the men would be known by name by the boss (in this case, his father). At some indeterminate point from the late 1870s onwards, the lumber companies deemed it necessary to install a 'dance hall', which became the barrelhouse. This quickly became a rural icon in the South and was often painted green, indicating 'Colored Only' (the large majority of blacks at that time were unable to read or write).

Silvester quotes pianist Little Brother Montgomery's recollections of the logging camp barrelhouse back in the late 19-teens and early 1920s. It was 'a combination dance hall, crap-game dive and whorehouse. This was known as the "barrelhouse", the "honky tonk" or the "juke joint". Furnished by the lumber company with drink and a piano, it was a rough, tough place... they'd have fights'n'cuts; sometimes one of them'd kill somebody and never stop gambling — just sit on him and keep a-gambling, and back in them days they didn't pay no attention... sometimes the women dance on top of the piano, all had a wonderful time. They shoot craps, dice, drink whiskey, dance, every modern devilment you can do, the barrelhouse is where it's at.' [39]

On 'Moon Going Down' [Paramount 13014], Charley Patton's raw and bruising vocal captures the atmosphere that surely prevailed in the barrelhouse of the 1920s:

> There's a house over yonder, painted all over green. *(x2)*
> *(Spoken)* Boy, you know I know it's over there.
> Some of the finest young women, Lord, a man most ever seen. [40]

Not surprisingly, one of the earliest forms of music in these establishments was soon referred to as 'barrelhouse piano'.

IV

US blues researcher Mack McCormick refers to the Texas variety of barrelhouse piano as 'erotic, exuberantly stomping music that once thrived in workingmen's roadhouses and tonks'. Both 'roadhouse' and '(honky) tonk' were alternative — usually white — names for the barrelhouse, although the name that finally stuck was the black term, 'juke (or jook) joint'.

Barrelhouse piano, as well as the guitar, harp and fiddle (which sometimes also featured in these establishments), imitated the sound or 'click' of the earlier railroads (remembering that this was long before the age of continuous rail which cancelled out the rhythmic 'clicketty-clack' of the old short-rail sections), as well as capturing the sudden contrasting sounds that a train made when travelling over a trestle bridge, going through a tunnel, passing a busy marshalling yard full of freight cars, or rolling over a myriad of crossovers and switches. These effects were often accomplished with the right hand. Some of this 'barrelhouse' style is present in the work of Will Ezell, Jabo Williams, Skip James, Roosevelt Sykes, Charley Taylor, Piano Kid Edwards, Walter Roland and Kid Stormy Weather, to name but a few. McCormick provides a more formal musicological description: 'A hard-hitting, physically heavy touch with fast releases and strongly stated initial themes; strong elements of ragtime, particularly in playing blues with rag syncopation and technique; occasional use of one-note bass passages in lieu of the walking bass; a tendency to rush and anticipate the beat', adding: 'It has no sharp definition nor proper name, though the pianists themselves (from East Texas) sometimes vaguely refer to their playing as in "the rambling style".' [41]

The 'walking bass' McCormick refers to is another name for boogie woogie, which seems to have evolved out of barrelhouse styles. Some blues singers referred to boogie woogie as 'Fast Western' and 'Dudlow Joe', amongst others. Reports vary as to when this piano genre was first heard but appear to reflect a time period from the turn of the Twentieth Century into the early 1900s. The celebrated blues and folk singer Huddie Ledbetter ('Leadbelly') commented in the introduction to his '4, 5 and 9' [2-LP *Last Session (Volume 2)*, Folkways FP-242) 1953] that boogie didn't get its name until 'the writers got 'old to it'. He claimed that piano players who couldn't read music were 'walkin' the basses' or 'speedin' ' as early as 1903. To this he added that 'they didn't know what they were doin' '.

Leadbelly gives a short description of those early days in a barrelhouse: 'You walk up to a man an' tell 'im to: "Walk the basses for me." Give 'im a drink or somethin'. He start to walkin' '. Soundin' good, the girls is jumpin' in the barrelhouse... I was walkin' 'em, too.'

He goes on to relate how boogie piano influenced the bass-oriented twelve-string guitar playing that was one of his trademarks: 'I want to play the guitar by a piano. I played piano time, piano rhythm. That's the reason I like the piano bass around my music. I'd always sit on the bass-side (ie the left-hand side) by the piano. Copied the jive the way the boys was playin', an' that's the way I play it.'

So, at some point after 1904, pianists who could read music (or 'writers') picked up on 'walkin' the basses'. '[There] was Meade Lux Lewis. There's old James P. Johnson, he used to walk the basses for a long time. *He* didn't know what 'e was doin'! But when the writers written it up, an' give it a name: 'the boogie woogie'. Now everybody can boogie then, what readin' boogie we was 'speedin' ', at that time. We didn't take time to read, which we wouldn't. We didn't want to read. We just speed.' [42]

Another writer, Peter Silvester, notes that Leadbelly 'first heard barrelhouse pianists playing boogie woogie walking the basses in 1899 (or 1901, depending on source). The author asserts that the singer 'might have heard these pianists and this music in the honky tonks of Shreveport's notorious Fannin Street, or perhaps in the juke joints of Caddo County's lumber camps'. [43]

But ultimately, it was the rhythms of the heavy freight and passenger trains which crossed and re-crossed the Southern countryside, certainly by the 1880s, that must have inspired the sensual and sometimes ominous rumblings of early left-handed boogie piano, so intriguing to Leadbelly. Also, the sudden clattering over the points and road crossings, etc, which flashed like the sparks of the snorting locomotive in the often brilliant decoration of the right hand. Certainly, by the late 1880's few working-class blacks were living out of earshot of the lonesome train whistle — and often literally alongside the tracks. As with the Southern countryside and its cities (where a large majority of blacks still lived in the early decades of the Twentieth Century), so too with major Northern locations, which were also hubs of the US railroad 'wheel'. As Harris says of Chicago-born Meade Lux Lewis: 'Having been brought up in a district where the trains thundered by every few minutes of the day and night, it was natural that his music should have been influenced by the rattle of the wheels in their ever-varying rhythms over the rails.' [44] But, although some blues writers and blues singers attribute the beginnings of piano blues and boogie to the log camp, they also include the levee and railroad construction camps. So, other factors need to be taken into consideration if my theory is to have any credence.

V

I am not, of course, attempting to trace the roots of the blues *per se* to the logging camps, although the latter were an important main starting point. It is the piano blues and boogie woogie which I hope to trace back to the barrelhouses deep in the piney woods. There are two main points which I will explore. Firstly, I need to establish that the barrelhouse started in the logging camp, rather than one of the other type of camps (levee, railroad construction, etc.). Secondly, that it was in the log camp barrelhouse that the piano was first utilised by the blues singers and their predecessors.

Even during the Civil War, the notorious convict-lease system *(see Chapter 6)* was used in levee and railroad construction camps, as well as in coal mines. This system endured long after 1865 — in some areas right up to 1928! The convict-lease system had no problem keeping men on the job, with armed guards as well as dogs being deployed. So, a facility such as a barrelhouse was not necessary. This system was undoubtedly used in railroad construction in the earlier post-bellum years. Indeed, Ayers points out that, in the South, 'railroad work on an expanded scale absorbed most of the penal labor *[of virtually every state]* in the 1870s.' [45]

Even in those camps where it was not used, these sites were normally located not far from some kind of town or other. As Silvester says of the Texas & Pacific, which had been laying tracks to Donaldsonville, La. since around 1901: 'It was in the barrelhouses of the railroad camps around Donaldsonville in 1904 (or 1906, depending on source) that the jazz pianist Richard M. Jones first heard boogie woogie played by Stavin' Chain.' [46] But this was in a more urban setting and, as Sam Charters observes, in the railroad camps 'the men lived in box cars, and they could get into a town or find some dancing and excitement without looking too far.' [47]

But the lumber industry, for a number of reasons, did not utilise convict-lease to anywhere like the extent to which levee and railroad builders did. This was in part due to increasing numbers of predominately black convicts being used in the mining industry in the 1880s and 1890s. Thus, the Southern lumbermen could only draw on the residue of black prisoners not already absorbed into mining and railroad building. Another approach was therefore required to keep the black working force in the logging camps. Hickman quotes an observer in 1895 and their comments on black lumber workers. According to this individual, all the African American wanted 'was fair treatment, plenty of food, and *a chance to frolic occasionally.*' [48] The emphasis is mine. This 'chance' was, I maintain, provided by the installing of the earliest barrelhouses.

But we need to briefly look at other rural scenarios to see if parallel scenes were also starting up elsewhere. Or, put another way: where else was a barrelhouse needed in the Southern countryside in the 1870s?

First off, it is relevant to remember that the 'official' Reconstruction era ran from 1867-77 — in other words, for most of the period under consideration. Briefly, Reconstruction was a genuine attempt by the US Federal Government to integrate the ex-slaves into free (white-dominated) society. Freedman Bureaux were set up in the Southern states for advice, general help and guidance. Federal troops were on hand to make sure things progressed as smoothly as possible. Blacks became US citizens, were given the vote, and gradually came to occupy responsible social and political positions such as policemen and state legislators. But the inevitable corruption (by both whites and blacks) soon made an appearance, and local white attitudes towards former slaves were slow — indeed difficult — to adapt to the entirely new situation in the post-bellum South. As early as 1872, Reconstruction had broken down or 'failed' in some states and it was a dead duck by the time the Hayes Compromise of 1877 was agreed. In effect, this was when the Federal Government pulled the troops out of the South and (on the understanding of white support for Rutherford Hayes for the next US President) left the region under the control of its all-powerful white plantation owner class.

For about a decade during Reconstruction, many blacks took to travelling about the countryside at will, just to reassure themselves they were actually 'free' *(see Chapter 10)*. While a large majority eventually resigned themselves to virtual agricultural slavery under the sharecrop system, a smaller but significant group rejected the white 'Protestant work ethic' and continued as itinerant wanderers. It was from these people that the blues singers finally evolved.

Indeed, many black workers would seek out the blues or its precursors in their leisure time. Two forms this would take were the country picnics and fish fries. The former (also known as 'frolics' or 'sukey jumps') were essentially an extension of the illicit 'arbor meetings', when slaves would congregate in the early hours of morning to hold their own (mainly religious) ceremonies before the Civil War. Often held in a clearing in the woods, a picnic could last for two, three or four days. A whole hog might be roasted on the spit over an open fire while the people drank cheap whiskey or moonshine liquor. Many would take to dancing to the musicians who would be hired for the occasion.

Sadly, I have not come across any early blues recordings which depict this phenomenon. An unissued Victor title from 1928, 'Country Spaces' by Ida May Mack, may well be an exception. Another side that has survived is 'Country Breakdown' [Columbia 14475-D] by the superb singer and twelve-string guitarist, Charley Lincoln (*aka* Charlie Hicks, elder brother of 'Barbecue Bob' Hicks), from his first session in Atlanta on an early November day in 1927. Although the lyric doesn't directly refer to a picnic or the woods, Lincoln could be describing the role of the blues singer at a picnic, where he might get nickels and dimes from an appreciative audience, and an endless supply of alcohol. Using mainly traditional 'floating verses', he injects some ironic humour that would have been much appreciated by revellers:

(Spoken) Lord, Lord! I'm gittin' drunk now, sure enough.
I'm leavin' here, mama. Cryin' won't make me stay.
Lord, I'm leavin' here, mama. Cryin' won't make me stay.
Ah! The more you cry, says, [the] further I'm goin' away.

> Soon as I get sober, I'll make me drunk again.
> Soon as I get sober, gonna make me drunk again.
> Says, I'm gon' leave the chicken, says, I'm goin' back to the hen.
>
> Did you ever wake up, 'twixt midnight an' day?
> Did you ever wake up, mama, 'twixt midnight an' day?
> Have your arms round your pillow where your good girl used to lay?
>
> I believe to my soul, my brown got a stingoree.
> Oh! I believe to my soul, my brown got a stingoree.
> When I woke up this mornin', says, she was stingin' poor me.

While he is playing, the blues singer catches a lot of eye-contact from the female dancers (whose husbands might be watching!), but meanwhile his own girlfriend has disappeared from view and he's worried she might be succumbing to the charms of another man out in the woods. So, he reminds her in his song that, as a hired blues singer, he has more money than anybody else at that picnic. For the duration of the latter, he is 'Thee Man!':

> Don't want no dollar, mama. Sure can't use no half.
> Don't want no dollar, mama. I sure can't use no half.
> Say, I got a brownskin, I can hear her laugh.[49]

The whole family would go along these affairs, and at one point — possibly as early as 1879 — W.C. Handy, the future self-styled 'Father of the Blues', also began attending such functions as a child. 'Handy's favorite uncle, Whit Waller, often played the violin at country frolics while his young nephew beat rhythm on the fiddle strings with a pair of knitting needles.'[50] Sometimes whites would hold these country frolics and employ black musicians. Or both races would be there, though they would be kept separate. So, two stages would be set up, with entertainment for blacks on one and for whites on the other. The celebrated bluesman, Big Bill Broonzy once recalled playing the fiddle, his first instrument, at such functions. Leadbelly and Yank Rachell also performed at these picnics. The latter was adept on both guitar and mandolin, and recalls how he and his brother played at a picnic 'out in a grove, like a shade — trees and everything. You had lights: they put corn oil in a Coca-Cola bottle — a Coca-Cola bottle used to be little then — you put some rag in there and soak it *[with kerosene or paraffin oil]* stick it there on a string, and we'd play at the picnic and have a big time, man. Them girls dancing, dust fly all over.'

But these picnics or frolics would not normally feature a piano. Like Handy's uncle, Big Bill, Leadbelly, Charley Lincoln and other musicians so employed, they played stringed instruments that were easy to carry around, keep dry and in tune, such as fiddles, mandolins and guitars.

And so too, at the rural 'fish fries'. These were often held at a farm on a Friday or Saturday night* and, while many would be dancing to the fiddle and mandolin, others would be using the nearby barn as a gambling room. Rachell continues: 'Ladies be in the kitchen cooking fish, put a table 'cross the door, and they'd be in there cooking. You want a fish sandwich, they'd give you a fish sandwich, then we'd be out there dancing, break the floor down dancing. Some guy out there in the barn shooting craps and losing money, come back, his wife dancing with somebody, he start a big fight, go to shooting and some of them jumping out of the window. I run in and stayed with a mule one night, got so rough there. Old mule say "whu" to me. I said "whu" right back to him.' [51]

Apart from the sheer impracticality of transporting a piano out to the woods, the vast majority of blacks in the closing decades of the Nineteenth Century were not able to afford such an instrument. Many also kept moving from place to place and from farm to farm in an effort to get a sharecrop deal that gave them fair treatment and some financial rewards, some eventually gravitating to Southern cities such as Atlanta, New Orleans, Birmingham and Memphis. By the late 1920s, fish fries in New Orleans were held on 'mostly Saturday night' — just like the one so graphically described by Louis Jordan.

Walter Lewis, a pianist who had moved to the Crescent City from Prarieville, La., some ten miles south-west of Baton Rouge, takes up the story: 'Somebody gave a supper and he'd hang a red light outside, so people would know that's where the supper is at. They used to call it 'fish fries'. When you go there, they got a piano, you go in and play' *(see Appendix I)*. Another informant, Alton Purnell, recalled for Karl Gert zur Heide that, around this period 'the piano in New Orleans was all the go, and there were a gob of pianists around in those days. Most every house had a piano in it.' [52]

This describes an urban scene in the late 1920s, but was this the case in the 1880s in New Orleans — or any other Southern city? Apparently not, as the celebrated pianist, 'Georgia Tom' Dorsey recalled that, a decade earlier down on Decatur Street, and in the black section of Atlanta generally, 'those who had pianos were kind-of scarce at that time. Everybody didn't have a piano.' [53]

It is generally accepted that the blues started out in the countryside — hence the terms used by writers since the 1960s, such as 'country' or 'rural'. This theory is well-supported by the recollections of older blues singers who were interviewed upon being 'rediscovered'. As the archetypal and fiercely intense singer, Bukka White — succinctly put it: 'Didn't have no jazz in the cotton fields. That's where the blues start from, back across them fields... It started right behind one of them mules or one of them log houses — one of them log camps — or the levee camp. That's where the blues sprung from.

---

* In the late 1940s, the highly popular R&B band, Louis Jordan & The Tympany Five, counted 'Saturday Night Fish Fry' [Decca 24725] amongst their successes.

I know what I'm talking about.' [54] And the well-known pianist, Clarence Williams (an accompanist as well as a bandleader in his own right), 'in his boogie portfolio... handed down the perception that boogie developed in the lumber camps, logging camps, turpentine camps, and railroad camps.' [55]

In those early days, while the blues was still emerging, the country frolic/picnic and the fish fry, as well as the travelling shows and itinerant string bands — including mandolin orchestras* — more than satisfied the demand in the rural South for entertainment and temporary escape from the monotonous drudgery of farm life. There were also, as early as 1871, railroad excursions which charged a cheap fare to major cities and 'jubilees' on public holidays such as Emancipation Day and July 4, as well as at lay-off periods, when all the crops were in, during the rest of the year. There was no apparent need for a barrelhouse, or a piano, in any of the country locations at this time, the sole exception being the logging camps of southern Mississippi, East Texas and elsewhere.

If boogie woogie is a part of the early blues, then it follows that *piano* blues must be where it originated from. If blues started in the countryside, then the logging camp barrelhouse must be the main contender for the earliest blues singers who accompanied themselves on a piano. Following on from the early barrelhouse styles, and inspired by the rhythms and sounds of the trains on the dummy lines in the forest, boogie was surely from somewhere in the woods. But it is a remarkably curious thing that vocal blues/piano, the most popular form after vocal and guitar, was not recorded in any depth until 1928 — this being some two years after male singers (who were the most common blues *musicians*) had reversed the female dominance on record of vaudeville-blues which had started in 1920. A study of the contents of *Blues & Gospel Records* for the years 1920-27 inclusive, reveals that, out of some of the five thousand blues listed (a conservative estimate), there are but 35 sides by 26 singers that bear the legend 'vo. p.' (ie 'vocal, piano'). Three of these are said to be 'prob. p.', as opposed to someone else providing this accompaniment; a further seven feature another instrument (cornet or fiddle) and one title with harmonica and kazoo; eight more feature the singer/pianist as part of a vocal duet, with added cornet on three Mike Jackson sides from 1926. In all, this yields a total of 50 examples (under 1% of the estimated total listed in *Blues & Gospel Records*) of blues or 'bluesy' piano on record up until the end of 1927.**

There seems to be one main reason for this low 'turnout' of singer/pianists during the first eight years of blues recordings. During the

---

* These 'orchestras' could often be some 20-strong and included all members of the mandolin family — the mandola, etc. Both blacks and whites featured this phenomenon.
** There are also six gospel items and a Mike Jackson performance with Thomas Morris & His Seven Hot Babies, plus two band recordings featuring Georgia Gorham, on which she is listed as 'poss. own p.' [56] These nine sides fall outside the vocal/piano blues argument being put forward.

antebellum period, the piano was generally associated with plantation owners' wives and daughters trying to perfect mainly classical pieces in their parlour. This more refined style of piano music would have been overheard by the slaves in the 'big house', who not unnaturally identified the instrument with the Southern aristocracy and the gentility of the drawing room. Bolles noted in 1878 that, in the USA at least, the piano was 'comparatively a recent invention, dating back no farther than 1760'.[57] It appears significant that the earliest reference to an African American playing a piano in the colonial or antebellum eras that I have come across in forty years is the following entry in the diary of a freedman aspiring to white bourgeois 'respectability' in the 1830s.[*]

William Johnson was a native of Natchez, Miss., and as well as being a barber, moneylender (to whites and blacks) and slave owner, also dabbled in the lumber business and speculated in capital investment. On 22 December 1835, Johnson recorded that he 'paid Mr. Maury $15 for repairing my Piano Forte and gave him orders to sell it for the Best price He could get for it. But that he must not sell it for less than $70.'[58] Johnson obviously bought another piano as, by 19 January 1838, he had written: 'Tonight I sent my piano to the Duchman *[sic]* to repair and play on it.'[59] While the fiddle, mandolin, and indeed all stringed instruments, were regarded by the upwardly mobile black middle classes — including the religious community — as the 'Devil's instruments', the piano seemed to be cloaked in (predominantly female) respectability.

On the flip side of this female coin, in the latter decades of the Nineteenth Century it was prostitutes who seemed to monopolise the piano/vocals. These women would normally be found in the 'sporting houses' and brothels in Southern cities, as well as out on the West Coast, where blacks had been migrating since the end of the Civil War. For example, one report stated that, in San Francisco, Ca. on Berry, Morton and Dupont Streets, 'the windows are left open, half-naked and brazenfaced, painted prostitutes are seated at pianos playing and singing lewd songs.'[60]

Whichever way the macho male blues singer looked at it, the piano was inextricably linked with women — certainly into the 1890s. So, around this time and into the 1900s, a male singer had to adopt a strong heterosexual stance if he wanted to accompany himself on the piano. Jazz pianist Jelly Roll Morton, who also featured blues, put it this way at a Library of Congress session in 1938: 'Of course, when a man played piano, the stamp was on him for life — the femininity stamp. An' I didn't want that on, so, of course, when I did start to playin' — the songs were kinda smutty a bit, not *so* smutty, but somethin' like this.'[61] He then sang an unexpurgated version of 'Winin' Boy Blues', which was every bit as blatantly sexual as Lucille Bogan's

---

[*] There are two other examples that I have discovered: an ex-slave and successful businessman in Kentucky and a woman music teacher in Tennessee; during 1863 and 1864, respectively (see *Slave Testimony* by John Blassingame *(Ed)*, Louisiana State University Press, 1998 *(reprinted)*).

unissued version of 'Shave 'Em Dry' (later released on the Various Artists LP, *Screening The Blues* [CBS 63288] 1968)[*], but without Bogan's joyous exuberance[**]. In fact, Morton's vocal approach was how I imagine Bing Crosby might have done it!

It was around 1895 that Jelly Roll Morton was introduced to the glories of the piano… at a surprisingly tender age [at] parties where he heard the talented pianist and blues singer Mamie Desdume and others. He insists, however, that Mamie was the one who impressed herself chiefly on his mind: 'My, but she could really play this number'":

Cow Cow Davenport, c.1925.

> Two-nineteen done took my baby away.
> Two-nineteen took my baby away.
> Two-seventeen bring her back some day'."

The piano cast its spell on him.' [62] (Significantly, Mamie's verse refers to trains so numbered.)

An attempt to disassociate himself from the 'femininity stamp' might explain why pioneer boogie pianist Charles 'Cow Cow' Davenport from Alabama (who, it is thought, derived his nickname from the cowcatcher on the front of US steam locomotives[***]) either sang or played — but never both — on most of the 56 sides (including alternate takes) that he and Dora Carr made between 1925 and 1938. He recorded four versions of his famous 'Cow Cow Blues' between 1925 and 1928. The two under his own name are instrumentals, with the added cornet of B.T. Wingfield on 'New Cow Cow Blues' [Paramount 12452] from January 1927. ('New' because he had

---

[*] A tamer version [Banner 33475] was commercially released in 1935.
[**] For the full text of 'Winin' Boy Blues' [General 4004] and 'Shave 'Em Dry', and an in-depth discussion on sexuality in the blues, see 'The Blue Blues' (Chapter 6 in *Screening The Blues* by Paul Oliver (Da Capo Press, 1989 (reprinted)).
[***] Before the use of fencing out in cattle country on the prairies, animals would often stray on to the single steel track. This would naturally sometimes cause accidents — or at the very least delays — in the train journey. So, in the early days, some railroad companies fixed a long iron spike to the front of their locomotives! Mercifully, an enlightened(?) industry replaced this gory appendage with the more 'friendly' and familiar apparatus termed a 'cowcatcher'.

already featured this title in two sessions with Dora Carr during 1925: Carr is the vocalist on one version accompanied by Davenport [OKeh 8250], and she is joined by him on his only vocal for 'Cow Cow Blues' on a pre-war recording for the other. Sadly, this Gennett side remains unissued.) Davenport did not even play piano at all on his first two sessions from 1924-25 with Dora Carr for the OKeh and Gennett labels, his stool being taken by William Smith and the better-known Clarence Williams.

The 'femininity stamp' might also explain why blues singers in these early years would normally only sing frankly sexual or 'smutty' songs when playing the piano. This naturally limited where, in the rural areas of the South, they could feature such material and present themselves as singer/pianists. One of the earliest such places, if not *the* earliest, was the juke joint/barrelhouse found in the logging camps and also on the 'turpentine farms'.

The turpentine industry, a spin-off from lumber operations since the early colonial era, was again predominantly black worker-oriented. Most of the turpentine camps were in Georgia, northern Florida and South Carolina, but they could also be found in East Texas, Louisiana, Alabama and elsewhere. While remembering the 'Dirty Dozens' (an old insult song particularly popular amongst male black teenagers), pianist Edwin 'Buster' Pickens recalled for Paul Oliver that, after usually starting off in the barrelhouse with a version of the 'Dozens', 'we had another number was called 'The Ma Grinder', that was first cousin to the Dozens. Well, that number originated in the barrelhouse. It limited itself to that kind of a life: in other words, you couldn't carry it any further. The barrelhouse was as far as you could carry it, because it was a pretty rotten song you know. So, it wouldn't fit just anywhere, but it sure worked when it was in the barrelhouse.' [63]

Another barrelhouse pianist, born in 1892, who was a contemporary of Charley Patton, Blind Lemon Jefferson *et al* was Rufus Perryman, better known as Speckled Red. It was his 1929 recording of 'The Dirty Dozen' [Brunswick 7116] which introduced this long-running theme to disc. 'But they was real bad words, you see. I was playing in one of them turpentine jukes where it didn't matter. Anything I said there was all right in there, you see. I had to clean it up for the record[*], but it meaned the same thing, but it was a different attitude.' Red also recalled the 'Ma Grinder', which had obviously travelled from the East Texas piney woods where Pickens came from, through Louisiana and Georgia, which Red often called home: 'I heard that for years. I don't know where I first heard it. In those days and in them places, you could say some of them smelly words and don't think nothin' of it.' [64]

Many such songs must have been extant in the early years of the barrrelhouse, but not many — unsurprisingly — made it onto wax. Apart from cleaned-up versions of 'The Dirty Dozens', 'The Fives' and a handful of

---

[*] For the full text of the unexpurgated 'Dozens' by Speckled Red, see 'The Blue Blues' (Chapter 6 in *Screening The Blues* by Paul Oliver (Da Capo Press, 1989 *(reprinted)*).

other songs, we can only surmise what 'The Ma Grinder', 'The Cows', etc. sounded like with the appropriate vocal/lyric accompaniment. Robert Shaw, often billed as 'The Last of the Texas Barrelhouse Pianists', recorded 'The Ma Grinder' in 1963 for Chris Strachwitz's Arhoolie label [LP *Texas Barrelhouse Piano*, Arhoolie F-1010], but sadly, although a fine stomping piano piece, it was totally instrumental.

Parts of 'Grinder' as well as 'Cows' were also featured in pre-war recordings by Rob Cooper and Joe Pullum, which also features Cooper's superb piano playing. Cooper's 'West Dallas Drag No. 2' [Bluebird B-5947] was also an instrumental, while Pullum includes a fine vocal on 'Cows, See That Train Comin'' [Bluebird B-5534] which, however, only hints at the 'smouldering' lyric content of the unexpurgated original.

Georgia Tom, c.1928.

Yet, it is significant that some of the most sexually-explicit blues that were not only recorded, but also issued featured male vocalists who accompanied themselves on a piano. Since they could not use expletives (or 'smelly words' as Speckled Red called them), these singers had to employ the art of vocal sensuality to flesh out their often-poetic verses. Although bluesmen such as Leroy Carr and 'Georgia Tom' Dorsey had made the piano an accepted instrument in blues by the end of the 1920s (albeit in conjunction with guitarists Scrapper Blackwell and Tampa Red respectively), it was still regarded warily by bluesmen in 1930, even though by the end of that year male pianists such as Lee Green, Little Brother Montgomery, Charley Taylor, Joe Dean and Roosevelt Sykes had all made a considerable contribution to the record scene. Indeed, on 'Kelly's Special' [Victor 23259] the latter artist (recording here as 'Willie Kelly') says to his piano: *'I'll play your part in a minute.'* Then while he is playing the 'piano's part' he says:

> *(Spoken)* You know, sometime, you know, this piano act contrary: She sorta play by herself. I can't understand that.[65]

Finally, in 1932, Alabaman pianist Jabo Williams set the pace with his fine 'Fat Mama Blues' [Paramount 13130]:

> I said: 'Oh! Fat mama, keep your great big legs off-a me.'
> I said: 'Oh! Fat mama, keep them big legs off-a me.'
> I said: 'Please, fat mama, keep them big legs off-a me.
> Oh! Fat mama, keep them big legs off-a me.
> Keep them great big things off-a me.'
>
> She got great big legs, she got whoppin' thighs.
> She got great big legs, she got... *(piano completes the line)*
> She got great big legs, she got whoppin' thighs.
> An' every time she shakes it, she makes my courage rise.
> An' every time she shakes it, she makes my courage rise.
>
> Says, I'm goin' away, mama, an' I'm goin' to stay.
> An' I'm goin' away, mama, I'm goin' to stay, Lord.
> I'm goin' away mama, I'm goin' to stay.
> Them big legs, baby, gonna keep me away.
> Them big legs gon' keep me away.[66]

Some two years later, fellow Alabaman Walter Roland cut his version as 'Big Mama' [Banner 33282], but still held back on 'barrelhouse-style lyrics' in his recordings until his first session in March 1935, when he cut 'Screw Worm' [Banner 33417] (named after an insect as deadly to cattle as the boll weevil is to cotton) and 'I'm Gonna Shave You Dry'. A.R.C. did not issue the latter, which rivals labelmate Lucille Bogan's likewise unissued 'Shave 'Em Dry' *(see pages 71-72)* (on which she was accompanied by Roland) for 'unbuttoned' sexual content.

1934 witnessed the emergence of the first of a group of vocal/piano blues which, as I have said, were amongst the most sensual and sexually blues ever released. Frank 'Springback' James cut his 'Snake Hip Blues' [Champion 16809, 50018] in this year and included such lines as *'My baby says I am a lightweight / Sometimes I weighs a ton'*... depending on his lover's sexual mood! Even his pseudonym was blatantly sexual! Other artists soon followed James' example. Walter Davis, for instance, recorded such titles as 'Root Man Blues' [Bluebird B-6040] and 'I Can Tell By The Way You Smell' [Bluebird B-6059] at his second session in July 1935. Davis had been recording since 1930, but had always used Roosevelt Sykes as accompanist until he took the plunge in 1935. His 'Think You Need A Shot' [Bluebird B-6498] the following year was a sensual masterpiece rivalled only by James' 'Snake Hip Blues'. Equally explicit was 'Whip It Up And Down' [Decca 7437] by Lee Green, cut in 1937. Like Davis, Green had been recording for some years — since 1929 in fact — although he had usually played his own piano accompaniment.

All these artists surely drew on an earlier tradition, which I maintain started out in the barrelhouses of the logging camps in the form of the admittedly loose format referred to as 'barrelhouse style'. Inspired by the sounds of the trains which served those camps, the unknown early pianists evolved the form commonly known as boogie woogie, as well as the piano blues proper. These styles and the songs they threw up then spread to other areas such as the levee camps and the brothels of Southern cities. Paul Oliver writes: 'Among the most colorful of the characters in blues history is the "barrelhouse" pianist who played for the loggers in sawmill towns and lumber camps. He has become almost a stereotype, conjuring up images of a tough figure in blue duckins playing fingerbusting blues on an upright piano in a saloon whose only other furnishings are barrels and a plank. Like most conventional pictures it is partly true, part distortion. The barrelhouse pianists did indeed play in such joints, but not solely in them.' I agree entirely, except that they played — and sang — in the logging camps before they introduced their 'fingerbusting blues' elsewhere. Oliver adds that, 'to distinguish themselves from the loggers they entertained and the camp-following women who accompanied them, they were inclined to dress smartly — or as well as their slender means and mode of travel would allow.' [67] Blues singers — certainly the recorded ones — all dressed smartly in the latest style, as their various publicity shots reveal.

To give some idea as to how easily even the most remote logging camps could be reached, let us consider East Texas — along with the Mississippi Delta one of the earliest sources of the blues — as a typical example. The Texan railroads were as important to the lumber industry in the late Nineteenth and early Twentieth Centuries as their counterparts in other Southern states. They were important too in the oral transmission of the early blues. This process found a vital route via the logging camps and visiting blues singers, which was speeded up by the spread of the railroads. The singers would appear in a sharp suit, not in 'dirty duckins' or overalls. They had an aura of self-confidence and the white 'bossman' would pay them some cash, give them room and board, and throw in some free liquor as well. To the black logger in a dirty and often dangerous occupation, and sometimes paid in company script only redeemable at the commissary, the blues singer was someone to admire and look up to. Many black worker-musicians would be inspired by a certain tune or turn of phrase and adapt it to their own particular style.

Ever-popular with the women, the blues singer was virtually his own boss as he travelled from camp to roadhouse to medicine show. Many of them rode trains of course, playing and singing the blues as the box cars rumbled along. Not surprisingly, the railroads which boasted the longest mileage often figured in the blues singers' repertoire. As well as the T&NO, the Santa Fe (Texas Division), the International & Great Northern, the Katy,

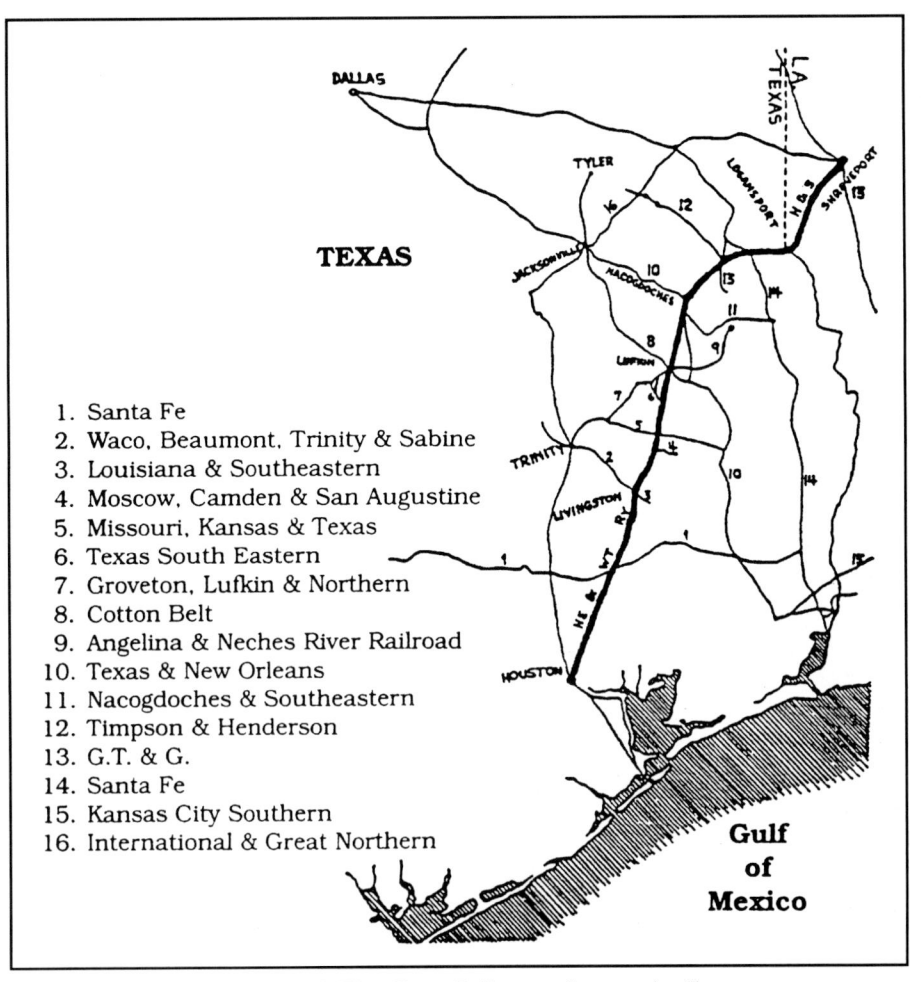

1. Santa Fe
2. Waco, Beaumont, Trinity & Sabine
3. Louisiana & Southeastern
4. Moscow, Camden & San Augustine
5. Missouri, Kansas & Texas
6. Texas South Eastern
7. Groveton, Lufkin & Northern
8. Cotton Belt
9. Angelina & Neches River Railroad
10. Texas & New Orleans
11. Nacogdoches & Southeastern
12. Timpson & Henderson
13. G.T. & G.
14. Santa Fe
15. Kansas City Southern
16. International & Great Northern

Houston, East & West Texas Railway and connecting lines.

the St. Louis & Southwestern ('the Cotton Belt'), the St. Louis & San Francisco ('the Frisco'), the T&P and the Fort Worth & Denver City railroads often featured in the early Texas blues. All of these roads had interests in the logging industry.

Following the example of the pioneering Houston, East & West Texas Ry. in 1877, the T&NO was the next railroad to enter the piney woods in East Texas. In 1881, it connected Beaumont in Hardin County near the Gulf Coast with New Orleans and gave a massive kick-start to the lumber mills in this region of the Lone Star State. Beaumont, in what became known as the Sabine Basin, was the lumber industry's 'principle *[sic]* milling point', and lumber 'then, and for many years after, its principle *[sic]* product.'[68] By 1883, the T&NO had reached the Sabine River and by 1908 had run into Port Arthur at the river's mouth on the Gulf of Mexico, as well as linking up with the city of Shreveport in Louisiana.

But major Texas roads such as the T&NO also had connections with short logging lines, which sometimes carried passengers as well as freight. For instance, the Shreveport, Houston & Gulf Railroad Co. was 'chartered June 19, 1906... to build from Prestridge to Houston a distance of 100 miles. By April they completed nine miles to Manning, Tex., and stopped there, where the Carter-Kelly Lumber Company operated a large sawmill. At Prestridge, the road connected with the Texas & New Orleans and the St. Louis, Southwestern Railroads.' [69] Prestridge is no longer on the map, but was located some ten miles north-west of the Neches River. The latter road, the 'Cotton Belt', also made connection with another small logging line, which became a common carrier officially in 1909: the Texas South-Eastern Railroad Company. 'Its principal traffic is lumber and its manufactures... the President is Arthur Temple of Texarkana, who is also President of the Southern Pine Lumber Co. and the Temple Lumber Co.' [70]

Bessie Tucker, c.1928.

The Frisco and the Santa Fe were involved with similar logging lines that ranged from a few miles to twenty or thirty, these roads connecting Texas logging camps with St. Louis and Los Angeles respectively, whilst one of the shortest logging roads serving the East Texas piney woods was less than six miles long. This was the Trinity Valley Southern Railroad Company chartered in 1901, 'originally a tram road... extending to Dodge on the I&GN.' [71] The I&GN had started life in 1875 by combining the Houston & Great Northern with the International Railway and was sometimes referred to as the 'Great Northern' by blues singers such as Peetie Wheatstraw. Dodge is some ten miles east of Huntsville, Tex. in Walker County. Huntsville was celebrated by Henry Thomas using the same verse on his 'Run Mollie Run' [Vocalion 1141] in 1927, as well as on 'Charmin' Betsy' [Vocalion 1468] from his final session in 1929. In 1899, there was even a 'Logging Camp' served by the Warren & Corsicana Pacific Railway Company. This was two miles from Campwood, and both were 'listed under these names in the Annual reports of the Commission'.[72] (Reed is here referring to the Railroad Commission of Texas.)

Another line which was for 'freight traffic only' was a comparative latecomer, being chartered at the beginning of 1929. This was the Hamlin & Northwestern Railway Company, which the Santa Fe and M-K-T both had links with. The 'Katy', as the latter was usually called, had its main line running from St. Louis (with a branch to Kansas City, Mo.) down into Parsons, Kan. via Dallas (reputedly Bessie Tucker's home town) down to Galveston on the Gulf, with various branches and connections including one with the Texas Midland Railroad. On her 'Katy Blues' [Victor V-38542], Tucker includes what might well be the only reference to the Texas Midland in the blues:

> Katy blowed this mornin', just about five miles from town.
> Mmmmmmm, just about five miles from town.
> Well it blowed so lonesome, almost blew the station down.
>
> Some say the Katy, some say the Santa Fe.
> Mmmmmmm, some say the Santa Fe.
> But that main line Katy fast enough for me.
>
> Katy's at the station, Santa Fe is in the yard.
> Mmmmmmm, Santa Fe is in the yard.
> I would catch that TP, if this Midland's got me barred.[73]

The phrase *'that main line Katy'* was a reference to this railroad's lines serving the logging camps, and it could even have been on the Katy that she was thrown off the 'dummy' as it shunted deeper into the longleaf pines of East Texas. Take 1 of 'Katy Blues' was a test pressing, with identical lyrics delivered in Tucker's usual superb 'moaning' vocal style, and an unidentified 'brass bass' (probably a tuba) adding a somewhat lighter touch to the proceedings. Her experience as a 'rambling woman' is intimated by her references to different railroads which were not all as well-known to her listeners as the Katy, unless they were from the areas served by them. The Texas Midland ran from Ennis, thirty-odd miles south of Dallas, in a north-easterly direction through Greenville and on to Paris. There it met the Santa Fe, whose own Texas main line ran a similar course to that of the Katy down to Galveston. Greenville, Tex. was also served by the Santa Fe, and the Katy crossed it there on the way from Mineola to Denison, which was then headquarters for the M-K-T. (Just maybe, the almost complete blank which is the total knowledge we have of Ms. Tucker could be at least partially filled in by a researcher's visit to Greenville.[*]) Bessie would have been able to catch the TP as an alternative if indeed *'this Midland's got me barred'* or was otherwise preventing her from bumming a ride, and travel down to Mineola,

---

[*] Continuing research by the author, attempting to trace some info/details on Bessie Tucker, is in progress. Any snippet of fresh info would be more than welcome.

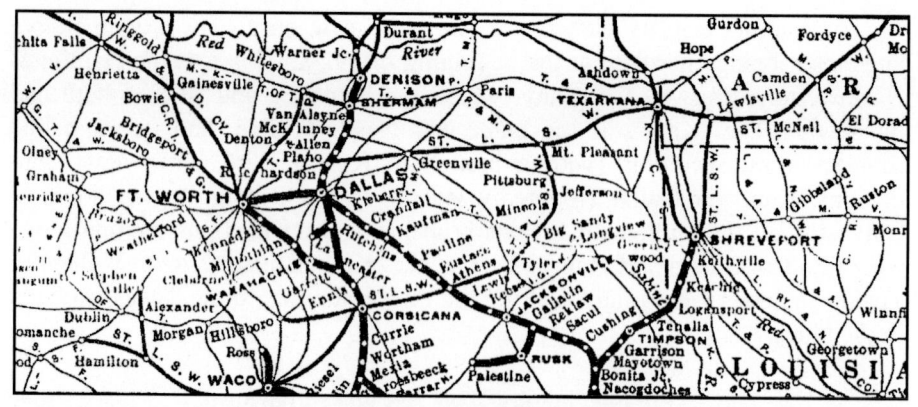

Part of the Mo-Pac system, c.early 1930s.

where she could change over to the Katy to get to Greenville.

Of course, as has already been stated, most of these railroads hauled lumber over their lines — the Santa Fe even lending its name to a body of pianists. The 'Santa Fe group' were so called because they travelled from barrelhouse to barrelhouse on or near this road, playing the piano and singing the blues in the piney woods area of East Texas. These included Rob Cooper, Andy Boy (his surname was Boy), Pinetop Burks and Son Becky — all of whom made it onto record in the 1930s — as well as countless others now beyond our vision who never got the chance. These pianists had certain 'set pieces' by which they were often judged as to their ability to hold down a job in a barrelhouse — 'The Fives', 'The Clinton' and 'The Ma Grinder' among them. Similarly in other Southern states which were blessed with vast tracts of yellow pine. In Mississippi, for instance, there were the '44's' and the related 'Roll And Tumble Blues', usually performed on a guitar[*]. Naturally, these songs shifted from place to place and so became familiar to musicians from other states — 'The Ma Grinder', for example, that Speckled Red learnt in a turpentine juke joint in Georgia.

Logging camps, sprang up in ever-increasing numbers on the relevant lines. In Mississippi for instance, the IC could claim in 1883 that there was 'a sawmill at every train stop of the railroad.'[75] After emerging from receivership in 1895, the Gulf & Ship Island RR 'soon became the artery for an extensive lumbering industry. Lumber camps, log yards and sawmills were located every few miles along the road, and by December 1896, the

---

[*] There is an ongoing discussion which argues the case for either the guitar or the piano as the original instrument to feature 'boogie runs' or the 'walking basses'. Jazzman Bunk Johnson favours the guitar. He is reported as saying that he 'heard the style used by pianists in the logging towns of Mississippi and Louisiana long before the Twenties, and that the insistent repetition of the bass patterns with the left hand, which is such a feature of piano boogie, quite obviously derives from an imitation of the guitar chording used by strolling singers.'[74] For an excellent account of the '44's', see 'The Forty-Fours' (Chapter 3 in *Screening The Blues* by Paul Oliver (Da Capo Press, 1989 *(reprinted)*).

railroad was operating five or six freight trains daily.' [76] The G&SI was ultimately absorbed into the Illinois Central in 1925, while Hickman notes that 'a large portion of the Mobile & Ohio was located in the longleaf pine counties of Greene, Wayne, and Clarke' [77] in south-eastern Mississippi.

The IC and the M&O, often referred to as 'sister railroads', were among the most popular railroads to appear in the blues during the 1920s and '30s. They served St. Louis, Mo. and/or East St. Louis, Ill. — both great railroad centres — as indeed were Birmingham, Atlanta, Memphis, Indianapolis, Cincinnati and the greatest of them all, Chicago. From these great railroad 'hubs' the blues came to be disseminated across the South, and eventually to all points on the US compass — a process initiated by those intrepid guitarists and pianists who travelled to perform in the barrelhouses of remote Southern logging camps in the late Nineteenth and early Twentieth Centuries.

Notes to Chapter 2

1	Hickman	Ibid, p.23
2	Trotter Jr, J.W.	p.25
3	Ibid.	p.25
4	Ibid.	p.130
5	Charters, S.B.	*The Country Blues*, p.198
6	Lomax, A.	Ibid, p.250
7	Ibid.	
8	Charters	*The Country Blues*, ibid, pp.198-98
9	Lomax	Ibid, p.66
10	Ibid.	p.253
11	Ibid.	p.229
12	Ibid.	p.216
13	'Levee Camp Moan Blues'	Texas Alexander - vocal; Lonnie Johnson - guitar (12 August 1927, New York City)
14	Lomax	Ibid. p.226
15	Ibid.	p. 216
16	Ibid.	
17	Wheeler	Ibid, p.95
18	Thigpen, S.G.	p.25
19	Hickman	Ibid, p.17
20	Ibid.	p.18
21	Thigpen	Ibid, p.34
22	Ibid.	pp.36-7
23	Ibid.	p.36

24	Bolles, A.S.	p.504
25	Ibid.	pp.504-5
26	'Log Camp Blues'	Ma Rainey - vocal; acc. Her Tub Jug Washboard Band: Georgia Tom - piano; Martell Pettiford - banjo; Herman Brown - kazoo/washboard?/tub drum; Carl Reid - jug (circa June 1928, Chicago, Ill.)
27	Bolles	Ibid, p.505
28	Cronon, W.	p.181
29	Ibid.	p.196
30	Hickman	Ibid, p.55
31	Ibid.	pp.55-6
32	'The Dummy'	Bessie Tucker - vocal; K.D. Johnson - piano (29 August 1928, Memphis, Tenn.)
33	Oliver, P.	Notes to Magpie PY-1815 (LP)
34	Ayers, E. L.	p.124
35	Clarke, V.S.	p.127
36	Hickman	Ibid, p.48
37	Ibid.	p.251
38	Ibid.	p.106
39	Silvester, P.	p.25
40	'Moon Going Down'	Ibid.
41	McCormick, M.	Notes to Arhoolie F-1010 (LP)
42	Ramsey Jr, Frederic	Interview with Huddie Ledbetter (Leadbelly) Notes to Melodisc MLP-12-113 (LP)
43	Silvester	Ibid, p.31
44	Harris, R.	p.156
45	Ayers, E.L.	p.1495 (*Encyclopedia of Southern Culture* - Wilson & Ferris (see *Bibliography*)
46	Silvester	Ibid, p.30
47	Charters	Ibid, p.199
48	Hickman	Ibid, p.244
49	'Country Breakdown'	Charley Lincoln- vocal, guitar, speech (4 November 1927, Atlanta, Ga.)
50	Wyatt, M.	Notes to Old Hat CD-1003 (CD), p.5
51	Rachell James 'Yank'	p.24
52	zur Heide, K.G.	p.24
53	Dorsey, 'Georgia Tom'	p.38
54	White, Washington 'Bukka'	p.279
55	zur Heide.	Ibid. p.13
56	Dixon, Godrich & Rye	Ibid, p.318
57	Bolles	Ibid, p.535
58	Johnson, W.	p.87

59	Ibid.	p.217
60	Daniels, D.H.	p.79
61	'Winin' Boy Blues'	Jelly Roll Morton - vocal, speech, piano (Library of Congress recording, 1938)
62	Harris	Ibid, p.141
63	Edwin 'Buster' Pickens	p.60
64	Rufus 'Speckled Red' Perryman	p.61
65	'Kelly's Special'	Roosevelt Sykes (as 'Willie Kelly') - piano, speech (17 November 1930, Memphis, Tenn.)
66	'Fat Mama Blues'	Jabo Williams - vocal, piano (c.May 1932, Grafton, Wis.)
67	Oliver, P.	Notes to Magpie PY-4411 (LP)
68	Reed	Ibid, p.230
69	Ibid.	p.471
70	Ibid.	p.477
71	Ibid.	p.481
72	Ibid.	p.487
73	'Katy Blues'	Bessie Tucker - vocal; K.D. Johnson - piano; Jesse Thomas - guitar; unk. brass bass (10 August 1929, Dallas, Tex.)
74	Harris	Ibid, pp.153-4
75	Hickman	Ibid, p.63
76	Corliss	Ibid, p.380
77	Hickman	Ibid, p.284

Discography – Chapter 2

'Country Breakdown'
(Charley Lincoln)

CD: *Charley Lincoln & Willie Baker (1927-30)*
[Blues Document BDCD-6027] 1992

'The Dummy'
(Bessie Tucker)

CD: *Bessie Tucker (1928-29)*
[Document DOCD-5070)] 1991

'Fat Mama Blues'
(Jabo Williams)

CD: *Boogie Woogie & Barrelhouse Piano (1928-32)* [Document DOCD-5102] 1992

'Katy Blues'
(Bessie Tucker)

CD: *Bessie Tucker (1928-29)*
[Document DOCD-5070] 1991

'Kelly's Special'
(Willie Kelly [Roosevelt Sykes])

CD: *Roosevelt Sykes – Volume 2 (1930-31)*
[Document DOCD-5117] 1992

'Levee Camp Moan Blues'
(Texas Alexander)

CD: *Texas Alexander – Volume 1 (1927-28)*
[Matchbox MBCD-2001] 1993

'Log Camp Blues'
(Ma Rainey)

CD: *Ma Rainey – Volume 5 (1928)*
[Document DOCD-5156] 1993

'Moon Going Down' 5-CD: *Charley Patton – Complete Recordings*
(Charley Patton) *(1929-34)* [J.S.P. JSP-7702] 2002

'Winin' Boy Blues' LP: *Copulatin' Blues* [Stash ST-101] 1976
(Jelly Roll Morton) CD: *Copulation Blues* [Trikont US-0277] 2000
  8-CD: *Jelly Roll Morton – The Complete Library of Congress Recordings by Alan Lomax (1938)*
  [Rounder 11661-1888-2BK01] 2005

Ah! When I leave here gonna catch that M&O

'M&O Blues' – Willie Brown (1930)

CHAPTER 3

THE MOBILE & OHIO RAILROAD AND THE BLUES

This chapter puts the spotlight on one of the two 'sister' railroads of the South — the Mobile & Ohio. As has previously been noted, the M&O was a major lumber carrier along with its 'sister' company, the Illinois Central. Indeed, in the late 1860s, when the South was generally still reeling from the aftermath of the Civil War and the lumber industry was slowing down or even declining, 'steam circular sawmills with an average capacity of 10,000 feet or less sprang up along the Illinois Central Railroad and the Mobile and Ohio.'[1] From these comparatively small beginnings both railroads, with the boost of the lumber trade, by the 1880s occupied fourth place *[as 'Mississippi Valley – the Illinois Central and the Mobile & Ohio']* in a list of 'ten major traffic corridors'.[2] Running from north to south, these railroads served Chicago, East St. Louis and St. Louis down through Tennessee to Memphis and on down to Mississippi and the Gulf of Mexico. In addition, the M&O ran through Alabama and some forty miles of Kentucky.

Although various books and articles have been written about the IC, the Katy, the L&N, etc — which are also popular railroads in the blues — very little has been set down in print about the M&O, and virtually nothing since 1936. In September 1940, the Gulf, Mobile & Northern 'merged' with the near-bankrupt M&O to form the GM&O. In 1953, a book titled after the latter was published, but concentrated on the GM&N and its predecessors. It

A southbound Gulf Coast Special on its way to Mobile, Ala., c.1926.

goes without saying that this and other books on Southern railroads make no mention of the blues. It was left to the blues singers who recorded in the 1920s and '30s to assure the M&O a place in history. The following 'journey' will hopefully illustrate the interaction between the world of the blues and the Mobile & Ohio Railroad in the early decades of the Twentieth Century.

The M&O was one of the oldest major lines in the South but, apart from the *Gulf Coast Special*, never operated a noteworthy fast train, unlike the IC or the Texas & Pacific, who ran several including the *Panama Limited* and the *Sunshine Special* respectively. Both of these trains are celebrated in the blues by singers such as Bukka White *(Chapter 1)* and Blind Lemon Jefferson, amongst others. There was however, a jointly-run named train which featured the purpose-built Pullman cars used in the *St. Louis World's Fair* of 1904: 'Composite car *Jefferson* and dining car *Monroe* operated in the 1906 *Havana Limited*, a once-a-week deluxe tourist service from Chicago to Cuba via the Chicago & Alton[*] and Mobile & Ohio railroads, in connection with the Munsen Steamship line *[sic]* from Mobile to Havana'[3] — the implication being that this joint venture had ceased by the following year. In any event, neither the *Havana Limited* nor the *Gulf Coast Special* appeared in a recorded blues. Nevertheless, the M&O seemed to have a special place in the hearts of many Southerners, both black and white.

The railroad's base was Mobile in Alabama. With the strong support of many Mobile businessmen and politicians, the M&O started life when it was chartered in 1848. The long-term plan was to connect with the agricultural trade and general commerce in the 'Old Western' states of

---

[*] The C&A eventually became part of the Gulf, Mobile & Ohio in 1947.

Chapter 3 — Ah! When I leave here, gonna catch that M&O

Kentucky and Missouri. The initial terminus north of Mobile was Columbus, Ky., but finally it ran through East Cairo, Ky. with an extension to Cairo and East St. Louis, Ill.. At first, work was laboriously slow — in fact, 'the main line from Mobile to East Cairo, Ky. was not opened until April 1861.' [4] By 1886, the main line had reached East St. Louis and the M&O soon acquired trackage rights[*] over the great Mississippi River across the Eads Bridge into the Union Station in St. Louis, Mo.. St. Louis was, of course, one of the major commercial 'crossroads' and an important blues centre in the 1920s and '30s. It was also a great railroad terminus.

Some two years after the M&O had been chartered, its board of directors, along with the leading citizens of Mobile, had persuaded the US Government to alter what was to be the first land grant to a railroad in the States. The original grant of this Federal-owned land was for the Illinois-based IC to lay its main line tracks further east, serving Chicago, the Great Lakes and Western states, rather than the South and the Gulf of Mexico. But the final grant of 20 September 1850 was altered to read as follows: *'An act granting a right of way and making a grant of land to the states of Illinois, Mississippi and Alabama in aid of the construction of a railroad from Chicago to Mobile.'* [5] It was this change, effected in December 1851, that enabled the M&O to become a reality — thus allowing, in due course of time, a group of musical legends and at least one railroad legend to surface in the 1920s and '30s on early blues records, some of which we will encounter later on.

The proposed North-South trunk line was seen as the vital link between Alabama and the mainstream of not only American, but also international trade. The state, which was almost completely rural at that time, possessed

---

[*] 'Trackage rights' refers to an agreement by one railroad company to let the trains of another company use its tracks. This was generally because the 'guest company' did not have the finances or permission from municipal authorities to establish its own road.

87

only one seaport, at Mobile. This is one of the oldest cities in the South, along with Charleston, S.C., Savannah, Ga. and New Orleans, La.. The city, like its main rival New Orleans, is situated upriver from the main coastline. Some twenty miles into Mobile Bay lay a natural deep sea harbour. One of the chief executives on the board of the Mobile & Ohio Railroad, the Rev. John Campbell, described it thus in 1854: 'The harbor is difficult of access, being obstructed by marshy islands and shoals, but within, deep and spacious enough for larger vessels. These, by a circuit around an island, in front of the city, anchor at its wharves.' [6] Two wharves extended from the city after the railroad had been given another (local) land grant of forty-nine acres on which depots were also to be built, and the M&O gained permission to 'run tracks through the commercial streets, that the cars may run to the warehouses or vessels of consignees.' [7] As the Chief Engineer, Colonel Childe, explained, any ships drawing more than ten feet of water had to anchor '16 to 25 miles below in the bay, where there is thirty square miles of water, two to nine fathoms deep... The Mobile & Ohio road will be extended to this deep water', adding — with a dig at Mobile's main rival — that M&O cars could then be brought 'alongside of vessels of 40 percent greater capacity than can get to New Orleans.' [8]

  The optimistic forecasts of potential trade in both imports and exports would eventually result in hundreds of stevedores being employed on the wharves to load or unload box cars, flat cars and refrigerator cars, and transfer products to and from the ships anchored alongside, from all parts of the world.[9] By the 1890s, the vast majority of these stevedores would have been black, and this remained the case into the earlier decades of the Twentieth Century. On the subject of Harlem, the *New York Times* reported in the spring of 1927 that: 'Strutting the streets of the "Black Belt" are Negroes of enviable physique, with slim waists and straight broad shoulders. Many of these have found jobs on the piers as stevedores. They receive good pay and can afford to wear good clothes.' [10] Although the work was hard, demanding and sometimes dangerous, wages were higher than could be earned as a sharecropper in the agricultural Southern hinterland. These stevedores would often sing worksongs to make their arduous tasks just a little bit lighter and to 'ease their worried minds', in blues-speak. In the earlier days, around the 1890s and 1900s, tall or sailing ships were still in use and foreign crews would also sing worksongs in the form of sea shanties whilst bringing their ship into dock, letting in sails, dropping anchor, etc. Often, these were 'checkerboard crews' — ie a mixture of black and white. Mobile, as well as other seaports along the Eastern seaboard of the US such as New Orleans, Houston in Texas and Savannah, Ga., all became a melting pot of cultural exchange. By the Twentieth Century, blues singers had also become part of this process.

  Attracted by the lure of lucrative busking sessions on the dockside and in the streets playing to the stevedores, many bluesmen like the legendary

Blind Lemon Jefferson from near Wortham in East Texas would make their way to Mobile and other ports. Not surprisingly, the stevedore also featured in a number of early blues recordings including Mary Dixon's 'Dusky Stevedore' [Vocalion 1199] from 1928 and Coot Grant's 'Stevedore Man' [Paramount 12379] from 1926:

> Woke up this mornin', 'bout half-past nine,
> An' I just could not keep from cryin'.
> I was worried about that stevedore man of mine.

Apparently, Grant's lover was also a part-time sailor, and she is concerned for his safety because it's *'rainin' an' hailin' out on the sea'*. For added 'human interest', she also frankly confesses to her listeners that she got her *'sweet man'* by trickery and deception:

> I stole that sweet man, stole him from my best friend.
> I stole my sweet man, stole 'im from my best friend.
> An' that woman done got lucky, Lord, an' stole 'er man back again.[11]

She was to record another version two years later as 'Stevedore Blues' [Cameo 9240], employing the same lyrics, but with a far superior accompaniment by a small section of the Fletcher Henderson band, including Charlie Green and Buster Bailey on trombone and clarinet respectively.

Interestingly, Grant had borrowed her last verse from a 1923 recording by the renowned vaudeville-blues singer, Ida Cox, called 'Worried Mama Blues' [Paramount 12085]. While Cox and Grant were the first on record (as far as we know) to use this 'floating verse'[*] in a blues, the great rural singer Blind Willie McTell also used these lines on 'Stole Rider Blues' [Victor 21124], from his very first session in 1927. On this very fine personal number, which was probably also inspired by the Ida Cox record, he 'mixes in' the dangerous theme of protest at the iniquitous peonage system with his

---

[*] The 'floating verse' is a set of well-known traditional lyrics which a singer could draw on if his/her inspiration ran dry during a performance (for example: *'I walked down the road, feelin' bad (x 2) / It's the worst old feelin' I've ever had'*).

personal relationship, so as to disguise his anger from casual white listeners[*]:

> I'm gonna grab me a train, ride the lonesome rail.
> Gonna grab me a train, ride the lonesome rail.
> Niggers [have] stole[n] my baby, she's in the lonesome jail.
>
> He took my mama, carried 'er to the town of Rome. *(x2)*
> Now, she's screamin' an' cryin': 'Papa let your mama come back home.'
>
> I stole my good gal from my bosom friend. *(x2)*
> That fool got lucky, an' he stole 'er back again.
>
> *(Spoken)* Do it good, Mr. So-an'-So!
>   Do it with a feelin'.
>   Do it good now.
>
> Now, the woman I love got a mouth chock full of good gold. *(x2)*
> Every time you hug an' kiss me, it makes my blood run cold.
>
> When you see two women runnin' hand in hand. *(x2)*
> Bet you my last dollar, one done stole the other 'un's man.
>
> I'm leavin town, please don't spread the news. *(x2)*
> That's why I've got these old 'Stole Rider Blues'.[12]

The *'He'* in the second verse refers to a white plantation boss, McTell giving a superb illustration of how to take a single verse from another blues and extend it into a personal statement of his own; he even draws on that verse for his new title.

In 1931, Mississippi's Skip James included the Ida Cox lines on his unique and chilling 'Devil Got My Woman' [Paramount 13088]. The subject of his composition, his 'cross-tuned' guitar and high-pitched, eerie vocal are seemingly at odds with the *'stole'* verse when read in print, but somehow this sounds just as harrowing as the other verses when one listens to the record. However, probably the best-known use of this verse was in Robert Johnson's 'Come On In My Kitchen' [A.R.C. 7-07-57] from 1936:

> The woman I love, took from my best friend.
> Some joker got lucky, stole 'er back again.[13]

---

[*] Peonage is basically agricultural/industrial slavery because of unpaid debt by the worker. Such 'debts' were often fictionalised by the white 'bossman', who would pursue any unfortunate worker who managed to escape — using guns and whips if necessary. The definitive book on peonage in the South, which became more widely recognised at the beginning of the Twentieth Century, is *The Shadow Of Slavery: Peonage In The South 1901-69* by Pete Daniel (University of Illinois Press, 1972).

Although it is almost bound to be the case that the use of the *'stole'* verse was due to the above recordings being heard at some stage, it is important to note that, even if blues had not been recorded, oral transmission could have acted in the same way for Coot Grant, McTell, etc.

'Coot' had been born Leola B. Grant in 1893 at Birmingham, Alabama and her father 'was owner of [a] local honky tonk'. She started to travel on the vaudeville circuit from around the age of eight[14], eventually meeting and marrying Wesley Wilson, a piano player from Jacksonville, Fla.. Together they formed a popular husband-and-wife team, Coot Grant & Kid Sox (or Socks) Wilson, and commenced recording in 1925. Like many other blues singers, they spent several years travelling the tent show and circus routes in the South *(Chapter 8)* and other parts of the US, predominantly by rail. Grant and her husband would almost certainly have used the M&O, both in her home state of Alabama and elsewhere. A contemporary of Ida Cox (who was born in 1896 in Toccoa, Ga.), Grant (or indeed any other black singer) may also have been the oral source for Cox's *'stole'* verse on 'Worried Mama Blues', as she is credited with writing the lyrics to 'Stevedore Man'.

Coot Grant, c.1925.

However, the M&O did not just serve the international market via the port of Mobile. From the beginning, they had their eye on the prospective home market, as Colonel Childe indicates after waxing lyrical about Alabama's 'noble rivers' (the ones that the M&O would have to cross) when projecting the future: 'In twelve hours, or less, citizens of Missouri, Ohio, Kentucky or elsewhere may leave Columbus, in Kentucky, the upper terminus, and arrive at Mobile with their produce in one-fifth of the time they could reach New Orleans.' [15]

The railroad was also a trading lifeline for countless small communities along its route out of Alabama. One example was Beaver Meadow in Mobile County. Local farmers would bring their produce to the depot, where an M&O box car would be left in the siding and the depot would become a mini-marketplace. Farmers and railroad officials would then negotiate a price for goods to be transported to Mobile or to St. Louis and other Northern destinations. When the freight train arrived to pick up this box car (sometimes referred to as a 'way freight train'), it also offered an ideal opportunity for a blues singer to *'ride the lonesome rail'* in McTell's words,

Chapter 3 — Ah! When I leave here, gonna catch that M&O

The M&O also served the large rural areas and picked up produce from local small farmers, as here at Beaver Meadow, Ala., c.1895. It would be easy for a singer/musician to 'grab a ride' from here and spread their style of blues across other states, north and south.

and influence — or be influenced by — differing styles of singing and playing elsewhere in the country.

Although the M&O bosses showed great enthusiasm in committees, newspaper reports, speeches, etc. after receiving their charter, actual progress in the beginning — for various reasons — was painfully slow. Indeed, by 1852 only some thirty-three miles of the projected main line had been completed. This brought the railroad to another small town called Citronelle. Nestling in the fertile lowlands, still in Mobile County, and home to a thriving turpentine industry, Citronelle was for the first few years the *de facto* 'upper terminus' of the M&O.[16]

Gradually, the railroad headed north-west into Washington County through the longleaf pines of Southern Alabama's forests which provided much employment for working-class blacks *(Chapter 2)*. On the way, it passed through other small towns such as Vinegar Bend and Yellow Pine, as it made its way to the Mississippi–Alabama border. Crossing this, the M&O train hit Stateline, Miss., snorting through drizzling rain skirting dense stands of yellow pine, via Waynesboro, Wayne County and Quitman in Clarke County. Quitman had, until the early 1930s, one of the largest lumber mills in the South, and doubtless attracted many blues singers to its environs, who would relieve black sawmill/logging workers of nickels and dimes when pay day arrived.

Passing on into Lauderdale County by the middle of the 1850s, the

Logging camp workers (probably from the Yellow Pine Lumber Co.) waiting for the train at Yellow Pine depot on the M&O near the Mississippi–Alabama border, c.1895. Note the banjoist, and possibly a fiddler.

M&O arrived at Meridian. Meridian was Mississippi's second largest city after Jackson, and soon became a large junction for several railroads. From as early as 1861, the Alabama & Vicksburg RR crossed the M&O at Meridian. After the Civil War ended in 1865, other railroads made their way to the junction and 'Meridian, as a railroad center, grew rapidly.' [17]

By the 1930s, 'numerous railroad tracks' near the centre of town made a natural division between the business and industrial sections. In 1935, 'with a view to building up the livestock industry of the county, the Meridian Union Stockyards were established... This plant occupies 14 acres of a triangle bounded by the tracks of the Southern, Mobile & Ohio, Illinois Central and Gulf, Mobile & Northern railroads, and its buildings and pens accommodate approximately 5,000 head of stock. This is the State's largest stockyard.' [18]

That same year, singer Robert Wilkins recorded his 'New Stock Yard Blues' [Vocalion 03223] in Jackson, Miss., with Little Son Joe (Ernest Lawlars) on second guitar and a spoons player known only as 'Kid Spoons'. The 'building up' of the livestock industry was only to become a practical reality with the coming of the railroads, and first and foremost was the Mobile & Ohio. Wilkins & co. capture the rolling rhythms of a freight train full of longhorn steers heading towards their ultimate end in the Meridian Union Stockyard, or perhaps mules to buy for working on the farm:

> When you wake up Monday morning with those stockyard blues,
> Come an' talk with Mr. Owen about his good-lookin' mules.
> When you wake up Monday morning with those stockyard blues,
> Have a talk with Mr. Owen about his good-lookin' mules.
>
> *(Spoken)* Come on, man. Tell him about his mules.
> Oh! Bid on that pair. Don't he look good?
> Yeah! I know he do.
>
> I know he's good, he's nice an' kind.
> Have a talk with him before you start to buyin'.
> I know he's good, I know he's nice an' kind.
> Have a talk with him before you start to buyin'.[19]

The inclusion of the prefix 'New' in Wilkins' title did not refer to a cover version of a song recorded earlier, as was often the case in blues, but presumably is to be taken in its literal sense. Leading blues authority Paul Oliver interviewed Wilkins in the 1970s and relates that: "Stockyard Blues' *[sic]*, formerly the 'Auction Day Blues'... told of the regular auctions held at the Owen Brothers' "Mule and Horse Commission" on West McLiammar Street where he used to work.'[20]

Could 'McLiammar' be an orally-transmitted interpretation of McLemore? For, where the A&VRR crossed the M&O in Meridian, 'their junction was to meet on McLemore's plantation.'[21] This referred to white businessman Richard McLemore, who had migrated from South Carolina in 1831. The plan for the railroad junction at Meridian was devised in 1854.

Given that he was a much-travelled bluesman from Hernando, Miss. and a former Pullman porter, I am inclined to think it too much of a coincidence that Wilkins recorded this side in the same year without knowledge of the huge Meridian project. I would suggest that he was inspired by the opening of the latter, and incorporated his title into a blues about his local stockyard in Memphis:

> The Union Stockyard is a good place to go
> Not for so much talk, but to spend your dough.
> The Union Stockyard is a good place to go
> Not for so much talk, but to spend your dough.[22]

The Union Stockyard was so called because of its location near the Union Station in Meridian at Front Street and 19th Avenue, which was served by the 'Mobile & Ohio RR, Yazoo & Mississippi Valley RR and the Southern RR.'[23] *[sic]* All these railroads were 'united' at this station or depot — hence 'Union'. A famous son of an M&O section gang foreman was the white country singer Jimmie Rodgers, who 'was born in Meridian in 1897'

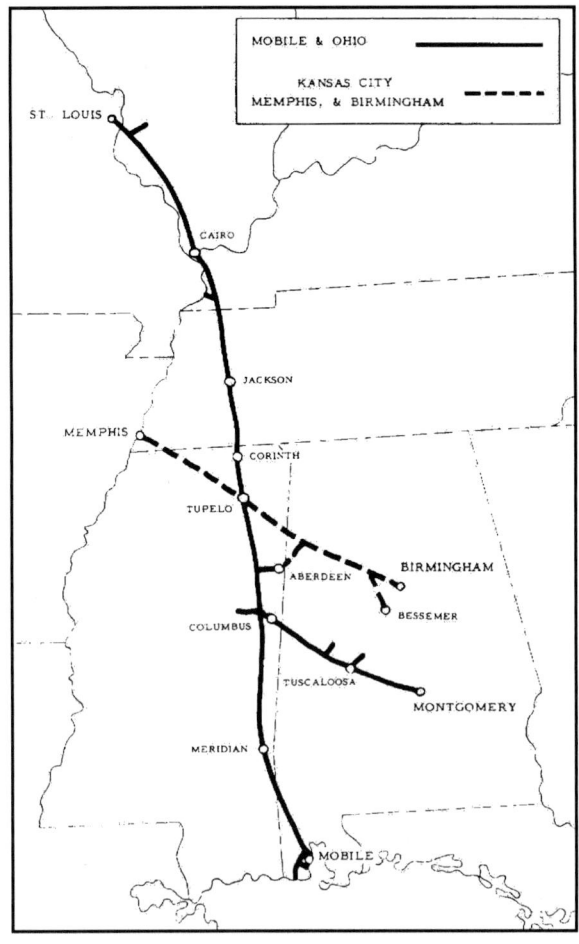

Chapter 3 — Ah! When I leave here, gonna catch that M&O

M&O map, 1900.

MOBILE & OHIO ———
KANSAS CITY
MEMPHIS, & BIRMINGHAM - - - - -

and was to learn about the blues from the black workers in the railroad yards of the M&O and down on 10th Street in the city.[24]

Leaving Meridian, the M&O trains rumbled on, passing more fertile lumber regions such as Electric Mills in Kemper County. The locomotive's whistle shrieking and moaning like a banshee in the Mississippi night. Travelling through the adjacent county of Noxubee, taking in Macon and skirting the fetid Knoxford Swamp near Crawford before finally pulling into Artesia in a hiss of steam. Both of these locations are in Lowndes County, and it was here in 1903 that the great blues singer known as 'Poor'/'Po' or 'Big' Joe Williams was born in Crawford into a farming family of sixteen children.[25] Famous for making the first recording of the classic 'Baby Please Don't Go' [Bluebird B-6200] in 1935[*], and his later invention of the nine-string guitar, Williams came to personify the popular concept of a blues singer. Quickly tiring of farm work, he learnt his instrumental skills early and started to roam, making his living at least in part from his music, playing at country picnics, outside train stations, on street corners, etc. But his favourite route for singing the blues in the barrelhouses and juke joints 'was down around Mobile, Meridian, Electric

---

[*] Although Joe made it to the record studio first, his onetime common law wife and blues singer, Bessie Mae Smith (*aka* St. Louis Bessie) claimed he stole the song from her. In any event, 'Baby Please Don't Go' has links going back to at least the turn of the Twentieth Century via 'Don't You Leave Me Here', 'Elder Green Blues', 'Another Man Done Gone', 'Alabama Bound', etc. (see Paul Oliver's *Songsters & Saints* (ibid. pp.115-7); and also *Baby Please Don't Go – Origins Of A Blues* by the author in *Acoustic Blues* No.6 (pp.10-14) and No.7 (pp.2-4), 1993 and 1994.

Mills, Shuqulak, and so on into Alabama.' [26]

Big Joe is getting his geography a little mixed up. But just the same, all the locations he mentioned were on the main line of the M&O between its Alabama terminus and Artesia, Miss..

From 1899, a branch of the Mobile & Ohio forked eastwards from Artesia, crossed the Tombigbee River and Highway 45 as it entered Columbus, Miss.. Cutting almost at right angles across the Frisco RR, it carried on eastwards over the state line and a second river, the Luxapalila, then made its way to Montgomery, Alabama. Big Joe met up with a local gangster, Totsie King, who 'ran things' in the 'M&O Bottoms' [27] and wound up organising gigs for Joe in the countryside around Tuscaloosa.

The 'M&O Bottoms' referred to the river 'bottoms', or adjacent land that was almost level with the water — in this case the Warrior River. The great Alabaman historian and chronicler, Thomas McAdory Owens, wrote a detailed description of these bottoms in 1921. He refers to three different 'terraces' which were present on the shores of all 'larger streams of the Coastal plain', and examines each in turn: 'The first terrace, or bottom, is subject to overflow and its soils are the sands and other materials periodically deposited by the stream. The second terrace, or bottom, is a few feet above high-water mark and consequently not subject to overflow, except in the depressions caused by erosion. The characteristic soils of these second bottoms are yellowish, silty loams increasing in sandiness from above downward. They average about a mile in width, and are always choice farm lands. Many of the great plantations of antebellum days were situated on this terrace. The third terrace is usually about 100 feet above the second, and averages some three miles in width, with soils of the ordinary lafayette type.' That is to say, sandy loam soils. Owen further comments that most of the river towns — including Tuscaloosa — are situated on this third terrace.[28]

John M. Barry provides an even more detailed description: 'The Mississippi River creates natural levees. When the river over-flows, it deposits the heaviest sediment first, thus building up the land closest to the river. Generally, these natural levees extend for half a mile to a mile from the riverbank. "Bottomlands" farther away are lower and often marsh and swamp.' [29] Barry adds that 'New Orleans was founded on a natural levee'.[30]

In 1909, F.H. Newell, a US Director of Land Reclamation, referred to this phenomenon as 'the high ground near the rivers'. He continued: 'The large amount of systematic work in the South has been in connection with the levee system in the lower Mississippi Valley, and especially in Louisiana, where drain ditches were dug leading back from the high ground near the rivers into the bayous, affording drainage of some of the swamp land.' [31]

Although Owen noticeably does not comment on the people who lived on the 'first terrace', it will come as no surprise that these would have been poorer working-class blacks. This lowest level was, of course, prone to malarial insects as well as periodic flooding. Due to the mixed sandy soil and also the 'overflows', cotton that these black farmers planted often did not have time to dry out before the next drenching, either by swollen river waters or torrential rains. Consequently, much of the crop would rot where it grew. In the last two decades of the Nineteenth Century and probably the beginnings of the Twentieth, a cotton picker had to 'clear' (pick) 100 lbs of good cotton per day before they were in a position to start earning any profit or wage. In 1940, folklorist John Lomax recorded a 79 year-old woman called Harriet McClintock for the Library of Congress. She admirably illustrates a blues in the making which has links with both the worksong and field holler — two of the earliest roots of the blues. In a little under one minute she conveys the near-hopeless conditions of trying to eke out a living in the sandy bottoms of the Warrior River:

> Way down in the Bottom
> All the cotton so rotten,
> You won't get your hundred here today.
>
> Way down in the Bottom
> All the cotton so rotten,
> You won't get your hundred here today.
>
> Poor little Johnny,
> He were a poor little feller.
> He won't get 'is hundred here today.

By the time of this recording, Harriet McClintock had moved twenty-odd miles west of the Warrior River in or near Sumterville, Alabama. This was near the Alabama–Mississippi border and was some two miles south of an M&O branch line which ran from Gainesville, Alabama to Narkeeta, Miss. on the main line. Lomax, using the prevalent custom of Southern whites at the time addresses his interviewee as 'Aunt' (because she was an elderly black woman) when asking her about this song, but he does so with respect:

JL:	'Uh, Aunt Harriet, where did you get this song?'	
HMc:	'My mama learn it to me.'	
JL:	'How long ago?'	
HMc:	'Ooh! I don't know. 'Cause she bin dead about near thirty years.'	
JL:	'Did you ever pick any cotton?'	
HMc:	'Me? Yessir!'	
JL:	'How much did you pick a day?'	
HMc:	'Oh! I pick about a hundred an' fifty an' a hundred an' twenty five.'	[32]

Aunt Harriet's last two replies are delivered with a youthful exuberance which belies her 79 years and reflects the indomitable spirit of the blues. It seems very likely, judging by her comments, that she learnt this song sometime in the 1880s when she was still a young girl.

Big Joe Williams invokes the M&O Bottoms in a 1941 song, 'Meet Me Around The Corner' [Bluebird B-8738], which was derived from an earlier song popular with East Coast/Piedmont bluesmen. With some variation, the following verse inspired the later song — a common occurrence in the blues:

> Meet me in the Bottom, bring me my boots an' shoes.
> Hey Lawdy, mama, good God Almighty.
> Meet me in the Bottom, bring me my boots an' shoes.
> My best girl have quit me an' I ain't got no time to lose.

The first African American to record it was Curley Weaver, who included it in his 'Oh Lordy Mama' [A.R.C., unissued] in 1933. The following year, fellow Georgian guitarist Buddy Moss cut his own version [Banner 33267], followed by a 'No. 2' [A.R.C. 6-04-56] in 1935. Weaver also re-cut the song in April of that year, which was issued as 'Oh Lawdy Mama' [Champion 50077]. 'Meet Me In The Bottom (Hey Lawdy Mama)' [Decca 7170] by Bumble Bee Slim, another Georgia singer, and 'Boots And Shoes' [A.R.C. 7-07-63] by North Carolina's Blind Boy Fuller, swiftly appeared in 1936 and 1937 respectively. Four years later, Big Joe, accompanied by William Mitchell on imitation bass, sang to an urgent attacking rhythm:

> Meet me around the corner, babe, bring my boots an' shoes.
> Meet me around the corner, bring my boots an' shoes.
> My best woman have quit me an' I ain't go no time to lose.

In a later verse, he even included a passing nod to the *'hey lawdy mama'* refrain:

> Early one mornin', just about the break o' day.
> She's not your mama, great God Almighty!
> Early one mornin', about the break o' day.
> I hug the pillow where my baby used to lay.[33]

Probably the earliest blues to feature the 'bottoms' in its title is 'The Black Bottom Blues' [OKeh 8050], a vaudeville-blues by Lizzie Miles recorded in February 1923. A rougher and more downhome singer even featured this geographical phenomenon as his pseudonym. Accompanied by master guitarist Scrapper Blackwell, 'Black Bottom' McPhail recorded four titles in 1932 including 'Down In Black Bottom' [Vocalion 1721]. At his second and final session in 1938, he revisited the theme with 'Don't Go Down In Black Bottom' [Vocalion 04317].

Again, as with the group of recordings which featured the *'I stole my woman from my best friend'* line, it is more than likely that the various versions of 'Meet Me In The Bottom'/'Lawdy Mama' were learnt from records, although the oral tradition would also have helped the spread this song from Georgia to North Carolina to Mississippi. Indeed, the M&O Bottoms would have seen sea-going commerce, as 'the Warrior River is navigable as high as Tuscaloosa' [34], thereby stimulating an international cultural exchange, in much the same way as Mobile, New Orleans and other ports on the Eastern Seaboard. The Tuscaloosa branch of the M&O itself continued on to Montgomery, Ala., where its tracks shared the Union Station with the L&N, the Western Railway of Alabama, the ACL, the SAL and the Central of Georgia.[35] All these railroads fanned out over the South, acting as a conduit for the oral transmission of the blues.

At the other end of this branch line (some 250 miles long!) the first place encountered after leaving Artesia, Miss., as has been noted, was Columbus, Miss.. It was around this area, including West Point (on the M&O main line) that the dark-voiced Bukka White played with the 'caterwauling' harp-blower George 'Bullet' Williams 'at local barrelhouses... 1934-35' and 'frequently worked streets/house parties *[in]* Aberdeen, Mississippi around 1935-37.' [36] Just north of West Point, an M&O branch to Aberdeen had opened in 1870. Bukka's father, John White, had been a railroad man for this company and had grown up near the railroad tracks. Bukka himself had been born in 1909 in Houston, Miss. in Chickasaw County, which was situated alongside the GM&N. So, 'trains is bound to be in my music, ain't they?' the bluesman summarised.

His repertoire certainly reflected this background with classics like 'Aberdeen Mississippi Blues' [OKeh 05743], recorded in 1940, 'The Panama Limited' [Victor 23295] from 1930, 'Black Train Blues' [Vocalion 05588] from 1940, and several other blues featuring railroads. Although none of his surviving earlier recordings (1930-40) referred specifically to the M&O, he made up for this on 1973's 'Gibson Hill' [LP *Big Daddy*, Biograph BLP-2049], cut some ten years after his 'rediscovery'. Describing a passion for two women, one of whom is Ora Lee, the singer stands on the main line at Gibson, Miss., hoping to attract the latter's attention by staring at her front door:

> I was standin' by the railroad [in] Gibson Town, standin' on that M&O.
> I was standin' by the rail...Gibson Town, standin' down on that M&O.
> Old deacon was on the way to the church,
>   he said: 'Son, where you plans to go?'

> I said: 'Be standin' down here on this M&O
>   tryin' to look in Miss Ora Lee's door.'
> He said: 'Don't you think it would be the best,
>   jest go up there an' knock on Miss Ora Lee's door?'
> He said: 'One of these old freight trains might come through
>   an' knock you out in the middle of the road.' [37]

Having taken the old deacon's advice, Bukka sadly relates that, though the lady in question answered the door, *'she didn't ax me in'*. This hypnotic blues is driven along at a furious pace on his National steel guitar, punctuated by urgent bottleneck on the upper strings, in the best tradition of the Mississippi Delta blues. LaVere comments: 'This fast blues about two lady friends was one of his most requested pieces.' [38]

Gibson lies about five miles due west of Aberdeen on the main line of the M&O, which then heads further north through Okolona and gently undulating countryside, arriving at Tupelo, Miss. — so named after 'tupelo' trees (a kind of palm) that grow there. With the businesses and stores lining either side, the M&O makes a diagonal cross where it meets the Frisco as the latter wends its way to Kansas City, Mo. via Memphis. In 1928, the aforementioned George 'Bullet' Williams, with his spoken introduction on the scorching train instrumental 'Frisco Leaving Birmingham' [Paramount 12651], may well have been the first to include a reference to the Mobile & Ohio on a blues record:

> *(Spoken)* I'm gittin' that Frisco when she leavin' Birmingham.
> She's blowin' into Tupelo, Mississippi.
> She's headin' for the M&O cross.[39]

Wardlow tells us that 'Williams was originally from west Alabama, near Millport, close to Columbus, Miss..' [40]

The first blues to feature this railroad in its title was 'M&O Blues' [Paramount 13090], recorded in 1930 by Delta bluesman Willie Brown. Brown, made famous in Robert Johnson's 'Cross Road Blues' [A.R.C. 7-05-81] and a superb artist in his own right, was a musical companion of Charley Patton and Son House. His opening lines describe the freedom of just jumping on a train and travelling to wherever he cares to go, his gravelly vocal almost jumping out of the grooves:

> I leave here, I'm gonna catch that M&O.
> Ah! When I leave here, catch that M&O.
> I'm goin' way down South where I ain't never been befo'.[41]

The Mobile & Ohio train leaves Tupelo and moans its way via Booneville and Corinth over the state line into Tennessee, heading for

Jackson. It was from here that John Lee 'Sonny Boy' Williamson rode the M&O in 1934 on his way to Chicago to set the pace and style for future post-war harp players like Little Walter, Dr. Ross and Junior Wells, as he relates on his 'Jackson Blues' [Bluebird B-7098]:

> Now, when I left out of Jackson, my baby was standin' in the door.
> Now, when I left out of Jackson, I rode that M&O.[42]

Williamson was to enjoy a highly-successful recording career before it was brutally terminated by an unknown assassin on Chicago's South Side in the early hours of a fateful morning in 1948.

James 'Yank' Rachell, one of Williamson's regular accompanists, was four years older and also a native of Tennessee, born twenty miles west of Jackson. A superb mandolin player, he began his recording career some eight years earlier than Williamson, when he entered the Victor studios in September 1929 for the first of several sessions with Sleepy John Estes (indeed, Estes later influenced Sonny Boy to some degree in the choice of songs he recorded). Rachell invokes the M&O on his 1941 'Katy Lee Blues' [Bluebird 34-0715] but prefers to take the slower steamboat, the *Katy Lee*. This theme of alternative transportation also occurred in 'Highway No. 61 Blues' [Banner 32844] by Jack Kelly & His South Memphis Jug Band from 1933, and 'Bluebird Blues' *(Take 1)* [Bluebird B-9037] recorded by Tommy McClennan in 1942. Kelly, based in Memphis, and McClennan, from Yazoo City in the Delta, both sang of the M&O as one of the choices available to them.

From Jackson the M&O swung in a north-easterly direction through Trenton, Tenn., crossing into the south-western tip of Kentucky, arriving at Cayce, Ky. shortly afterwards where, in the mid 1870s, one John Luther Jones had arrived from 'the Missouri backwoods'. Inspired by watching 'steam locomotives draw water from tanks alongside the Mobile & Ohio tracks'[43], he joined that company as a telegrapher and adopted the name of his home base, Cayce (pronounced 'Kay-see'), which was soon corrupted to 'Casey'.

But Casey Jones had his eye on higher things and soon joined the M&O's sister road, the Illinois Central. On the IC, he was to achieve legendary status as an engineer on the fast mail *(Chapter 9)* that travelled from Chicago down to New Orleans. It was on the crack express known as the *Cannonball*, 'officially as *No. 1, The New Orleans Special*'[44], that Casey rode into history on that fateful day in 1900, when he became the sole fatality in a train wreck at Vaughan/Vaughn[*], Miss., some fifteen miles north of Jackson. This event was well chronicled in white country song or 'hillbilly', as well as in the blues of Furry Lewis, Mississippi John Hurt and the Cincinnati-based pianist, Jesse James — the ultimate source of inspiration for

---

[*] Both spellings are used.

Chapter 3 — Ah! When I leave here, gonna catch that M&O

The locomotive Casey Jones wrecked at Vaughan.
Inset: Engineer Jones

all these offerings being a poem written shortly after the crash by a black engine cleaner, Wallace Saunders, who worked in the roundhouse where Jones' locomotive had been based.

One contributing factor to this accident — like many at that time — was the fact that, even by 1900, around 93% of railroad miles in the US still only consisted of a single track. The major cause, however, was Jones' reckless and irresponsible speeding on the *No. 1* or *Cannonball* fast mail train.

On the day of the accident, 30 April 1900, Jones was behind time to the tune of 'ninety-five minutes' when he left Memphis, Tenn..* As there were no stops until he got down to Jackson, Miss. and the IC had a 'straight level track' all the way, Jones saw an opportunity to make up this deficit, simultaneously enhancing his already-growing reputation as a 'fast runner' on the railroad. The only trains scheduled further down the line would not be met until he reached Vaughan.

Now, the railroad at this Mississippi town featured a passing loop. In other words, a length of track left the single main line and ran parallel to it, rejoining it a little further down. This parallel line or siding was long enough to accommodate a freight train, which would then wait until the express train had passed by.

---

* According to the IC Accident Report, Jones was five minutes late leaving Goodman (the stop some ten miles before Vaughan) and two minutes late when he got to Vaughan. White's statement that he was '95 minutes late' in Memphis doesn't seem to square with this report, which also states that Jones actually arrived on time in Goodman, Miss. — a distance of some 140 miles from Memphis. But there is a missing section of this Accident Report which might clarify this point.

Unfortunately, on this occasion there were two freight trains! One, *No. 83*, was running south, while *No. 72* was travelling north towards Casey's train.* Both of these trains were in the right place according to their timetable. As *Nos. 83* and *72* were too long to fit in the loop, the engineers had to perform a 'saw by' operation[45]: briefly, both trains were to enter the loop and position themselves so that at least one of the two points or switches (where this loop joined the main line) would be clear — in this case, the northernmost one. Casey's train could then gently ease over this switch until it was clear and then stop before arriving at the next switch, where several box cars of *No. 72* overlapped onto the main line, blocking its path. The clear switch would then be thrown to allow both freight trains to move onto the main line Casey had just vacated, thereby clearing the southernmost switch. The *Cannonball* could then continue on its journey down to Jackson. This was an operation familiar to the freight train crews. Indeed, they reportedly 'performed the manoeuvre successfully with a local passenger train just before Jones' train appeared on the scene.'[46] However, while they were attempting to relocate on the passing loop as just described, 'an air hose** between two of the cars broke, and the trains were stalled, with several cars protruding onto the main line from the north rather than the south end of the siding.'[47]

Jones had been wired from Vaughan advising him of this 'saw by' operation, so that he could start to slow down. After the breaking of the air hose, 'a flagman walked 3,200 feet north of the switch. Torpedoes *[bright shooting flares]* were fixed to the railhead 500 feet south of that point... Jones, however, was moving rapidly toward a scene that called for caution, not speed, yet he sailed by the flagman at 70 miles per hour — too fast to slow down, much less to stop. The freight train crew scattered when they heard him coming'.[48]

Simm T. Webb, the black fireman on the IC fast mail***, and the passengers managed to jump off before impact, 'but the engineer, Casey Jones, was killed, another victim of fast running on a single-track railroad.'[49] Had Jones remained a telegrapher on the M&O, he would arguably have had a longer, if less prestigious, life span; and Southern country music, as well as the blues, would have been deprived of one of its most enduring epic ballads.

---

* The official IC Accident Report stated that these trains were at Vaughan due to an earlier fault connected with *Train No. 83* causing both it and *No. 72* to be delayed. The final sentence as a summary of the Report by General Superintendent A.W. Sullivan ran: 'Engineer Jones was solely responsible for the collision by reason of having disregarded the signals given by Flagman Newberry' from *No. 83*.

** This refers to the air brake system, which immediately locks 'on' if a break or bad leak occurs, as part of a failsafe function.

*** The IC Report, in 1900, identifies the fireman as *'Simon Webb (colored)'*. I am greatly indebted to an unidentified US rail historian for providing a copy of this report by the Illinois Central RR.

Upon leaving Casey Jones' hometown of Cayce, the M&O line proceeded almost directly due north, its trains rattling through Moscow, Ky. before eventually easing into the original planned northern terminus of Columbus, Ky. (actually located in South Columbus, a mile or so to the east) in 1861 — ten days after the outbreak of the Civil War. The line now stretched over 470 miles from Mobile and was 'operated practically without change or alteration for more than twenty years.' [50] It was not until the beginning of November 1881, that another '19·12 miles... was opened for traffic' [51] to East Cairo, Ky..

Prior to this, however, the eighteen- or twenty-mile stretch (depending on which source you choose) of the Mississippi River between Columbus, Ky. and Cairo, Ill. was served by the M&O by means of ferry boats. A similar arrangement existed between Columbus and Belmont, Mo. Owen observes that Belmont, 'the southeastern terminus of the St. Louis, Iron Mountain & Southern Railway *[and the M&O]* was supplemented by steamers, which received and delivered cars without breaking bulk.' [52] Some forty years earlier, historian Thomas Scharf had already noted that the St.LIM&S met the ferry at Belmont, where it 'connects with the Mobile & Ohio Railroad for Mobile and intermediate points in Mississippi and Alabama, also with New Orleans.' [53] These ferries were also referred to as 'car floats' and 'transfer boats', and they 'were normally stop-gaps — cheaper, temporary expedients resorted to only because capital was not available to bridge a river.' [54] Such 'transfer boats' were to be found all over the North American railroad system in the latter part of the Nineteenth Century and well into the Twentieth, from the Great Lakes down to Louisiana.

One such boat[*] operated on the Tennessee River between Huntsville and Decatur in northern Alabama on the Nashville, Chattanooga & St. Louis Railway in 1904 (which had actually 'merged' with the L&N in 1880). Another was at Friar's Point, Miss., only a few miles south-west of Lula, both in Coahoma County.

Lula, on the Illinois Central, was a sometime home to Charley Patton and his common-law wife, Bertha Lee. In addition to the infamous *Big Kate Adams* it can be presumed that other transfer boats were still operating in 1934, when Ms. Lee waxed her fine 'Mind Reader Blues' [Vocalion 02650]. Here, she watches helplessly as her man and his new lover travel across the swirling yellow-brown waters to the Arkansas side of the great river, her 'hollered' vocals placing her firmly in the country/downhome blues mould *à la* Bessie Tucker:

> Baby, I can see just what's on your mind. *(x2)*
> You got a long black woman, with her gold teeth in her face.

---

[*] The steamboat *Big Kate Adams* (one of three so named) was a US Mail boat built in 1899, which from 1922 spent some time on the Lee Line out of Memphis and became notorious as a floating brothel.

Floating bridge at Coal Grove, Ohio–Scioto Valley Railway, c.1890.

> I take a long look, right smack down in your mind. *(x2)*
> An' I see poor Bertha comin' up an' down the line.
>
> I remember days when I was livin' in Lula Town. *(x2)*
> My man done many wrongs, 'til I had to leave the town.
>
> Down by the riverside, my man got a transfer boat. *(x2)*
> An' last time I seed 'im, he 'ad a gal way up the road.[55]

Car floats were essentially barges propelled by steamboats, or actual steamboats themselves, adapted to carry locomotives as well as freight and passenger cars as well as locomotives. Tracks on the deck had to be lined up with those on the 'transfer bridge', which was 'intermediate between the track *[on the riverbank]* and the car float.' [56] Also called 'float bridges', these could be adjusted as necessary. As Droege explained in 1925: 'The float bridge must be constructed to accommodate itself to the varying levels of the car float, due to tides, which range from 4 to 12 ft, and the difference in the depth of water drawn by the float itself, when fully loaded and when light.' [57] He goes on to describe what must have been quite a tricky operation using electric winches to make sure all the tracks were strictly in line before the transfer of freight cars commenced.

Of course, accidents occurred from time to time, and Tennessee's Sleepy John Estes' 'Floating Bridge' [Decca 7442] from 1937 probably relates to one that occurred in the early 1930s. But first, let Droege fill in the background of the illustration: 'The float is brought up to the transfer bridge and made fast by ropes or chains drawn taut by winches. There is one rope or chain at each side, and these draw the float up snug, so that the tracks on the float and on the transfer bridge are in approximate horizontal alinement *[sic]*. The final adjustment is made by a ratchet working a screw, by which the tracks on the bridge can be slid over a few inches. The bridge is raised or lowered before the float comes in, until the tracks are in approximate vertical alinement with those on the float'. He also comments that 'it is comparatively rare for cars to be lost from floats while in transit; most of the accidents occur while at the dock.' That is to say, on the 'transfer' or 'floating bridge'.

He goes on to describe a scenario which became actual reality for Estes: 'The engineman of the yard locomotive sometimes misunderstands or fails to obey the trainman's stop signal, if given, and backs a string of cars up against the bumper. If this holds, the force is usually enough to break the ropes which make the float fast, and the float is driven out from the dock and the cars may be dropped between the bridge and the boat' [58] — into the water in other words, and any hobos concealed inside the cars in question would be extremely lucky to escape drowning, as Estes so movingly relates, his high-crying vocal beautifully carried by Hammie Nixon's harmonica:

> Now, I never will forget that floating bridge. *(x3)*
> Tell me five minutes time an' the water I was in.
>
> When I was goin' down I threwed up my hands. *(x3)*
> Please take me on dry land.
>
> Now, they carried me in the house an' they laid me across the bank. *(x3)*
> 'bout a gallon [and a] half of muddy water I had drank.
>
> They dried me off an' they laid me in the bed. *(x3)*
> Couldn't hear nothin' but muddy water runnin' through my head.
>
> Now, my mother often told me: 'Quit playin' a bum.' (or 'box'?)
> Now, my mother often told me: 'Quit playin' a bum.' (or 'box'?)
> Now, my mother often told me: 'Son, quit playin' a bum. (or 'box'?)
> Go somewhere, settle down an' make a crop'.
>
> Now people standin' on the bridge screamin' an' cryin'.
> People on the bridge was screamin' an' cryin'.
> Now, people on the bridge, they screamin' an' cryin':
> 'Lord! Have mercy whilst we gwine.' [59]

Some time after his 'rediscovery' in the early 1960s, Estes told Paul Oliver that this song referred to a 'personal experience of an accident when

Clyde two-line skidder in southern Mississippi, unknown date.

the car in which he was travelling skidded on a temporary bridge at Hickman, Ky..' [60] Hickman lay some fifteen miles south of Columbus, Ky. and around ten miles west of Cayce on the M&O main line. Situated on a bend of the Mississippi River, the small town by 1883 boasted a car float operated by the 'Northwestern Railroad' (presumably the Leavenworth, Atchison & Northwestern which had become part of the Missouri Pacific in 1880), in conjunction with the Merchant's Southern Line Packet Company. From 1870, this steamboat business operated from St. Louis down to New Orleans and also connected 'at Columbus with the Mobile and Ohio Railroad' [61] amongst other ports of call on the way to the Crescent City. As many of these car floats survived well into the 1940s, most notably between New Orleans and Algiers in Louisiana, it is reasonable to assume there could have been one still operating from Hickman in the late 1930s at the time 'Floating Bridge' was made. As White points out: 'The car float system was certainly well used.' Indeed, statistics published in 1912 showed that there were still 'six thousand men and nearly two thousand car floats active in the New York railroad navy, which handled ten thousand freight cars each day.' [62]

I maintain that Sleepy John Estes was referring to an accident on a float bridge at Hickman, rather than one in an automobile. His expression 'temporary bridge' almost certainly relates to this almost-obsolete railroad phenomenon. In addition, two of the words used would seem to clinch it. The first is 'car', which of course is the common US term for a railroad passenger or freight vehicle. The second is the less-obvious 'skidded'. Back in the 1890s, loggers deep in the piney woods started replacing the ox-driven

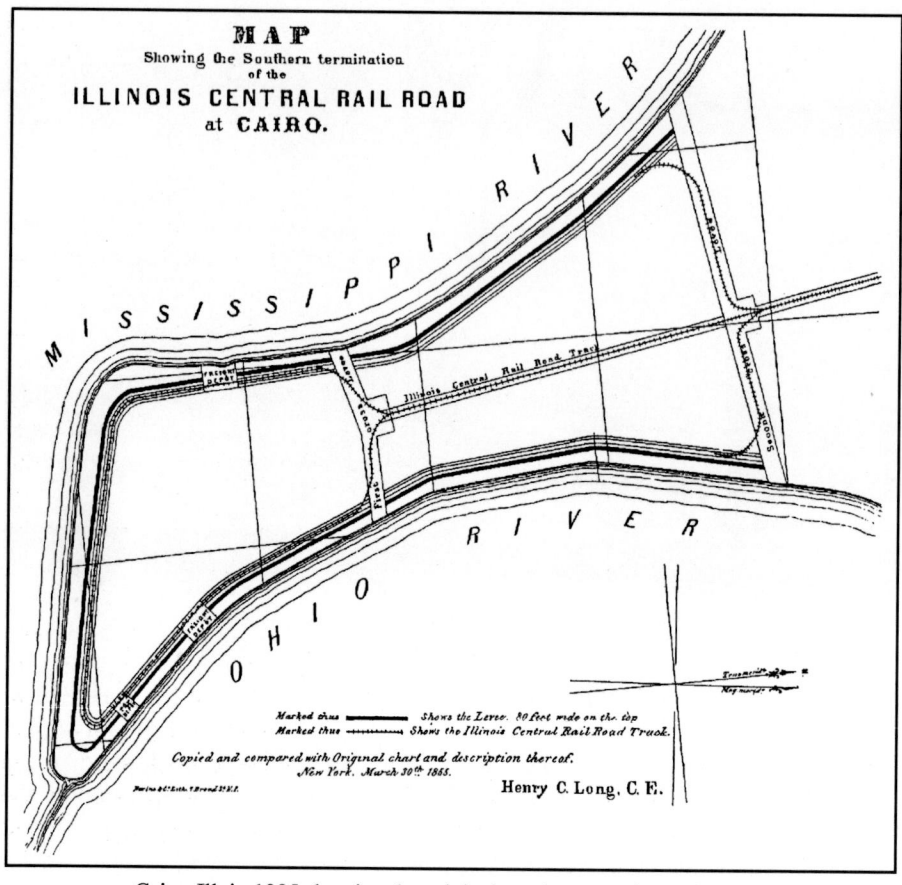

Chapter 3 — Ah! When I leave here, gonna catch that M&O

Cairo, Ill. in 1885 showing the original southern terminus of the IC prior to the M&O being included in the US Federal land grant of 1851.

'skid' used to bring logs to the riverside *(Chapter 2)* with steam operated machinery. The steam 'skidders' would fix strong steel cables around a tree trunk and drag or 'skid' it towards the railroad track, ready for loading onto the waiting flat cars. Anything from a one- to four-line machine was used. As Hickman explains: 'The skidders were set up near the spur tracks *[dummy lines]* where timber was thick. The steel wire cables, with varying lengths up to 1,000 feet or more, were unwound from the drums and attached to the logs in the woods. As the revolving drums reeled in the cables, four or five logs or more were skidded to the spur track at one pull-in.' [63]

The word 'skidder' soon got corrupted back to 'skid', as when Bolles used the term in the 1870s *(Chapter 2)*, and these machines were adapted to operating the float bridge, as Droege so aptly describes. It is easy to see how Paul Oliver's interpretation *(ref. 60 above)* came about.

However, let us now return to our imaginary M&O train, which we left panting steam and smoke at South Columbus, Ky. depot. As has been noted, by 1881 it could head ever northward and arrive at the shores of the Ohio River in East Cairo, Ky.. Although the original twenty-mile or so river journey was greatly reduced, the car float/float bridge operation was still needed to cross the river into Cairo, Ill.: 'The Mobile & Ohio Railroad ferried its cars directly across the river to the incline of the Wabash Railway Company below the Halliday Hotel *[in Cairo]* for a number of years.' [64] Of course, the Illinois Central was already there and had been serving Cairo for a quarter of a century or so. They too had to use a car float for many years — right up to 1889 in fact, when funds were finally found to build a bridge. It would be another decade or so before the M&O struck an agreement with the IC for the use of this bridge.

Cairo lies in a rough sort of 'V' shape between where two mighty rivers converge: on the western 'leg' is the Mississippi and on the eastern is the Ohio. Founded initially in 1818, it was not until the third attempt in 1846 that Cairo finally became established as a town. As the chronicler Lansden said, the town was really built for the Illinois Central (in agreement with the Trustees of Cairo): 'It was their city by birth.' [65] Indeed, the original plan had been to locate the southern terminus of the IC in Cairo. This was thwarted of course, when Mobile persuaded the US government to change the original land grant, as has already been related *(see page 87)*. Lansden also points out that, despite being a Northern town, the easy pace of life in Cairo was more Southern in character — as was the climate: 'Summers begin early and end late, making the long or hot season a long one comparatively.' But, combined with the close proximity to two major rivers, this extended hot season also brought malaria 'quite sufficient for home consumption'! He concludes: 'The geography and topography of the place make it more of a Southern town than a Northern town.' [66] Of course, Cairo would not have thrived as it did, had its railroad system not also included the M&O and its all-important connection to Mobile Bay. Most likely it would have remained just another stop on the IC line to Chicago via St. Louis.

It was to the latter city that the singer Henry Spaulding migrated from his native Cairo. Probably the founder of the heavy string-snapping and percussive guitar style found in the St. Louis area, Spaulding only ever recorded two sides, in 1929: 'Biddle Street Blues', about a location in his new home town, and 'Cairo Blues' [Brunswick 7085], one of the most haunting of the early rural blues to be committed to wax. Spaulding concedes that he may quite like St. Louis, but *'Cairo is my baby's home'*:

> Oughta know, she take my lovin' on.
> Know my babe, she will take my lovin' on.
> Know by that, I swear I won't be here long.
> Cairo, Cairo is my baby's home.
> I'm goin' home an' I swear an' it won't be long.
> Mmmmm, babe, Cairo, mmmm, babe. [67]

Another guitarist, who also started recording in 1929, adopted and extended Spaulding's style. A native of Shelby, Miss., Henry Townsend also called Cairo his home for a while, even though his family soon moved to St. Louis in the late 1920s. He had not yet reached his twentieth birthday when he first walked into the Columbia studios in Chicago and laid down a remarkable collection of blues songs that always echoed the insistent rhythms of his Mississippi birthplace[*]. He continued recording throughout the remainder of the Twentieth Century and is still alive at the time of writing.

All aboard! Time to leave Cairo amidst a swirl of hissing steam and the barking coughs of the M&O locomotive as it pulls out of the depot, its whistle shrieking and moaning out a challenge to all-comers. How could this not be the stuff that blues is made of?

By the beginning of 1886, the M&O had also taken out a lease on a shorter line, the St. Louis & Cairo Railroad. The latter ran from Cairo up to East St. Louis, Ill. — a distance of some 170 miles. The lease was for 45 years, ending on 'January 1, 1931', which coincided with the termination of the agreement to use the IC bridge across the Ohio River at Cairo mentioned on the previous page. Writing in 1910, Lansden observed that 'this change in the method of transfer' from the float bridge/car float arrangement 'has been of a very great advantage to the company, giving as it does, an all-rail line from Mobile to the great city of St. Louis.' [68]

Travelling an almost parallel route to that of the mighty Mississippi River and passing through Illinois towns like Hodges Park, Murphysboro, Red Bud, and Millstadt Junction, our M&O train with its smoke- and oil-blackened engine rumbles and grumbles over a myriad of switches and crossovers as it enters the unlovely conurbation of East St. Louis. Originally known as Illinoistown (its name was changed in 1861), it had started out as 'a settlement made by Capt. James Piggett, who in 1797 established a ferry at this point between the east and west banks of the river.' [69] By the early Twentieth Century, it had grown into a city that was home to thousands of

---

[*] In 1999, an autobiography appeared by Henry Townsend (as told to Bill Greensmith). *A Blues Life* (University of Illinois Press, 1999) is a remarkable account of the early blues in St. Louis, and is highly recommended.

Chapter 3 — Ah! When I leave here, gonna catch that M&O

blacks, who lived in dire conditions in what was rapidly becoming an industrial wasteland, largely ignored by the municipal authorities including the police. As has been related by other writers, it was the scene of one of the most horrendous race riots in 1917. Many black citizens were massacred and many more were seriously injured. The scars apparently have not completely healed, even to this day.

In his autobiography, Townsend mentions that, around the time of the riot, East St. Louis 'was a major migration area for people from the South. And everybody out of the South *[ie blacks]* had a .45 or a .38 or something' [70] to defend themselves with in the concrete jungle. These migrants would normally arrive by train, as many railroads converged on the city. These included the M&O, IC, C&A, B&O and the Cairo Short Line. The latter was a vital connecting road shared by several railroads and its full name was the St. Louis, Alton & Terre Haute RR. It also had a strong alliance with the IC. Another such connecting road was the East St. Louis & Carondelet Railway which was 'used chiefly… for all lines terminating at East St. Louis'. [71]

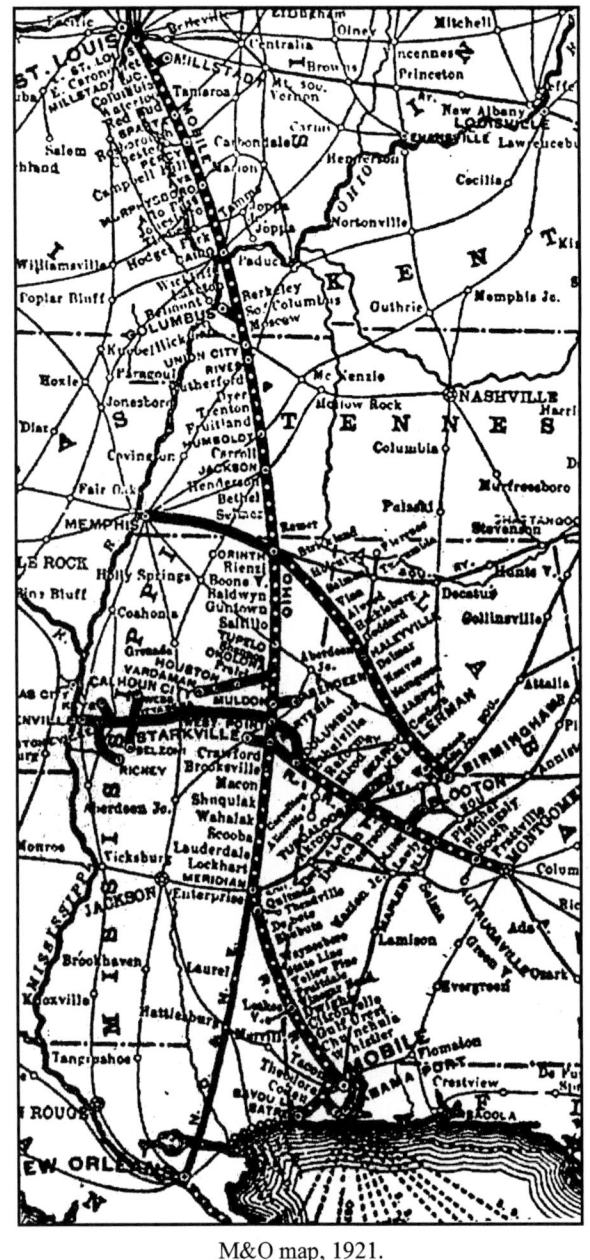

M&O map, 1921.
Trackage rights to Birmingham for freight trains only.

Although employment prospects were bleak, in the 1920s and '30s many blues singers would converge on the city, playing for nickels and dimes

Eads Bridge from St. Louis side, c.1880.

on the streets, in dilapidated barrelhouses or at house-rent parties. It was immortalised in several versions of 'East St. Louis Blues' by singers as varied as Bumble Bee Slim (Amos Easton), Luella Miller, Johnnie Temple, Faber Smith and Blind Willie McTell, as well as sides recorded for Library of Congress by William Brown (not the Paramount artist) and a group of unidentified singers, probably from Mississippi. Some of these artists were from Georgia, though Smith and Miller were based in St. Louis. Although recordings were mainly responsible for spreading this song, the vast complex of railroads carrying blues singers from place to place undoubtedly also played a part in its proliferation. As Scharf says, East St. Louis was 'the real western terminus of the roads centering in St. Louis from the East, and their several freight yards and depots being there'. [72]

By 1874, the Mississippi River crossing to St. Louis was spanned by the mighty Eads Bridge, an impressive two-level structure — the lower one for the railroad and the other for 'horse railways, wagons, and foot-passengers.' [73] On the Illinois side of the river, the railroad tracks which had previously run at the same level as the 'roadways' rose above the latter, due to the easier grading of their embankments. 'At Third Street, East St. Louis, the highways are terminated on the level of the street.' [74]

Third Street was a particularly impoverished part of the city. Traffic fumes and industrial emissions mingled with the soot and smoke from nearby trains, adding to the general pandemonium and the fast-growing decay of grimy slum tenements that housed teeming numbers of blacks. In the winter, thousands of coal fires spewed forth thick white smoke, creating a pall over the city that added to the misery of its inhabitants. Unlike their neighbour across the river, the city fathers of East St. Louis steadfastly refused to adopt smokeless fuels even into the late 1940s.

Billed as the 'High Sheriff From Hell' and the 'Devil's Son-In-Law', East St. Louis resident Peetie Wheatstraw was a popular bluesman in the 1930s and played both piano and guitar. Recorded in 1937, his 'Third Street's Going Down' [Decca 7379] reflects the sheer hopelessness of living there.

Peetie Wheatstraw, c.early 1930s.

On his 'Santa Fe Blues' [Vocalion 03231], cut at an earlier session in 1936, Wheatstraw employs the 'alternative transport' theme referred to on page 101, musing that he might travel on the Santa Fe or the 'Great Northern'. The latter was a Southern term for the International & Great Northern Railroad, which ran from St. Louis down to Houston, as well as branching off to Laredo in Texas. Accordingly, Henry Thomas — a 'professional' hobo if ever there was one — could easily head back to the Lone Star State, having first arrived in St. Louis by way of Mobile. Leaving his East Texas home by the Southern Pacific and switching to the L&N in New Orleans on the way to Mobile, he finally ends up in the freight yards of the M&O in East St. Louis. On 'Cottonfield Blues' [Vocalion 1094], in 1927, desperate to escape from this industrial hell, he declares himself ready to *'ride the rods' (see Chapter 10)* on a Texas-bound freight:

> I'm goin' to Texas, have to ride the rods.
> I'm goin' Texas, have to ride the rods.
> Just sure [as] the train leaves out of that Mobile [& Ohio] yard.[75]

As Mack McCormick points out in his superb notes to the *Ragtime Texas* LP [Herwin 209], a variation of this verse also appeared in Thomas' 'Bull-Doze Blues' [Vocalion 1230], made at a later session in 1928. He speculates that the 'Mobile' reference is more likely to indicate the M&O rather than the Alabama seaport, and in particular 'the Mobile & Ohio Railroad yards, possibly in East St. Louis.'[76] This is almost certainly bound to be the case. By the singer's own admission in his autobiographical

Chapter 3 — Ah! When I leave here, gonna catch that M&O

The *Abraham Lincoln*, on the C&A, backing into St. Louis station, c.1935.

'Railroadin' Some' *(Chapter 10)*, he probably travelled through St. Louis to Chicago on at least the four occasions that he recorded for Vocalion between 1927 and 1929[*].

To leave East St. Louis, Thomas could have chosen at least three other railroads that had a direct route into Texan towns such as Fort Worth, Dallas, Denison, Corsicana or San Antonio: all were served variously by the Frisco, the Missouri Pacific and the Cotton Belt. Or he could have caught the St. Louis, Iron Mountain & Southern which ran through Texarkana, Ark., where he could change over to the T&P, which would take him back to Dallas.

Having crossed the Eads Bridge over the Mississippi, our imaginary M&O train clatters into the Union Station in St. Louis, beads of water from condensing steam flecking its beleaguered boiler. Hissing triumphantly and filling the depot with eye-watering smoke and soot after emerging from a mile-long tunnel, the locomotive comes to a halt at the platform, having completed some 689 miles through five states.

Like its neighbour on the east side of the river, St. Louis, the great crossroads for commerce and railroads, was also home to countless blues singers in the 1930s. Guitarists like Henry Townsend, Big Joe Williams and Jaydee Short; women singers such as Mary Johnson, 'Little' Alice Moore and Edith North Johnson; and pianists Roosevelt Sykes, Sylvester Palmer, Henry Brown and Walter Davis.

More than most railroads, the M&O, along with its 'sister road', the IC, seemed to inspire blues singers. We have already come across the abrasive Willie Brown with his sensual sliding bass notes, and Bukka White's

---

[*] His October 1927 visit to Chicago involved two sessions (thus making five in all). But, since they were so close together — on 5 and 7 October — it is reasonable to assume that Thomas 'stayed over' in the Windy City, rather than making two separate trips from his home in East Texas.

Chapter 3 — Ah! When I leave here, gonna catch that M&O

impassioned, frenetic post-war side celebrating Gibson, Mississippi. Walter Davis, at his debut in 1930, committed to wax the first of three versions of his poignant 'M&O Blues' [Victor V-38618] (a different song to Brown's) with Roosevelt Sykes taking the piano chair:

> My baby's gone an' she won't come back no more. *(x2)*
> Ah! She left me this mornin', an' she caught that M&O.[77]

Davis was an almost-instant hit with the blues-buying public (largely the black community, of course) and continued to record steadily for Victor until 1952. He had hoboed his way to St. Louis around 1925, and would have most likely caught a slow, rumbling freight train on the M&O to get there. Fittingly, his 'M&O Blues' was to inspire a whole group of recordings in the pre-war era. Covers of his hit were made by Georgia Tom Dorsey, Big Bill Broonzy and Bumble Bee Slim, while Blind Willie McTell borrowed the melody for his 1933 recording, 'My Baby's Gone' [Vocalion 02668], which was itself reinterpreted by Tommy McClennan, Champion Jack Dupree and others.

North Carolina's Blind Boy Fuller also used the melody for his 'My Best Gal Gonna Leave Me' [Vocalion 0334] in 1937, and in 1938 he borrowed a verse from Davis' 'M&O Blues No. 3' [Victor 23333] for his 'Bye Bye Baby Blues' [Vocalion 04843], as well as including a further reference on the otherwise unrelated 'Big Bed Blues' [A.R.C. 6-11-71] in 1936. In passing, it is entirely possible that prior to 1926 (when our knowledge of his earlier life is an almost complete blank), Fuller may have spent some time within earshot of the Mobile & Ohio — perhaps in Jackson, Tenn., Mobile, Ala., or somewhere along the main line in eastern Mississippi.

A very moving 'I Hate That Train Called The M and O' [A.R.C. 6-02-04] was recorded in 1934 by Lucille Bogan (as 'Bessie Jackson'), which caused Cohen to remark that the 'closest *[the M&O]* came to Bogan's hometown of Birmingham was about fifty miles'.[78] However, a glance at the map of the M&O system in 1921 *(see page 111)* clearly shows the railroad had trackage rights — be it freight only — into Birmingham, Ala.. Furthermore, one of the many minor roads which the

M&O had absorbed by 1920 was the Fairfield & Macon Rail Road Company. Fairfield is some fifty miles north-west of Tuscaloosa and lies just outside Birmingham, approximately five miles from the city centre. A train to Tuscaloosa would connect you with the Montgomery branch of the Mobile & Ohio to Artesia, Miss., where you would pick up the main line. So, Ms. Bogan's blues about her man leaving on the M&O was factually correct and points to her likely residence in Fairfield — a possible avenue of research — rather than Birmingham itself.

The subject of Bogan's song was either the engineer (or, more likely on a Southern road, the fireman) and may well refer to her first husband, Nazareth Bogan, who was a railroad man. This beautiful blues is a slowed-down version of the 'My Baby's Gone' tune, sung with heartfelt conviction with a hint of the field holler, and accompanied by Walter Roland — on guitar this time — interweaving unerringly with the second guitar, probably played by Bob Campbell. You can almost see the tail-lights of the train as they fade towards the horizon and finally disappear...

> I was sorry, I was sor-sorry to my heart.
> I was sorry, I was sorry to my heart.
> To see that M&O train an' me an' my daddy part.[79]

Notes to Chapter 3

1	Hickman	Ibid, p.57
2	White, J.H.	*The American Railroad Freight Car*, p.10 (quoted from a list published in *Principles of Inland Transportation* by Stuart R. Daggett, p.202. New York. 1928)
3	Dubin	Ibid, p.385
4	Rowland, D.	p.560
5	Lansden, J.M.	p.101
6	Campbell, Rev. J.P.	p.47
7	DeBow, J.D.B.	p.533 (Volume II)
8	Ibid.	pp.533-4
9	Loree, L.F.	p.37
10	Schoener, A.	p.70
11	'Stevedore Man'	Leola B. Wilson (as 'Coot Grant') - vocal; with unk. cornet; trombone; clarinet; piano (c.May/June 1926, Chicago, Ill.)
12	'Stole Rider Blues'	Blind Willie McTell - vocal, guitar, speech (18 October 1927, Atlanta, Ga.)
13	'Come On In My Kitchen'	Robert Johnson - vocal, guitar, speech (23 November 1936, San Antonio, Tex.)

14	Harris, S.	p.197
15	DeBow	p.57 (Volume I)
16	Moore, J.	p.4
17	W.P.A.	p.228
18	Ibid.	p.231
19	'New Stock Yard Blues'	Robert Wilkins - vocal, guitar, speech; Little Son Joe (as 'Son Joe') - guitar; Kid Spoons - spoons (10 Oct. 1935, Jackson, Miss.)
20	Oliver, P.	Notes to Wolf WSE-111 (LP)
21	W.P.A.	Ibid.
22	'New Stock Yard Blues'	Ibid.
23	W.P.A.	Ibid, p.227
24	Russell, T.	p.188
25	Charters	Ibid, p.198
26	zur Heide	Ibid, p.12
27	Charters	Ibid, p.199
28	Owen, T.M.	pp.1254-5 (Volume II)
29	Barry, J.M.	p.40
30	Ibid.	
31	Newell, F.H.	p.578
32	'Poor Little Johnny'	Harriet McClintock - vocal, speech; unacc.; John Lomax speech (Library of Congress recording, 29 October 1940, near Sumterville, Ala.)
33	'Meet Me Round The Corner'	Joe Williams - vocal, guitar; William Mitchell - imitation bass (27 March 1941, Chicago, Ill.)
34	Owen	Ibid, p.1333
35	Ibid.	p.1045
36	Harris	Ibid, p.552
37	'Gibson Hill'	Bukka White - vocal, guitar (July 1973, West Memphis, Ark.)
38	LaVere, S.	Notes to Biograph BLP-12049 (LP)
39	'Frisco Leaving Birmingham'	George 'Bullet' Williams - harmonica, speech (c.May 1928, Chicago, Ill.)
40	Wardlow	Ibid, p.54 (*Devil's Music*)
41	'M&O Blues'	Willie Brown - vocal, guitar (28 May 1930, Grafton, Wis.)
42	'Jackson Blues'	Sonny Boy Williamson - vocal, harmonica; Joe Williams - guitar; Robert Lee McCoy - guitar (5 May 1937, Aurora, Ill.)
43	Wilson, C.R., & W. Ferris	p.508
44	Botkin, B.A., & A.F. Harlow	p.43
45	White, J.H.	Ibid, p.90
46	Ibid.	p.91
47	Ibid.	

48	Ibid.	
49	Ibid.	
50	Owen	Ibid, p.1016
51	Ibid.	p.1017
52	Ibid.	p.1016
53	Scharf, J.T.	p.1175 (*Volume II*)
54	White, J.H.	Ibid, p.102
55	'Mind Reader Blues'	Bertha Lee - vocal; Charley Patton - guitar (31 January 1934, New York City)
56	Loree	Ibid, p.38
57	Droege, J.A.	p.245
58	Ibid.	pp.245-6
59	'Floating Bridge'	Sleepy John Estes - vocal, guitar; Hammie Nixon - harmonica; Charlie Pickett - guitar (2 August 1937, New York City)
60	Oliver, P.	*Blues Fell This Morning*, p.225
61	Scharf	Ibid, p.1121
62	White, J.	Ibid.
63	Hickman	Ibid, p.165
64	Lansden	Ibid, p.222
65	Ibid.	p.60
66	Ibid.	p.121
67	'Cairo Blues'	Henry Spaulding - vocal, guitar (9 June 1929, Chicago, Ill.)
68	Lansden	Ibid, p.223
69	Scharf	Ibid, pp.1867-8
70	Townsend, H.	p.14
71	Scharf	Ibid, p.1202
72	Ibid.	p.1842
73	Ibid.	p.1202
74	Ibid.	p.1084
75	'Cottonfield Blues'	Henry Thomas - vocal, guitar (30 June 1927, Chicago, Ill.)
76	McCormick, M.	Notes to Herwin 209 (LP)
77	'M&O Blues'	Walter Davis - vocal; Roosevelt Sykes (as 'Willie Kelly') - piano (12 June 1930, Cincinnati, Oh.)
78	Cohen, N.	p.445
79	'I Hate That Train Called The M and O'	Lucille Bogan (as 'Bessie Jackson') - vocal; Walter Roland - guitar; prob. Bob Campbell - guitar (31 July 1934, New York City)

Discography – Chapter 3

'Cairo Blues'
(Henry Spaulding)
CD: *St. Louis Country Blues (1929-37)*
[Document DOCD-5147] 1993

'Come On In My Kitchen'
(Robert Johnson)
CD: *Robert Johnson – King Of The Delta Blues Singers* [Columbia CK-52944] 2004

'Cottonfield Blues'
(Henry Thomas)
4-CD: *Texas Blues – Early Blues Masters From The Lone Star State*
[J.S.P. JSP-7730] 2004

'Floating Bridge'
(Sleepy John Estes)
CD: *Sleepy John Estes – Volume 2 (1937-41)*
[Document DOCD-5016] 1990

'Frisco Leaving Birmingham' [Take 3]
(George 'Bullet' Williams)
CD: *Too Late, Too Late Blues (1926-44)*
[Document DOCD-5150] 1993

'Gibson Hill'
(Bukka White)
LP: *Big Daddy* [Biograph BLP-12049] 1974
CD: *Big Daddy* [Shout! Factory DK-34010] 2004

'I Hate That Train Called The M and O'
(Bessie Jackson [Lucille Bogan])
CD: *Lucille Bogan – Volume 3 (1934-35)*
[Blues Document BDCD-6038] 1993

'Jackson Blues'
(Sonny Boy Williamson)
CD: *Sonny Boy Williamson – Vol.1 (1937-38)*
[Document DOCD-5055] 1991

'M&O Blues'
(Walter Davis)
CD: *Walter Davis – First Recordings (1930-32)*
[J.S.P. JSP-605] 1992

'M&O Blues'
(Willie Brown)
5-CD: *Charley Patton – Complete Recordings (1929-34)* [J.S.P. JSP-7702] 2002

'Meet Me Around The Corner'
(Big Joe Williams)
5-CD: *Big Joe Williams And The Stars Of Mississippi Blues (1935-51)*
[J.S.P. JSP-7719] 2003

'Mind Reader Blues'
(Charley Patton)
Charley Patton – Complete Recordings (1929-34) [J.S.P. JSP-7702] 2002

'New Stock Yard Blues'
(Robert Wilkins)
4-CD: *Masters Of Memphis Blues (1927-39)*
[J.S.P. JSP-7725] 2004

'Poor Little Johnny'
(Harriet McClintock)
CD: *Field Recordings – Volume 4: Mississippi & Alabama (1934-42)*
[Document DOCD-5578] 1997

'Stevedore Man'
(Coot Grant [Leola B. Wilson])
CD: *Coot Grant / Kid Wilson – Volume 1 (1925-28)* [Document DOCD-5563] 1997

'Stole Rider Blues'
(Blind Willie McTell)
5-CD: *Blind Willie McTell – The Classic Years (1927-40)* [J.S.P. JSP-7711] 2003

Chapter 3 — Ah! When I leave here, gonna catch that M&O

She's givin' it away

'She's Givin' It Away' – Sam Theard (1929)

CHAPTER 4

REFRIGERATOR CARS, BANANAS AND THE BLUES

The M&O had a direct as well as indirect influence on the blues — as indeed did many other railroads — not just through the sounds emanating from them that inspired imitation on musical instruments, but also the powerful poetic imagery and symbolism used by the singers in their lyrics, Charley Patton's black smokestack that 'shines like gold', for example. Of course, railroads in general were to largely shape the US in both economic and social structure as well. Their development, not only in route mileage, but also in technology, also gave inspiration to the blues. A phrase such as *'I'm gonna eat my breakfast here, an' my dinner a thousand miles below'* might have drawn on poetic licence in an earlier century, but the actual concept of covering such a distance in so short a time was due to the increasing standardisation, the extended mileage and, above all, the speed of the railroad.

The railroad, I have already noted, is one of the major themes in the blues and one particular technological advance was to lend itself to another such theme — that of sexuality. The advent of the much-improved refrigerator car in the 1880s brought a hitherto 'exotic' fruit to the market place of towns and cities in the Southern interior. This was the phallic-shaped banana.

At the core of the blues is the 'two-way communication' which exists between singer and listener. For instance, Rube Lacy, who recorded the starkly beautiful 'Mississippi Jail House Groan' [Paramount 12629] in 1928,

Chapter 4 — She's givin' it away

From the 1890s, a reefer in the Philip Armour fleet.

confessed in later years that he actually had never done any time in prison, but he knew it would 'hit' many blacks out there listening in Mississippi. By the same token, a singer using the banana by way of sexual symbolism in a blues would not have been able to complete this two-way link unless their audience was familiar with the fruit in question.

While it is true that bananas had found their way inland many decades earlier, they were still very much a luxury item until the late 1880s and '90s. For example, freedman William Johnson of Natchez, Miss., thought it worth mentioning both bananas and oranges in an 1851 entry to his diary on 21 April. One of his slaves[*], Edd, had come up on a steamboat 'from New Orleans this morning and brot the Children Some Bananahs & a Box of Orranges.'[1] Over a decade later, the banana did not figure in a list of eighty imports received by the city of Memphis during a twelve-month period, although it did include apples, limes and oranges. Coulter reports that, around 1878 there 'arose the Northern drummer[**] who came South to scatter his wares over the country, first to introduce widely a thousand knicknacks and exotic products like bananas.'[2] It was only with the improved efficiency of the refrigerator car that this fruit was to become a common sight throughout the South by the 1900s, and a favourite amongst the black population. It was then — and only then — that the banana lent itself to potent sexual imagery in the blues of Bo Carter, Memphis Minnie, Sam Theard and others.

Ever since the 1840s, railroads and other industrial companies had been exploring the possibilities of using refrigerated cars to convey perishable

---

[*] As a successful barber in Natchez, Johnson employed assistants as well as slaves, some of whom were taught the trade with a view to becoming independent and free themselves.

[**] In the US during the Nineteenth Century, the term 'drummer' referred to travelling salesmen (who 'drummed up' business by knocking on doors).

goods — in particular citrus fruits. The concept of a fast freight line was known and had been advertised prior to the Civil War. The idea was for the companies involved to transport such goods between one railroad and another at priority speed. It was at these points that freight trains could get bogged down for hours, as often a change of railroad also meant a change of gauge and missed connections due to the myriad of local times then in operation[*]. More often than not, the fast freight lines 'talked a good talk' but were unable to transform their claims into actual results. It was not until after the Civil War that private companies realised there was a viable business in running refrigerator cars, or 'reefers' as they were often called. These companies owned the majority of this new rolling stock, as most of the railroads were not keen to invest money in this new market at the time.

The idea of shipping fresh beef, pork and other types of meat over long distances without it deteriorating was a major inspiration to these companies. One of the first was George H. Hammond, who based himself in Hammond, Ind.. He started out in 1868, and by 1900 owned 1,300 reefers, which delivered vast quantities of freshly-preserved meat to all the major US cities. He is described by William Cronon as a 'Detroit packer who... used a special refrigerated car — an icebox on wheels originally designed for fruit shipments — to send sixteen thousand pounds of beef to Boston'[3], but Cronon was almost certainly referring to the large fruit grower, Parker Earle from Cobden, Ill.. Earle first shipped strawberries in 1858 in a reefer to Chicago, some three hundred miles away. Others, like Swift and Armour, were soon to follow suit. The latter became one of the largest of the fast freight lines by the 1900s, when Philip D. Armour 'ran no fewer than seventeen car lines and twelve thousand cars.'[4] However, in an early Twentieth Century pre-run of the recent Microsoft scenario, the US Government declared itself unhappy with the virtual monopoly enjoyed by Armour's 'empire' and in 1919 'the Federal Trade Commission ruled that Armour had gained an unfair advantage *[and]* ordered the sale of the Armour subsidiary'[5] (ie the meat-packing arm of the operation, Armour & Company).

It seems that, like many large companies (George Pullman's, for example), Armour lines were poor payers when it came to employees' wages, which doubtless accounted for some of their success. There was a street in Chicago named 'Armour Avenue', and this crops up in a small group of blues titles in the early 1920s — presumably in the form of veiled protest. Pianist Jimmie Blythe (as 'James Blythe') restricted himself to an instrumental piece, 'Armour Ave. Struggle' in 1924 [Paramount 12207], while Maggie Jones cut 'The Gouge Of Armour Avenue' b/w 'The Chicago Gouge' [Paramount 12209] in June of the same year. Recording as 'Faye Barnes' (her real name was Fae

---

[*] Before 1883 and introduction of the current US time zones, all cities and large towns (at least, those served by a railroad) operated local 'sun times', which decreed that it was 12:00 noon when the sun was directly overhead.

Barnes), she disguised the subject as a new dance craze; however, the definition of a 'gouger' given by Partridge — a slang term in criminal circles from 1924 — is 'a swindler; one who takes excessive profits'.[6] Perhaps George Hammond was also a mean employer and Lillian Miller's 'Hammond Blues' just a little too outspoken... which might explain why it was the only side from her 1928 session that Gennett decided not to issue.[*]

In any event, reefers (generally painted a bright yellow) were here to stay. Shipping bananas, however, required a great deal more care than other perishable foods, allowing only a five degree variation in temperature[**]. As John Droege, General Manager of the New York, New Haven & Hartford RR, explained circa 1912: 'For bananas the minimum temperature is 55, for safety against chill with a usual refrigerator temperature of 58 to 60. Other fruits require temperatures ranging from 34 to normal. Meats are often frozen.' [7] This meant using more expensive and sophisticated equipment — which was one of the main reasons the railroads let private companies such as Hammond, Swift and Armour buy and run most of the reefers themselves. The Armour Refrigerator Line had used many pseudonyms to help disguise their growing monopoly in the 1890s including 'Barbaroza, Brittain's Provision, Dubuque, Kansas City Fruit Express *[and]* Tropical and Fruit Growers Express.' [8]

In 1920, the year after Armour's defeat in the courts, ten major railroads got together and adopted the last title for a new corporation: Fruit Growers Express, or FGE. The companies included the Southern, ACL, Pennsylvania, B&O and Norfolk & Western. The railroad industry had

Maggie Jones/Faye Barnes, c.early 1920s.

---

[*] Alternatively this title might indicate Ms. Miller's origins in Hammond, Louisiana.
[**] All references to temperatures are in Fahrenheit.

Chapter 4 — She's givin' it away

Typical rail yard scene in 1885-90, near New York.
(from *Scribner's Magazine*, May 1889, showing various 'colour' fast freight lines).

finally realised that the refrigerator car was here to stay and, more importantly, could be a lucrative source of income via the fast freight line. Some railroads, however, had been 'sneaking into' the fruit and frozen meat transportation business ever since the end of the Civil War. They achieved this by setting up what John White calls 'pseudo-private car lines'. These were generally named after colours, such as the Blue Line, White Line or Green Line. The first of these — the Red Line* — was set up by the New York Central in October 1865. The Red Line was actually a form of cooperative which, besides the NYC, also included 'all its associated lines to the north and west'. White adds that 'each railroad was required to furnish three new cars per mile of line. They were painted an English vermilion, coated with varnish.' [10]

Since the term 'highball' came to refer to an express passenger train *(Chapter 1)*, it seems inevitable that a fast freight on the Red Line would become the 'redball'. Indeed, by 1892, the Santa Fe had inaugurated its own fast freight line dubbed the 'Red Ball Service'. The term soon entered railroad slang to signify any fast freight, and also surfaced on a couple of

---

* This name was probably chosen as various shades of red adorned the box car and its ventilated variant, a precursor of the reefer. The main reason for this — which will come as no surprise — was that red paint was cheapest to buy: 'Natural pigments were the only coloring agents available to the Nineteenth Century painter. One of the most abundant of these was red oxide, which was derived from iron ore.' [9] The box car was far and away the most numerous freight car on the US railroad system.

Library of Congress recordings. Eugene Foster sang a 'Red Ball Turning Over' in Montgomery, Ala. while languishing in Kilby Prison during 1934, and in the previous year someone referred to only as 'Old Man' committed a vocal/harp train blues to wax as simply 'Red Ball', down in New Orleans.

Another expression, 'hot shot', was soon to become even more popular, certainly in black usage. It stems from 'hot box', a term describing the frequent overheating of wheel axle bearings on the outside of earlier cars, especially when pushing the locomotive to its limits. One guitarist became Hobson 'Hot Box' Johnson when accompanying singers like Curtis Jones and Lillie Mae Kirkman, on record in the late 1930s[*], whereas Kingfish Bill Tomlin (who might also be the pianist on 'Hot Box' [Paramount 13034]) revealed a greater-than-average knowledge of the railroad when he sang this unique verse in 1930, more than hinting at a free ride *(see Chapter 10)* on a fast freight line:

> I got the railroad blues, hot boxes on my mind.
> I got the railroad blues, babe, hot boxes on my mind.
> I ain't got no railroad fare, but [if] *No. 1* pass I'll blind [it].[11]

Because bananas were more prone to decay on long hauls, they were often run in complete trains (or 'manifests') of reefers in the quickest possible time to reach their destination. For example, some two years after introducing the Red Ball Service, the Santa Fe reportedly 'ran a *hot-shot* banana special from Galveston to Chicago *[1,385 miles]* in fifty-three hours, for an average speed of 26 mph' [12] — more than twice the usual average for freight trains at the time.

The expression 'Hot shot' was also used to denote sexual prowess, as in the ubiquitous Willie McTell's words on his plangent 'Scarey Day Blues' [OKeh 8936] from 1931, where he invokes the L&N that ran down to Atlanta, Ga., and also the Central of Georgia, which served his home base of Statesboro:

> Said, my baby got a bed, it shines like a mornin' star.
> My good mama got a bed, it shines like a mornin' star.
> An' when I crawls in the middle, it rides me like a Cadillac car.
>
> I said she got that mojo, an' she won't let me see. *(x2)*
> An' every time I start to lovin', she try to put them jinx on me.
>
> *(Spoken)* Play it a little bit, Mr. So-An'-So, 'cause I know you like it.

---

[*] Johnson holds the honour of being the first electric guitarist to feature on a blues recording session, having backed Curtis Jones on two titles, 'Sweetheart Land' [Vocalion unissued] and 'It's A Low Down Dirty Shame' [Vocalion 04027] on 1 March 1938. He was followed shortly after by white player George Barnes on a Jazz Gillum session for Bluebird on 14 March.

Chapter 4 — She's givin' it away

Well, she shakes like the Central, she wobble like the L&N.
I said she shake it like the Central, she wobble like the L&N.
Well, she's a hot-shot mama an' I'm scared to tell 'er where I bin.[13]

McTell recorded this out of contract for OKeh Records and used a pseudonym (a common practice among bluesmen) — on this occasion 'Georgia Bill'. On the previous year's 'Mama Let Me Scoop For You' *(Chapter 1)*, however, he'd used 'Hot Shot Willie'.

Although Houston, some fifty miles away, was rapidly increasing the competition, Galveston (with the help of the Santa Fe's 'hot shot' freight trains) remained the major handling port in Texas for bananas right up to the 1940s. As well as the Santa Fe, there were four other major roads out of Galveston. These were the Southern Pacific, Missouri Pacific, the Katy and the Chicago, Rock Island & Pacific or 'Rock Island line' — the latter made famous by Leadbelly's recording in several versions, the first cut in 1937 for the Library of Congress[*]. Lonnie Donegan's version of the song, cut during the UK skiffle craze of the mid-Fifties, went 'gold' (ie sold a million copies) after reaching No. 1 in the US pop charts — the first time ever that a British artist had achieved this.

One of the main companies that controlled the dockside movement of bananas and other cargo on the railroads in Galveston was the Galveston Wharf Company, formed in 1860. However, even as late as 1872, when the state legislature granted the company authority to 'operate a railroad between the railroad

Rock Island ad, 1879.

---

[*] The first-ever recorded version of 'Rock Island Line' was another Library of Congress side: a fine accapella performance recorded in 1934 by a group of prisoners led by Kelly Pace at Camp No. 5, Cummins State Farm, Gould, Ark.. The first song to mention this railroad was 'Rock Island Blues' [Vocalion 1111] by Furry Lewis, recorded in April 1927 in Chicago.

Chapter 4 — She's givin' it away

Papa Charlie Jackson, c.1924.

depots and their wharves', the city was far from being a major rail centre: these lines linked up with the Galveston, Houston & Henderson RR, 'then the only railroad in Galveston.' [14] As Reed points out, the five major roads (Santa Fe, etc) that later served Galveston also ran into Houston. Many early blues singers from East Texas must surely have stolen a ride in a box car on a journey from the Galveston Wharf Company's freight yards and their forty-seven miles of track *en route* to Houston, Dallas and points north, east and west, spreading the blues across the land.

One such early exponent was Aaron 'T-Bone' Walker who, along with B.B. King, later became one of the 'fathers of modern blues guitar'. Born in 1910 in Cass County not far from the Texas–Arkansas border, the Walker family soon after moved into Dallas. There, in December 1929, he recorded his first two blues sides as 'Oak Cliff T-Bone'. One of these told of the Trinity River, which cuts through the centre of Dallas before flowing south-eastwards, flooding its banks. Both 'Trinity River Blues' and 'Wichita Falls Blues' [Columbia 14506-D] also featured piano accompaniment (provided by Douglas Finnell). It is known that Walker travelled quite extensively in his earlier years, mostly by rail.

Although the box car was the preferred method of travel if one was 'riding free', the more adventurous would sometimes use the reefer. This required a little more care, as Walker explains: 'When those railroad guards walk the top looking for you, you get down inside a "reefer" — that's the refrigerator car, where they put the produce. On a car like that, there's a part that raises, so that when all the stuff aboard is unloaded, it can be opened and aired out. Well, when you climb down onto the reefer, if you don't know what to do, the guard can close the top on you and you can smother to death in there, because it's airtight. So, you take a spike with you and jam it so that whatever he does on top, it won't go down, and neither will it go back up — or only if you remove the spike. A lot of times he guesses what has happened, but it's a moving train and he's got to worry about his movements, too.' [15]

To return to the 'pseudo-private car lines' mentioned earlier: by the 1890s, some railroads also ran fruit trains under their own name. One of the

Chapter 4 — She's givin' it away

Built in 1891, these cars were mainly used for the 'banana specials' from New Orleans to Chicago.

most prominent of these was the Illinois Central, whose 'banana specials' gained something of a reputation as one engineer competed with another to make the long haul (some 914 miles) from New Orleans to Chicago in the shortest possible time.

One resident of the Crescent City at the turn of the Twentieth Century was the obscure 'Papa' Charlie Jackson. Thought to have been born in the late 1880s, Jackson started his recording career in 1924 with Paramount and ended it just over a decade later with A.R.C., leaving behind a legacy of some 75 sides. Much of this material was a mixture of vaudeville, minstrelsy and country blues played in the main on a six-string banjo. Jackson had migrated to Chicago sometime before 1924, to become one of the first on the city's blues scene along with guitarist Big Bill Broonzy from Mississippi and pianist Cripple Clarence Lofton from Tennessee. It could well be that Jackson 'grabbed' one of the IC's banana specials to get to his destination, as that railroad had set up a regular timetable for its fast freight line by 1896.

Interestingly, once in the Windy City, he spent some time living on Maxwell Street, which was not only a famous focal point for black street singers, but also home to a large open-air market. Having revealed his address on 'Maxwell Street Blues' [Paramount 12320], he intimates on 'If I Got What You Want' [OKeh 8957] that he may have spent some time as a market stall-holder, featuring among his wares the 'exotic' banana:

> (Spoken) 'Say babe, do you know I'm in business now?
> People attend from miles an' miles around to get my stuff.'
>
> 'What kind of stuff are you havin'?'
>
> 'Apples, oranges an' bananas.'
>
> 'An' I got somethin' else, too.
> But I'll tell you about it later on — yeah, man.'

Unloading bananas in Chicago, 1910.
Some of these would soon be going to the famous Maxwell St. market.

'Oh! Lay it, papa.'

'Think I ain't.'

'You tellin' me?'

(Vocal refrain) Now, if I got what you want, come on an' get it.
Please, baby, don't you know you're welcome to [it]?
If I got what you want, come on an' get it.
Please, baby, don't you know you're welcome to [it]?[16]

Jackson was to die some four years later in 1938. It is odd that, although acknowledged as 'Father of Hokum Blues' *(Chapter 8)* — a genre which revelled in *double entendre* — he did not see fit to use the obvious sexual symbolism of the banana until near the end of his recording career.

The first recording by a black artist to feature the name of this fruit in the title was an early 'answer' to a 1923 English music hall song, 'Yes! We Have No Bananas'* called 'I've Got The Yes! We Have No Banana *[sic]* Blues' [OKeh 4927], cut by Eva Taylor in August that same year. Despite the

---

* For further coverage of the influence on blues from early music hall in the UK, see *English Music Hall Connection* (dissertation by the author, Lancaster University, 1992). Also *Blacks, Whites And Blues* (with update) by Tony Russell, featured in *Yonder Come The Blues* by Paul Oliver, Robert M.W. Dixon *et al* (Cambridge University Press, 2001).

title, which was a vaudeville ditty, Taylor was really more of a popular/jazz singer who jumped on the blues bandwagon in the early 1920s (as did many other singers of course), rather than a blues singer *per se*. She was the wife of pianist/composer and sometime record boss Clarence Williams, who was probably instrumental in getting her on disc.

A much more convincing artist with a strong vocal style was Rosa Henderson, who recorded some 110 sides between 1923 and 1931. Within a fortnight of Eva Taylor's release, Henderson adapted the theme for her remarkably assertive 'If You Don't Give Me What I Want' [Vocalion 14652]. Backed by Fletcher (no relation) Henderson's jaunty piano, she incorporates the banana as part of a 'market stall' scenario in which her lover is the salesman:

Rosa Henderson, c.1923.

> It's pickle to pickle an' dill to dill,
> If you don't give me, someone will.
> You may refuse to give me chops,
> But I know all the butchers' shops.
>
> *Refrain:* So, if you don't give me what I want,
>   I'm gonna get it somewheres else.
>   If you don't give me what I want,
>   I'm gonna get it somewheres else.
>
> It's pepper to pepper an' salt to salt,
> If you don't give me, ain't my fault.
> For weeks and days I heard you say,
> Yes, we have no bananas today.
>
> *Refrain:* But if you don't give me what I want,
>   I'm gonna get it somewheres else.[17]

Some four months later Lucille Hegamin recorded a version [Cameo 461], and in June 1924 Edna Hicks with Fletcher Henderson and two of his Big Band revisited Rosa Henderson's recording, leaving out a couple of verses and changing the original music hall phrase to *'You've had no bananas all this week'*[18] [Paramount 12090]. It would appear that the English music

Chapter 4 — She's givin' it away

A Tiffany reefer from 1879, but of similar design to Honeyboy's 'carboxes'.

hall was the source for these three vaudeville-blues records, and that Papa Charlie Jackson's title represented a belated male response.

Like T-Bone Walker, David 'Honeyboy' Edwards from Mississippi — one of several bluesmen whose path crossed that of the allegedly 'satanic-influenced' Robert Johnson in the 1930s — 'used to ride the reefer, too.' A self-confessed hobo, his travels would have seen him jumping on both the M&O and the IC. In 1997, he recalled the technique for riding in the ice bunkers situated in the back of refrigerator cars (or 'carboxes', as he called them): 'They'd have a hole in the back end of one of them carboxes where they put two or three hundred pounds of ice to keep the cargo cold. Like the banana cars up from New Orleans, before they load them with the bananas, they'd put two or three hundred pounds of ice in there to keep that whole carbox cool. So, when you catch one of them reefers empty, you jump down in where they put that ice and pull the handle down and close the door. Now you got the handle inside and ain't going to let nobody in there.' [19]

Edwards describes the ice bunkers as 'a hole', and indeed on most reefers that was about the size of it. Even for a person of average height, the conditions would have been extremely cramped and not at all conducive to riding on the reefer for any great distance. As John White noted, in one design 'ice bunkers two feet deep and four feet long were placed at either end, and an inclined drip floor and pipes carried away the water from the melting ice. Roof hatches were provided above the ice bunkers.' Neither would changing to another reefer have been much of an improvement, as White refers to the foregoing description as 'the general arrangement of the standard refrigerator car'.[20]

These comments refer to the 'wood car era' which lasted from the early Nineteenth Century until around 1910 officially, when steel-bodied freight cars began coming into vogue. Nevertheless, time often moves very slowly in the South and the old-fashioned rolling stock was still in use some twenty years later on, when Honeyboy Edwards was riding the rails in Mississippi, Alabama and elsewhere.

So, from the time of its introduction in the US as an exotic fruit in the early Nineteenth Century, and to freedman William Johnson in the early

1850s, via the drummers up to the 1880s, the banana had spread throughout the South and into Northern cities too by the beginning of the 1900s. So much so, that certainly by the 1910s this fruit was a familiar sight and readily accessible to the public at large — including, of course, the working-class black community. Initiated by the Illinois Central's banana specials, and spread ever wider by other roads* such as the M&O and L&N, the 'exotic fruit was made commonplace and popular by cheap long-distance transport, aided by some imaginative marketing.' [21]

It is not surprising that blues singers growing up in the 1900s drew on the erotic symbolism of the banana, which began to appear on records from the 1920s onwards. It was from this period that their audiences would have known *just what I'm talkin' about'*, when listening to the likes of Rosa Henderson, Edna Hicks and Papa Charlie Jackson.

Apart from that group of recordings which directly or otherwise drew on the English music hall, another banana-related song emerged in the late 1920s which was of the 'home-grown' variety. Also emanating from a vaudeville background, but a with rougher, more 'country' blues vocal, 'Givin' It Away' [Gennett 6829] — by the superb boogie/barrelhouse pianist Cow Cow Davenport — made its first appearance at the beginning of April 1929. Born in 1894 in Alabama, Davenport was one of the first generation of blues singers and a highly-influential musician. The theme of his song is hard times — where things that you used to be able to sell, you can't even sell dirt cheap, and so now you are giving them away — and included jelly roll (a kind of jam sponge or Swiss roll), meat and hair grease as wares viewed from a sexual perspective.

Another Alabaman who sometimes recorded with Davenport was Sam Theard, often billed as 'Lovin' Sam From Down In 'Bam'. Theard, who does not appear in any 'Blues Who's Who', did not play an instrument on his sessions, but was an excellent scat vocalist and often drew songs from vaudeville and the minstrelsy stage. Two weeks after Davenport's session, he cut a version of this song as 'She's Givin' It Away', which Brunswick decided not to issue. However, his second attempt on 1 May did see the light of day [Brunswick 7073]. With his grainy and essentially 'blues' vocal, Theard describes the 'financial' plight of various street traders in Birmingham, Ala. and also on Chicago's South Side:

> Aunt Sue runs a bakershop back of the jail.
> A sign on the window: 'Jelly roll for sale'.

---

* Because of the more complex make-up of a reefer, which made even 'the cheapest refrigerator car... half again as costly as an ordinary box car', the railroad companies were content to allow private car lines such as Hammond, Armour, etc. to own and operate 'most refrigerator cars before around 1910. After that time, railroads began to enter the field more aggressively because they had more capital available, realized that the demand for this type of car was not a temporary fad, and saw that a fair return on capital was possible.' [22]

> She can't sell her jelly, so they say.
> Down there givin' her jelly away.
>
> *Refrain:* She's givin' it away;
> She's givin' it away.
>
> Uncle Ned runs a market on 18th Street.
> He don't sell nothin' but the best of meat.
> He can't sell his meat, so they say.
> Round town givin' good meat away.
>
> *Refrain:* He's givin' it away.
> He's givin' it away.
>
> Tony runs a fruit wagon all day long.
> You ought to hear 'im sing that song.
> He can't sell bananas, so they say.
> Down there givin' his banana away.
>
> *Refrain:* He's givin' it away.
> He's givin' it away.

Note how Theard emphasises the sexual suggestion of the song by referring to Tony's 'banana' in the singular.

18th Street is in the black section of Birmingham and wasn't far from the Union Station where the trains of the M&O, L&N, Southern, Frisco, ACL and others terminated. The singer also makes a pointed comment when comparing Georgia's female cotton field workers 'hollering' instructions to their mules (and at least, by implication, eking out some sort of living) with the lack of 'honest' employment for women on Chicago's State Street:

> Women in Georgia hollerin': 'Whoa! Haw! Gee!'
> Women on State Street hollerin': 'Who wants me?'
> They can't sell nothin', so they say.
> They're down there givin' everything away.
>
> *Refrain:* They're givin' it away.
> They're givin' it away.[23]

Guitarist Tampa Red, who accompanied Theard on the above, recorded his own version of 'Givin' It Away' [Vocalion 1409] the very next day. Accompanied by Georgia Tom (Dorsey) on piano, he borrows lines and verses from both Davenport and Theard. Although he follows the latter more closely, Red sings 'bananas' in the plural, seemingly in a fit of atypical coyness (Red and Dorsey were the main creators of the risqué hokum hit of

Bo Carter, c.mid-1930s.   Tampa Red, c.1940.

1928, 'It's Tight Like That' [Vocalion 1228]). He also uses Theard's *'Women in Georgia'* verse, which, along with the general sexual theme, can be seen as a form of protest against a white-dominated system which left black working women and men on the bottom of the wage-earning table.

The personal references in the 'Givin' It Away' group of songs to *'Aunt Sue'* (who appears in all three versions), Davenport's *'Papa Joe'* and *'Uncle Ned'*[*], and Theard's *'Bill'* and *'Tony'* give them a ring of authenticity. *'Tony'* and his fruit wagon are also mentioned on the Tampa Red side. This could indicate a Birmingham locale for the mysterious Sam Theard. (In passing, it should be noted that the Birmingham Jug Band's 'Giving It Away' [OKeh 8908] from 1930 is a totally unrelated song which makes no mention of street traders, bananas or indeed the title itself, though it may of course have been inspired by these recordings.)

In 1931, the peerless Bo Carter cut 'Banana In Your Fruit Basket' [Columbia 14661-D], and although he sings *'then I'll be satisfied'*, things are not working out the way he planned:

> Mmmmmmm, gonna let my banana spoil now.
> Mmmmmmm, let my banana spoil now.
> I can see by the way you carryin' on you don't want my banana nohow.[24]

---

[*] In 1930, Cow Cow Davenport recorded 'Now She Gives It Away' [Gennett 7275] accompanied by singer Ivy Smith. In effect, this is a monologue by Davenport which abandons the melody, and where he tells of a bootlegger called Lisa Green who waters down her booze, finally ending up with no customers!

Memphis Minnie meanwhile returned to the scenario of Davenport/ Theard's marketplace on her 1934 'Banana Man Blues' [Decca 7019]. Subtitled 'I Don't Want That Thing', the song portrays Minnie surveying the different stalls or 'stands' and finding fault with nearly all of the items on offer:

> *Spoken:* 'Now, say what you got there, man?'
> 'A rug.'
> 'What do you want for it?'
> 'Fifteen dollars?'
>
> *Vocal:* I don't want that thing.
> I don't want that thing.
> I don't want that thing,
> I wouldn't have it layin' around on my floor.
>
> *Spoken:* 'Ooooh! What a pretty bed.'
> 'Pretty mattress.'
> 'No springs?'
> 'No?'
>
> *Vocal:* I can't use that thing, etc.

One such 'item' is a one-legged man — apparently a war veteran — whom she callously rejects:

> *Spoken:* 'What's the matter with that man [in] the corner over yonder?'
> 'Crippled? Peg-leg? Same war?'
>
> *Vocal:* No, I can't use that thing.
> I can't use that thing.
> I can't use that thing.
> I don't want 'im hoppin' all over my floor.*
>
> *Spoken:* 'Look, what a pretty dove.'
> 'What you want for 'im?'
> 'Ten dollars!'
> 'For that?'
>
> *Vocal:* I don't use that thing, etc.

---

* Louisiana historian Joe Gray Taylor notes: 'Amputations were the only type of surgery in which Civil War surgeons were truly expert, and the one-armed or one-legged Confederate veteran was a fixture of many Southern communities for decades after the fighting was over.'[25] This would take us into the 1910s and '20s, and so Minnie's scorn would most likely have been directed at a war veteran but may equally have been used as an opportunity by Minnie to 'have a go' at a white man without being too obvious.

until finally she shoves her way through the thronging crowds to the fruit stall:

Spoken: 'Ooooh! What's that man sellin' over yonder?'
'Bananas? Sure enough?'

Vocal: Yes, I wants that thing.
Yes, I wants that thing.
Yes, I wants that thing, an' I finally don't care where 'e go.

Spoken: 'Banana man, sure I will!' [26]

Memphis Minnie was one of the few female guitarists to record in the pre-war era and stands today as one of the finest singers of either sex. Her acrid vocals and stinging guitar caused Big Bill Broonzy to make the admittedly chauvinistic but admiring comment that she sang and played blues 'just like a man'. Her earlier recordings, often with onetime husband Joe McCoy (on which they billed as 'Memphis Minnie & Kansas Joe'), are especially recommended.

Pianist Peetie Wheatstraw perpetuated Minnie's favourite stall-holder on his 1938 title, 'Banana Man' [Decca 7465], while on 'My Baby' [Bluebird B-8495] from 1940, Bo Carter complained of his girlfriend's 'interest' in several street traders — although it was the man on the banana stand who stirred up the strongest of his jealous feelings:

I taken my baby to the banana stand,
She got a fool about the banana man.
I'm talkin' about the little sweet girl of mine.
I taken my baby to the banana stand,
She got a fool about the banana man.
I'm talkin' about the little sweet girl of mine.
(Spoken) Yes! Baby.[27]

Carter (real name Armenter Chatmon) was one of the large Chatmon family, many of whom formed a travelling string band. A trio derived from this family group, which also included Walter Vinson, recorded from 1930-35 as the Mississippi Sheiks, with Carter sometimes playing on their sessions. The Sheiks' big hit was 'Sitting On Top Of The World' [OKeh 8784], made at their first session and much-copied over the next thirty years by blacks and whites alike. However, Carter was to rise to even greater fame — or, more accurately, notoriety — when he embarked on a solo career that saw him cut nearly 120 sides between 1930 and 1940. A superlative finger-picker, he laid down some of the most sensitive of blues ever recorded, but these were often overshadowed by his predilection for *double entendre* titles such as 'Banana In Your Fruit Basket' [Columbia 14661-D], 'Ants In My Pants' [OKeh 8897],

A country store in Marietta Street, Atlanta, Ga., 1900. Note bananas hanging next to trace chains and the ad for Pearline, a popular soap of the day – now defunct.

'Ram Rod Daddy' [OKeh 8897] and 'She's Your Cook But She Burns My Bread Sometimes' [OKeh 8870], amongst many others. But, whatever his choice of material, Bo Carter produced some of the finest blues in the pre-war era.

It was Carter who acted as a booking agent for fellow Mississippian, 'Sonny Boy Nelson' (*aka* Eugene Powell from Hollandale) on his only known recording session, down in New Orleans in 1936. Accompanied by a second guitarist called Willie Harris Jr.* the duo laid down half-a-dozen excellent sides for the Bluebird label on 15 October. They presumably also accompanied Powell's wife, Matilda, on the four songs she cut that day as 'Mississippi Matilda'. Three of these were released, including a lowdown and mean blues about the Alabama & Vicksburg RR, 'A&V Blues' [Bluebird B-7908]. The fourth may have been inspired by the recording location in New Orleans, from whence the Illinois Central banana specials ran. Whatever the reason, possibly the most explicit title concerning this fruit and sexual symbolism, 'Peel Your Banana', sadly remains unissued.

Clearly, it was the banana's incredible spread throughout the South — including land-locked Hollandale — and the increasing popularity of this 'exotic' fruit, that was responsible for this and the other songs being recorded at all. As well as being a popular part of the Southern black diet and a favourite icon for sexual symbolism in the blues, the banana occasionally even acted as a life-saver for desperately hungry hobos in the early 1930s, as the prolific blues composer and bassist Willie Dixon explained. He had travelled with a friend from his home in Vicksburg, at the southernmost tip of the Mississippi Delta, down to New Orleans, looking for work: 'We came damn near to starving to death, and if it wasn't for a few banana cars down there, we would have starved to death. We ate bananas every damned day — I didn't know you could eat so many bananas and lose weight... We sat down and actually cried, eating them bananas and actually crying. Most of 'em were green. They had two long lines of banana cars there.' But the story has a happy ending. After several unsuccessful attempts to find some employment, he finally 'got a job down at the wharf and they paid off every night.' [28]

Thanks to the development of the fast freight lines and the evolution of the refrigerator car by the 1880s, not only the poetry but story of the blues itself was greatly enriched thanks to the 'Pullman of the freight cars' — the yellow reefer.

Notes to Chapter 4

1	Johnson, W.	Ibid, p.785
2	Coulter, E.M.	p.202
3	Cronon	Ibid, p.233
4	White, J.H.	*The American Railroad Freight Car*, ibid, p.130
5	White, J.H.	*The Great Yellow Fleet*, p.143
6	Partridge, E.	p.301

---

* Harris also recorded one song at this session, 'Low Down' [Bluebird B-7091], with accompaniment on second guitar probably provided by Carter.

7	Droege	Ibid, p.413
8	White	*The Great Yellow Fleet*, ibid.
9	White	*The American Railroad Freight Car*, ibid, p.235
10	Ibid.	p.130
11	'Hot Box'	Kingfish Bill Tomlin - vocal, poss. piano; or unk. piano (c.Nov. 1930, Grafton, Wis.)
12	White	*The American Railroad Freight Car*, ibid, p.119
13	'Scarey Day Blues'	Blind Willie McTell (as 'Georgia Bill') - vocal, guitar, speech (23 Ocober 1931, Atlanta, Ga.)
14	Reed	Ibid, p.491
15	Dance, H.O.	p.33
16	'If I Got What You Want'	Papa Charlie Jackson - vocal, banjo, speech, scat vocal (3 Nov. 1934, Chicago, Ill.)
17	'If You Don't Give Me What I Want'	Rosa Henderson - vocal; Fletcher Henderson - piano (21 August 1923, New York City)
18	'If You Don't Give Me What I Want'	Edna Hicks - vocal; Fletcher Henderson's Trio: Joe Smith - cornet; prob. Don Redman - clarinet; Fletcher Henderson - piano (early January 1924, New York City)
19	Edwards	Ibid, p.72
20	White, J.H.	*The American Railroad Freight Car*, ibid, p.272
21	Ibid.	p.271
22	Ibid.	p.29
23	'She's Givin' It Away'	Sam Theard - vocal; prob. Cow Cow Davenport - piano; Tampa Red - guitar (1 May 1929, Chicago, Ill.)
24	'Banana In Your Fruit Basket'	Bo Carter - vocal, guitar (4 June 1931, New York City)
25	Taylor, J.G.	p.196
26	'Banana Man Blues'	Memphis Minnie - vocal, guitar, speech (24 April 1934, Chicago, Ill.)
27	'My Baby'	Bo Carter - vocal, guitar, speech (12 February 1940, Atlanta, Ga.)
28	Dixon W.	pp.39-40

Discography – Chapter 4

'Banana In Your Fruit Basket'
(Bo Carter)
CD: *Bo Carter – Volume 1 (1928-31)*
[Document DOCD-5078] 1992

'Banana Man Blues'
(Memphis Minnie)
5-CD: *Memphis Minnie (1929-37)*
[J.S.P. JSP-7716] 2003

'Hot Box'
(Kingfish Bill Tomlin)
CD: *Barrelhouse Piano Blues & Stomps (1929-33)* [Document DOCD-5193] 1993

Chapter 4 — She's givin' it away

'If I Got What You Want' CD: *Papa Charlie Jackson – Vol. 3 (1928-34)*
(Papa Charlie Jackson) [Document DOCD-5089] 2

'If You Don't Give Me What I Want' CD: *Rosa Henderson – Volume 1 (1923)*
(Rosa Henderson) [Document DOCD-5401] 1995

'If You Don't Give Me What I Want' CD: *Edna Hicks / Hazel Meyers / Laura Smith
(Edna Hicks) – Volume 2 (1923-27)*
 [Document DOCD-5431] 1996

'My Baby' CD: *Bo Carter – Volume 5 (1938-40)*
(Bo Carter) [Document DOCD-5082] 1992

'Scarey Day Blues' 4-CD: *Blind Willie McTell – The Classic Years
(Georgia Bill [Blind Willie McTell]) (1927-40)* [J.S.P. JSP-7711] 2003

'She's Givin' It Away' CD: *Lovin' Sam Theard (1929-34)*
(Lovin' Sam Theard) [Document DOCD-5479] 1996

Chapter 5 — Goin' where the Southern cross the Yellow Dog

Goin' where the Southern cross the Yellow Dog

'Yellow Dog Blues' – Sam Collins (1927)

CHAPTER 5

THE YAZOO & MISSISSIPPI VALLEY RR, FREIGHT TRAINS AND THE BLUES

The reefer also contributed to one of the most famous — and certainly the earliest — icons in the blues, the 'Yellow Dog'. It was at the depot in Tutwiler, Mississippi that the well-known bandleader/composer, W.C. Handy heard this, the first blues we have any knowledge of, in 1903.

After some nine hours of waiting for a train, Handy had dozed off, only to be woken up by a peculiar sound: 'A lean, loose-jointed Negro had commenced plunking a guitar beside me while I slept. His clothes were rags; his feet peeped out of his shoes. His face had on it some of the sadness of the ages. As he played, he pressed a knife on the strings of the guitar in a manner popularised by Hawaiian guitarists who used steel bars. The effect was unforgettable. His song, too, struck me instantly: *"Goin' where the Southern cross the Dog."* The singer repeated the line three times, accompanying himself on the guitar with the weirdest music I had ever heard. The tune stayed in my mind.[*] When the singer paused, I leaned over and asked him what the words meant. He rolled his eyes, showing a trace of mild amusement. Perhaps I should have known, but he didn't mind explaining. At Moorhead, the eastward and the westbound met and crossed the north and southbound trains four times a day. This fellow was going where the

---

[*] Handy was to compose his 'Yellow Dog Rag' in 1914, which soon became 'Yellow Dog Blues'. The most famous recording of this song was made by Bessie Smith in 1925 [Columbia 14075-D].

All that was left of the depot at Tutwiler in 1993 was the concrete base surrounded by scrub vegetation. Sadly, the old Y&MV/IC track has seen no rail traffic for many years.

Southern cross the Dog, and he didn't care who knew it. He was simply singing about Moorhead as he waited.' [1]

There can be little doubt that the phrase 'yellow dog' originated on the railroads. A string of empty box cars was often referred to as a 'dog' and, by extension, a train of empty reefers would qualify as a 'yellow dog' (in the late Nineteenth and early Twentieth Centuries, 'a yellow car was sure to be a refrigerator car' [2]). By the same token, a train running through the Delta hauling tank cars — which usually carried gasoline or oil — was known as the 'black dog', since these freight vehicles were traditionally painted black. Indeed, Mississippi's Rube Lacy and white hillbilly guitarist Bayless Rose both recorded a 'Black Dog Blues' in 1930. We can only surmise the content of Lacy's Columbia recording[*], as it was never issued and is probably now lost; Rose's record [Gennett 7250] was a fine slide instrumental.

---

[*] The East Coast guitar genius Blind Blake recorded a 'Black Dog Blues' for Paramount around March 1927, but his title is a rare — if not unique — use of the term for a rival lover, usually referred to as a 'mean black snake' or 'mean black cat'. Referring to the late Eighteenth Century in England, Gerzina notes that a 'deliberate confusion of black men and dogs appeared in literature as well as in real life towards the end of the century. William Goodwin, known for his radically liberal views as well as for his son-in-law Percy Shelley, repeatedly demeans black people in his 1799 novel, *St. Leon: A Tale of the Sixteenth Century*, and draws a scene of a black servant weeping over the corpse of a black dog with whom he feels a racial kinship. Maria Edgeworth, in her 1802 novel, *Belinda*, portrays a handsome young West Indian, whose black manservant and black dog are both named Juba.' [3]

The term 'dog' also referred to short railroad branch lines, and many of these were simply known by names originally bestowed upon them by black logging workers at the turn of the Twentieth Century, particularly in the state of Mississippi. Dummy trains were also called 'short dog trains' and the dummy lines *(Chapter 2)* 'rickety short dogs'. Writing in 1948, McIlwaine noted that: 'In the Mississippi Delta these short-dog trains were so ridiculed and appreciated by the lumbermen that they nicknamed them the Black Dog; the Biggety Ben (its engineer was a pompous old coot with a yard-long beard); the Pea Vine, an all-Negro train; and the Yellow Dog, made famous by W.C. Handy.' [4] In due course, the term 'peavine' passed into general railroad slang for any winding branch line (White Mississippian Betty Carter noted that 'mules by the carlot were delivered to sidings of the peavine railroads that followed the meandering contour lines through the river-built land' [5]). The name derived from the twisting and turning of this particular crop, which adorned the edges of a 1929 Paramount ad for Charley Patton's 'Pea Vine Blues' [Paramount 12877].

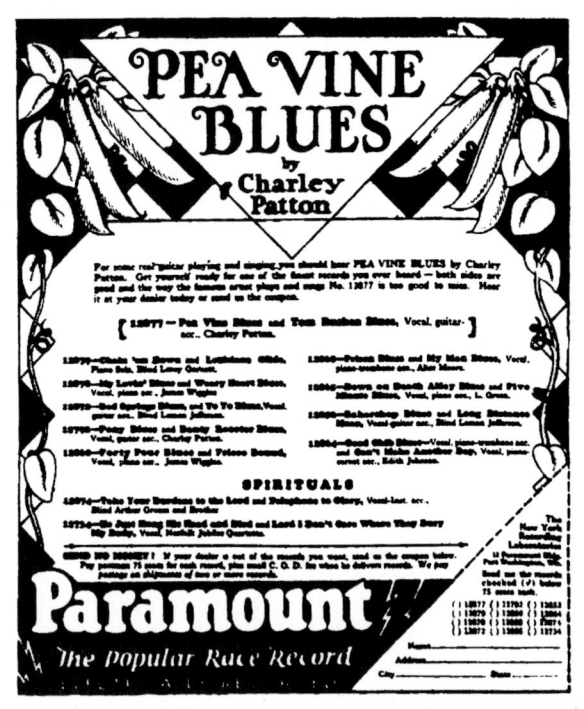

Charley Patton ad, *Chicago Defender*, 1929.

While there is a paucity of recorded blues about the 'Black Dog', this is understandable: few singers would care to bum a ride on such a train, simply because of the dangerous inflammable cargo it carried! The reasons for the same scarcity of blues featuring the 'Yellow Dog' are not immediately apparent[*], but digging a little deeper reveals a darker origin than merely a string of reefer cars. While McIlwaine's 'Biggety Ben' singles out a particular train and engineer (who would have been white), the 'Yellow Dog' phrase appears to refer to the actual railroad company itself.

Lucille Bogan gives more than a gentle hint where the trouble lies on her heartfelt 'Pay Roll Blues' [Brunswick 7051]:

---

[*] Bertha Lee's 'Dog Train Blues' [A.R.C., unissued] might be a song about the Yellow Dog, or at least make reference to it. Recorded on 31 January 1934, this recording has never been found.

> Pay day on the Southern, pay day on the Yellow Dog. *(x2)*
> An' I want to meet that payroll an' try to make a water-haul.
>
> Mens out on the Southern, they make dollars by the stack. *(x2)*
> An' I have money in my stocking when that payroll train gets back.[6]

Ms. Bogan's payroll train invokes the phenomenon of the pay-car which, it seems, first appeared at the end of the Civil War. This car would be hauled for many miles to rendezvous with workers on the track far from the railroad company's offices. Often almost literally 'stuffed with money' which might constitute a couple of months' wages for the section gang, 'the pay-car, a joyful sight in the days of old, for obvious reasons did all of its traveling in the day-time.'

Inevitably, payroll trains also attracted unwelcome visitors from time to time. On 11 October 1866, an incident occurred which 'involved the wrecking and subsequent robbing of the L&N pay-car at Bristow, Ky. — about five miles north of Bowling Green.' Overturning the train, 'the wily daylight robbers... disappeared into the shrubbery with some $8,264.70.' The relevant Annual Report from the Louisville & Nashville relates that, 'through his judicious conduct', the paymaster, G.W. Craig, 'saved $6,222.65 of the funds aboard.'[7] This indicates a payload in the region of $15,000 in wages — a vast sum back in 1866. These 'daylight robbers' appear to have been precursors of the Jesse James gang who specialised in train robberies in the following decade.

But, with the advent of stronger, more secure pay-cars, by the 1890s they were not such an easy target. Herr refers to 'an unsuccessful attempt to wreck a pay-car in the fall of 1893 on the high fill south of Mt. Vernon, Ky.'.[8] So, other ways and means needed to be found to get hold of the contents.

More successful than the train robber, the prostitute could derive a steady income from this source. Lucille Bogan is known to have worked in this profession for at least part of her life in Alabama, and her second verse, where she brags that she will have money *'in her stocking'* when the pay-car/payroll train arrives back in town, confirms her superiority over *'daylight robbers'*.

Her reference to a *'water-haul'* draws on a railroad scenario for some sexual symbolism where *'water'* signifies semen. Back in earlier times, when the major railroads were still being constructed — particularly across desert terrain — the workers would often find themselves in locations far from the nearest source of water. The train crew living in a tent or a box car as temporary accommodation 'had to haul it on their cars, in barrels, from springs thirty to fifty miles distant.'[9] Indeed, even as late as the first decades of the Twentieth Century, water would still be hauled — if only for a few miles — for the section gang waiting for the pay-car.

Chapter 5 — Goin' where the Southern cross the Yellow Dog

Another blues which alluded to the Yellow Dog without including the name in the title was 'Green River Blues' [Paramount 12972] by Charley Patton. Like Bogan's 'Pay Roll Blues', this also had earlier connections with roustabout songs on the river. Patton reputedly worked in a logging camp (or more likely sang in its barrelhouse for the other lumbermen) at some point in the 1920s. With his magnificent gravelly vocal and the rolling rhythm of his guitar, he generates a flowing, 'bobbing' feeling as he sings the very lines that Handy heard some twenty-six years earlier:

Charley Patton, Father of the Delta Blues, 1929.

> I'm goin' where the Southern cross the Dog.
> I'm goin' where the Southern cross the Dog.
> I'm goin' where the Southern cross the Dog.

Another verse refers to the earlier log camp operation of 'rafting' *(see page 58)* on the river before railroads became widespread:

> I'd rather be up Green River floating like a log.
> I'd rather be up Green River floating like a log.
> I'd rather be up Green River floating like a log.[10]

By the time he recorded this song in 1929, Patton was working at Dockery's plantation, some ten miles north of the Yellow Dog's famous crossing with the Southern Railway at Moorhead. As already stated, the 'Yellow Dog' referred to a particular railroad company which ran through the Mississippi Delta. This was the Yazoo & Mississippi Valley Railroad, which ran its first tracks in 1884 from Yazoo City, in the county of the same name, to Jackson, Miss. As a chronicler of the time related, it was 'built as a feeder to the Illinois Central RR.'[11]

Construction had started as early as 1882, and some three years later the Delta town of Moorhead was founded at what was to become the site of the best-known railroad crossing in the blues. The Y&MV on approaching

Chapter 5 — Goin' where the Southern cross the Yellow Dog

Yazoo City station sometime before 1900.

Moorhead connected up with a small independent line built by one Chester H. Pond who, with some financial support, had laid 'some twenty miles of track'. Pond named the site after a nearby bayou called Moorhead, itself named after a lumberman who had passed through the area sometime prior to 1885. This stretch of line, according to DeCell & Prichard, (as with the Y&MV) soon became known as the 'Yellow Dog'. Pond's railroad is thought to have reached Sunflower to the north and Markham to the south — both in Sunflower County. His short stretch of line also soon became known as the 'Yellow Dog' because of 'a chain of flat cars pulled by a second-hand locomotive.' [12]

Meanwhile, the Y&MV line reached Greenwood, Miss. and — presumably in the same period (1884-86) — 'branched off from Yazoo City slightly to the northwest on its way north to Tutwiler.' [13] It was around this time that Pond's line was merged into the Y&MV. By 1892, the successful 'Yellow Dog' had come to the notice of the IC, who duly took it over but to all intents and purposes ran it as an independent line. It was also in this year that the IC bought out a line running from New Orleans to Jackson, Miss.. This was the Louisiana, New Orleans & Texas RR. which was then renamed the 'Yazoo & Mississippi Valley Railroad'. [14] The IC then commenced extending the Y&MV 'to Tutwiler on the north and to Belzoni on the south'. [15] It was in the latter town that Charley Patton sang about being jailed for drunkenness in his 'High Sheriff Blues' [Vocalion 02680] in 1934.

In 1893, about a year after the IC pushed the Y&MV to Tutwiler, the railroad's land commissioner, Edward P. Skene, changed the wording of land adverts to encourage purchase by potential customers from the West and North: 'On all railroad circulars advertising the Illinois Central's Mississippi lands, he changed the name "Yazoo Delta" to read "Yazoo Valley", believing that the term "Delta" had connotations of a place continually flooded.' [16]

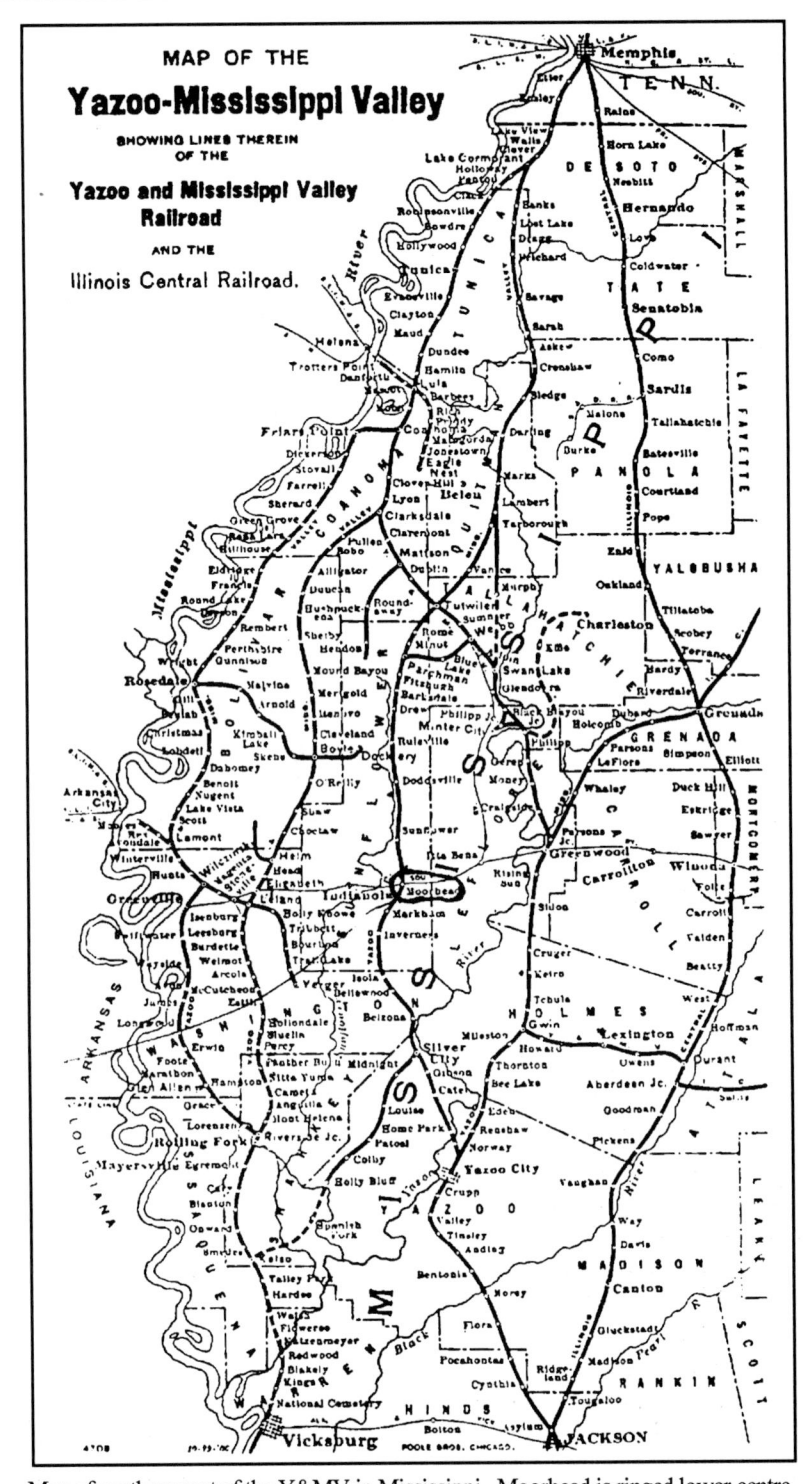

Chapter 5 — Goin' where the Southern cross the Yellow Dog

Map of southern part of the Y&MV in Mississippi. Moorhead is ringed lower centre.

The former title not only put off property speculators, but also caused some confusion as to the name of the railroad known as the 'Yellow Dog'. Norm Cohen refers to the 'Yazoo Delta RR' as being given this name which was already applied to the Y&MV. He notes that in August 1897 this railroad 'first consisted of 20.5 miles of track between Moorhead and Ruelville [sic] to the north.' By 1899 this 'had been extended in both directions — 21.5 miles to the north to Tutwiler, and 15 miles to the south to Lake Dawson.'

As I intimated earlier, the origins of the term 'Yellow Dog' also have a darker side. Chester Pond's initial 'twenty miles of track', the Y&MV and indeed the LNO&T may all have used non-union labour, for smaller railroads could get away with paying markedly lower wages than some of the major companies like the IC or the Southern, which were almost 100% unionised — hence Lucille Bogan's pointed verses on her 'Pay Roll Blues'. Before Philip A. Randolph's Brotherhood Of Sleeping Car Porters in the mid-1920s *(Chapter 1)*, virtually all of the most powerful unions represented craft or skilled workers (who were invariably white), but one which did appeal to unskilled labourers, such as those involved in railroad construction, etc, was the Knights Of Labor.

Setting out to attract workers of all races, this union had its beginnings 'as a small society of garment workers in 1869... *[which]* evolved into a national organisation numbering 700,000 members.' [16] In Mississippi, despite resistance from employers and communities, many blacks and whites joined the Knights Of Labor and the latter 'achieved some success', with the result that 'in 1888 there were thirty-three locals *[branches]* in the state.' However, due to 'intensified employer resistance' — which included the ploy of the 'yellow dog contract'[*] — the use of unionised labour was vastly reduced, resulting in the Knights Of Labor becoming 'almost extinct as a national union' by 1900. One definition of a 'yellow dog contract' reads: 'The employee is required to sign a card stating he is not a union member and would not join a union as long as he worked for the company.' [19] The 'intensified resistance' mentioned above ranged from instant dismissal to severe beatings by hired thugs, and on occasion even to murder. The phrase 'yellow dog' in its most derogatory form referred to a coward[**] or, in union

---

[*] In this context, the term 'yellow dog' probably alluded to the buff colour of the form (the contract) which workers had to sign in order to relinquish their right to join a trade/labor union. This practice spread from the railroads to other industries which included (or had formerly included) a union presence.

[**] I believe the use of 'yellow' to mean 'cowardly' derives from the US Army's Nineteenth Century custom of not only stripping a court-martialled soldier's uniform of buttons, medals, etc, but also painting a broad yellow stripe down the centre of the back of his jacket. Interestingly, another term used in the old American West was 'yaller belly'. Partridge lists 'Yellow Belly' and states: 'A native of the fens, orig. and esp. the Fens in Lincolnshire;'. One example given is: 'the frogs, which are yellow-bellied'.[17] The earliest definition of 'yellow' is from *A New Canting Dictionary* in 1725 which asserts that ' "yellow", jealous, was orig. a *c.* term: this is prob. correct'.[18]

parlance, a 'scab'. Consequently, 'it stigmatised the conduct of the individual willing to be bound by such an agreement.' [20]

Some idea of the strength of anti-union feeling in the US can be gleaned from the attitude of a Northern capitalist who had moved to the South near Greensboro, N.C. and opened a cotton mill and a company store. After shutting down his premises, effecting a short lock-out, Caesar Cone claimed he would rather burn his mill down than 'submit to' the unions. He then 'resumed work with non-union labor under a yellow-dog contract.' [21] As has been suggested, such contracts were widespread outside the railroad industry. In lumber for instance, in 1915 'the Southern Pine Operators' Association maintained records of all workers applying for jobs in the southern lumber companies, and forced the workers to sign away their right to organise through the acceptance of a 'yellow dog contract'.' [22] So, it transpires that the 'Yellow Dog' nickname doesn't merely originate from a short string of reefers on the tracks; it is also irrevocably associated with blood, brutality and intimidation, and we should perhaps not be surprised that many blues singers did not care to sing about this particular line.

The first blues about the 'Dog' was made by Lizzie Miles from New Orleans. This was the W.C. Handy composition, which Ms. Miles cut as 'The Yellow Dog Blues' [OKeh 8052] in February 1923 while staying over in New York City. It was to be another two years before Bessie Smith committed her more famous version [Columbia 14075-D] to wax, accompanied by Fletcher Henderson's Hot Six. As Handy's songs were published in sheet music form, they would have been readily available to any singer, especially vaudeville-blues artists like Lizzie Miles and Bessie Smith who worked a more urban circuit. Indeed, two of the characters Lizzie and Bessie sing about are Susan Johnson and Jockey Lee, whose names they 'borrowed from Shelton Brooks' song, 'I Wonder Where My Easy Rider's Gone'.' [23]

Some of Handy's lyrics (which Smith did not include) run:

> I know the Yellow Dog district like a book.
> Indeed, I know the route that rider took.
> Ev'ry cross-tie, bayou, burg and bog.
> Way down where the Southern cross the Dog.
> Money don't 'zactly grow on trees.
> On cotton stalks it grows with ease.
> [In] every kitchen there is a cabaret:
> Down there the boll weevil works while the darkies play
> This 'Yellow Dog Blues' the live-long day.[24]

— the words in print exuding a 'plantation melody' atmosphere that is in stark contrast to Bessie's lowdown and blues-drenched vocal on her 1925 recording. Only the couplet about *'money don't 'zactly grow on trees'* hints at the often turbulent and violent world of railroad employment in the South, especially for black workers.

Chapter 5 — Goin' where the Southern cross the Yellow Dog

In February 1929, 'The Yellow Dog Blues' was recorded by the Nonpareil Trio [Columbia 14403-D]. They took their name from an early class of American locomotive ('the Nonpareil, built by the Beaver Meadow Railroad[*] in 1837 or 1838, was probably the first 0-6-0[**] constructed in the country' [25]). In 1930, Lizzie Miles reworked the song for Victor as 'Yellow Dog Gal Blues' [unissued at the time, but later released on the Various Artists LP *Singin' The Blues* (Camden CAL-588) 1953], and this was the last example to appear on a blues record.

In 1927, however, a guitarist from Louisiana called Sam Collins, recorded a different 'Yellow Dog Blues' [Gennett 6146], which did not follow Handy's song in either melody or lyric. Collins, who spent a great deal of time in McComb, Miss. (south of the Delta), played slide guitar, most likely placed across his lap, Hawaiian-style. The guitarist that Handy had heard in Tutwiler also employed this technique, and Collins' interpretation was probably very similar to the performance Handy had witnessed. Indeed, with his high-crying vocal and eerie accompaniment, Collins may well have committed the earliest version of the original 'Yellow Dog Blues' to wax:

> Be easy mama, don't you fade away. *(x2)*
> I'm goin' where that Southern cross the Yellow Dog.
>
> I seed 'im(?) here when 'e was fightin' all round the hall.
> Lord, I seed 'im here when 'e was fightin' all round the hall.
> An' I felt so rowdy an' I didn't wanna ride no train.
>
> I would ride the Yellow Dog, but wary of [her] Mary Jane[s]
> I wanna ride the Yellow Dog, but I was wary of Mary Janes.
> I dug deep in my saddle, an' I don't deny my name.
>
> Dug deep in my saddle, Lord, an' I don't deny my name.
> Just as sure as the train leaves around the curve.[26]

What Collins is singing about in the third verse has only just become clear to me — in March 2006! 'Mary Janes', it turns out, were in fact a brand name of 'slippers' (ie slip-on shoes) with wood or steel toecaps! The celebrated white Mississippian author, Eudora Welty, refers to them in her first collection of short stories published in 1941. Written in the mid-1930s under the umbrella title, *A Curtain Of Green*, one of these stories was called *The Key*. Here, she describes one Ellie Morgan patiently waiting for a train at a little railroad depot at Yellow Leaf, Miss., near Jackson: *"Her hands were*

---

[*] This was in Pennsylvania and should not be confused with the Beaver Meadow in Alabama referred to on page 91.
[**] For those unfamiliar with railroad terminology, '0-6-0' refers to the wheel formation of the locomotive, the figure in the middle indicating the number of driving wheels, the others the number of trailing wheels in front and behind.

tight and wrinkled with pressure. She swung her foot a little below her skirt, in the new Mary Jane slipper with the hard toe".[27] In other words, the singer is rather wisely keeping an eye on those hard caps in case she lets fly with some potentially damaging high-kicking.

The rather confusing second verse seems to include a third person (the ' 'im that was 'fightin' all round the hall') — an unidentified male who might be waiting to take Collins' place. By the third verse, however, he seems to have solved the 'third party' problem and still intends to ride the Yellow Dog. As a face-saver, he claims that he sticks to his guns and states: *'I don't deny my name'* (this latter phrase recalls a Barbecue Bob title, 'Easy Rider Don't You Deny My Name' [Columbia 14257-D], recorded in the same year of 1927). Collins' original lyrics and unique vocal/guitar combined to create one of the finest downhome blues records of the 1920s. For all we know, he may have been Handy's 1903 guitar hero from Tutwiler, Miss.!

As regards the yellow dog contracts themselves, various acts and cases in the US Supreme Court had, from 1898 onwards, gradually driven nails into the coffin of this iniquitous practice in Southern industries, and the railroads in particular. Eventually, the *Railway Labor Act* of 1926 'was amended in 1934 to outlaw "yellow dog contracts".'[28]

In 1930, three months after Lizzie Miles' remake of her 1923 recording, Yank Rachell recorded what is probably the last reference to a 'Yellow Dog' railroad before this amendment was passed. On 'Sweet Mama' [Victor 23318], his last title with Sleepy John Estes and Jab Jones (on guitar and piano respectively), Rachell sings that he's *'goin' up the country where the Southern done cross the Dog.'*[29] However, it is more than likely that many employers on short railroads (which were usually not unionised) would have been dragging their feet to comply with the amended Federal law. Certainly, only a couple of months into the new year of 1935, Big Bill Broonzy saw fit to 'disguise' his version of 'Yellow Dog Blues' by naming it after the major line which made up the 'cross' at Moorhead: 'The Southern Blues' [Bluebird B-5998].

> When I got up this mornin', I heard the old Southern whistle blow. *(x2)*
> Says, I'm-a thinkin' 'bout my baby, Lord, I sure did wanna go.
>
> I was standin', lookin' an' listenin',
>   watchin' that Southern cross the Dog. *(x2)*
> If my baby didn't catch that Southern, she must-a caught that Yellow Dog.

Like Lucille Bogan on her 'Pay Roll Blues', Broonzy implies that pay on the Southern was better than on the non-union Y&MV:

> I'm gwine to Moorhead, get me a job on the Southern line.
> Said, I'm gwine to Moorhead, get me a job on the Southern line.
> So that I can make some money, just to send for that brown of mine.

> Said, the Southern cross the Dog at Moorhead, mama,
> Mama, Lord, an' she keeps on through. *(x2)*
> I said my baby's gone to Georgia, I believe I'll go to Georgia too.[30]

Even his *'baby'* preferred travelling on the Southern, which served large areas of Georgia as well as other states, rather than the Yellow Dog. Bill's biting guitar and Black Bob's rolling piano give a solid urban feel to this blues, which indicated how the music was evolving in the middle 1930s. Their fine performance constitutes the only other departure from Handy's composition, along with that of Sam Collins.

Two other recordings (from 1937 and 1942) made reference to the Yellow Dog, apparently alluding to a partial failure by the state legislature to enforce the Federal law. Big Bill's reference to Georgia, calls to mind James 'Kokomo' Arnold, who hailed from the Peach Tree State. Possibly the fastest slide-guitar player on record, Arnold was very much his own man and also ran a successful bootlegging business in the 1920s and '30s. Having spent some of his earlier life in the Mississippi Delta, he recorded for Decca at a 1937 session, and appropriated the line Handy had first heard at Tutwiler in 1903 for his own original verse in 'Long And Tall' [Decca 7306]:

> Now, she's long an' tall, shaped just like a cannonball. *(x2)*
> Says, I found that woman where the Southern cross the Yellow Dog.[31]

The 'cannonball' in this case referred to the wood/coke-burning stove which supplied heat to so many Southern homes in the 1920s *(see also page 286)*, and Arnold's inclusion of the reference to the Yellow Dog was to be the last on a pre-war commercial blues record. However, the very last mention was to appear on a 1942 recording for the Library of Congress.

In that year, Alan Lomax supervised a session in Sledge, Miss. featuring the great fife-and-drum band leader and lowdown fiddler, Sid Hemphill. Sledge was Hemphill's home town and was also a stop on the Y&MV. Amongst a fascinating group of songs, which included many rooted in the Nineteenth Century, was one titled 'The Carrier Railroad'. Rye tells us that this was 'the Sardis & Delta Railroad, a logging line serving the operation of one Robert Carrier.'[32] The S&D served Panola County and ran from Burke through Ballantine and Malone, joining the main line of the IC at Sardis on its way, via Hernando to Memphis. Only Ballantine and Sardis were still shown on a more modern map from the mid-1990s.

Somewhere in or around 1902, engineer Dave Cowart was warned about his reckless speeding on many occasions and Carrier finally transferred him from the *No. 7* (presumably his regular run) to *No. 9*, the Ballantine train heading towards Sardis:

> Mr. Carrier said: 'No, Dave Cowart, [I'll] tell you in time.
> Can't let you run the 7 no more.'
> 'Well, I'll have to run the 9.'
>
> *Refrain:* Oh, my honey babe... *(voice trails off)*
>
> Last one Monday mornin', it come a shower of rain.
> 9 come to Ballantine blowing like a fast train.
>
> *Refrain:* Oh, my honey babe...

Inevitably, there is an accident, and the wreck puts the line out of action for some considerable time, causing workers to drift off to look for other employment on local farms, or possibly the nearby Y&MV. Carrier tries to warn them of their folly, obviously hoping to get his own line running again as soon as possible and realising he will need experienced labour ready to go to work immediately. He purposely 'mistakes' his own train, *No. 9,* for one from the Y&MV, perhaps intimating that he would employ cheaper 'scab' labour from the Yellow Dog. The singer also implies that Carrier had a serious 'cash flow' problem and couldn't afford to pay the men's wages, offering to pay them off *'in brass'*:

> When the 9 got over to Sardis, with a large old load of logs,
> Mr. Carrier told the people at the plant:
> 'Yonder train off the Yellow Dog.'
>
> *Refrain:* Oh, my honey babe...
>
> Oh! They couldn't pay 'em no greenbacks.
> Couldn't pay 'em no gold.
> Couldn't pay 'em no silver.
> All his banks done closed.[33]

This was to be the last mention of the Yellow Dog on a blues record for some two decades[*].

In the pre-war era, eleven sides were recorded which featured this railroad in the title and/or the lyrics, and it appears fairly obvious that the common link between these recordings, whether direct or indirect, is the state

---

[*] In 1947, a post-war recording at Parchman Farm was made by an unidentified prisoner while cutting a live oak with an axe. His worksong, 'Katy Left Memphis', refers to the *Big Kate Adams* steamboat, but the concluding line advises: *'Buy you a ticket and catch, well, the Yellow Dog'.*[34] For a more detailed discussion and full transcription of 'The Carrier Railroad' see the excellent liner notes in CD *Afro-American Folk Music (From Tate & Panola Counties, Mississippi)* [Rounder Library of Congress Series 18964-1515-2] 2000.

'Where the Southern cross the Dog' –
Moorhead, Miss., c.1963.

of Mississippi. Not only that, but a particular area – Yazoo County — and a single railroad: the Yazoo & Mississippi Valley or 'Yellow Dog'. As the line serving the Yazoo Delta, it was sometimes referred to as the 'Yazoo Delta line'*. Nearly half of the recordings (that is to say, the two versions by Lizzie Miles, plus the titles by Bessie Smith and the Nonpareil Trio) are versions of W.C. Handy's 1914 composition, 'The Yellow Dog Rag', which he drew from an impromptu performance by a guitarist in 1903 at the depot in Tutwiler, Miss.. In fact, only one of the five blues using 'Yellow Dog' as a title departs from the Handy song, and that is the 1927 Sam Collins disc.

Collins was reputedly born in Louisiana in 1887, but spent some considerable time living and playing in McComb and the surrounding area in southern Mississippi. Lucille Bogan was originally from this state and at one time married to a railroad man who worked on the M&O, as well as possibly the Southern and/or the Yellow Dog. Big Bill was also originally from Mississippi and, of course, Charley Patton and Sid Hemphill were 'denizens of the Delta'. This leaves Kokomo Arnold and Yank Rachell. Arnold, like Collins, spent some time living in Mississippi, in the Delta and around the Jackson area. Rachell was from near Jackson, Tenn., but he was based for a while in Memphis, which is on the Mississippi–Tennessee state line. Much of the blues scene down on Beale Street was made up by guitarists who had more in common with the Delta styles — Furry Lewis, George Torey and Allen Shaw, among them. Indeed, the city had such a close 'affiliation' for everything Mississippian in the early Nineteenth Century, it tried to become

---

* There was a Yazoo Delta RR. which existed briefly from 1896-1900 before being 'fully merged with Y&MV in 1900'. (*The Green Diamond* (Official Publication of the Illinois Central Historical Society) No. 71 (December 2004, p.72).

part of that state when it was created in 1819, albeit unsuccessfully. Indeed, Rachell himself, when exchanging his more well-known mandolin for a guitar, often played with a heavy Delta 'feel'.

The question arises, why were there not more blues recorded which referred to the yellow dog contract on other railroads, and in other Southern states? In the first place, the powerful white railroad unions (in collusion with the railroad companies) successfully kept blacks from joining a union and so no other 'contract' was needed. Secondly, some two decades after the virtual demise of the Knights Of Labor, the Brotherhood Of Sleeping Car Porters was successful in gaining nationwide recognition, with the result that most major railroads in the US, which employed black Pullman porters in varying numbers, did not attempt to resort to non-union tactics such as the yellow dog contract. As has already been stated, the Illinois Central which took over the Y&MV was almost 100% unionised. Maybe the earlier efforts in Mississippi to organise workers by the Knights Of Labor had bred a more militant stance than in other states, so at least blues singers would include the Yellow Dog in their repertoire. In the case of Sid Hemphill, he might have thought it was now 'safe' to include the railroad in his 'The Carrier Railroad', as the yellow dog contract had been outlawed for some eight years and the accident on the S&DR was about forty years in the past at the time he recorded this song.

Finally, despite the aforementioned connection with the Magnolia State, in July 1961 a guitarist from North Carolina recorded 'Goin' Where The Monon Crosses The Yellow Dog' [LP *Blues Before Sunrise* (77 LA-12-4) 1960].[35] This was Scrapper Blackwell, erstwhile partner of the famous pianist Leroy Carr. Like the Tennessee-born Carr, Blackwell was firmly based in Indianapolis at the time of his pre-war recordings, and was still there in 1961. The 'Monon'[*] referred to the Chicago, Indianapolis & Louisville Railway, which ran almost entirely within the state of Indiana. Apart from its southern terminus at Louisville, Ky., it had two legs heading north which crossed diagonally at Monon, Ind., with one going to Chicago and the other to Michigan City, Mich.. Blackwell sang of this crossing on his 'Down South Blues' [Champion 16452] in 1931:

> I'm goin' where the Monon crosses the L&N *(x2)*
> An' catch me a freight train an' go back home again.[36]

Because of part-ownership of the Monon by the L&N, the rolling stock of both would often be seen on the L&N as well as the CI&L lines, particularly on freight trains. But by 1961 Blackwell's memory was failing him, because the Monon never came within 450 miles of the Yellow Dog in Mississippi. He probably meant to repeat the above-quoted verse from 'Down South

---

[*] 'Monon' is a Potawatomi word meaning to tote, to carry. By extension, the 'Monon' railroad may be thought of as being a 'carrier of coal' — the main freight transported by both the CI&L and the L&N.

Blues' made some three decades earlier. Either that, or he was confusing the latter with the early versions of W.C. Handy's composition by Lizzie Miles *et al.* A third interpretation may be that the Monon was itself a non-union road which had used the yellow dog contract in the past.

In any event, we will never know for sure what Scrapper Blackwell intended singing about, as he was shot by an assassin 'early in the morning of 6 October and died in the morning of 7 October 1962.' [37]

Thus ends the saga of the Yellow Dog on blues recordings, a grim finale to the bloody early days on the Y&MV. Small wonder that Handy's 'ragged Negro' looked at the middle-class bandleader 'showing a trace of mild amusement', for Handy was obviously totally unaware of the often brutal conditions for working-class blacks (and whites) on a non-union railroad. Yet, that 1903 guitar player left a message for those who did understand, that his blues was about the Yazoo & Mississippi Valley Railroad, known — with good reason — 'by blacks and whites' [38] as the 'Yellow Dog'.

Notes to Chapter 5

1	Handy, W.C.	p.74
2	White, J.H.	p.23 (*The Great Yellow Fleet*), ibid.
3	Gerzina, G.	pp.108-9
4	McIlwaine, S.	p.254
5	Carter, B.	p.22
6	'Pay Roll Blues'	Lucille Bogan - vocal; Tampa Red - guitar; poss. Georgia Tom - piano (8 August 1928, Chicago, Ill.)
7	Herr, K.A.	p.26
8	Ibid.	p.69
9	Ambrose, S.E.	p.372
10	'Green River Blues'	Charley Patton - vocal, guitar (circa October 1929, Grafton, Wis.)
11	Wilson, J.B.	p.49
12	Briegar, J.	p.460
13	DeCell, H., & J. Prichard	p.351
14	Brandfon, R.L.	p.80
15	Briegar	Ibid.
16	Mosley, D.	Ibid, p.250
17	Partridge, E.	p.1061 (*Historical Slang*)
18	Ibid.	
19	Mosley	Ibid.
20	Adams, J.T.	p.504

21	Woodward, V.	p.422
22	Todes, C.	p.97
23	Handy	Ibid, p.123
24	'Yellow Dog Rag'	From W.C. Handy, ibid, p.83
25	White, J.H.	p.66 (*Locomotives*)
26	'Yellow Dog Blues'	Sam Collins - vocal, guitar (23 April 1927, Richmond, Ind.)
27	Welty E.	p.73.
28	Risher	Ibid, p.26
29	'Sweet Mama'	Yank Rachell - vocal, mandolin; Sleepy John Estes - guitar; Jab Jones - piano (30 May 1930, Memphis, Tenn.)
30	'The Southern Blues'	Big Bill - vocal, guitar; prob. Black Bob - piano; unk. train whistle (25 February 1935, Chicago, Ill.)
31	'Long And Tall'	Kokomo Arnold - vocal, guitar (12 January 1937, Chicago, Ill.)
32	Rye, H.	Notes to Document DOCD-5577 (CD)
33	'The Carrier Railroad'	Sid Hemphill - vocal, violin; Lucius Smith - banjo; Alec Askew - guitar; Will Head - bass drum (Library of Congress recording, 26 July 1942, Sledge, Miss.)
34	'Katy Left Memphis'	Unk. male vocal, axe-cutting
35	Leadbitter, M., & N. Slaven	p.103
36	'Down South Blues'	Scrapper Blackwell - vocal, guitar (24 November 1931, Richmond, Ind.)
37	van Rijn, G., & H. Vergeer	Notes to Agram AB-2008 (LP)
38	McIlwaine	Ibid, p.331

Discography – Chapter 5

'The Carrier Railroad'
(Sid Hemphill)

CD: *Afro-American Folk Music (from Tate & Panola Counties, Mississippi)* [Rounder Library of Congress Series 18964-1515-2] 2000

'Down South Blues'
(Scrapper Blackwell)

CD: *Scrapper Blackwell – Vol. 1 (1928-32)* [Blues Document BDCD-6029] 1993

'Green River Blues'
(Charley Patton)

5-CD: *Charley Patton – Complete Recordings (1929-1934)* [J.S.P.-7702] 2002

'Katy Left Memphis'
(Unk. male vocal)

LP: *Murderer's Home* [Pye Nixa NJL-11] 1959
CD: *Murderer's Home* [Rounder ROUCD-1714] 2004

'Long And Tall'
(Kokomo Arnold)

CD: *Kokomo Arnold – Volume 3 (1936-37)* [Document DOCD-5039] 1991

'Pay Roll Blues' CD: *Lucille Bogan – Volume 1 (1923-30)*
(Lucille Bogan) [Blues Document BDCD-6036] 1993

'The Southern Blues' 5-CD: *Big Bill Broonzy (1928-37)*
(Big Bill) [J.S.P. JSP-7718] 2003

'Sweet Mama' 2-CD: *Sleepy John Estes – Gus Cannon*
(Yank Rachell) *(1928-30)* [J.S.P. JSP-3406] 2002

'Yellow Dog Blues' CD: *Sam Collins (1927-31)*
(Sam Collins) [Document DOCD-5034] 1991

An' that thing don't keep a-ringin' so soon

'Last Fair Deal Gone Down' – Robert Johnson (1936)

CHAPTER 6

SOUTHERN PRISONS AND RAILROADS

If life on the Southern railroads could sometimes be brutal and bloody when working to a 'yellow dog' contract, such conditions became the norm under the grim and evil convict-lease system. This was an arrangement whereby convicts in the state penitentiary were hired out to private contractors to work on construction/commercial projects, railroads, in coal and phosphate mines, plantations, etc. In return, these companies undertook to clothe, feed and shelter the men in their charge and also supply medical treatment when necessary. However, the reality was far different and the convict-lease system represented a nadir in the history of African Americans, sometimes equalling the horror and atrocities committed by the Ku Klux Klan and other 'white power' groups. Some of the major lessees were the railroads, and the majority of convicts leased to them were black.

Contrary to one popular school of thought, amongst its many other roles in working-class black life, the blues *was* a vehicle for protest. This protest could not be high-profile (with some exceptions), but nevertheless was protest just the same. In this chapter, I shall be considering some examples of this as it applied within the Southern penal system, particularly within the context of railroads.

Probably the earliest form of corporal punishment or 'correction' used in the towns and cities of the newly-formed United States was the whipping

Chapter 6 — An' that thing don't keep a-ringin' so soon

post — a public punishment meted out to both black and white wrongdoers. It was certainly used in the earlier decades of the Eighteenth Century, when America was still a British colony. A one time butcher and a member of the New York Historical Society, Thomas De Voe, reported the opening of Broadway market in 1738 near Liberty Street in the city. Plantation owners, farmers and millers 'that came by water from a distance were obliged to have their slaves to assist them.' These slaves would also bring their own items of produce to sell, grown on the plantations, and this soon developed into 'an illegitimate sort of traffic with the Indians and many negro slaves in the city, who had spare, or stolen, time enough to make a little spending-money.' Finally, in August 1740, a law was passed 'to prohibit Negroes and other Slaves vending Indian corn, Peaches, or any other fruit within this City'. The reasons given were that this 'pernicious practice is not only detrimental to the masters, mistresses and owners of such slaves, in regard they absent themselves from their service, but is also productive of increasing, if not occasions, many and dangerous fevours [sic], and other distempers and diseases in the inhabitants'! The transparency of this false premise seems beyond belief from a Twenty-First Century viewpoint, but New York's city fathers blithely decreed: *'Be it enacted and ordained, That any negro, Indian, or mulatto slave be convicted before the Mayor, Recorder, etc. of any of the above acts, shall be publickly whipped at the whipping post, unless the master, mistress, shall pay to the person or officer informing of such an offence the sum of six shillings, current money of this Colony: one half thereof to such informer, and the other half to the Treasurer of this City.'* [1]

This proviso for exception from the whipping post became the *raison d'être* for subsequent practices within the Southern prison system — notably convict-lease — as a source of state income. The two years following the end of the Civil War could be seen as part of an evolutionary process in the penal codes, especially as far as Southern blacks were concerned; certainly in Georgia and Alabama. According to Owen, a Governor of the latter state, John Gayle, 'is probably due the credit of having first recommended that the old and barbarous methods of punishment be substituted by other forms more consonant with the dictates of humanity.' Owen adds that it was Gayle's opinion that 'the whipping post, the pillory, the branding iron, and all such instrument [sic] of savage and barbarian cruelty, accord neither with the enlightened and humane spirit of the age, nor with the principles of our free institutions.' [2]

The state of Georgia obviously concurred, as their 1868 constitution outlawed the whipping post 'as a punishment for crime'. But despite fine words, rousing sentiments and actual legislature — doubtless sincerely intended — the replacement methods of punishment turned out to be often just as 'savage and barbarian'. In Georgia, for example, 'the switch could [sic] be from whipping post to chain gang.' [3]

Indeed, the chain gang soon supplanted the old 'road duty' —

involuntary servitude which misdemeanour prisoners were subjected to for varying periods of time. This idea dated back to the new United States in the last decades of the Eighteenth Century (the premise being that the authorities — be they state, county or municipal — could maintain their road system at a minimum cost to themselves), but lent itself equally well to the construction of railroads. Indeed, one of the main reasons that the Georgia legislature adopted the chain gang so readily was to help maintain and expand the Western & Atlantic Railroad — a rare example of a state-owned line in the US. The objective was to build and connect with other, privately-owned railroads and eventually achieve a complete system within Georgia which would then extend to a larger Southern network. The W&A already linked Atlanta with Chattanooga in Tennessee.

On the chain gangs, convicts remained shackled together twenty-four hours a day, spending their waking hours grading embankments for the rails using only picks and shovels, with sweat running through their eyes and the chains chafing their bodies until the blood ran. The brutality of these conditions was reflected in several private recordings made in the 1920s by folklorist Lawrence Gellert. Originally from Hungary, Gellert first lived in New York before moving to the South for health reasons. He settled in the black section of Tryon, N.C., where he lived with a black woman, and soon started touring East Coast states recording black singers in the prisons (before the Lomaxes!), as well as chain gangs on the road. He apparently told the (white) guards that he was only interested in spirituals and worksongs, but what he actually got were some of the most outspoken protest lyrics that have come down to us from those times. In return for this important body of song, Gellert promised the prisoners absolute anonymity which, as far as I'm aware, remains the case to this day.

The first of these, 'I Been Pickin' And Shovellin' ', performed in 1926 by an unidentified male guitarist in Spartanburg, S.C., runs:

> Babe, I been worked all day long.
> I been pickin', shovellin' babe, I mean the whole day long.
> For you mistreated me woman, I mean mistreat me on the road.

implying that his lover/wife was entertaining another man while he was working on the gang. He conveys some of the horrors of convict-lease without actually describing them, greatly enhanced by his moaning vocal and Delta-style guitar:

> Mm, I'd rather see my coffin, brownie, come rollin' in my door.
> Mm, I'd rather see my coffin, baby, come rollin' in my door.
> I'd be afraid(?) same as if I didn't have to pick an' shovel
>   for that W.P. no more.[4]

Chapter 6 — An' that thing don't keep a-ringin' so soon

Ramblin' Thomas, c.1928.

The 'W.P.' probably refers to a railroad, but which one is not known for certain. The most likely candidate seems to be a small rail connection which is not officially described by these initials! This line was an addition to the Raleigh & Gaston RR. in North Carolina. In 1838, the R&G had proposed building through the town of Warrenton, N.C., which lies some 65 miles north-east of Raleigh. However, the townspeople objected to having a railroad, so 'the engineers modified their plans and laid out the track of the Raleigh & Gaston RR through Warren Plains, three miles to the north, instead… Many years later, a new generation of Warrenton realized the folly of their forefathers, and thus caused the Warrenton Railroad to be organized in 1876 and completed in 1884 as a rail connection to Warren Plains.'[5] The latter location, in Warren County, N.C., might have lent itself to a colloquial abbreviated nickname, the 'Warrenton Plains railroad' or 'W.P.' for short (it was quite a common practice to give railroads nicknames in this earlier era — for example, the M&O was commonly called the 'Milk & Onion route'). The R&G came to form part of the nucleus of the Seaboard Air Line in 1900. Interestingly, Raleigh is some 200 miles north-east of Spartanburg, S.C., where our anonymous guitarist recorded his song. And the Warrenton RR itself was still operating as late as the mid-1960s.

Some two years earlier, in 1924, another unknown guitarist cut a song called 'Pick And Shovel Captain', a theme extended in 1928 by a third unidentified musician on 'Shootin' Craps And Gamblin' ':

> Captain, captain, please don't be so mean, so mean.
> Because a pick an' a shovel sure don't run by steam.[5]

Some seven years later, a washboard player known as Bull City Red (real name George Washington), temporarily switched to guitar and borrowed this verse for his fine 'Pick And Shovel Blues' [A.R.C. 6-06-55].

Although usually reported by historians as commencing after 1865, the chain gang was already thriving in antebellum Mississippi, as a contemporary black diarist's entries clearly illustrate. Freedman William Johnson owned slaves in Natchez, one of whom, Steven, was always getting drunk and running away. By 30 October 1840, Johnson declared: 'I had Steven put in the Chain Gang today after dinner.' [6] The sentence might have been thirty days, as the next diary entry concerning this slave was made on 5 December, just a week after he would have completed such a sentence; when Johnson noted: 'Steven Runaway.' [7] A further reference appears in the New Year, when an entry for 2 January 1841, reads: 'Mr. McDanial, Chain Gang man, runaway from Natchez and took all of this force.' [8]

However, the earliest method of 'crime control' outside the state penitentiary was the convict-lease system, which initially replaced the whipping post, and was in turn superseded by the chain gang and the county farm. Perhaps the first reference to the horrendous convict-lease was the one concerning an ironworks in Maryland: 'Even though the Baltimore Company continued to acquire numerous indentured servants, hired seasonal laborers for wood cutting, and convict labor when necessary, throughout the 1760s and 1770s the company came to place a heavy reliance upon a large core of slave iron-workers.' [9] Nevertheless, it seems it was Louisiana that gave convict-lease its real start. The Governor of the state, Isaac Johnson, whose term ran from 1840 to 1850, founded a new state penitentiary which proved to cost far more than had been envisaged. According to Wall: 'The solution was to 'farm out' the prisoners, which greatly lessened the expense and sometimes returned the state a small profit. Thus was born the convict-lease system that was to become such a scandal in the years following the Civil War.' [10] This 'farming out' of prisoners spread from the state pen. to the county jail, and then to virtually any Southern town that possessed a jailhouse.

As has already been stated, the vast majority of prisoners who were hired out were black — the main reason being that white convicts were incarcerated for serious crimes such as murder, armed assault, bank robbery, etc, and were therefore kept behind bars. Blacks, on the other hand, were often arrested on the slightest pretext: being a stranger in town, walking on the 'wrong' (ie white) side of the street, or — one of the most popular with a local sheriff — the 'crime' of vagrancy. Basically, if you were in a strange town with no visible means of support (in other words, cash), you could be locked up for thirty days. The sheriff might then hire out such an unfortunate black citizen to a plantation owner for a fee, and the prisoner might end up picking cotton for anything between thirty and sixty days until the white farmer had finished with him. Willard 'Ramblin' ' Thomas from Logansport, La. sings of just such a vagrancy (or 'vag') charge with more than a hint of irony, as he was looking through a local newspaper for a job when the police picked him up! On 'No Job Blues' [Paramount 12609], he finds himself in a prison uniform out in *'the ice an' snow'* and comments bitterly: *(Spoken) 'Now, boys you oughta see me in my black an' white suit. It won't do!'* [11], his spine-chilling slide guitar increasing the atmosphere of protest a thousand times more effectively than if he had shouted explicit rhetoric and slogans. Instead, Thomas produced a beautiful slice of oral culture which has become

Chapter 6 — *An' that thing don't keep a-ringin' so soon*

Convict labourers, probably on the Western North Carolina RR near Ashville, N.C., between 1885 and 1915. From a postcard (the original caption read 'Stripes but no Stars' – a humorous reference to blacks in military service).

timeless. If the listener has a knowledge of the socio-economic circumstances of African Americans from slavery up until at least the 1940s, he or she will appreciate and understand the sheer artistry of the best of the early blues singers — Charley Patton, Blind Lemon Jefferson, Blind Willie McTell and Lucille Bogan, among many others. Thomas' understated rising indignation on his unjust imprisonment simply because of his skin colour manifests itself when he has to put on the then-current striped US prison garb and ceases to be a civilian.

This theme was developed by the intense Mississippi singer Bukka White when he recorded his 'When Can I Change My Clothes' [Vocalion 05489] in 1940. Half of the verses are concerned with the trauma of losing his *'citizen's clothes'*. His stark vocals with 'hammered on' dirty vibrato, together with his brooding yet driving guitar, impart some of the horrors of being imprisoned on Parchman Farm, the Mississippi state penitentiary[*]:

> So many days I would be staring down,
> I would be staring down, lookin' down on my clothes.
>
> *Refrain:*   I-iiiii wonder how long, babe,
>   'fore I can change my clothes.
>   I-iii wonder how long, 'fore I can change my clothes.

---

[*] For excellent accounts of Mississippi's state pen., interested readers should check out *Down On Parchman Farm* by William Banks-Taylor (Ohio State University Press, 1999). Also *Worse Than Slavery* by David M. Oshinsky (Free Press Paperbacks, New York, 1997). Both have much to intrigue blues and railroad lovers.

> So many days when the day would be cold,
> You could stand an' look at the convicts' clothes.
>
> *Refrain:* I-iiii wonder how long before I can change my clothes.
> I-iii wonder how long 'fore I can change my clothes.
>
> So many days I would be walkin' down the road,
> I can hardly walk with lookin' down on my clothes.
>
> *Refrain:* I-iiiiii wonder how long, before I can change my clothes.
> I-iii wonder how long 'fore I can change my clothes.
>
> Never will forget that day when they taken my clothes,
> Taken my citizen's clothes an' throwed 'em away-eee.
>
> *Refrain:* Wonder how long before I can change my clothes.
> I-iii wonder how long 'fore I can change my clothes.[12]

White's powerful performance is the epitome of poetic protest delivered in the raw Delta blues style. Poetic? Yes — but protest just the same.

The convict-lease system was adopted in Georgia in 1866, when that state 'abandoned the penitentiary system in favor of leasing felony convicts to private authorities, particularly railroad corporations. For misdemeanour[*] convicts, public authorities adopted either a local counterpart to convict-leasing or, increasingly, the chain gang.'[13] Soon, convict-leasing spread to virtually all states in the country, and to many railroads which served Alabama, Georgia, Mississippi, Texas, Tennessee and Louisiana, amongst others.

Even prior to the Civil War there were damaging reports about convicts used by the Virginia Central RR, which highlighted the appalling conditions the men had been subjected to. The VC was one of the components which came to form the later Chesapeake & Ohio. Around 1878, two white men who were writing and sketching all that was beautiful in the countryside made a journey on the C&O to Goshen Pass in Virginia, some forty miles north-west of Lynchburg. Leaving Goshen Pass and heading west, author G.W. Bagby says they were 'whirled along the new highway' (the C&O) and, as well as the natural grandeur of Virginia he recorded: 'Striped convicts, clinking at the drills, poise their sledges as we pass to catch sight of the very antithesis of their restraint — the rushing locomotive.'[14]

Also around that time, in the state immediately to the south, the Western North Carolina RR progressed towards the town of Murphy in Cherokee County 'with the labor of hundreds of convicts from North Carolina

---

[*] 'Felony' and 'misdemeanour' refer to criminal and civil offences respectively.

Chapter 6 — An' that thing don't keep a-ringin' so soon

A rolling cage and chain gang in North Carolina, 1910.
Note the black guitarist standing outside the cage.

state prison... and by January 1882 the rails reached Paint Rock and the Pigeon River. Tracks reached Waynesville in 1884, and Charleston (now Bryson City) in 1886.' Circa 1892, the road arrived at Murphy, and soon after 'the Richmond & Danville, which had controlled the Western North Carolina for fourteen years, was forced into receivership.' [15] Both these roads were among several which were to be amalgamated into the new Southern Railway in 1894. The latter was a premier line in the South and was the one that 'crossed the Dog' at Moorhead.*

It was also the subject of a blues by pianist Lee Green from Vicksburg, Miss.. Although Green had long been a resident of St. Louis, he never seems to have lost sight of his Mississippi roots and included many fascinating lyrics and archaic-sounding blues in his recorded repertoire of some 45 sides between 1929 and 1937. On his 'Southern Blues' [Decca 7032] from 1934, which features some laid-back barrelhouse and boogie piano, Green uses the phrase *'murderers' home'*, which was also used by one of Gellert's unknown guitarists, his vocal harking back to the bad old days in the closing years of the Nineteenth Century when the newly-formed Southern seemed to cling to its evil

---

* Technically speaking, it was the Columbus & Greenville that crossed the 'Yellow Dog' *(Chapter 5)*. The Southern owned it and ran their trains over C&G tracks to reach Greenville on the Mississippi River. As the major road, the Southern was therefore seen as the one to cross the line at Moorhead. It lost control of the C&G in 'August 1923'.[16]

legacy from smaller roads such as the Western North Carolina:

> There's a place on the Southern, they call the murderers' home. *(x2)*
> I don't care if a graveyard down there, baby, I'll be down there before long.
>
> Got my suitcase packed, mama. My trunk's already gone.
> Got my suitcase packed, babe. My trunk's already gone.
> Well, I'm goin' down on the Southern, so long, so long.
>
> Babe, down on the Southern, oh, is a long old lonesome town.
> Babe, down on the Southern, babe, is a long old lonesome town.
> If you ain't careful down on the Southern,
>   somebody's go down an' carry you down.[17]

The *'murderers' home'* refers to the penitentiary, and in this instance is a long row of shacks akin to the old slave quarters, which Green describes as *'a long old lonesome town'* — presumably built by the Southern to house the convicts. Although the singer knows this fact, and that he could get killed, out of bravado for his lover's benefit he is going to seek work on this railroad just the same.

Only four days after the Lee Green recording, Milton Sparks (recording as 'Flyin' Lindburg') adapted the theme for his 'IC Train Blues' [Decca 7066]. Sparks, however, transferred the murderers' home to *'Detroit, Michigan'*.

Other prison 'accommodation' was also used, including 'great rolling cages that followed construction camps and railroad building, hastily built stockades deep in forest or swamp or mining fields, or windowless log forts in turpentine flats.'[18] The Southern, via the C&G, crossed Mississippi from west to east, and most of its deep South mileage lay in Alabama and Georgia. The latter state was one of the main sources of turpentine, largely worked by blacks, whether as free individuals or unfortunate leased convicts.

Although composed and performed by a male vaudeville-bluesman and professional songwriter in 1925, 'Georgia Stockade Blues' [Columbia 14082-D] has the same ring of truth about it as more downhome/country items such as Lee Green's 'Southern Blues'. In an appropriately worn-down vocal with some fine, sympathetic piano from Fred Longshaw, Tom Delaney paints a deceptively casual picture as a 'chipper' on a turpentine farm. This activity involved attaching boxes to longleaf and slash pines, then making a deep cut in the trunk above the box to allow gum to drip down into the box. 'The area thus wounded, or chipped, was known as the face.' The boxes could hold about 'three pints of crude gum' and one face or 'streak' would run dry after seven days, when a new one would be inflicted on the pine's trunk. The tool used by the chipper was called 'a hack' and had a flat steel blade '2½ inches wide which was bent into a U-shape measuring an inch between the sides. The blade of a hack was about two inches in diameter.' The other end of the handle was weighted with a 3 lb piece of iron. Hickman's quote, from 1877, adds: 'This weight... enabled the workman to cut a deep streak into the tree with a minimum of effort.' [19]

But the 'minimum of effort' required for one streak when repeated a hundred times or more as a convict worked from sun to sun in temperatures of 100 degrees and intensely high humidity, caused Delaney to groan he couldn't raise his arm from his side at the end of the day:

> Days are dreary, nights seemed long,
> Down in Georgia on a stockade farm.
> Doing time for a crime,
> They found me guilty without one dime.
>
> Guards all around me with their guns,
> Shoot me down like a rabbit if I try to run.
> Five long years in a special pen,
> Working from sun to sun.
>
> Evenin' goes, mornin' comes,
> My daily task is never done.
> Chipperin' boxes, Lord, on a turpentine farm,
> At night can't raise my arm.
>
> Both legs shackled to a ball an' chain,
> Pleading for mercy, but it's all in vain.
> Ankles all swollen, can't wear no shoes,
> I've got the meanest kind of 'Georgia Stockade Blues'.[20]

Set in a vaudeville atmosphere, the apparent innocence of this recording is belied by words that referred to a stark reality. As one writer has already observed, the grim and inhuman facts of convict-lease would be unbelievable, were it not for the reports by white health inspectors, prison superintendents and surgeons, as well as other state officials. Often standing knee-deep in freezing water during the winter months or waist-high in malarial-infested swamps in the summer whilst working for railroad contractors, mine owners and lumber/turpentine bosses, the mortality of these predominantly black prisoners was understandably very high. At night, they were often penned into box car shacks still chained, and had to lie in their own faeces and urine. Vann Woodward described this barbaric system as parallel 'only in the persecution of the Middle Ages or in the prison camps of Nazi Germany.' [21] Complaints recorded included that of excrement in the food, and worms in rotting meat. Many railroads were guilty of criminal negligence at the very least. Large and small companies were involved in this system — among them the Memphis Branch Railroad, the Marietta & North Georgia, the Southern, the T&P, the Richmond & Danville of Virginia, the Washington County RR in East Texas, and the South Western Car Company of Jeffersonville in Indiana.

Nor were sentences limited to between thirty and sixty days. They could extend to years — sometimes even for life — as Tom Delaney indicated. One such example, 'Ninety-Nine Year Blues' [Victor 20658], was set down by an excellent finger-picking guitarist, Julius Daniels, who appears to have been one of the first recorded bluesmen from the East Coast/Piedmont region. Daniels travelled from Pineville, N.C., a few miles south of Charlotte, to the studios of Victor Records in Atlanta, Ga. in 1927. Over his dazzling guitar accompaniment, he expresses first his anger, then his sorrow, about his trial and sentence:

> Bring me my pistol, three rounds of ball,
> I wanna kill everybody [who] whopped this poor boy, Lord.
> Poor boy, Lord.
> Poor boy, Lord. Poor boy, Lord.
>
> On a Monday I was arrested, on a Tuesday I was tried,
> And the judge found me guilty, an' I hang my head an' cried.
> Lord, an' cried. Lord, an' cried. Lord, an' cried.
>
> Says, I asked the judge, what would be my fine.
> Says: 'A pick an' a shovel way down in Joe Brown's coal mine.'
> Coal mine, coal mine, coal mine. Coal mine, coal mine.

though the hard edge of the blues philosophy permits him to inject some grim humour in his closing line:

> Be light on me judge, I ain't bin here before.
> 'Give you ninety-nine years, don't come back here no more.'
> No more, no more, my Lord.[22]

If this superlative performance didn't echo Julius Daniels' personal experience, then it certainly mirrored that of hundreds of other black citizens. In many ways, these blues and blues-songs were far more effective as a form of protest than direct action. They have stood the test of time and are a culturally artistic reminder of how things were — and will hopefully never be again.

Chapter 6 — *An' that thing don't keep a-ringin' so soon*

As I have already stated, mortality rates were high within the convict-lease system. In Texas, a *State Penitentiary Report* from 1888 grimly stated that 'the chief causes of death were tuberculosis, typhoid and malarial fevers, pneumonia, and gunshot wounds, in that order.' [23] Another such report from South Carolina some eight years earlier resulted in charges being brought against the railroads concerned, the Edgefield & Trenton Branch RR and the Greenwood & Augusta. This report showed that, between 24 September 1877 and 7 April 1879, the G&A had received 285 prisoners. Of these, 128 had died while working for this railroad — 44·9% of the total! But death also followed the convicts back into jail: 'Out of those prisoners returned to the penitentiary, sixteen died within ten days after arrival, and if counted would make the death rate 50·52 per cent instead of 44·91.' [24] On a happier note, a further 27 were either discharged or 'pardoned', while another 39 made good their escape during this period.

Of course, there were many more hapless prisoners who remained in jail for years, often dying there. Under the guise of vaudeville-blues once again, a male singer from New Orleans called Willie Jackson cut a record as a tribute to them called 'Long Time Men' [Columbia 14432-D] Although it was inspired by the imprisonment of his *'only pal'*, he extends his sympathy to all long-term inmates:

> It's like a grave, is any jailhouse door,
> Where men come in an' don't go out no more.
> My only pal was sent away,
> That's why you hear me say:
>
> When they work you in the snow,
> An' you just barely can go.
> When you think your work is done,
> You have only just begun.'
>
> *Refrain:* I'll be thinkin' of you, long time man.
>
> When you hear the hammers ring,
> An' you hear the poor boys sing.
> When they don't bring you no mail,
> An' you doin' life in jail.
>
> *Refrain:* I'll feel sorry for you, long time man.
>
> When the sun is beating strong,
> And the days seems, oh so long.
> When you want to cry so bad,
> But you just too doggone sad.
>
> *Refrain:* I'll be sorry for you, long time man.

> When the jailer's cruel an' mean,
> An' the grub you eat ain't clean.
> When you can't get no parole,
> You're uptight an' walled-up so...
>
> *Refrain:* I'll be sorry for you, long time man.

Jackson even promises to look after his friend's wife, with no ulterior motive in mind, vowing to end her life if she starts sleeping around with other men!

> I'll look after your gal, too,
> Long as she is true to you.
> An' I'll kill her, you can bet,
> If she proves to be all wet.[*]
>
> *Refrain:* I'll be sorry for you, long time man.[25]

This evil system could not have survived without corruption in high places, and this was certainly rife in the Nineteenth Century. This involved not just politicians, but also industrialists, some of whom were only interested in power and making as much money as possible for as little effort or expense as possible. These included state inspectors and senators, one of the latter being Joseph M. Brown of Georgia — the 'Joe Brown' referred to by Julius Daniels on his 'Ninety-Nine Year Blues'. Brown was one of the state's two major lessees (having a twenty-year lease), and was the son of Civil War Governor of Georgia (1857 to 1865) Joseph E. Brown. In 1880, he was elected to the United States Senate as a Democratic representative, and by the beginning of the 1890s had acquired several companies which included the Western & Atlantic RR, the Southern Railway & Steamship Company, and the Dade Coal Company. By this time, he was ranked 'among the leading industrialists of the South.'[27] This was largely achieved through his enthusiastic espousal of convict-lease, as well as fraud and corruption. He was president of the Western & Atlantic which was maintained/built by prisoners in chains. The W&A served the Dade coal mines, which he also owned. Although Brown was probably not directly involved with running the convict gangs at his mines, an unidentified victim of this system (yet another Gellert recording) knew exactly where to place the blame for his sufferings:

> Joe Brown (uh-huh), Joe Brown, (uh-huh) he's a mean (uh-huh) white man.
> He's a mean (uh-huh) white man, (uh-huh) I know, (uh-huh).

---

[*] The phrase *'to be all wet'* derives from a slang term popular at the turn of the Nineteenth Century. Partridge defines it as: 'to get a wet bottom; do a wet 'un; do, have or perform a bottom-wetter (of a woman); to have sexual intercourse.'[26]

Chapter 6 — An' that thing don't keep a-ringin' so soon

Seemingly endless coal/ore trains at Maunch Chunk and Mount Pisgar in Pennsylvania, 1875.

Honey, he put (uh-huh) them shack-(uh-huh)-les around my leg (uh-huh)
And they made (uh-huh) my leg (uh-huh) go sore (uh-huh).[28]

    Brown must surely have been aware of the horrendous conditions that existed in his Dade mines. Over a hundred convicts mutinied in 1886 and were eventually starved into submission. Six years later, an investigating committee discovered filthy bunks in the mining camp and men being forced to work standing in water. As with many other powerful industrialists/politicians who used the convict-lease, Joe M. Brown could not fail to make a large amount of money over the years. He was 'guaranteed by his twenty-year lease *three hundred able-bodied long-term men*' to work in his coal mines, for which he paid the state about eight cents per head per day.' [29]

In his very thorough book on the US coal industry, Eavenson describes the beginnings of this mine in Georgia. Coal was to be found only in the north-west corner of the state, immediately south-west of the state line and Chattanooga in Tennessee. It was part of a massive coalfield stretching down from Pennsylvania in a south-westerly direction that took in huge chunks of West Virginia, Kentucky, Ohio, Tennessee and Alabama, plus this tiny pocket inside Georgia, where 'the first mines were in the vicinity of Cole City in Dade County.' As well as the W&A, these mines were also served by another railroad. Eavenson reports that, in 1860 'the first coal was hauled by wagon from the mine about six miles to Shellmound on the Central Railroad of Georgia… This coal probably came from the base of Round Mountain.' [30]

By the beginning of the last decade of convict-lease in Georgia (it was abolished there in 1907), Joe Brown's coal mines in Dade County were the only ones still operating in the state and he had been Georgia's largest lessee of prisoners over the past fifty years. Indeed, the size and extent of his operation was impressive. Trains that hauled his coal could be anything up to 500 wagons long, which apparently was not unusual. Bunce noted the scene on the Lehigh Valley RR* at Mauch Chunk, Pa. in 1874: 'Ceaselessly day and night the long, black coal-trains come winding round the base of the hills, like so many huge anacondas, often with both head and tail lost to the eye, the locomotive reaching out of sight before the last car comes swinging round the curve. These trains are of marvellous length, sometimes, when returning empty, numbering over two hundred cars' [31], while John White intimates that 547 cars was not unusual in 1879. In fact, in July of that year 'a train of 593 jimmies** was operated on the same railroad.' As White commented: 'One always thinks of trains in Nineteenth Century America as being short, but here is a train in 1879 measuring more than 1·5 miles long!' [32]

---

* The Lehigh Valley RR also ran a named express passenger train from 1896, appropriately called *Black Diamond*, then a popular term for coal. Running from New York City to Buffalo on Lake Erie, and then on to Niagara Falls, this train inspired the powerful preacher, Rev. A.W. Nix to feature it on his 'Black Diamond Express To Hell', which ran to six parts between 1927 and 1930 on the Vocalion label.

** The 'jimmies' referred to by White had four wheels and were very short, about half the length of an average US freight car. They evolved in the 1870s from an earlier period prior to the Civil War. As they were not readily adaptable to carrying other products, jimmies usually formed single-unit trains and these open wagons were used almost entirely for transporting iron ore and coal — including that produced by the Dade County mines. In a massive demolition exercise, the jimmy abruptly disappeared without trace in 1899, and was replaced by the far larger and more efficient eight-wheel hopper car.

Chapter 6 — An' that thing don't keep a-ringin' so soon

On 'Rolling Mill Blues' [Columbia 14438-D], Peg Leg Howell, a gruff singer from Eatonton, Putnam County in central Georgia, recalls seeing such a train which was hauling the coal (to be converted into coke at the rolling mill and used to reduce the iron ore in the manufacture of pig iron[33]) leaving the mine for the last time:

> The rolling mill, baby, it's done closed down.
> They ain't shippin' no iron to town.
> The longest train I ever seen
> Run round Joe Brown's coal mine.
>
> The engine was at the Four-Mile [pit] head,
> An' the cab[in]* had never left town.[34]

If *'town'* referred to Atlanta, where Howell was recording and was generally based, then his train would have been about 100 miles long! Not only that, the Dade County mines were taken over in 1900 by the Alabama Steel & Wire Company of Birmingham, yet, as far as the singer was concerned, they were still owned by the infamous Joseph M. Brown in 1929.

The tune and the rambling fiddle on 'Rolling Mill Blues' gives this piece a white country feel, and the phrase *'the longest train'* is an alternative title to a theme popular with white hillbilly singers known as 'In The Pines'. Also related to 'Reuben' and various other hillbilly titles an enduring verse alludes to a railroad accident involving a woman, where *'her head was found in the drivin' wheel, and her body have never been seen'* [36], adding a gruesome touch seldom found in the blues or early black music generally.

Interestingly, these lines are featured by twelve-string guitarist Charley Lincoln on his 'Chain Gang Trouble' [Columbia 14272-D] from 1927, Sam Collins on 'Lonesome Road Blues' [Banner 32669] from 1931 and by Willie Williams, who recorded 'Railroad Wreck' in the state pen at Richmond, Va. for the Library of Congress in 1936. Lincoln was a resident of Atlanta, and Collins, I believe, also lived there for a period, in the 19-teens. 'In The Pines' is often given a Georgia origin in hillbilly music, so some cross-cultural fertilisation or oral transmission seems to have taken place in and around Atlanta before the arrival of the recording era *(see Appendix II)*.

Sadly, politicians and other 'people in high places' who were as corrupt as Brown existed in most other Southern states at this time. In Louisiana for instance, one Samuel L. James was also granted a long lease for convicts — twenty-one years — in 1870. Together with 'a well-bribed clique of legislators and other officials' who helped and protected him, they are described by a writer as 'Louisiana's James Gang', which, although not

---

* Not all railroads used the term 'caboose' for the end car on a freight train. John White notes that 'some preferred…'conductor's car', 'way car' or 'cabin car'.[35] The Central of Georgia had used 'cabin car' since about 1870, which Howell abbreviated to 'cab'.

A 'yard full of jimmies' on the Central Railroad of New Jersey, c.1890.

related to the famous train robbers of the time, was 'perhaps more predatory and certainly more lethal.' [37] Hundreds of black prisoners consigned to the unscrupulous James and his henchmen were employed on the railroads, in the lumber camps and on the levees, where 'the overworked, underfed convicts received only marginal medical care, when they received any at all.'

A leading newspaper in New Orleans, the *Daily Picayune,* was sufficiently horrified to suggest in 1884 that 'anyone sentenced to a term of over six years ought to be given the death penalty instead, as a humanitarian gesture, as the average convict lived no longer than six years anyway'! This was supported by the grim statistics for 1892, when 'over 20 percent of all convicts died of disease, exposure, or maltreatment.' [38]

In 1896, after a ten-year renewal, the 'James convict lease established a new record for brutality, with 216 reported prisoner deaths... out of a total convict population of 840.' [39] Although Samuel James did not live to see the ten years out (he died a multi-millionaire in 1894), his group of supporters perpetuated his callous projects.

At the beginning of the Twentieth Century, blacks in the South (where the great majority still lived) were virtually powerless in free society, and indeed had been disenfranchised by various underhand methods as well as overt intimidation by Southern whites. Once a black member of the community had been jailed and lost his 'citizen's clothes', his or her predicament became a nightmare of complete subjugation, frequent brutality

Chapter 6 — *An' that thing don't keep a-ringin' so soon*

No.1 'Sewanee', c.early 1880s.

and sheer hopelessness on a scale we can hardly begin to contemplate in this day and age.

Yet Charley Lincoln's 'Chain Gang Trouble', delivered in a darker-than-black vocal with his otherworldly twelve-string guitar oddly invoking the banjo, imparts a recorded oral document of beauty amongst all the horror, and, yes, inspires hope that a human being can overcome the worst travesties of justice thrown at him or her:

> The train run off nine miles from town, an' killed lil' Lula dead.
> Her head was found in the driving wheel, her body have never been seen.
>
> I cried, I moaned. I cried, I moaned.
> I asked: 'How long? How long?'
>
> I asked my captain for the time o' day.
> Sayin', he throwed his watch away.
>
> If I listened at my mother – uh – an' father dead,
> I never woulda been here today.
>
> How long, how long?
> How long, how long?
> How long 'fore I can go home?
>
> I rise with the blues, an' I wake with the blues.
> Nothin' I can get but sad news.[40]

Lincoln later ended up in a penitentiary in Cairo, Ga. for shooting a man — he claimed in self defence. Although he continued performing after his release, he sang only religious songs until his death in 1963.

Yet another contractor to avail himself of the convict-lease system was a resident of Nashville, Tenn., one William H. Morrow. Via a route of political corruption in the city, he became one of its richest men by the time of his death in 1895. He achieved this by becoming 'a partner and eventually a major shareholder in Cherry O'Conner & Company, which had been granted the right to lease convict labor from the state.' This company built freight cars for railroads and 'subleased the convicts to Tennessee Coal & Iron, of which Morrow owned a substantial share.' [41] This referred to the Tennessee, Coal, Iron & Railroad Company of Nashville, which had started life as the Sewanee Mining Company (chartered in 1852) and, after acquisitions and mergers in the 1880s including 'the important Southern States Iron & Land Company' eventually became part of the giant United States Steel Corporation early in the Twentieth Century.

As 'one of the largest owners of mineral lands and furnaces in the South', the TCI was 'a large employer of convict labor' [42] and also exerted enormous influence in the mining and steel industries of Alabama. As one of the state's most avid chroniclers, Ethel Armes, put it, its arrival in the Birmingham area in 1886 was 'perhaps the most significant event in Southern coal and iron records of this interesting year.' [43] Some nine years earlier, a rich coal deposit known as the 'Browne coal seam' had been found by a Mr. Aldrich, later of the TCI, 'to underlie the vast *[Warrior]* field for miles and miles. Its name was at length changed from Browne to Pratt in honour of Daniel Pratt, whose moneys were to be used in its first large development.'

Daniel Pratt was a major entrepreneur in the progress of industrialisation in Alabama, and Pratt City — later to become part of Greater Birmingham — was named after him. The latter was featured in two blues titles as 'Pratt City Blues' by Bertha 'Chippie' Hill in 1926 [OKeh 8420] and by Alabamian boogie/barrelhouse pianist Jabo Williams in 1932 [Paramount 13141]. Pratt was also remembered in the name of the first large coal mining company to appear in Alabama. This was the Pratt Coal & Coke Company, founded in January 1878. 'Its original officers were H.F. DeBardeleben, president; J.W. Sloss, secretary and treasurer; T.H. Aldrich, superintendent and mine manager.' [44] This followed on from the major success of the experiment to make iron with coke (pig iron) at the Oxmoor furnace. By 1886, the Pratt Coal & Coke Co. had been taken over by the TCI, though it would appear that this had been on the cards for some three years. During 1883, treasurer Sloss had visited the iron-producing areas at Cowan in Tennessee. He noted in a report that, at the furnace in Cowan, they used convict labour and yet claimed that iron cost them $12.50 per ton to produce. Sloss explained his interest in this furnace as it was owned by the TCI. The idea of convict labour attracted Sloss, as it was cheaper (in both money and human lives) to operate. He concluded: 'I believe, when we take into consideration the convict-labor, iron ought to be made at Cowan… for $11.90 per ton.' [45]

In fact, most coal mines were owned by railroad companies, or *vice versa*, as with the TCI. By the beginning of the 1880s, over half of the prisoners in Alabama were being leased out to the mines — the majority of whom, of course, would have been black. As well as being cheap labour, convicts were also used as strike-breakers.

This grim background seems to be reflected in some of the most primitive (in the best sense of the word) recordings by harp-blowers Jaybird Coleman, Ollis Martin and George 'Bullet' Williams, a plethora of acappella groups rivalling those of Norfolk, Va., some archaic piano players like Cow Cow Davenport and Jabo Williams, and the sparse but superb guitarist, Ed Bell. There was also more of the 'under-developed' or proto-blues about some of these artists, especially in the 'field holler' approach of Coleman or Martin. While he sounds as if he were born around the 1860s, the singer Blind Jesse Harris seems to go back to when the blues first saw the light of day. Performing thirteen selections for the Library of Congress in 1937 on the piano accordion — an instrument rarely used on early black recordings — he appears to almost pre-date the archaic Henry Thomas! Russell observes that 'as a musician, Harris was probably only a shadow of his younger self, yet these performances seem to connect us by a dim, crackly telephone line to an age before records.' [46]

One of the Harris sides was a version of 'Railroad Bill', a black hero who often adopted a 'Robin Hood' approach of helping poor blacks by leaving parcels of food and drink outside their cabin doors in the middle of the night. He was able to do this with money he acquired from robbing trains, especially those on the L&N, and during his violent life killed several white sheriffs and their deputies. While various versions of this blues-ballad exist in the Library of Congress vaults, only one crops up in the commercial pre-war blues. This constituted one side of the only release by the otherwise obscure Will Bennett in 1929 [Vocalion 1464], who accompanied himself on guitar.[*]

Nor is much known of Railroad Bill himself, so L&N chronicler Kincaid Herr's comments are a rare insight into this legendary figure who was a member of the real world at the end of the Nineteenth Century: 'Crime rode the rails in the Gay Nineties and on the L&N it was personified by such characters as Morris Slater alias "Railroad Bill", Gus Hyatt, Harry Lester and many others... The case of Morris Slater... supplies an excellent example of the difficulty of finding a rather vicious needle in a haystack. "Railroad's" usual habitat was the pine woods and swamps of southern Alabama and northwestern Florida and in them he led a charmed existence for a number of years, eking out a living by 'working' on the railroad at periodic intervals. "Railroad Bill" was a Negro and it was commonly believed by members of his race that it would take a silver bullet to kill him. After a long and varied career as a bandit and a plunderer of our depots and freight cars, he was

---

[*] Will Bennett reputedly hailed from Loudon, Tennessee, which lies nearly ten miles east of the L&N main line from Knoxville — where Vocalion 1464 was recorded.[47] The railroad then ran down into Alabama through Birmingham and Mobile, terminating at New Orleans.

As the legend on the box car says, this celebrates
the first shipment of steel from Ensley, Ala., in 1899.

finally killed, however, by an ordinary bullet at Atmore, Ala. on March 7, 1897.' [48] The L&N had a branch which crossed its main line at Flomaton, Ala. and ran on down to the seaport of Pensacola, Fla. on the Gulf of Mexico. Presumably, the Flomaton area, being a busy railroad junction, was part of Railroad Bill's hunting grounds, as well as the stretch of line going down to the Florida coast.

But there are always two sides to every story, and it is quite likely that the L&N was such a regular target for Morris Slater because of that railroad's involvement with the hated convict-lease system which broke and ultimately killed so many of his fellow African Americans. As has already been noted, the Pratt, Coal & Coke Co — by now the Pratt Coal & Iron Company — was taken over by the TCI&RR in the mid-1880s. One of the instigators of this takeover was John H. Inman, the TCI&RR's ultimate boss: 'Inman was also serving as a director of the L&N Railroad and was anxious to expand the Tennessee Company's coal and iron operations into the booming fields of Alabama.' [49]

This expansion was a success — in a large part due to the cheap labour (and blood) of black convicts. The Birmingham Mineral Railroad (owned and run by the L&N) and the South & North Alabama RR (which was later taken over by the L&N) virtually monopolised the iron and coal traffic in the Birmingham area. Another railroad, the Birmingham Southern, was formed in 1899 'in order to acquire the old Pratt mining line that ran from Birmingham to Pratt City.' The TCI promptly bought this railroad, extending it 'to the new furnaces at Ensley' [50], twenty-eight miles from the Magic City and named after the mining entrepreneur Enoch Ensley. This town was the place where the first steel 'in commercial quantities was made in Birmingham by TCI in late 1899.' [51] In turn, the L&N and the Southern took over the Birmingham Southern 'which they operated jointly until 1907', when the TCI once again resumed control of most of this railroad.' [52]

However, since the 1880s, opposition to this form of penal correction had been steadily growing from powerful unions, miners, members of state legislatures, church and social leaders (black and white), as well as many ordinary, decent white Southerners. Some mining companies started employing black operatives in addition to whites, especially in Alabama.

This was happening in other states too, and between 1915 and 1932 the mining/railroad companies gradually distanced themselves from the convict-lease system, which was finally legally abandoned by the last state to use it in 1928. That state of course was Alabama, where the TCI had so much invested in the coal and ever-growing steel industry. 'In their growing efforts to stem the tide of working-class militancy and discontent, the major coal companies sponsored mine safety programs, hired social workers, and subsidised the public school system[*], as well as supporting private churches, social clubs, and fraternal organisations.' [53]

The churches would have been the home of such ensembles as the TCI Women's Four and the TCI Sacred Singers. The former acappella group cut two sides in 1927, 'That Great Day' b/w 'I Got A Home In That Rock' [Paramount 12491], while the social clubs and fraternal organisations could have spawned the secular coupling by the TCI Section Crew made at the same session, 'Track Linin' b/w 'Section Gang Song' [Paramount 12478]. As Cohen observed, these recordings 'strongly suggested that these singers were... a choir — either from a commercial firm (such as the Tennessee Coal & Iron Company *[sic]*) or from some school that was re-creating several pieces, both sacred and secular, for commercial purposes.' [54] The IC Glee Club was to perform for the Illinois Central Railroad in much the same way over the following three years on OKeh. As well as sacred items, also performed acappella, the quartet featured secular numbers like 'I'm Going Home On The Chicasaw *[sic]* Train' [OKeh 8710], while other sides extolled the *Seminole Limited* ('Riding On The Seminol' *[sic]* [OKeh 8929]) and the *Panama Limited* ('Panama To Chi' [OKeh 8929]); all three were express trains on the IC in the earlier Twentieth Century.

II

The Gulf & Ship Island RR was a notorious acquisition of the Illinois Central in 1925, which became a source of anger and protest in the blues. The G&SI owed its existence to the deaths of many black prisoners employed, via the convict-lease system, to build it. Ship Island is one of several islets lying off the Mississippi coast and was described in 1938 as 'a low white sandy bar

---

[*] In the US, 'public schools' were/are municipally-run schools which are open to the general public — the exact opposite of British 'public schools', which are exclusive, fee-paying private schools.

lying between the Mississippi Sound and the Gulf of Mexico... approximately seven miles long and half a mile wide, its length roughly paralleling the mainland east to west... The place is rich in early history and legend.' [55] Part of this history involved its use as a prisoner-of-war camp during the Civil War.

    The G&SI had some high-flying ambitions to start their line on Ship Island and bridge across to the Mississippi coast. The distance was some twelve miles and the railroad finally settled for a southern terminus on the mainland, where they built the city of Gulfport. The city's beginnings 'can be dated exactly at May 3, 1887.' [56] Construction of the railroad started a year earlier, and around this time 'to hasten the work' the state of Mississippi made an unprecedented agreement with the G&SI. It passed an act on 17 March 1886 'authorising the transfer of the state penitentiary to the Gulf & Ship Island.' [57] The state legislature had leased convicts in the past five years to three influential and powerful individuals, but they had been treated abominably. Some had already been privately 'sub-leased' to the railroad in what was probably an illegal agreement. Now, the G&SI temporarily 'owned' these prisoners officially, paying the state less than a dollar a week per head for their labour. In spite of some writers' claims that the railroad treated them more humanely from this point onwards, the death rate increased horrifically. In 1887, after just one year, this figure rose to 'more than 15 out of a 100, while the rate within the penitentiary walls was only two percent... the high death rate attributed to overwork and to lack of ordinary sanitary care' [58] (McLemore carefully omits the overriding factor — murder by gunfire and severe beatings). As another writer said at a later date, the railroad was simply obligated to return the men to the penitentiary dead or alive.

    A Georgia guitarist who sometimes played with Curly Weaver and Buddy Moss put the brutality of this prison system in no uncertain terms on his harrowing 'De Kalb Chain Gang' [Banner 32784], recorded in 1933. Be it a chain gang in Georgia or a convict camp in Mississippi, Fred McMullen's message is starkly clear, the emotion and rich timbre of his voice with his slide guitar sending icy ripples down the spine of the listener:

> Well, they beat me an' they slashed me, forty-five in my side.

His closing lines referred to the vicious leg-irons which were never removed — not even at night — often causing running sores and festering wounds into which gangrene could set in:

> Break these ring-chains from round my legs.
> Take these rings an' chai-eeens from around my legs.
> Well, I believe [to] the Lord, these gonna kill me dead.[59]

Companies who leased convicts also employed armed guards to watch over them — often poor whites of questionable intelligence and even less humanity. As Lemly says: 'In many instances it was easier to take back a dead convict than it was to explain how one was allowed to escape. This fact, coupled with the necessity of forcing the men to work, created conditions of appalling brutality wherever [these] convict camps were set up.' [60]

Leased prisoners usually worked in railroad camps, on plantations or in mines, and were not normally visible to the general public. So, the previously-mentioned sighting of a convict gang in 1878 on the C&O trackside by two travelling artists was more the exception than the rule. Of course, this was true not only of Virginia or Mississippi, but every state. As Tindall reported, in South Carolina 'convict leasing was almost altogether a system for the leasing of Negro prisoners', but that 'it was also difficult for the public to become concerned over a problem with which it was not familiar.' [61] All the same, South Carolina outlawed convict-lease at the beginning of 1880 after only 2½ years. It would be nearly another fifteen years before Mississippi followed suit.

In 1884, a group of eighteen prisoners was marched down the main street in Vicksburg, Miss. in the middle of a bleak winter day *en route* to a hospital in Jackson. They were emaciated and virtually naked, with ragged clothing, their bodies showing signs of extreme torture and struggling to walk in bare feet. The temperature, which often drops to 20° Fahrenheit at that time of year, had resulted in several of the men suffering from severe frostbite in their fingers and toes. These unfortunates had been working on a plantation in the Delta but, according to a report by a committee of the House of Representatives, their pitiful condition was matched by many prisoners labouring on farms and railroads generally. This incident, reported in at least one Mississippi newspaper, led to a public outcry against the convict-lease system. But despite the groundswell of public opinion, the G&SI picked up the baton for this cruel penal practice with the blessing of the state legislature two years later in 1886. This railroad had originally been granted a lease until February 1892, but by 1888 increasing public pressure and bad publicity saw the convicts returned to the penitentiary.

Nor did the inhuman conditions which convicts endured whilst on lease to the G&SI go unreported in black song. In 1933, an unidentified convict group recorded 'The Gulf Is A Long Railroad' for the Library of Congress at Parchman Farm, Miss.. This song probably dates back to the mid-1880s, when the G&SI commenced construction in 1886 'and some twenty miles of track north out of Gulfport was completed through the contract labor of 700 convicts from the Mississippi State Penitentiary.' [62] This carried the rails as far as Saucier in Harrison County and took until 1891 to achieve — every foot of the way must have seemed like a thousand miles to the prisoners. Another jailhouse song, 'It Makes A Long Time Man Feel Bad', probably dates from the same period. This appears in several

Black convict lease victims in Birmingham, Ala.,1907. They had to sleep in their chains.

recordings made by the Library of Congress in the 1930s including one in 1934 at Cummins State Farm in Gould, Ark.. One verse in particular seems to be well-known in Arkansas, Mississippi and Louisiana:

> Alberta would you cry about a dime? *(x2)*
> If you cry about a nickel, you will die about a dime.
> Alberta, oh Lord, would you cry, oh Lord, about a dime? [63]

A version of the song survived into the late 1940s at Parchman Farm, and was recorded for the Library of Congress by a group of inmates led by a young man known only as '22':

> Oh, Captain George — he was a hard — oh, drivin' man. *(x3)*
> Oh, my Lord, Lordy — out on the Gulf — and Ship Island Road. [64]

Largely built with the blood, sweat and tears of black convicts, the G&SI had still only got as far as Hattiesburg by 1897 — just 65 miles from Gulfport. Like many Southern towns and cities, Hattiesburg (chartered in 1885) was a product of the railroads, and they brought the logging trade

Chapter 6 — An' that thing don't keep a-ringin' so soon

The combined G&SI hotel & passenger depot at Hattiesburg, Miss., c.1906 – affordable mainly thanks to the convict lease system.

through once the G&SI finally reached Jackson, Miss. in 1901. In Hickman's words: 'The Gulf & Ship Island meant the beginning of south Mississippi's lumber boom.' [65]

Hattiesburg was right in the middle of the vast longleaf pine forests and was served by four railroads, all of whom invested heavily in logging. These lines, the Mississippi Central, the New Orleans & Northeastern, the Gulfport & Ship Island and the Mobile, Jackson & Kansas City (later Gulf, Mobile & Northern) formed a hub in the Southern railroad network, and Hattiesburg duly became known as 'Hub City'. In the surrounding area, there were 'fifty-nine sawmills with a daily output of 1,000,000 board feet' [66] by 1893, and the G&SI became one of the most important lumber carriers in the US. By 1907, 'about one-tenth of all yellow pine lumber manufactured in the Southern states, or about 800,000,000 board feet, was transferred by the Gulf & Ship Island line.' [67]

In 1902, the year after the railroad reached Jackson, the company had dredged a 22-feet deep channel from Ship Island to Gulfport, where they had just finished building the harbour. By 1911, 'Gulfport shipped more yellow pine than any other port in the world.' [68] It was in this year that Robert Johnson, 'the cult figure of the blues', was born in Hazlehurst surrounded by the greenery of the longleaf piney woods that permeated Copiah County. Hazlehurst was a stop on the Illinois Central about thirty miles south of Jackson and forty miles north of McComb. These two Southern lumber towns were part of a 'blues circuit' that also included Summit, Tylertown, Norfield,

Crystal Springs, Magnolia and Kokomo. Recording artists such as the guitarists King Solomon Hill, Sam Collins and Tommy Johnson, as well as pianists Little Brother Montgomery and Cooney Vaughn and washboard player Chasey 'Kokomo' Collins would often be seen in these areas, playing in the barrelhouses or out on the streets. There was also a whole host of unrecorded musicians working the same circuit. Montgomery recalled that five of these came up from Hattiesburg on the Gulf & Ship Island RR, while Cooney Vaughn, who recorded with the Mississippi Jook Band in 1936 in the city, was a long time resident there. Additionally, several of these towns had also long been 'principal shipping points' on the logging routes. These included McComb, Summit, Crystal Springs and Hazlehurst, amongst others. As far back as 1888, there had been 'seventy-five mills within a thirty-mile radius of McComb.' [69]

The Gulf & Ship Island and the lumber industry must have loomed large to these rural communities — both black and white — and to Robert Johnson. Like other bluesmen, he too could draw on a rich oral tradition which included songs from the Southern penal system. Judging by the lyrics of 'From Four Until Late' [A.R.C. 7-09-56], the G&SI seems to have made a particularly strong impression on the young singer:

> From four until late I was wringin' my hands an' cryin'. *(x2)*
> I believe to my soul that your daddy's Gulfport bound.[70]

Another of his blues, 'Last Fair Deal Gone Down' [A.R.C. 7-04-60] from 1936, utilised the tune of a Henry Thomas recording, 'Red River Blues' [Vocalion 1137]. Made about nine years earlier, Thomas' recording was itself inspired by one or more songs from Southern prisons in the Nineteenth Century[*] — the 'Red' in the title alluding to the waters often mixed with the blood of severely beaten or murdered prisoners, as well as the red clay deposits on the river bed.

In 1959, another group of convicts was recorded by Harry Oster in Angola State Penitentiary in Louisiana. One of them, Guitar Welch, sang 'Alberta Let Your Bangs Hang Low'[**] [Various Artists LP *Prison Worksongs* (Louisiana Folklore Society LFS A-5) 1959] to a tune which followed that of 'It Makes A Long Time Man Feel Bad'. Singing acappella with support from Hogman Maxey and Andy Mosely, Welch included a quote from the *'dime'* verse:

> If you cry 'bout a nickel, Alberta, you'll die 'bout a dime.[71]

---

[*] It is quite likely that the title 'The Gulf Is A Long Railroad' is a version of 'It Makes A Long Time Man Feel Bad'. The latter's tune lent itself to Thomas' recording and therefore indirectly to Johnson's 'Last Fair Deal'. Unfortunately 'Gulf' remains unissued.

[**] The title (which also has other variants including 'Alberta Let Your Bangs Hang Down' and 'Alberta Let Your Bangs Grow Long') refers to a young girl's/woman's pigtails.

Robert Johnson also used it on 'Last Fair Deal Gone Down', substituting 'Annabelle' for the more traditional 'Alberta'. Basically, the inmate, who hasn't received any mail from home, feels that if his loved one *'cries'* (balks) at spending five cents on a postage stamp to write to him, then she would surely die if she had to pay out double this amount. Johnson slightly speeded-up the song and gave it a different title, which no doubt accurately captured the unfortunate convict's frame of mind on being leased to the notorious Gulf & Ship Island RR in 1887.

The singer also recalls another verse of the old prison song about this railroad, which he refers to as *'the Gulfport Island Road'*:

> My Captain's so mean on me. *(x2)*
> My Captain's so mean on m-mmmm, good Lord.
> On this Gulfport Island Road.

Many of the convicts who were killed remained 'disappeared persons', and Johnson reports such a case as bluntly as he dares[*]:

> That cal *[sic]* ain't been an' seen.
> Gal ain't been an' seen.
> That gal ain't been an' seen, good Lord;
> On that Gulfport Island Road.[73]

A sense of anger pervades Johnson's voice as he refers to yet another undetected murder of a black prisoner in the Southern penal system — in this case a woman.

During the late Nineteenth and earlier Twentieth Centuries, female convicts in the South constituted only a small percentage of the total state pen population, but in any case they were overwhelmingly black, be it in Mississippi, East Texas, Florida or any other Southern state. Indeed, in 1890, a 'Captain of the Florida Convict Camp' in North Florida stated that there was only one white woman in the pen.[74] Statistics for women prisoners in local jails, county farms, etc. — if they were ever recorded — are not known, but these inmates likewise would have been predominantly African American.

In 1935, a white Delta planter observed that the black women convicts 'exhibit a ferocity as bloody and as savage as that exhibited by the men'.[75] They lived in the same filthy and insanitary conditions and frequently worked in the fields alongside their male counterparts — just as in slavery times. As more than one writer has noted, the 'sanctity' of Southern womanhood did not extend to the 'lower caste'. As well as this grim lifestyle while in prison, black women suffered sexual abuses from the guards, many

---

[*] It would have been fascinating (and possibly more illuminating) if Take 2 of this song were available to listen to. But *Blues & Gospel Records* states that, although Take 2 has been claimed on past LP reissues, 'it is very doubtful whether it was actually released'.[72]

of whom were white, sometimes giving birth while working in the fields.

Given this horrific background, it's not surprising that many blues with a prison theme were recorded by women in the 1920s and '30s, including Bessie Smith's 'Jail-House Blues' [Columbia A-4001] (recorded in 1923, and possibly the earliest example of the genre) and the better-known 'Send Me To The 'Lectric Chair' [Columbia 14209-D] from 1927; Little Alice Moore's[*] 'Prison Blues', [Paramount 12868], 'Cold Iron Walls' [Paramount 12973] and 'Serving Time Blues' [Paramount 12947], all from her first two sessions in 1929; Ma Rainey's 'Booze And Blues' [Paramount 12242] (amongst others); and Mae Glover's 'The County Farm Blues' b/w 'Hoboken Prison Blues' [Champion 16268] *(see page 293)*. Also noteworthy are 'Jail Break Blues' [Brunswick 7044] made in 1927 by a female singer known only as 'Texas Tommy', who sang with unusual relish to the accompaniment of a string band with a brass bass, and 'Rock Pile Blues (Mama's Prison Yard Blues)', recorded for Columbia in 1925 by Clara Smith, but sadly still unissued.

Besides these commercial outings, the Library of Congress recorded some very fine examples in penal institutions in the 1930s and early '40s. One release in particular is worth seeking out. This is an LP called *Jailhouse Blues* [Rosetta RR-1316][**], which consists entirely of songs by black women prisoners at Parchman Farm in the late 1930s, collected by Herbert Halpert and John Lomax.

Significantly, the unexplained disappearance of black convicts — both male and female — remained a recurring theme in the blues. For example, Texas Alexander sang on 'Penitentiary Moan Blues' [OKeh 8640] in 1928:

> I wonder what's the matter with po' Annie Lee.
> Lord, the Captain whupped her, an' she ain't been seen.
> Mmmmmmm-mmmm.
> Lord, the Captain whupped 'er an' she ain't been seen.[77]

The last line was picked up by Robert Johnson to form the preceding verse in his blues about the G&SI. It is probable that Alexander had spent some time in the pen when he wasn't working as a field hand or rambling from town to town singing the blues, and his powerful, moaning vocal reflected his experiences there.

In a similar style, Bessie Tucker — who possessed one of the strongest and most moving voices in the blues — recorded her graphically-titled 'Key To The Bushes Blues' [Victor 23385] in 1929 with piano and guitar accompaniment:

---

[*] Recently discovered information on Moore, which appeared in an excellent article by Guido van Rijn, reveals that she was arrested three times in 1925-26.[76]

[**] As far as I am aware, this 1987 album compiled by the Mississippi Department of Archives and History has not yet made it onto CD, but interested readers could try the 1987 address: Rosetta Records, 115 West 16th Street, New York, NY 10011.

Chapter 6 — An' that thing don't keep a-ringin' so soon

> Captain, captain. Ha-haaaah. What's te matter with Sal?
> Captain, captain. Ahhh-haaaah. What's te matter with Sal?
> You have worked my partner, you have killed my pal.

Her anger at yet another senseless murder in the Texas prison system reaches boiling point:

> Captain got a big horse-pistol. Ah-haah, an' he think he's bad.
> Captain got a big horse-pistol. Hah-haaaah, and he think he's bad.
> I'm gonna take it this mornin' if he make me mad.[78]

In 1947, back on Parchman Farm, 'B.B.' and six fellow inmates immortalised yet another 'disappeared' black female prisoner in a worksong while using dull-bladed axes to split up a live oak tree (for logs) lying in the early morning mud, the chill of the mist running down their spines:

> Did you hear about — Louella Wallace?
> Did you hear about — Louella Wallace?
> Did you hear about — Louella Wallace?
> Poor gal dead. Lawdy, poor gal dead.'
> *(Spoken – unknown male)* Mud! [79]

The last announcement betrays a sense of triumph at not only finally cutting through the fallen oak, but also at having maintained a sense of self-respect throughout their task and not allowing themselves to be crushed down into the same mud by the harsh conditions then still extant at Parchman Farm. Lomax noted at the time: 'About the life and death of Louella Wallace, no accurate information exists.' [80]

Much later still, in the wake of a national scandal in the late 1960s, Calvin Leavy recorded 'Cummins Prison' [Soul Beat 100], a lid-lifting blues about an untold number of murdered convicts discovered buried in unmarked graves at Cummins State Farm, the main penitentiary in the Arkansas penal system, down in Gould, Ark..[*]

On his 'Last Fair Deal Gone Down', Robert Johnson drew on a long 'tradition' of cruelty that stretched back much farther than the beginnings of the G&SI, placing himself in the situation of a hapless prisoner at Gulfport in the late 1880s, in sight of Ship Island (on a clear day), who is having to work back up the line to his home in Hattiesburg or Jackson, Miss.:

> I'm workin' my way back home. *(x2)*
> I'm workin' my way back home, good Lord.
> On this Gulfport Island Road.[81]

---

[*] For more information, see 'Calvin Leavy – The Story of Cummins Prison Farm' by Jeff Kuhn (*Juke Blues* No.52, Winter 2002/03).

His concluding verse takes us back to the antebellum days when slaves were awakened by one of them blowing a giant conch shell — later replaced by a bell of even greater proportions. It would still be dark as the slaves were made to walk a mile or more to the fields, arriving there just as the sun rose in the east. The penalty for not responding to this 'morning call' was often a severe beating with a whip. As an ex-slave born in 1850 in Vicksburg, Miss., recalled in the late 1930s: 'When that big bell rang at four o'clock you'd better get up, 'cause the overseer was standin' there with a whippin' strap if you was late. My daddy got a whippin' most every morning for oversleeping.' [82]

Compare this with the following report from a white worker on the WPA writers' project in 1938, which was then intended to cover most of the Southern states. He or she is describing a 'scene' on one of the many tours arranged at the time. 'Tour 7' took in Delta towns like Ruleville, Drew and Cottondale — all on the Y&MV and the stomping grounds of the likes of Charley Patton, Willie Brown and Kid Bailey, as well as the younger Robert Johnson. Lying some two miles equidistant between Ruleville and Doddsville, Cottondale 'is a group of neatly whitewashed tenant cabins clustered around a spreading, white frame plantation big house. The plantation bell in the yard is typical of the Delta, being used to summon hands from the fields. When rung, its noisy clang is heard to the most remote corners of the plantation.' [83]

The 'noisy clang' was soon referred to by slaves as the 'ding dong', which was carried over into the post-bellum period and featured in a number of prison songs in the South. The most famous of these is 'Midnight Special' which includes the well-known line *'Get up in the morning, hear the ding dong ring'*. Often attributed to Leadbelly, who learnt it while incarcerated at Sugar Land, Tex., its origins seem to lie at least partly in an existing oral tradition. This tradition would take it back at least to the early 1920s, although Leadbelly didn't record the first of his several versions until 1934[*].

Singing unaccompanied, Henry Truvillion recorded 'Who's Dat Knockin' On De Old Ding Dong' for the Library of Congress in 1933 at Wiergate, Tex., while another unrelated song by an anonymous singer/guitarist, 'Ding Dong Ring', was collected by Lawrence Gellert in Atlanta, Ga. possibly in 1928, or more likely around the same time as Leadbelly's initial recording of 'Midnight Special'.

However, 1928 was definitely the year when Frank Stokes laid down 'Stomp That Thing' [Victor 21738] — an enduring classic featuring a memorable and unique vocal with a heavy, 'gritty' flavour backed up by some of the most beautifully sensitive guitar on a blues record. A former

---

[*] The first recording of 'Midnight Special' (as 'Midnight Special Blues') was made by Sam Collins in 1927 [Gennett 6307]. Like Leadbelly, he was from Louisiana and round the same age. An earlier 'Midnight Special' was made by Sodarisa Miller in 1925 [Paramount 12306], but is a different song.

Chapter 6 — An' that thing don't keep a-ringin' so soon

blacksmith from Whitehaven in Shelby County, Tennessee, Stokes was one of the most popular bluesmen on Beale Street in Memphis. Born in 1888, he also featured songs from medicine shows and circuses *(Chapter 8)*, sometimes with another guitarist, Dan Sane (or Sing), in some of the tightest guitar duets ever. 'Stomp That Thing' commences in the guise of an anti-Prohibition statement:

> Bring round the bottle, Stud(?), let's bottle some beer.
> The town done got too dry round here.
>
> *Refrain:* For me to stomp that thing,
> I mean the same thing.
> I done getting' tired tellin' you about hearin' them ding dongs ring.

but the song's title actually refers to the singer having a good time, getting drunk and being free to do as he wants. But running against the existing Prohibition law could mean winding up on a gang in prison uniform, where they change your name for a number, as well as taking away your citizen's clothes:

> Now, mama said one thing, my papa said the same:
> Stompin' that thing is about to change your name.
>
> *Refrain:* Ah, help me stomp that thing,
> I mean that same thing.
> An' I'm gettin' sick an' tired o' hearin' them ding dongs ring.[84]

Diplomatically, the WPA writer had concentrated on the bell sounding the return from the fields at the end of the day. And Robert Johnson, in his role as a convict on the G&SI, just can't wait for that evening 'ding dong' to ring — alluding not only to resting his wearied and bloodied body down for the night, but also to the day of that final bell which means he would be free from the convict gang working on the Gulf & Ship Island Railroad. That ding dong surely could not ring *'so'* (too) soon:

> An' that thing don't keep-a ringing so soon, good Lord.
> That thing don't keep-a ringing so soon.
> On that Gulf-an'-port Island Road.[85]

Notes to Chapter 6

1	De Voe, T.	p.264
2	Owen, T.M.	p.384 (Volume 1)
3	Wallenstein, P.	p.198
4	'I Been Pickin' And Shovellin' '	Unknown male - vocal, guitar (1926, Spartanburg, S.C.)
5	'Shootin' Craps And Gamblin' '	Unknown male - vocal, guitar (1928, Atlanta, Ga.)
6	Hogan & Davis	Ibid, p.303
7	Ibid.	p.310
8	Ibid.	p.314
9	Lewis, R.	p.185
10	Wall, B.H. (Ed.)	p.131
11	'No Job Blues'	Ramblin' Thomas - vocal, guitar, speech (c.February 1928, Chicago, Ill.)
12	'When Can I Change My Clothes'	Bukka White - vocal, guitar; Washboard Sam - washboard (7 March 1940, Chicago, Ill.)
13	Wallenstein	Ibid, p.197
14	Bagby, G.W.	p.356 (Volume 1)
15	Davis, B.	p.197
16	Rowland	Ibid, p.559
17	'Southern Blues'	Lee Green - vocal, prob. piano; or unk. piano (20 August 1934, Chicago, Ill.)
18	Woodward, C.V.	p.?
19	Hickman, N.	Ibid, pp.122-3
20	'Georgia Stockade Blues'	Tom Delaney - vocal; Fred Longshaw - piano (18 June 1925, New York City)
21	Woodward	Ibid, pp.214-5
22	'Ninety-Nine Year Blues'	Julius Daniels - vocal, guitar (19 February 1927, Atlanta, Ga.)
23	Rice, L.D.	p.249
24	Tindall, G.B.	p.271
25	'Long Time Men'	New Orleans Willie Jackson - vocal; Ernest Elliott - clarinet/alto sax; J.C. Johnson - piano (12 December 1927, New York City)
26	Partridge, E.	*Penguin Dictionary of Historical Slang*, p.1036
27	Woodward	Ibid, p.15
28	'Joe Brown's Coal Mine'	Unknown male - vocal, speech; acc. by unk. male group vo.; unaccompanied (1933-37, possibly Atlanta, Ga.)
29	Woodward	Ibid, p.215
30	Eavenson, H.N.	p.327
31	Bunce, O.B.	*Picturesque America*, Vol. 1, ibid, p.110
32	White	*The American Railroad Freight Car*, ibid, p.303

33	Cline, W.	p.109
34	'Rolling Mill Blues'	Peg Leg Howell - vocal, guitar; unk.- violin (10 April 1929, Atlanta, Ga.)
35	White	*The American Railroad Freight Car*, ibid, p.410
36	Howell	Ibid.
37	Wall	Ibid, pp.219-220
38	Ibid.	p.220
39		Ibid, p.227
40	'Chain Gang Trouble'	Charlie Lincoln (as 'Laughing Charley') - vocal, guitar (4 Nov. 1927, Atlanta, Ga.)
41	Doyle, D.H.	p.109
42	Clark, V.S.	p.242
43	Armes, E.	p.360
44	Ibid.	p.273
45	Ibid.	p.305
46	Russell, T.	Notes to Document DOCD-5578 (CD)
47	Dixon, Godrich & Rye	Ibid, p.53
48	Herr, K.A.	Ibid, p.68
49	Cline	Ibid, p.143
50	Ibid.	p.165
51	McMillan, M.C.	p.66
52	Cline	Ibid.
53	Trotter, J.W.	Ibid, p.65
54	Cohen	Ibid, p.646
55	W.P.A.	Ibid, p.303
56	Ibid.	p.196
57	Corliss	Ibid, p.378
58	McLemore, R.A. (Ed.)	Ibid, pp.15-16 (Volume 2)
59	'De Kalb Chain Gang'	Fred McMullen - vocal, guitar; Curly Weaver - guitar (18 January 1933, New York City)
60	Lemly J.H.	p.287
61	Tindall	Ibid, p.273
62	Stover J.	p.293 (*Illinois Central*)
63	'It Makes A Long Time Man Feel Bad'	Kelly Pace - vocal; unk. vocal group; unk. male - speech (Library of Congress recording, circa 5 Oct. 1934, Camp No. 5. Cummins State Farm, Gould, Ark.)
64	'It Makes A Long Time Man Feel Bad'	'22' - vocal; unk. male group - vocal; unaccompanied (Library of Congress recording, 1947, Parchman Farm, Parchman, Miss.)
65	Hickman	Ibid, p.213
66	Ibid.	p.177

67	Ibid.	p.157
68	W.P.A.	Ibid, p.196.
69	Hickman	Ibid, p.65.
70	'From Four Until Late'	Robert Johnson - vocal, guitar (19 June 1937, Dallas, Tex.)
71	'Alberta Let Your Bangs Hang Low'	Guitar Welch - vocal; Hogman Maxey - vocal; Andy Mosely vocal; unaccompanied (1959, Louisiana State Penitentiary, Angola, La.)
72	Dixon, Godrich & Rye	Ibid, p.477
73	'Last Fair Deal Gone Down'	Robert Johnson - vocal, guitar (27 November 1936, San Antonio, Tex.)
74	Powell, J.C.	(see pp.334-335)
75	Oshinsky, D.M.	p.169
76	van Rijn, Guido	'Lonesome Woman Blues – The Story of Alice Moore' (*Blues & Rhythm* 208, April 2006)
77	'Penitentiary Moan Blues'	Texas Alexander - vocal, speech; Lonnie Johnson - guitar (16 November 1928, New York City)
78	'Key To The Bushes Blues'	Bessie Tucker - vocal; K.D. Johnson - piano; Jesse Thomas – guitar
79	'Old Alabama'	'B.B.' - vocal; acc. six unk. males – vocal with axes; unk. male - speech (1947, Parchman Farm, Parchman, Miss.)
80	Lomax, A.	Notes to Pye Nixa NJL-11 (LP)
81	'Last Fair Deal Gone Down'	Ibid.
82	Young L.	p.336
83	W.P.A.	Ibid, p.408
84	'Stomp That Thing'	Frank Stokes - vocal, guitar (28 August 1928, Memphis, Tenn,)
85	'Last Fair Deal Gone Down'	Ibid.

Discography – Chapter 6

'Chain Gang Trouble'
(Laughing Charley [Charley Lincoln])

CD: *Charley Lincoln & Willie Baker (1927-30)* [Blues Document BDCD-6027] 1992

'De Kalb Chain Gang'
(Fred McMullen)

CD: *Georgia Blues (1928-33)* [Document DOCD-5110] 1992

'From Four Until Late'
(Robert Johnson)

CD: *Robert Johnson – King Of The Delta Blues Singers (Volume 2)* [Columbia CK-92579] 2004

'Georgia Stockade Blues'
(Tom Delaney)

CD: *Male Blues Singers Of The Twenties (1923-28)* [Document DOCD-5532] 1997

Chapter 6 — An' that thing don't keep a-ringin' so soon

'I Been Pickin' And Shovellin' '
(Unknown male)

CD: *Field Recordings – Volume 9: Georgia, South Carolina, North Carolina, Virginia, Kentucky (1924-39)* [Document DOCD-5599] 1998

'It Makes A Long Time Man Feel Bad'
(Kelly Pace)

CD: *Field Recordings – Volume 2: North & South Carolina, Georgia, Tennessee, Arkansas (1926-43)* [Document DOCD-5576] 1997

'It Makes A Long Time Man Feel Bad'
(22)

LP: *Murderer's Home* [Pye Nixa NJL-11] 1959
CD: *Murderer's Home* [Rounder ROUCD-1714] 2004

'Joe Brown's Coal Mine'
(Unknown male)

LP: *Negro Songs Of Protest* [Rounder 4004] 1973

'Key To The Bushes Blues'
(Bessie Tucker)

CD: *Bessie Tucker (1928-29)* [Document DOCD-5070] 1991

'Last Fair Deal Gone Down'
(Robert Johnson)

CD: *Robert Johnson – King Of The Delta Blues Singers* [Columbia CK-52944] 2004

'Long Time Men'
(New Orleans Willie Jackson)

CD: *Male Blues Singers Of The Twenties (1923-28)* [Document DOCD-5532] 1997

'Ninety-Nine Year Blues'
(Julius Daniels)

CD: *Georgia Blues & Gospel (1927-31)* [Document DOCD-5160] 1993

'No Job Blues'
(Ramblin' Thomas)

4-CD: *Texas Blues – Early Masters From The Lone Star State* [J.S.P. JSP-7730] 2004
Covers the period 1927-40.

'Old Alabama'
(B.B.)

LP: *Murderer's Home* [Pye Nixa NJL-11] 1959
CD: *Murderer's Home* [Rounder ROUCD-1714] 2004

'Penitentiary Moan Blues'
(Texas Alexander)

CD: *Texas Alexander – Volume 2 (1928-30)* [Matchbox MBCD-2002] 1993

'Rolling Mill Blues'
(Peg Leg Howell)

4-CD: *Atlanta Blues (1926-49)* [J.S.P. JSP-7754] 2005

'Shootin' Craps And Gamblin''
(Unknown male)

CD: *Field Recordings – Volume 9: Georgia, South Carolina, North Carolina, Virginia, Kentucky (1924-39)* [Document DOCD-5599] 1998

'Southern Blues'
(Lee Green)

CD: *Lee Green – Volume 2 (1930-37)* [Document DOCD-5188] 1993

'Stomp That Thing'
(Frank Stokes)

'When Can I Change My Clothes'
(Bukka White)

4-CD: *Masters of Memphis Blues (1927-39)* [J.S.P. JSP-7725] 2004

5-CD: *Legends Of Country Blues – The Complete Pre-War Recordings of Son House, Skip James, Bukka White, Tommy Johnson, Ishmon Bracey* [J.S.P. JSP-7715] 2003

Chapter 6 — An' that thing don't keep a-ringin' so soon

Runnin' down to the station

'Ramblin' On My Mind' – Robert Johnson (1936)

CHAPTER 7

FAST MAIL DEPOTS AND LEAVING BLUES

If the 'ding dong' as an icon had grim connotations for black prisoners working on the G&SI (or any railroad for that matter), the 'fast mail' was seen as the peak of symbolic freedom. Starting out as a train named the *Fast Mail*, it soon entered the annals of both hillbilly/country music as well as the blues. The line used in this chapter heading is concluded by Robert Johnson as *'catch the fast mail train I see'*. The fast mail and the station, or depot, were very important to both black and white communities in the South from the earlier Nineteenth Century up to the 1940s. Indeed, towns often came into being around where a particular railroad decided a depot was to be situated, and the fast mail train was their communications link with the rest of the country. As the railroads spread, the depots became the scene of emotional farewells (as chronicled by numerous blues singers who claimed that the railroad in question and the 'low-down fireman an' cruel old engineer' had 'taken their baby away'). But first, our path takes us back to the very beginnings of US railroads in the 1830s.

Ever since the days of the Pony Express, the idea of getting the mail through to its destination over long distances and against sometimes seemingly impossible odds, has intrigued and fascinated the population of the predominantly rural areas in the US — no more than in the South. With the advent of the railroad, which of course has its own magic, it was only a matter of time before mail would gravitate to the train. Indeed, mail was 'first carried on the Camden & Amboy and Saratoga & Schenectady Railroads in

Chapter 7 — Runnin' down to the station

1832.'[1] In the decades that followed, several roads offered a rapid mail service, but only with limited success. It wasn't until 1875 that the New York Central RR inaugurated its legendary *Fast Mail*.

Probably the most historic precursor of this train can be seen in the experiment conducted at the beginning of the 1860s on the Hannibal & St. Joseph. Often referred to as the 'St. Jo line', it was 'notable as the railroad that toted the mail across Missouri to connect with the Pony Express. During the line's first trip... over the Hannibal to St. Joseph distance of 206 miles, the mail was carried in slightly over four hours, a record that stood for many years.'[2] The St. Jo line is generally attributed with introducing the sorting of mail in transit on US railroads and, although the experiment was never extended much to other lines for various reasons, the original Railway Post Office (RPO) car 'was operated on the Hannibal & St. Joseph Railroad between Quincy, Ill. and St. Joseph, Mo.'[3] Other roads, including the Chicago & North Western RR in 1867, made sporadic attempts, but these were only moderately successful and remained fairly localised.

One of the main reasons why the railway postal service had not spread out nationally was the Federal Government's reluctance to inject anything like the funding required to make it viable. During this period, the railroad express companies were expected to pay from fifty to seventy cents per mile for the 'privilege' of operating postal cars on their lines, while the Government only paid them twenty cents a mile. Indeed, 'until 1873 some of them got as low as seven cents.' Harlow quotes a scathing attack on the Government's' attitude from the *Railroad Gazette* in January 1874: 'There was no profit for the major railroads in mail-carrying. They did it just for prestige and to outdo the other fellow.'[4] It was in the same year of 1874 that the general superintendent of the Railway Mail Service, George S. Bangs, approached William H. Vanderbilt of the New York Central RR with the idea of an express all-mail train from New York to Chicago that would complete the journey in twenty-four hours. This came to fruition in September 1875 in the form of the *Fast Mail*.

The deal included a subsidy from the Government for handling US mail at such a high speed. The projected twenty-four hours for the *Fast Mail*'s trip meant a reduction of around twelve hours compared to the then-fastest regular passenger trains plying between New York and the Windy City. Thus, the way was paved for the inauguration of the 'most spectacular express that America had seen up to that time.'[5] Four postal cars and 'one drawing room coach' for top railroad officials including Bangs made up the first express all-mail train. All the cars were 'painted white, trimmed in cream, and ornamented with gilt; each car was named after the governor of a state, the RPO cars being designated the *Tilden, Dix, Allen* and *Todd*. The name of the car and the words *'United States Post Office'* were included within large gilt ovals, while *The Fast Mail* and the railroad name were lettered on sides and ends.'[6] Holbrook observed: 'From its first trip, the *Fast*

Chapter 7 — Runnin' down to the station

Arrival of the *Fast Mail* in Chicago, 1875.

Mail, running over tracks of the New York Central and the affiliated Lake Shore & Michigan Southern, was a success.' [7]

It was only on this inaugural run that the *Fast Mail* carried passengers — officially anyway! The introduction of this service — and a parallel one on the Pennsylvania RR called the *Limited Mail* — had a far-reaching effect in economic, social and cultural spheres of American life. The latter of course included the blues. Although there was a 'blip' in these services when the Federal Government withdrew funding in July 1876, it was restored the following year. Soon the cream-and-white cars of the *Fast Mail* were to be seen all over the Eastern states (and also, indeed, in the West), though by the 1900s the original distinctive livery had virtually been replaced by standard colours of the respective railroads (the Rock Island, IC, Atlantic Coast Line, L&N, Southern, C&NW, CB&Q and New York Central, as well as many others all over the US) and the 'fast mail train' had become a major Southern icon in both hillbilly music and the blues.

A stop on the IC between Natchez and Jackson, Miss. called Red Lick is where bluesman John Byrd reputedly called home. This is in Jefferson County, and a fast mail train thundering towards the river town of Natchez on the Mississippi must have been a familiar sight by the 1920s. In 1930, Byrd recorded a song which has links going back to the middle of the Nineteenth Century. He wove the fast mail into his story of a mischievous goat who loved eating red shirts off the clothesline, 'Billy Goat Blues' [Paramount 12997]. Hitherto recorded by white singers, John Byrd's version identifies the goat as a black anti-hero or trickster in Br'er Rabbit mould, as he claims the animal was from Harlem!*

> Oh, that Harlem goat, mama, sure was feelin' fine.
> Oh, that Harlem goat, honey, sure was feelin' fine.
> Now, when 'e eat six red shirts right off of Sally's clothes-line.

---

* 'Goat is a frequent character in Negro folktale. Among the Hausa, for instance, he can outwit both Lion and Hyena. The Yoruba have a legal story in which Goat outwits Leopard.' [8] Both tribes from West Africa 'contributed' members in the Atlantic slave trade to the Americas during the Seventeenth, Eighteenth and Nineteenth Centuries.

> Now, she grabbed a stick, an' she broke that Harlem's back.
> Now, grabbed a stick, Lord, an' broke 'er Harlem's back.
> An' she tied old Harlem to the railroad track.
>
> Lord, a fast mail train, honey, was 'pproachin' nigh.
> Oh, the fast mail train, Lord, was 'pproachin' nigh.
> An' that Harlem goat, he was doomed to die.
>
> Lord, he gave a curse, it was such a pain.
> Lord, he gave a curse, it was such a pain.
> An' 'e coughed up red shirts, mama, tried to flag the train.

As in many of the early blues, a multi-layer of meanings existed in the lyrics. In the two closing verses, Byrd sees the situation through the eyes of Sally, and the 'Harlem goat' becomes a layabout lover as well as a four-legged farmyard nuisance:

> Lord, I love my goat, better than I love myself.
> Yes, I love my goat, better 'n I love myself.
> I'm gonna kill my goat [or] kill somebody else.
>
> Lord, it was early in the mornin', 'bout the break of day
> Oh, it's early in the mornin', mama, 'bout the break of day.
> Laid my head on the pillow where my poor goat used to lay.[9]

As stated earlier, this theme had previously been recorded by hillbilly artists. It was first waxed by Fiddlin' John Carson in 1923 under one of its earliest titles, 'Papa's Billy Goat' [OKeh 49941] and again in 1934 [Bluebird B-5787]. Uncle Dave Macon also used this title on a 1924 recording [Vocalion 5041], while Mac & Bob cut another early variant, 'Rosenthal's Goat' [Vocalion 5322], in August 1928. Usually featuring 'red flanneled shirts' in the different variants, an earlier text from around 1920 was remembered as drawing on an older oral tradition:

> The whistle blow, the train drew nigh,
> Bill Grogan's goat knew he must die.
> He gave three bleats of mortal pain,
> Coughed up the shirts and flagged the train.[10]

Cohen likens 'Papa's Billy Goat' to the 'droll minstrel stage or music hall'.[11] He dates the original song possibly back to the 1880s, but not later than 1910, and opines that 'there is no concrete evidence to push back into the Nineteenth Century'.[12] Some sheet music entitled 'The Tale Of A Shirt' was published in 1904, but Cohen is reasonably confident that this text is a rehash and not from the original.

A 1949 *Dictionary of Folklore, Mythology & Legend* contains an interesting entry for 'Goat that flagged the train'. As well as including the usual red shirt-eating goat which gets tied to the railroad track, it also states that this theme was the 'subject of a favourite American barbershop quartet song entitled 'The Goat', sung to the same tune as the drinking song, 'When I Die', in close harmony and with echo imitation.' [13] In John Byrd's fifth verse, his 'Harlem goat' incorporates the theme of this drinking song, if not the melody:

> He said: 'When I die, don't bury me at all.
> Lordy, when I die, don't bury me at all.
> Just pickle my body up in alcohol.' [14]

This would seem to date the origins of the Byrd recording back to around the turn of the Twentieth Century, when barbershop quartets first became popular — as indeed Cohen has already intimated. Byrd's verse also appears in Papa Harvey Hull's 'Hey! Lawdy Mama – The France Blues' [Gennett 6106], cut during April 1927, which is otherwise a totally unrelated song. Dixon, Godrich & Rye also list a 'When I Die' by John Williams collected by Library of Congress in the Darien area of Georgia about 1926, which unfortunately remains unissued and unheard.

But, in fact, 'Billy Goat Blues' appears to draw on a tradition started back in the 1850s — ever since the first Federal land grants were made to the IC and the M&O in 1851 *(Chapter 3)*. Many millions of acres were to be acquired by the railroad bosses in the ensuing years, and often they weren't too fussy how they handled negotiations with civic authorities or in their treatment of the public living along the projected routes. Many farmers especially grew to distrust and often hate the railroad companies, even though the twin rails potentially promised to increase their market trade a hundredfold. To add insult to injury, they saw 'their' black labourers leaving the cotton fields for much better wages on the new railroads.

In these earlier days, it was not compulsory for farmers to fence their land, and so cattle and sheep wandered where they pleased. This was harmless enough — until the railroad arrived. There followed many accidents where livestock strayed onto the line and were hit by an oncoming train. Allen Trelease observes that 'most cases of animal injury *[on railroads]* were accidental and were regretted by all parties involved'. However, he adds that it was 'a widely held belief around the country that some farmers derived secondary incomes from such accidents'. He refers to a quote from the *American Railway Times* in 1864, who 'remarked with more than a trace of bitterness, that for such farmers the best way to sell an otherwise unsaleable animal was to lead him onto a railway track, then sue the railroad and depend upon anticorporation jurors to award substantial damages. It is suggested that some stock owners in Alabama (at least) deliberately salted the tracks* in order to entice animals to them' [15], while in Texas in the same year it was reported that 'a certain community in Texas had made it a pretty frequent practice to get all the money they could from the railroad corporation thereabout, by allowing their cattle to get upon the track and obtaining damages when they were killed by the locomotive.' [18]

During the 1870s, Alabama 'at least' still had some farmers deliberately enticing livestock onto the tracks. 'Public hostility to railroad corporations... made itself felt in many ways.' This included damaging track and other property and 'shooting at railroad trains'.[19]

It is readily apparent that, with the approval of the first railroad land grants, the seeds for the theme of 'Papa's Billy Goat'/'Billy Goat Blues' were sown. The wind of oral transmission scattered them far and wide between Alabama and Texas, and probably as far as North Carolina — at least, the part of the song concerning the tying of an animal to the railroad track. The 'red shirts' and the fast mail, on the other hand, appear to have been inspired by an incident which happened much further north, in New York State.

Back in 1854, a resident of Owego called Mrs. Silas Horton could open her front door and look out on the tracks of the New York & Erie RR, which had recently opened a line from Piermont on the Hudson River, and whose original main line ran close to the borders between New York, New Jersey and Pennsylvania. Running through Owego in Tioga County, roughly mid-way between Binghampton and Elmira, the new service terminated at Dunkirk on the shore of Lake Erie**.

One fine spring morning, so the story goes, Mrs. Horton saw that 'an immense tree had been blown down across the Erie tracks, on a sharp curve of the line. A train was due, and was even whistling for the curve. Grabbing the first thing that came to hand, the public-spirited Mrs. Horton dashed out of the

---

* An unidentified writer describing the 'Levee of New Orleans' in the late 1830s observed: 'The states of Kentucky, Indiana, Illinois, Missouri, Arkansas and Louisiana, and the republic of Texas, annually sent more than twenty thousand head of horned cattle to this market *[in New Orleans]*. Arkansas, Missouri and Texas raise numerous herds, which run wild over their extensive praries, and are tamed and caught with salt.' [16]

Before a uniform train signal code (one whistle for 'stop', etc) was adopted in the South at the Southern Time Convention in 1884, railroads had various different versions, which often caused confusion and sometimes led to accidents. One whistle code listed in 1879 by the Catasauqua & Foglesville Railroad Co. was: *'Irregular and prolonged whistling signifies that cattle are on the track, and is a signal to apply the brakes.'* [17] The C&F was based in Pennsylvania, but this particular whistle code was used all over the South. As late as 1959, an engineer on the Bonhomie & Hattiesburg Southern in Mississippi gave an awesome demonstration (recorded by the British Argo label) on a journey from Hattiesburg to Beaumont, Miss. The listener is transported back to the beginnings of the blues as skilfully interpreted by harp-blowers such as Noah Lewis, Palmer McCabee, George 'Bullet' Williams, etc, back in the 1920s.

** The NY&E opened in 1851 and was a predecessor of the Erie Railroad Co. or 'the Erie', celebrated by Milton Sparks on his 'Erie Train Blues' [Bluebird B-6529] from 1935. This road was to connect Jersey City, N.J. to Hammond, Ind., with trackage rights into Chicago, by the earlier Twentieth Century.

house and down the tracks towards the oncoming train, flagging it down and becoming without doubt the first such heroine in railroad history. Her "flag" was a pair of her own red woollen undergarments, commonly called "drawers".' This was prior to the introduction of the *Fast Mail* in 1875, but the train stopped by Mrs. Horton apparently was a mail train. Holbrook adds: 'Out of Mrs. Horton's brave deed must have come the countless stories, the poems, the songs, the "true" anecdotes about the flagging down of the *Fast Mail* or *Lightning Express* by waving a pair of red flannel drawers, womens, that have long since become a part of our folklore.' [20] Unfortunately, Holbrook cites no examples.

It is quite likely that Mrs. Horton was white, for the majority of blacks in New York State at that time lived in the New York City area. So, it is reasonable to assume that the first singer of 'Papa's Billy Goat' would probably also have been white and, so as not to offend white folks' sensibilities of the time, changed the 'red flannel drawers' line to something less 'vulgar' — like a shirt.

Norman Cohen suggests 'O'Grady's Goat', a poem written by the successful composer Will Hays around 1890 or earlier, as a possible source (or early link?). The verse he quotes includes the goat and the two red flanneled shirts which it ate, but makes no reference to a train or a railroad track. Kincaid Herr, however, states that 'Will S. Hays, of Louisville, then river editor of *The Courier*, had also written a song titled 'No. 29', which immortalized a locomotive on the L&N named the *Southern Belle*[*]. This was built in 1871 and was 'widely acclaimed as one of the most beautiful engines of the day.' [21] Presumably Hays' song was written in the same year, so conceivably his poem about O'Grady's goat could be of similar vintage. It seems likely, therefore, that John Byrd drew on a version of the earliest form of this song for his 'Billy Goat Blues' and added a 'contemporary' fast mail

---

[*] Blues/boogie pianist Wesley Wallace recorded a 'No. 29' in 1929 [Paramount 12958], but this is a piano solo with spoken comments, rather than a song. Some of these comments refer to the train going to East St. Louis via Troy, Ill.. This was on the IC. The L&N could only reach Troy via trackage rights on another railroad.

Chapter 7 — Runnin' down to the station

The *Fast Mail* on the CB&Q, 1886.

reference. Another tantalising thought is the possibility that Mrs. Horton may have been the 'Sally' mentioned in the first verse.

John Byrd's record appears to be the only 'black' variation on the theme, although Spark Plug Smith cut a 'Billy Goat Blues' in 1933 for A.R.C. This could also be related, but frustratingly remains unissued. It seems Smith was an older singer (his pseudonym reputedly referred to a racehorse, or possibly a freight train on the Southern, rather than to an automobile part), while his musical approach and lyrics were once described as lying 'far afield from blues tradition, except in their indifference to the King's English'.[22]

If Will Hays wrote any poems about the *Fast Mail*, I have not come across them. However, over a dozen plays, and at least one painting *(see previous page)* celebrated this railroad innovation. One railroad company — the CB&Q — even sponsored a popular song, 'The Fast Mail', in 1899. Newspapers and illustrated weeklies, which featured accurately-drawn engravings, devoted pages of print to the latest exploits and speed achievements of this train. Comparative statistics from the 1870s reveal just how fast these trains were perceived to be by the beholder: the average speed for passenger trains was around 35 mph, freight trains just 15 mph, while the *Fast Mail* often reached dizzying speeds of between 75 and 80 mph! Even with more advanced locomotives and greatly improved tracks, the fast mail was still the 'hot shot' of the railroad in the 1920s and 1930s, its only rivals being the 'name' trains such as *The Twentieth Century Limited* and *The Chief* (amongst a few others), running on the New York Central and the Santa Fe respectively.

The fast mail had the distinct advantage of being given top priority on the right of way by the railroad companies, even over such luxury expresses. At least one report from the early 1890s states how the *Fast Mail* was held in awe by working-class blacks and hobos of both races. Teachers in trackside (ie black) schools would interrupt the class — the vibration and noise from the train would interrupt them anyway — so that the children might see the *Fast Mail* go thundering by, belching orange sparks, spewing black smoke and screaming its presence via its multi-toned whistle. Not surprisingly, the speed and power of these trains captured the imagination of the black community, and this awe-inspiring railroad image inevitably found its way into some early blues like John Byrd's 'Billy Goat Blues''.

Although *Fast Mail* as a designation 'was dropped sometime after 1883' [23] — probably nearer 1890 — the name 'fast mail' stuck to most mail trains in much the same way that vacuum cleaners of whatever brand came to be called 'hoovers'. The fast mail trains not only served major cities such as Atlanta, Birmingham and Memphis, but also delivered mail to small-town depots scattered across the countryside. The method used was to have a special crane on a platform at the depot which had a mechanical device to 'snatch' mailbags from the train as it thundered by. These trains were scheduled to run both by night and by day, and everybody knew what time the morning or evening mail came through their town.

By the early 1910s — the dawn of the golden age of passenger trains in the US — they had become 'exalted stars of the rails. No longer were they *Limiteds* or *Fast Mails*. Better, more descriptive names were required.' [24] As well as the *Sunnyland*, immortalised in 1931 by Walter Davis on his 'Railroad Man Blues' [Victor 23291] *(see also pages 217-8)*, Sonny Boy Williamson's 'Sunny Land' in 1938 [Bluebird B-7500], and by Elmore James in post-war years [Flair 1057], they also included the *Kansas City–Florida Special*. Like the *Sunnyland,* this train ran on the Frisco from Kansas City, Mo., carrying the US mail down through to Memphis and coming to a halt in the Union Station in Birmingham, Ala.. From there, the Southern took over and 'rolled into Jacksonville, Fla. via Atlanta and Macon.' [25]

As well as being given more exciting names, the trains also carried numbers — mainly for administrative and maintenance purposes. The Frisco's fast mail was allocated *106* for the daytime run northwards from Birmingham, and the *105* started from Kansas City after the sun went down and headed south. 'Steamin' an' a-screamin' ', the *Kansas City–Florida Special* sped on through the night to dump the mail off in the early hours of 'near-dawn' in Memphis as it went streaking by on its way with the rest of the letters and parcels to Birmingham, Atlanta and Jacksonville.

Some of those who waited in the most anxious anticipation of the sonorous moan of the mail train shattering the early morning air were black prisoners longing for just one word from the outside world. In the South, blacks were often jailed on the flimsiest of pretexts, or for no reason at all — other than being black *(Chapter 6)*. On 'Waitin' For The Evenin' Mail' [Columbia 13002-D] from 1923, Clara Smith, one of the finest of the vaudeville-blues singers, paints a dramatic scenario of one such individual, whom she spies one morning as she passes by the jailhouse. Looking through the bars of his cell, the prisoner's only link with the 'real world' is the hopeful delivery of his bail sent by his girlfriend down in Jacksonville, and every morning he waits for the piercing whistle of the *Kansas City–Florida Special* to announce his imminent release. The day Clara hears his 'moan' through the bars is exactly one year since he wrote to his *'one-dime baby'* (the price of a postage stamp) and now he waits in vain for that Frisco train, which he calls the *'evenin' mail'*. Ms. Smith, the 'Queen of the Moaners', shows some racial solidarity by referring to him as a *'hard-luck brother'* and hums to portray his lowdown state of mind as only she can. This title may have been composed by a professional songwriter, but such is Clara Smith's artistry, I swear you can see the early morning sun glinting on the steel bars as well as on the gleaming brass bell of the approaching train:

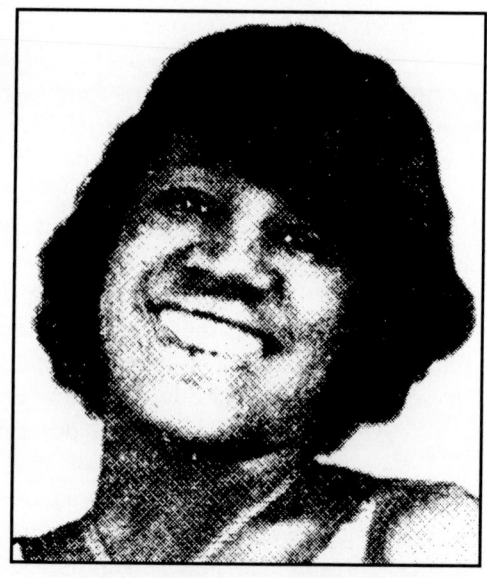

Clara Smith, 'Queen of the Moaners', c.1923.

> Passing by the jail this morn,
> [I] heard a hard-luck brother moan:
> 'I'm in here, right where I don't belong.
> I never did no wrong.'
>
> As I passed by his window
> I could hear him moanin' his song:
> 'Mmmmm-mmm.
> Sitting on the inside, looking at the outside;
> Waiting for that evenin' mail.
>
> 'Oh, [my] heart's inner feeling.
> Lordy, what a feelin'.
> Just the mean old lowdown jail
> Separating me from everything but that evenin' mail.

'I wrote my one-dime baby
Down in Jacksonville.
Sayin': "Sweet baby, I'm in jail.
Baby, please don't fail me.
Hurry up an' mail me bail."

'That's just a year ago today
An' I'm still on the inside, looking at the outside.
Waiting for that evenin' mail.

'Mmmmmmm-mmmmm.
Mmmmmmmm-mmmm.
Mmmmmmm-mmmm,mmmm-mmmm-mmm.
Mmmmmm-h'mmm. Mmmmmm-h'mmm-mm-h'mm.

'Mmmmmmm-h'mmm-mmm.
Now, now, I'm still on the inside, looking at the outside
Waiting for that evenin' mail.' [26]

Although Lucille Hegamin recorded this some four months earlier [Cameo 343], she had a much lighter voice, and the Columbia star's performance must rate as the definitive version.

A rare and fascinating description of working on a fast mail train was written by L.E. Davis, a clerk who actually worked on the *Kansas City–Florida Special* or *'evenin' mail'* back in the 1930s. The baggage and mail-sack handlers were nearly always black and they loaded up the mail cars at the beginning of the journey. The clerks were white and did the administrative work, as well carrying out the delicate operation of delivering mailbags at high speed to trackside cranes: 'The night was coal black, and it was awkward holding onto the mail-sack with one hand, the other on the crossbar... watching for the faint glow of the light of the crane... The wind tried to steal your breath away... There was both relief and satisfaction when I heard the 'whing' of the pouch as it was snatched.' Davis waxes poetical as he recollects: 'And on through the night the train rushed from station to station, like the song 'Blues In The Night'. From Thayer to Hoxie; from Hoxie to Jonesboro; from Jonesboro to Memphis... The progressive stages of life awakening: a few early risers in this town with a sprinkling of lights, and half the town awake at the next station... Darkies filing out to the cotton fields... As a grand finale, the Mississippi, muddy and turbulent.' [27] (Thayer, Mo. was situated just north of the Missouri–Arkansas state line, and the Frisco ran a fairly direct route through the towns of Hoxie and Jonesboro before crossing into Tennessee and arriving at Memphis.)

Two years after Clara Smith's recording, another of the main four female vaudeville-blues singers cut her 'How Long Daddy, How Long'

[Paramount 12325]. This was the heavy-voiced Ida Cox. Accompanied by the syncopated banjo of Papa Charlie Jackson (played in stop-time *à la* Blind Blake), she sang:

> It takes a good engine to pull a fast mail train.
> How long, how long, daddy how long?
> It takes a brownskin man to run a woman insane.
> How long, how long, daddy how long? [28]

An obvious precursor of Leroy Carr's famous 'How Long – How Long Blues' [Vocalion 1191] made some three years later, this could well be the earliest direct reference to the fast mail in recorded blues. Of course, the above verse — if not the entire melody — of Ida Cox's song was probably drawn from rural blues already extant, via oral transmission. The first line of her song assumes total familiarity with the fast mail train and its high speeds by her listeners, the black blues-buying public. This would seem to indicate several years of existence for this and similar verses in other blues then doing the rounds.

One of these, 'The Mail Train Blues' [OKeh 8345], was recorded by Sippie Wallace, in the following year of 1926. Some mail trains ran as a permanent unit or consisted of RPOs and could be considered the most 'authentic' fast mails, but others on less populous routes included a few postal cars in amongst the standard passenger rolling stock. Wallace sings of catching one of the latter and, in a unique reference, seems to acknowledge that the locomotive itself was really in charge of the train, the all-powerful engineer figure (usually white in the South) becoming superfluous to requirements or otherwise redundant. She has 'lost' her man, who has left town, and is so desperate to find him that she wants to catch 'the fastest train that runs':

Ida Cox ad, *Chicago Defender*, 1926.

> I'm goin' to have me a ticket when the mail train rolls around.
> I don't care where it go to, my man must be found.
>
> I wanna dance, hop,
> Don't stop.
> Don't care if there's a engineer or not.
> I'm gonna ride on the mail train 'til I run my daddy down.[29]

Fellow Texan Blind Lemon Jefferson cut 'Booster Blues' [Paramount 12347] around the same time as the Sippie Wallace recording. This includes the first reference to the fast mail in early recorded rural blues. His lover has also gone and he implies with sad resignation that this parting may be final:

> I thought I would write, but it's best to telephone.
> I say, I thought I would write, it's best to telephone.
> But that fast mail train can carry your sugar so far from home.[30]

Some eighteen months later, Jefferson again featured this train on his magnificent 'Gone Dead On You Blues' [Paramount 12578]. Here, he calls it the *'fast mail rambler'*, only this time around he has heard that his girlfriend is dying and he needs to catch the wind on the twin silver steel if he is to have any chance of reaching her in time to say his last goodbye:

> Mmmmmmmm-mmm, mailman's letter brought misery to my head.
> Mmmmm, it brought misery to my head.
> I got a letter this morning, my pigmeat mama was dead.

But the singer, like many newly-bereaved, cannot accept that she has gone. The notion that maybe they made a mistake and meant she was still clinging on to life spurs him into positive action to ride the fast mail, urging the engineer to make the train go even faster:

> I jumped a fast mail rambler, almost went a-flyin'.
> I jumped a fast mail rambler an' I almost went a-flyin'.
> Hurry engineerman, for my pigmeat mama is dyin'.

In his state of shock-ridden emotional terror, his self-delusion takes over and he rings the exchange to get in touch with his girlfriend's doctor. Jefferson's supreme artistry makes the simple act of walking up to a telephone hanging on a wall to *'pull the receiver down'* one of the most indescribably poignant moments on a blues record, his minimalist, strangely-piercing high notes on the guitar seeming to come from some other world out in the deep black yonder:

> Walked to the telephone an' I pulled the receiver down.
> Walked to the telephone, pulled the receiver down.
> 'Hello Central, won't you please ring Doctor Brown?'

In his numbed state of mind, the brief pause while the exchange connect him seems like an eternity.

> 'Mmmmmmm-mm, Central what's the matter now?
> Mmmmmmmmm-mmm, Central what's the matter now-ow?'
> I rang so hard can't get no doctor nohow.

But when he finally gets through to the doctor, he is confronted with the awful reality — the one that sub-consciously he feared the most:

> 'Oh, Doctor, Doctor, what can a good man do?
> Oh, Doctor, Doctor, what can a good man do-oo?'
> [He] said: 'Your girl ain't dyin', but she's done gone dead on you.'[31]

Interestingly, Jefferson may have drawn inspiration for two of his verses from an Ida Cox record, 'Long Distance Blues' [Paramount 12307], made two years earlier.* These both concerned the Central telephone exchange:

> Hello Central, give me long distance please. *(x2)*
> I'm beggin' with tears in my eyes an' down on my bended knees.

> Hello Central, give me Mr. Henry Brown. *(x2)*
> What? You say you're sorry, 'I can't make no num[ber], wires all down'? [33]

Blind Lemon Jefferson's recordings were already well-known in the late 1920s, and had become even more widespread by the mid-1930s. James 'Iron Head' Baker would almost certainly have been aware of 'Gone Dead On You Blues' when the Library of Congress recorded him at the Sugar Land penitentiary about the same time as Leadbelly *(Chapter 6)*. One song that he recorded twice (in 1933 and 1934) was 'Shorty George'. This was about a train that performed a similar service for love-craving prisoners in Texas as

---

* 'Long Distance Blues' is credited to Jesse Crump, who was a regular accompanist to Ida Cox for over a dozen years and eventually married her. Crump 'was a Texas-born pianist who became a performer in carnivals and tent shows before graduating to the vaudeville stage.'[32] A superb musician, Crump probably spent some time playing in juke joints on Central Tracks in Dallas, where he would surely have heard Blind Lemon Jefferson, from whom he may have got this lyric first-hand. It should be noted that Jefferson also recorded a 'Long Distance Moan' at his last session in 1929 [Paramount 12852], although this is unrelated to Cox's 'Long Distance Blues', despite its similarity in title.

the *Midnight Special* in the Mississippi Delta *(Chapter 1)*, bringing wives/lovers to enjoy their 'conjugal rights'.* But the visits were always too short, as the *Shorty George 'taken all the women an' left the men behind'*. Baker interprets Jefferson's words from a more practical standpoint: he claims that the letter *he* got had been a little premature with the sad news of his *'baby's'* death:

> Ah well, I got the train an' the train went a-flyin'. *(x2)*
> Uh, baby she wasn't dead, but she slowly dyin'.**
> Uh, well your baby ain't dead, but she slowly dyin'.
> Uh, well your baby ain't dead, an' she slowly dyin'.
> Uh, tell me how can you bring a poor man from cryin'? [36]

Another Ida Cox song, 'Death Letter Blues', appears to be the recorded source of the actual theme in 'Gone Dead On You Blues'. Three versions were made by vaudeville-blues singers before Jefferson cut his masterpiece. Both Clara Smith and Helen Gross recorded covers of the Cox original, who cut the first of two versions of 'Death Letter Blues' around August 1924 [Paramount 12220].

Cox had met up with Texas pianist Jesse Crump the previous year and their first sessions (of several) took place in December 1923. It is quite likely that Crump brought a version of the original 'Shorty George' with him from Texas and may have learned it from a live performance by Blind Lemon Jefferson down on Central Tracks. The seven versions of this song recorded between 1923 and 1933 for the Library of Congress and commercial companies are all by Texas artists. Additionally, Leadbelly, who spent time in the state pen at Sugar Land, cut three versions of 'Shorty George' between 1935 and 1941. He also extended 'Death Letter Blues' to two parts, adding his own usual narrative style and extra lyrics, as well as a different tune [LP *Good Mornin' Blues* (Biograph BLP-12013) 1969]. Leadbelly, of course, worked with Blind Lemon down alongside the Houston & Texas Central RR

---

* The subject of 'Shorty George Blues' [OKeh 8106] by Sippie Wallace from 1923 was transposed was transferred to a man of that name who has left her for another woman. The prison-oriented text used by James 'Iron Head' Baker may well reach back into the 1880s, along with other prison songs such as 'It Makes A Long Time Man Feel Bad' *(Chapter 6)*. The song was credited to the unrecorded Texas pianist, Peg Leg Will, by Robert Shaw, who recalled that Will 'was famous for his song, 'Shorty George'.' [34]

** The phrase *'slowly dyin''* seems to have only been used by Southern black singers when rendering versions of the Eighteenth Century English ballad, 'Bonnie Barbara Allen'. It is also used by these performers on 'related' themes such as 'Death Letter Blues', 'Shorty George' and 'Gone Dead On You Blues'. There is an apparent thematic link (albeit vestigial) between 'Bonnie Barbara Allen' and these songs when they appeared on record by Ida Cox (1924), James 'Iron Head' Baker (1933 and 1934), Mose 'Clear Rock' Platt (1933) and Blind Lemon Jefferson (1927) respectively. However, the last-named singer omits the word *'slowly'* which is in keeping with the original(?) ballad first published in England in 1740. One verse of the latter runs: *'Slowly, slowly she got up'*. [35]

in Dallas, from whence 'Central Tracks' got its name.

In 1937, North Carolina's Blind Boy Fuller used Lemon's *'fast mail rambler'* and a phrase from Ida Cox's 'Long Distance Blues' on an entirely different song, 'Wires All Down' [A.R.C. 7-08-73]. Here, Fuller softens the *'gone dead on you'* theme and sings that his woman has quit him and *'done left town'*. While he does not quite reach the emotional depths of Blind Lemon Jefferson, this is still a very fine blues. Indeed, Fuller maintained a consistently high standard during his prolific recording career and certainly never made even one bad disc.

British blues writer Mike Rowe has attributed Jefferson with originating the phrase *'fast mail rambler'*. In the late 1940s, another famous Texas blues singer, Lightnin' Hopkins, was to perpetuate Blind Lemon's memory, as well as that of the fast mail, in his 'Fast Mail Rambler' [Aladdin 204] — actually a very fine version of 'Gone Dead On You Blues'. Hopkins later recalled seeing Jefferson play as a young boy, and being encouraged by the great bluesman in his youthful attempts to play the guitar.

On 'Shorty George', James 'Iron Head' Baker also sings: *'Well, I'm goin' to Galveston, work on the mail road line.'* [37] This refers to the fast mail trains which ran on the Santa Fe and the Southern Pacific. Both of these roads started from Galveston and headed through the Brazos Bottoms past Sugar Land on their way to various destinations on the West Coast.

Of course, Texas wasn't the only state served by the fast mail. Another route ran from Washington, DC by way of Virginia and the Carolinas, then cut through Waycross, Ga. and Jacksonville, Fla. on its way down to New Orleans. The *Coast Line Florida Mail* had started as early as 1879 on the 'Atlantic Coast Line Fast Mail Passenger Route' [38] and by the 1920s was 'one of the oldest of main line passenger trains' on the ACL. However, its grand title was usually supplanted by the number system as already mentioned, *'Nos. 80* and *89* performing the local work between Washington and Tampa.' [39] Number *89*'s sister train became known as the *'Big 80'* and the unique Blind Willie McTell makes a reference to it on his 1928 classic, 'Statesboro Blues' [Victor V-38001] *(Chapter 9)*: *'Big 80 left Savannah, Lord, an' did not stop'*. As he is going *'up the country'*, this would take him north out of Savannah, Ga. through Rocky Mount, N.C. and Richmond, Va., heading for Washington, DC. Fellow Georgia singer Bumble Bee Slim subsequently recorded a 'Big 80 Blues' in 1935 [Vocalion 03090] and a 'New Big 80 Blues' [Vocalion 03267] a year later.

Heading south from Savannah, the ACL or 'Coast Line' had one main line running through Tallahassee, Fla. on the way to Mobile and New Orleans. Louis Washington (in the guise of 'Tallahassee Tight') was one of only a handful of known blues singers from Florida who recorded prior to 1943. Although he employed the well-known tune of Leroy Carr's 'How Long — How Long Blues', the singer's gritty vocals, strange guitar and odd turns of phrase on 'Coast Line Blues' [Banner 32968] lend an air of originality to his blues — probably the only one to allude to the ACL in its title:

Chapter 7 — Runnin' down to the station

The *Big 80's* 'little sister', *No. 89*, passing Rocky Mount, N.C.
on its way to Port Tampa, Fla. in 1924.

> I went down the Coast Line depot.
> Catch me a Coast Line train.
> Told my baby sadly, that we goin' again *[ie splitting up]*
>
> *Refrain:* I told 'er: 'Bye-bye; woman, bye-bye.
> You got the whole round world in your hand.' [40]

The fast mail train was also introduced by Sam Collins into a white song from Georgia, 'In The Pines' [Banner 32669] *(Chapter 6)*, and its final appearance in a pre-war setting occurs in Robert Johnson's rendition of 'Ramblin' On My Mind' [A.R.C. 7-05-81] from November 1936. One of his finest blues, it epitomised the whole psyche of the wandering blues singer and the importance of the railroad and the fast mail train to her/his real freedom:

> Runnin' down to the station, catch the fast mail train I see.
> *(Spoken)* I reckon I hear 'er comin' now.
> Runnin' down to the station, catch that old fast mail train I see.
> I got the blues for Miss So-an'-So, an' the sow 'as got the blues about me. [41]

This brilliant composition also highlights the importance of the station or depot in the blues genre, which is the concern of the remainder of this chapter.

II

The theme of going to the station to catch the fastest train on the railroad seems to have first appeared on a song called 'Down South Blues', five versions of which were recorded by vaudeville-blues singers in 1923. Alberta Hunter cut it in May [Paramount 12036], followed in June by Rosa Henderson [Vocalion 14635], a powerful-voiced singer who remains under-appreciated by Twenty-First Century blues collectors/fans. Accompanied by Fletcher (no relation) Henderson's bouncy piano, she echoes sentiments that must have struck a chord with many blacks who had migrated to the North after the First World War and discovered that life there could be just as tough as 'down in Dixie'. You couldn't hunt for possum or rabbits in Harlem or Chicago's South Side if you had no job. To cap it all, there were the freezing winters which cut through light Southern clothing like a knife through warm butter:

> I'm goin' to the station, get the fastest train that goes. *(x2)*
> I'm goin' back South where the weather suits my clothes.[42]

One month later, Clara Smith cut her version of the song [Columbia A-3961], and perpetuated 'the fastest train' image the following year on two titles, 'Chicago Blues' *b/w* '31st Street Blues' [Columbia 14009-D]. This focused specifically on the run from New York City (where she was recording) to Chicago — the original route of the *Fast Mail* back in 1875.

In 1923, 'Down South Blues' was also recorded by Hannah Sylvester [Pathé Actuelle 032007] and Lena Wilson [Ajax 17014] during September and November[*], while in 1928 Luella Miller employed a more downhome approach with backing by an unknown fiddler and pianist, and possibly Al Miller on mandolin, for her 'Chicago Blues' [Vocalion 1234] — not the Clara Smith song, but including a variation of the verse from 'Down South Blues':

---

[*] A 'Down South Blues' [Brunswick 7112] was recorded by Coletha Simpson in 1929, but this is a different song, with no reference to either a train or station.

The *Nickel Plate Limited* leaving Englewood, just outside Chicago, c.1935.
Clara Smith could have been on this train! As she sings on her 'Chicago Blues' from 1931:
'When you reaches ol' Englewood, then I'll be feelin' mighty good.'

> I'm goin' to the station, catch the fastest train that goes. *(x2)*
> I wouldn't stay in Chicago to save your doggone soul.[43]

At the beginning of 1930, Tampa Red became the first male singer to use the *'fastest train'* phrase on his 'Station Time Blues' [Vocalion 1456] and, by altering it slightly, provided the basis of Robert Johnson's version on his 'Ramblin' On My Mind' [A.R.C. 7-05-81] in 1936. One of the most accurate — and most beautiful-sounding — bottleneck guitarists to record, he does not disappoint here:

> I'm goin' to the station an' catch the fastest train I see. *(x2)*
> An' that's the train baby, that' gonna carry me.[44]

A few months later, Kaiser Clifton (with jug band accompaniment) used the same opening line on 'Fort Worth And Denver Blues' [Victor 23278] but substituted a reference to the *Sunshine Special* (which ran on the T&P) to complete his verse. This, and the title 'Fort Worth & Denver Blues' (not the Bessie Tucker song), indicate a possible Texas origin for Clifton.

In 1931, Walter Davis recorded his poignant 'Railroad Man Blues' [Victor 23291]. Here, Henry Townsend plays some stinging guitar reminiscent of his initial 1929 sides, while Roosevelt Sykes keeps things 'too tight' with his rock-solid piano. As with 'Gone Dead On You Blues', this has a sequential storyline that somehow emphasises the near-pathological hatred the singer expresses for this particular Frisco train:

> *Sunnyland, Sunnyland*, that runs on the Frisco line. *(x2)*
> Have come through here, stole that girl of mine.
>
> Every time I look at her picture hangin' up in a frame. *(x2)*
> It makes me think about that low-down dirty *Sunnyland* train.
>
> Every time I hear that lonesome *Sunnyland* blow. *(x2)*
> It make me have a feeling that I've never had before.

The heartbreak he feels over the loss of his lover is laid squarely at the door of the Frisco's *Sunnyland* fast mail train. The eternal reminders of this 'fact' are about to drive him crazy. As he sees it, there is only one option: get out of there as soon as possible. Fortunately, the fast mail is nearly due:

> I'm goin' to the station, catch the fastest train that I see.
> I'm goin' to the station, catch the fastest train I see.
> An' that's the train baby, that's goin' to carry me.[45]

Four days before Robert Johnson etched the fast mail train into blues history in San Antonio, Tex., the raunchy Lil Johnson made 'Crazy About My Rider' [Vocalion 03397] in Chicago, declaring that she was going to *'catch the fastest train leavin' town'*. She was heading out to Detroit, Michigan — probably on the CB&Q — in search of her wandering man.

III

Let us now turn our attention to the railroad station or depot, whose iconic status was on a par with the trains themselves. While many blacks — especially male blues singers — would go 'down in the yard' to check out the next freight train being made up for departure *(Chapter 10)*, there were also many who were able to travel as fare-paying passengers and make the depot their point of departure — as most of mainstream US society, of course.

The importance of the railroad depot in the first three decades of the Twentieth Century cannot be overstressed, and nowhere was this truer than in the South. As has been stated, the location of a depot could make or break a rural town or village. For example, when discussing Hazlehurst, Miss. (the birthplace of Robert Johnson) in 1938, a WPA writer noted that the town 'begins with the history of Gallatin, seven miles w., chartered in 1829; when the railroad was put through in 1857 the people of Gallatin moved closer to the new depot, which was named for George Hazlehurst, chief engineer of the New Orleans, Jackson & Great Northern RR.'[46] Gallatin simply disappeared from the map.

The NOJ&GN had been merged into the Illinois Central by the time Johnson started recording. As Gates astutely points out: 'Towns were certain to develop along the route of the Illinois Central wherever stations were established.' [47] This was also true of course in regard to other major railroads. He goes on to describe a town's 'birth' once the land ads had been widely distributed: 'The construction of freight and passenger stations at the selected locations was followed by an inrush of small tradesmen and mechanics who had been especially attracted by the land advertisements. Some enterprising individuals would then put up a "commodious" hotel. Next would follow the construction of small flour mills, sawmills if there was timber in the vicinity, packing houses, and grain elevators. Churches and school buildings were soon required, and their construction frequently led to the development of brick-making, quarrying and lumber yards.' [48] There would also be a fair smattering of liquor saloons and grog shops. Of course, all of these would attract workers, and then the itinerant musicians including the blues singers would arrive in town to take a 'cut' of those workers' wages by playing on the street corners or at the depot for nickels and dimes.

Many of these itinerants (who also included gamblers, prostitutes and criminals) were regarded as 'undesirable' elements and were forced to live in flimsy shacks near the depot on a narrow strip of land parallel to the tracks, which Stilgoe calls the 'metropolitan corridor', that was not viewed by the 'good' citizens as being part of their town. Often, these shacks or shanties were provided by the railroad companies themselves for retired employees, as well as temporary accommodation for maintenance workers looking after the tracks. The latter were known as 'section hands' or 'gandy dancers' — 'a nickname resulting from their rhythmic motions in swinging sledgehammers, picks, and other tools manufactured by the Gandy Tool Company* of Chicago.' [49]

Shanties situated in the Northern and Midwestern states generally housed Italian Americans in 1900, but by the 1930s were 'chiefly Polish American'. Stilgoe quotes from a 1938 play called *Our Town*: 'Up here is Main Street,' says the narrator with a wave of his hand toward backstage. 'Way back there is the railway station; tracks go that way. Polish Town's across the tracks.' [50] But in the Southern states these gandy dancers were predominantly black, and some roving blues singers had picked up a derogatory term for Polish immigrants, rendering it as 'Polock'. This word crops up in several earlier blues including 'The Snitchers Blues' [Q.R.S. R-7049] by James 'Stump' Johnson in 1928 and also provided the title for Jabo Williams' 1932 recording, 'Polock Blues' [Paramount 13130].

Williams, who does not feature either in *Blues Who's Who* or in most

---

* Along with celebrated US railroad historian, John White Jr (throughout many years' search), I have not come across a company with this name from the later Nineteenth or early Twentieth Century. Possibly 'gandy' was just a slang term used by section hands at the time.

Chapter 7 — Runnin' down to the station

blues literature to date, was a rough-hewn barrelhouse and boogie pianist thought to be from the Birmingham area in Alabama. He cut a solitary session in 1932 for Paramount and seems to have then disappeared off the face of the earth (an unfortunately familiar story in the blues). On 'Polock Blues' he accompanies his raw vocals with a punchy piano and a 'good-rocking' boogie beat. In the song, he has been raided at his *'playhouse'* following a tip-off and now wants to leave the big city for the safer confines of a shanty town way on down the line. The *'playhouse'* in question appears to be a barrelhouse, where he supplied liquor and prostitutes as well as the blues:

> Gon' spend all my days way down in Polock Town.
> Spend all my days way down in Polock Town.
> 'Cause womens an' bad whiskey have tore my playhouse down.

His operations were obviously lucrative, as he pawns his *'diamonds'* in order to buy a ticket on a southbound train and doubtless drop off somewhere else along the metropolitan corridor to start up another barrelhouse near the anonymous depot:

> I said: 'Mr. Ticket Agent ease your window down.
> Mr. Ticket Agent ease your window down.
> I got my ticket, I'm goin' to Polock Town.' [51]

'Polock' seems to be a rural black derivation of 'Polak' or 'Polack' — an early Twentieth Century term in criminal circles referring to white slave traders, some of whom were Polish, 'who deal in Polish Jewesses'. (It was also used as a general term for *any* Polish national.) Partridge quotes a later source from 1940 which states: 'The traders from eastern Europe who dominate the business are known to the trade as "Polacks".' [52]

But the depot was not just a focal point for the seamier side of life; it was also the inspiration for several blues which described the 'leavin' scene' in graphic terms about lost love of the deepest kind. In around three minutes on a 78 rpm shellac disc sheer poetry is revealed, sometimes harrowing in its poignancy, but never descending into the mawkish or purely sentimental.

Probably the best-known

example in the world of the blues is a 1937 recording by Robert Johnson titled 'Love In Vain Blues' [Vocalion 04630]. Set to the melody of the popular Leroy Carr song, 'When The Sun Goes Down' [Bluebird B-5877], Johnson's vivid lyrics transport the listener to the station where the singer is carrying his woman's suitcase in a final declaration of his love, while night's darkness symbolically descends upon them as they slowly walk together for what is probably the last time. No amount of words can describe the sheer tragic beauty of Johnson's blues, on which he plays fittingly subdued and lonesome guitar strings:

> I followed her to the station, with 'er suitcase in my hand.
> An' I followed her to the station, with her suitcase in my hand.
> Well, it's hard to tell, it's hard to tell... when all your love's in vain.
> All my love's in vain.
>
> When the train rolled up to the station, I looked her in the eye.
> When the train rolled up to the station an' I looked her in the eye.
> Well, I was lonesome. I felt so lonesome... an' I could not help but cry.
> All my love's in vain.

In the penultimate verse, the singer describes watching the disappearing lights of the caboose through misty eyes as the train finally departs:

> When the train it left the station, with two lights on behind. *(x2)*
> Well, the blue light was my blues, an' the red light was my mind.
> All my love's in vain.
>
> Eeeeeeee-eeeeh! Oooooh! Willie Mae[*].
> Ohhhhhh-heyyyy! Ooooh! Willie Mae.
> Ey-ey-heyyyyyy-hey-hey! Ooooh! Willie Mae, woah.
> All my love's in vain.[53]

In doing so, he echoes the poetic license first used back in 1926 when Blind Lemon Jefferson sang on his 'Dry Southern Blues' [Paramount 12347]:

> My train at the depot, the red an' blue light behind.
> Train's at the depot, the red an' blue light behind.
> Well, the blue light's the blues, the red light's a worried mind.[54]

The caboose, as the last car on the train, had marker lights when running on double tracks with two-way traffic. These were 'red to the rear on the outside and green to the rear between the tracks'.[55] Back in 1922,

---

[*] The 'Willie Mae' in the song turned out to be a real part of Robert Johnson's life. During the 1970s, white US researchers discovered her whereabouts and, after hearing 'Love In Vain', she broke down in tears, saying she had been unaware of the record until that moment.

Chapter 7 — Runnin' down to the station

L.F. Loree, who was chairman of the Kansas City Southern RR, had already observed 'it is well to note that the lamps carried on the rear of the train are combination lamps, the red signal for rear protection, the green signal the marker.' [56] This detail was faithfully reproduced in the same verse on the completely unrelated 'The Flying Crow' [Decca 7307], recorded by Black Ivory King and Dusky Dailey in the same year of 1937, and in Washboard Sam's 1941 remake, 'Flying Crow Blues' [Bluebird B-8844].

Of course, Johnson's 'Love In Vain Blues' gained much wider popularity when the Rolling Stones recorded it in the late 1960s, so a closer examination of the origins of this 'love song of the blues' is warranted. Johnson may have been familiar with an early Sippie Wallace record, 'Suitcase Blues' [OKeh 8243] from 1925. Here, she used mostly traditional lyrics, but put her own original vocal stamp on the song — as she generally did. Featuring irregular verses, she opened with the following lines:

> My suitcase is packed, trunk's all gone.
> Know by that I ain't gonna be here long.

— and concluded by asking her upset lover for her case, as the train is ready to leave:

> The train whistle's blowin', I'm goin' on my way. *(x2)*
> Give me my suitcase, I'll see you some old day.[57]

Johnson would no doubt have been aware of the ever-popular Memphis Jug Band and their 1927 record, 'I Packed My Suitcase, Started To The Train' [Victor 21412]. Or, as another guitar man, the unique Robert Wilkins may have been inspiration to Johnson's lyric on 'Love In Vain'. Wilkins was one of the finest bluesmen from the state of Mississippi and he too had one of his records covered by the Rolling Stones in the late 1960s. This was the incredible 'That's No Way To Get Along' [Brunswick 7125], from his third session in 1929, which he remade as 'The Prodigal Son' in 1964 [LP *Memphis Gospel Singer*, Piedmont PLP-13162].

Equally awesome was 'Rolling Stone (Parts 1 & 2)' [Victor 21741], cut at his very first recording session in September 1928 — some twenty years prior to the similar title by Muddy Waters from which the English group

Chapter 7 — Runnin' down to the station

took their name. Using a sparse, hypnotic guitar accompaniment, Wilkins — like Johnson — conveys a real sense of standing expectantly on the station platform waiting for the train to roll up in a cloud of hissing steam. His verses, being couplets, lend a pre-blues feel to his song and emphasise the drone of his guitar:

> Come run, bring my suitcase please, an' let me go.
> Come run, bring my suitcase please, an' let me go.
>
> Oh, the train rolled up, got them way too lonesome blues.
> Oh, the train rolled up, got them way too lonesome blues.
>
> Hon[ey], come kiss me goodbye, my time alone come to go.
> Hon come kiss me goodbye, my time alone come to go.
>
> When the train rolled off, she waved her hands at me.
> When the train rolled off, she waved her hands at me.
>
> I looked out the window, friends, as far as I could see.
> I looked out the window, friends, as far as I could see.[58]

Equally moving was 'The Train Is Coming' [Decca 7483], recorded in 1938 by Roosevelt Sykes, which may have been inspired by both Wilkins and Johnson. Subtitled 'No More Baby Talk', this offering lacks the melodic beauty of 'Love In Vain', but more than makes up for it with the allure of the descriptive lyrics and the 'stalking' piano that was virtually Sykes' trademark, as well as hinting at the style of his home base at the time, St. Louis.

The lines describing in detail the very act of the train leaving the station are a rarity in recorded blues. His words invoke the smell of damp steam and dirty oil that constitute the 'breath' of the snorting locomotive about to spirit his lover away; yet, unlike many other blues singers, he does not blame either the train or the crew for his misfortune:

> The train is comin' an' my baby is got to go.
> The train is comin' an' my baby's got to go.
> I believe she's leavin' me not to come back no more.'

Chapter 7 — Runnin' down to the station

Chicago Union Station in 1919.
The sight that would have greeted migrating blues singers like Red Nelson as they arrived.

> The porter wave 'is hand an' the fireman ring the bell. *(x2)*
> When the drivin' wheels start turnin' over, my poor heart begin to swell.
>
> I stood an' looked at the train until it went around the bend. *(x2)*
> I says: 'I don't believe I'll see my baby's smilin' face again.'

Having watched the train disappear from sight, the screaming silence of the sleepy small-town depot brings the singer back to awful reality. He feels emotionally and spiritually alone on the planet and, although he contemplates walking out of the station to sit under the shade of a tree, his feet seem rooted to the platform at the point where he saw his woman exit from his life forever. Only the slight chill of early evening and the setting of the sun remind him just how long he has stood there looking down the empty tracks:

> The sun begin sinkin' down behind the western horizon. *[sic]*
> The sun is sinkin' down behind the western horizon. *[sic]*
> The evenin' dew began to fall an' I'm all alone.
>
> I would go an' sit down under the old oak tree.
> I would go out an' sit under the old oak tree.
> But I ain't got nobody to talk baby talk to me.[59]

Chapter 7 — *Runnin' down to the station*

Entrance to Chicago Union Station, 1919.

The traumatic scenario of the 'depot leaving' occurred in a great many blues — sometimes as one or two floating verses, as in Charley Patton's 'Pony Blues' [Paramount 12792] from his initial session in 1929 or Joe Pullum's 'Cows, See That Train Comin'' [Bluebird B-5534] from 1934. This theme's first appearance on a blues record might well have been on Rosa Henderson's 1924 recording, 'Barrel House Blues' [Vocalion 14831][*]:

> It was late one evening, the sun was going down. *(x2)*
> It was then my baby stepped on the eastern-bound.
>
> The whistle blew like it never blew before. *(x2)*
> I'll tell the world I hated to see him go.[60]

It was not only the station that was so prominent in the blues – there was also the figure central to its operation. Usually a white male, the depot or ticket agent was looked up to by the whole community, and was perceived to have the whole workings of 'his' particular railroad at his fingertips. With his communications link of first the telegraph, and later also the telephone, he was seen as a person of importance, influence and 'inside information'. The local people, black and white, also viewed him as a sort-of 'father figure' who

---

[*] Two 'Barrel House Blues' were recorded earlier, by Ma Rainey [Paramount 12082] and Ed Andrews [OKeh 8137], in 1923 and 1924 respectively. These are both different songs and do not include references to either a depot or a railroad.

A streamline train on the NYC – the *20th Century* – leaving Chicago's La Salle St. Station in 1938.

would give advice and lend a sympathetic ear to their problems. They also believed he had knowledge of their loved ones' whereabouts when they chose to travel by train to make their getaway. One verse that features in many blues is a variant of these lines:

> Mr. Ticket Agent, don't tell me no lie.
> Did my woman/man stop here, or did she/he ride on by?

In 1935, a recently-settled Chicago resident from Mississippi, Nelson Wilborn, made his record debut. Reportedly a guitarist as well as a pianist, he cut his 'Streamline Train'[*] [Decca 7171] the following year as 'Red Nelson' but apparently did not accompany himself on any instrument; nor did he on subsequent sessions. Instead, on this song he was backed by the superb and extrovert Cripple Clarence Lofton, who beat out the rhythms of the wheels on the piano keys. But Nelson, not knowing which of the many trains he could catch out of the Chicago Union Station, puts absolute trust in the ticket agent — or rather the train caller (referred to by Red as the *'call-boy'*), who took his orders direct from the ticket agent:

---

[*] A streamline train was one whose locomotive had been modified so that it offered the least wind-resistance when in motion. For example, reducing the height of the smokestack so that it was flush with the top surface of the engine, and rounding the front end to give it a bullet-like appearance.

Chapter 7 — Runnin' down to the station

> Goin' to the Union Station, act just like a child.
> Ask the call-boy, mama: 'What train do I ride?'
>
> *Refrain:* I'm gonna leave in the mornin',
> Baby, on that streamline train.
> Onliest thing I could say mama:
> 'Get your mind off of this thing.' [61]

The ticket agent even took on a supernatural aura on 'Ticket Agent Blues' [Bluebird B-5675], when Noah Lewis asked him to reposition his depot!

> Depot Agent, turn your depot, turn your depot 'round indeed, Lord.
> Depot Agent, please turn your depot 'round.
> *(Spoken - unknown male)* 'Why?'
> My woman done quit me, an' I goin' to leave your town. [62]

The surreal atmosphere is heightened by Noah's moving vocal and the haunting jug band backing which includes his own ethereal harp, Yank Rachell's mandolin and some fine, booting jug from Ham Lewis.

Some two years earlier, 'Mother of the Blues' Ma Rainey put a slightly different angle on the 'depot leaving' theme on her fine 'Traveling Blues' [Paramount 12706], which also included some great jug-blowing as well as crazy 'jazzhorn' and kazoo. Here, Rainey also consults the ticket agent on the whereabouts of her man, whom she refers to as *'my child'*[*]:

> Train's at the station, I heard the whistle blow.
> The train's at the station, I heard the whistle blow.
> I done bought my ticket, an' I don't know where I'm goin'.
>
> I went to the depot, looked up an' down the board. *(x2)*
> I asked the Ticket Agent if my child's on this road.
>
> The Ticket Agent said: 'Woman don't sit an' cry.'
> Ticket Agent said: 'Woman, don't sit an' cry,
> Your train blowed at the station, but she keeps on passin' by.'

She tortures herself by thinking of her *'daddy'* talking in loving and intimate tones with another woman, which makes her feel desperate as well as *'dangerous an' blue'*:

> I hear my daddy callin' some other woman's name. *(x2)*
> I know 'e don't need me, but I'm goin' ask her just the same.

---

[*] It has been often reported over the years that Ma Rainey was not only bisexual, but also heavily attracted to young men — including those in their early teens. In this instance however, she apparently uses 'child' as a simple term of endearment (like 'baby').

> I'm dangerous an' blue, can't stay here no more. *(x2)*
> Here come my train, Walton(?), I've got to go.[63]

Rainey's biographer mentions that this song was her favorite blues during the 1930s, 'which she acted out in performance' — that is to say, she came out on stage dressed in a coat and hat, carrying a suitcase. Putting this down, she would deliberate for a moment as if wondering which train to catch, 'just to let 'em see what I was about. Then I sing. You could jes' see them jiggs[*] wantin' to go some place else.'[65]

Finally, there is also a group of songs which refer to the railroad track running through the station. The Mississippi Sheiks, usually fronted by singer/guitarist Walter Vinson, were one of the most famous black string bands to record, and featured many fine blues in their repertoire along with a wide range of material ranging from waltzes to hokum songs. 'River Bottom Blues' [OKeh 8843], from their fourth session in 1930, contains an apparently unique verse which makes reference to the sound of the vibration of the twin steel rails and creosote-coated sleepers or 'ties' — faint at first, so as to be almost imagined, but undeniably growing in volume and finally singing in his ears, announcing the imminent arrival of an oncoming train. Is his girlfriend on this one? Will it even stop? Vinson's rich vocal is replete with the most exquisite blues poetry:

> I heard the railroad poppin', an' the ties begin to cry. *(x2)*
> Wondered did it bring me my baby, or leave her pass on by.[66]

In the early decades of the Twentieth Century, many US railroads — and Southern ones in particular — owned track that left much to be desired with regard to smooth running, not to mention safety. This was sometimes due to cost-cutting or a more general lack of finances, but often just sheer negligence on the part of a section foreman. In 1922, L.F. Loree, one of the prominent US railroad men of the early Twentieth Century, analysed shortcomings in the national railroad freight operation in his excellent book, *Railroad Freight Transportation*. The fact that he was President of the Delaware & Hudson as well as Chairman of the KCS did not stop him familiarising himself with these roads 'on the ground' to the same extent as any gandy dancer, and his comments about the state of the track are suitably enlightening: 'One of the offenses of the track foreman, still prevalent, is to bring one rail to the grade line set for it and then, discarding the track level *[spirit level]* to attempt to bring the other rail into the same horizontal plane by 'sighting across'. Not one man in a hundred can do this successfully. The result is a waving track, rolling the cars as they pass over it.'[67] Another

---

[*] Partridge gives one definition for 'jig' as a 'jocular' colloquialism when it is 'applied to a person, a domestic animal, etc.', used during the Eighteenth and Nineteenth Centuries.[64]

malpractice when 'grading' or otherwise laying out the road bed on which the rails and ties will rest, resulted in what Loree terms 'lumpy track'.

In his 'Wartime Blues' [Paramount 12425] from 1926, bluesman Blind Lemon Jefferson also spots this problem, though the Texan railroad in question would have been under the auspices of the US Federal Government at the time the song is set (the First World War) — the nearest the USA got to a nationalised system prior to Amtrak in the 1970s:

> Well, they tell me that south-bound train had a wreck last night.
> Lord, that south-bound train had a wreck last night.
> Lord, that south-bound train had a wreck last night.
> Said to the section foreman: 'You ain't treatin' your railroad right.' [68]

Elsewhere in his book, Loree deplores the state of rails in stations, which often creep out of alignment as 'a result of changes of track in order to run round station platforms' — that is, the engine has to be uncoupled and go from one end of the train to the other in order to make a return journey. Under the heading 'Track Kinks' (or deformation of the alignment), he says that these kinks have to be 'carefully handled by proper curvature, *[otherwise]* considerable resistance to train movement may result... Such deformation may oppose serious difficulties to starting a train, and unfortunately are most apt to occur where trains are frequently stopped.' [69]

Once again, Blind Lemon the Rail Watchdog leaps into action! In 'Rambler Blues' from 1927 [Paramount 12541], he arrives at the depot to discover that his train is unable to depart due to one of these kinks:

> Well, it's train time now an' the track's all out of line.
> Well, it's train time now, track's all out of line.
> An' I come 'ere soon [as] I wanna catch that *No. 9.*[70]

Big Boy Cleveland featured the same 'track's out of line' imagery on 'Goin' Away To Leave You Blues' in 1927 [Gennett 6108], as did Cannon's Jug Stompers on their 'Big Railroad Blues' [Victor 21351] the following year; Charlie 'Specks' McFadden used it on 'Harvest Moon Blues' [Brunswick 7146] in 1929 and, at the tail-end of 1941, the tough, two-fisted pianist, Big Maceo also featured it on his 'I Got The Blues' [Bluebird B-8939], albeit in connection with a freight yard. Switch engines used for moving or shunting rolling stock from track to track would create the same sort of problem as at the station, the yard also qualifying as a place 'where trains frequently stopped'. Indeed, it is from this railroad phenomenon that we get the phrase 'out of line', meaning someone who is speaking out of turn or whose behaviour is out of order. The excellent pianist Andy Boy from Galveston, Tex. recorded an 'Out O' Line Blues' [Bluebird B-6940] in 1937, though purely in the latter context and without any other railroad references.

IV

In the late Nineteenth and earlier Twentieth Centuries, the railroad depot or station had a multi-purpose role in Southern US society for both blacks and whites, though it was much more centrally focused in the South than in other parts of this vast country. This was mainly for two reasons. Firstly, the huge expanse of land below the Mason–Dixon line colloquially known as 'Dixie' was predominantly a rural one. As a quick example, even as late as 1992 the state of Mississippi had a population of only some two million people. Compare this to England and Wales, which cover roughly the same area but are home to some fifty million-plus inhabitants. And there are many other states in the South like Mississippi in both size and population. Secondly, there was the inherited racial situation stemming from the 'Peculiar Institution', as slavery was sometimes called. There is no parallel, over such a large land mass, to the close-knit black communities spread across the South — either in Western states with similar profiles, or anywhere else in the world for that matter. We are talking here of an area equivalent in size to that of southern Europe and the UK combined. From 1865 onwards, the harsh Jim Crow laws, sharecropping and prison systems all kept the large majority of black citizens locked into an impoverished and undeniably second-class society, which ultimately only strengthened their solidarity and will to survive. Of course, black solidarity extended to the cities in both the North and the West once the mass migrations began — to Chicago, Los Angeles, New York, Detroit and so on. It was, and continues to be, a major source of strength to the African American population today.

This solidarity was particularly strong in the early blues, as has already been noted. It didn't matter whether Robert Johnson or Roosevelt Sykes had actually experienced the trauma of watching a loved one leave on a fast-disappearing train. They, and other singers, knew full well that, in Rube Lacy's words, 'it hit' *somebody* — many hundreds or thousands of fellow black citizens in fact. The success of a blues performer in the 1920s and '30s depended to a large extent on what they sang being readily identified with by an audience, whether heard live in a barrelhouse or at a train station, or via a recording on a phonograph in somebody's home. After all, the blues is primarily a vocal tradition. So, Blind Lemon Jefferson could sing with confidence about train times while waiting at the depot with his girlfriend who is about to leave him:

> Tell me, what time do the trains come through your town?
> I wanna know what time do the trains come through your town?
> I wanna laugh an' talk with a long-haired teasing brown.

> One goes south at eight, an' it's one goes north at nine.
> One goes south at eight, one goes north at nine.
> I got a hour to talk with that long-haired brown of mine.[71]

This recording of 'Black Horse Blues' [Paramount 12367], with its long guitar-break in the middle, ranks among his finest, alongside classics such as 'Got The Blues', 'Match Box Blues', etc.

Another guitarist, originally from Kentucky, was Clifford Gibson, and on 'Drayman Blues' [Victor V-38562] he too could sing of a 'multiple choice' of trains to leave on once the drayman[*] (who almost certainly would have been black) had hauled his trunk to the station:

> Mr. Drayman, Mr. Drayman back your truck up to my door. *(x2)*
> Take my trunk down to the station [I'm] checkin' out, like, here no more.
>
> I'm in bad luck now, wanna catch somebody's train. *(x2)*
> Take this whole world through, my luck will be bound to change.
>
> *53*'s done run, *54*, what do I care?
> *53*'s done run, as long as *54* is here.
> *55* done gone, *56* ain't goin' to leave me here.[72]

An excellent finger-picker, who is said to have greatly admired Lonnie Johnson's style of playing, Gibson made his base in Johnson's home town of St. Louis. No mere imitator, however, he also featured many unusual lyrics in his songs.

Both Jefferson and Gibson can claim confidently that their audiences 'know what I'm talkin' about' — a key factor in the strength of the blues. Similarly, on his 'Hurry Down Sunshine' [Vocalion 02741] Leroy Carr could include a poetic line inspired by the particular duration of a locomotive's whistle or bell. There were many 'calls' for different operations on the railroad and these were universally recognised by all the companies in the US. Two long whistles indicated that the engineer was about to release the train brakes and slowly haul the train out of the station. Carr's myriad of fans would all have known this was the moment of parting and many would surely have empathised with his words:

> Now, I never got worried until the fireman rang his bell. *(x2)*
> Two keen long whistles bid me long farewell.[73]

If it was true of smaller rural depots in the South that they facilitated the oral transmission of the different songs and styles within the blues, then

---

[*] A drayman would do short journeys with a two- or four-wheel pony and trap — or later on, a small truck. Main business was to and from train stations in the 1920s.

how much greater was the influence of the Union Stations in the cities? Massive centres of railroad exchange such as the ones in Chicago or St. Louis, and only slightly lesser ones in Memphis, Birmingham and Atlanta, witnessed the comings and goings of dozens of railroads that fanned out all over the United States. Inevitably, the 'Union Station' crops up in blues by various singers such as Bukka White and Red Nelson. Sometimes, a city would name this large building of social, civic and architectural importance the 'Terminal', as was the case with Cincinnati and Atlanta. The Atlanta Terminal (opened in 1905) makes an appearance on Barbecue Bob's 'She's Gone Blues' [Columbia 14461-D], underscored by a pounding twelve-string rhythm and bittersweet bottleneck fills:

> I was standin' at the Terminal, arms folded up an' cryin'. *(x2)*
> Cryin': 'I wonder what train takin' that brown of mine?' [74]

With as many as thirty tracks or 'stubs' at the end of the line, it is hardly surprising that Bob didn't know which train his lover took out of Atlanta. Where they did know, of course, blues singers often berated a particular railroad — for example Walter Davis' attack on the *Sunnyland* (and, by implication, the Frisco, over whose lines it ran) in 'Railroad Man Blues' [Victor 23291], Leroy Carr's 'Big Four Blues' [Vocalion 03349] and Peetie Wheatstraw's 'C and A Blues' [Vocalion 1672].

In many cases, the *'fastest train that goes'* was the fast mail or evening mail, and, if the train was a symbol of a chance for escape, hope and freedom, then the depot was often the place where you could grab that chance. It is not surprising therefore that Robert Johnson was carrying on a traditional attitude that had started in 1875 with the *Fast Mail*, continuing with Sippie Wallace carrying her suitcase down to Ma Rainey's depot to catch Robert Wilkins' train with Blind Lemon's red and blue lights on behind. The very image of the singer moving rapidly towards the depot and seeing a tiny white wisp of smoke etched against a leaden Mississippi sky, denoting the approach of the fastest train on the line, surely evokes the pinnacle of the black concept of freedom itself — never to more telling effect than when Johnson uttered those immortal words: *'Runnin' down to the station, catch the fast mail train I see.'*

Notes to Chapter 7

1	Harlow, A.F.	*Old Post Bags*, p.310
2	Bowman, H.W.	p.87
3	Farrington, S.K.	pp.49-50
4	Harlow, A.F.	*The Road Of The Century*, pp.294-5

5	Hungerford, E.	p.263
6	Long, B.A., & W.J. Dennis	p.124
7	Holbrook, S.H.	Ibid, p.314
8	Jameson, R.D.	p.456
9	'Billy Goat Blues'	John Byrd - vocal, guitar (c.March 1930, Grafton, Wis.)
10	Cohen, N.	Ibid, p.291
11	Ibid.	p.275
12	Ibid.	p.291
13	Jameson	Ibid, pp.456-7
14	Byrd	Ibid.
15	Trelease, A.W.	p.77
16	De Bow, J.D.B.	p.137 (Volume 2)
17	White	*The American Railroad Freight Car*, ibid, p.82
18	Kirkland, F.	p.365
19	Doster, J.F.	p.7
20	Holbrook	Ibid, p.67
21	Herr, K.A.	Ibid, p.193
22	Calt, S., & J. Miller.	Notes to Yazoo L-1040 (LP)
23	Long & Dennis	Ibid, p.125
24	Cline, W.	Ibid, p.256
25	Ibid.	
26	'Waitin' For The Evenin' Mail'	Clara Smith - vocal, humming; Fletcher Henderson - piano (1 October 1923, New York City)
27	Long & Dennis	Ibid, p.91
28	'How Long Daddy, How Long'	Ida Cox - vocal; Papa Charlie Jackson - banjo (September 1925, Chicago, Ill.)
29	'The Mail Train Blues'	Sippie Wallace - vocal; Louis Armstrong - cornet; Hersal Thomas - piano (3 March 1926, Chicago, Ill.)
30	'Booster Blues'	Blind Lemon Jefferson - vocal, guitar (c.March 1926, Chicago, Ill.)
31	'Gone Dead On You Blues'	Blind Lemon Jefferson - vocal, guitar (c.October 1927, Chicago, Ill.)
32	Cowley, J.H.	Notes to Document DOCD-5324 (CD)
33	'Long Distance Blues'	Ida Cox - vocal; acc. Lovie Austin & Her Serenaders: Bob Shoffner - cornet; Jimmy O'Bryant - clarinet; Lovie Austin - piano (August 1925, Chicago, Ill.)
34	van Rijn, G., & co.	Notes to Agram AB-2012 (LP)
35	Botkin, B.A. (Ed.)	pp.302-3
36	'Shorty George'	James 'Iron Head' Baker - vocal; unacc. (Library of Congress recording, 21 May 1934, Central State Farm, Sugar Land, Tex.)

37 Ibid.
38 Prince, R.E. p.181
39 Ibid. p.182
40 'Coast Line Blues' Tallahassee Tight - vocal, guitar (18 January 1934, New York City)
41 'Ramblin' On My Mind' Robert Johnson - vocal, guitar; speech (23 November 1936, San Antonio, Tex.)
42 'Down South Blues' Rosa Henderson - vocal; Fletcher Henderson - piano (c.28 June 1923, New York City)
43 'Chicago Blues' Luella Miller - vocal; 'Mr. Jimmy' - piano; poss. Al Miller - mandolin; unk. violin (1 August 1928, Chicago, Ill.)
44 'Station Time Blues' Tampa Red 'The Guitar Wizard' - vocal, guitar (c.28 January 1930, Chicago, Ill.)
45 'Railroad Man Blues' Walter Davis - vocal; Roosevelt Sykes (as 'Willie Kelly') - piano; prob. Henry Townsend - guitar (10 June 1931, Louisville, Ky.)
46 W.P.A. Ibid, p.394
47 Gates, P.W. p.122
48 Ibid. p.124
49 Stilgoe, J.R. pp.212 and 214
50 Ibid. p.214
51 'Polock Blues' Jabo Williams - vocal, piano (c.May 1932, Grafton, Wis.)
52 Partridge, E. *A Dictionary of the Underworld*, ibid, pp.522-3
53 'Love In Vain Blues' Robert Johnson - vocal, guitar (20 June 1937, Dallas, Tex.)
54 'Dry Southern Blues' Blind Lemon Jefferson - vocal, guitar (c.March 1926, Chicago, Ill.)
55 Webster, G. p.?
56 Loree, L.F. Ibid, p.499
57 'Suitcase Blues' Sippie Wallace - vocal; Clarence Williams - piano; Buddy Christian - banjo; unk. clarinet (c.25 August 1925, New York City)
58 'Rolling Stone (Part 1)' Robert Wilkins - vocal, guitar (7 September 1928, Memphis, Tenn.)
59 'The Train Is Coming' Roosevelt Sykes - vocal, piano; unk. drums (31 March 1938, New York City)
60 'Barrel House Blues' Rosa Henderson - vocal; Fletcher Henderson - piano (24 May 1924, New York City)
61 'Streamline Train' Red Nelson - vocal; Cripple Clarence Lofton - piano (4 February 1936, Chicago, Ill.)

62	'Ticket Agent Blues'	Noah Lewis' Jug Band: Noah Lewis - vocal, harmonica, speech; Sleepy John Estes - guitar; Yank Rachell - mandolin, speech; Ham Lewis - jug (26 November 1930, Memphis, Tenn.)
63	'Traveling Blues'	Ma Rainey - vocal; acc. Her Tub Jug Washboard Band: Georgia Tom - piano; Martell Pettiford - banjo; Herman Brown - kazoo, washboard; Carl Reid - jazzhorn, jug (12 June 1928, Chicago, Ill.)
64	Partridge, E.	*Penguin Dictionary of Historical Slang*, ibid, p.491
65	Lieb, S.	p.46
66	'River Bottom Blues'	Mississippi Sheiks: Walter Vinson - vocal, guitar; prob. Lonnie Chatmon - violin; Bo Carter (*aka* Chatmon) – guitar (12 June 1930, San Antonio, Tex.)
67	Loree	Ibid, p.?
68	'Wartime Blues'	Blind Lemon Jefferson - vocal, guitar (c.November 1926, Chicago, Ill.)
69	Loree	Ibid, p.10
70	'Rambler Blues'	Blind Lemon Jefferson - vocal, guitar (c.September 1927, Chicago, Ill.)
71	'Black Horse Blues'	Blind Lemon Jefferson - vocal, guitar) (c.April 1926, Chicago, Ill.)
72	'Drayman Blues'	Clifford Gibson - vocal, guitar (26 November 1929, New York City)
73	'Hurry Down Sunshine'	Leroy Carr - vocal, piano; Scrapper Blackwell - guitar (20 February 1934, St. Louis, Mo.)
74	'She's Gone Blues'	Barbecue Bob - vocal, guitar (26 October 1928, Atlanta, Ga.)

Discography – Chapter 7

'Barrel House Blues' (Rosa Henderson)
CD: *Rosa Henderson – Volume 2 (1924)* [Document DOCD-5402] 1995

'Billy Goat Blues' (John Byrd)
CD: *Rare Country Blues – Vol. 2 (1929-43)* [Document DOCD-5641] 1999

'Black Horse Blues' (Blind Lemon Jefferson)
4-CD: *Blind Lemon Jefferson – All The Classic Sides* [J.S.P. JSP-7706] 2003

'Booster Blues' (Blind Lemon Jefferson)
4-CD: *Blind Lemon Jefferson – All The Classic Sides* [J.S.P. JSP-7706] 2003

'Chicago Blues' (Luella Miller)
CD: *Luella Miller with Lonnie Johnson (1926-28)* [Document DOCD-5183] 1993

'Coast Line Blues' — CD: *East Coast Blues & Gospel (1933-34)*
(Tallahassee Tight) [Document DOCD-5387] 1995

'Down South Blues' — CD: *Rosa Henderson – Volume 1 (1923)*
(Rose Henderson) [Document DOCD-5401] 1995

'Drayman Blues' — CD: *Clifford Gibson (1929-31)*
(Clifford Gibson) [Blues Document BDCD-6015] 1991

'Gone Dead On You Blues' — 4-CD: *Blind Lemon Jefferson – All The*
(Blind Lemon Jefferson) *Classic Sides* [J.S.P. JSP-7706] 2003

'How Long Daddy, How Long' — CD: *Ida Cox – Vol. 3 (Apr. 1925–c.July 1927)*
(Ida Cox) [Document DOCD-5324] 1995

'Hurry Down Sunshine' — CD: *Leroy Carr – Volume 4 (1932-34)*
(Leroy Carr) [Document DOCD-5137] 1993

'Long Distance Blues' — CD: *Ida Cox – Vol. 3 (Apr. 1925–c.July 1927)*
(Ida Cox) [Document DOCD-5324] 1995

'Love In Vain' — CD: *Robert Johnson – King Of The Delta Blues*
(Robert Johnson) *Singers (Vol. 2)* [Columbia CK-92579] 2004

'The Mail Train Blues' — CD: *Sippie Wallace – Volume 2 (1925-45)*
(Sippie Wallace) [Document DOCD-5400] 1995

'Polock Blues' — CD: *Boogie Woogie & Barrelhouse Piano*
(Jabo Williams) *(1928-32)* [Document DOCD-5102] 1992

'Railroad Man Blues' — CD: *Walter Davis – First Recordings*
(Walter Davis) *(1930-32)* [J.S.P. JSP-605] 2003

'Rambler Blues' — 4-CD: *Blind Lemon Jefferson – All The*
(Blind Lemon Jefferson) *Classic Sides* [J.S.P. JSP-7706] 2003

'Ramblin' On My Mind' — CD: *Robert Johnson – King Of The Delta*
(Robert Johnson) *Blues Singers* [Columbia CK-52944] 2004

'River Bottom Blues' — CD: *Mississippi Sheiks – Volume 1 (1930)*
(Mississippi Sheiks) [Document DOCD-5083] 1991

'Rolling Stone (Part 1)' — 4-CD: *Masters Of Memphis Blues (1927-39)*
(Robert Wilkins) [J.S.P. JSP-7725] 2004

'She's Gone Blues' — CD: *Barbecue Bob – Volume 2 (1928-29)*
(Barbecue Bob) [Document DOCD-5047] 1991

'Shorty George' — CD: *Field Recordings – Volume 6: Texas*
(James 'Iron Head' Baker) *(1933-58)* [Document DOCD-5580] 1997

'Station Time Blues' — CD: *Tampa Red – Volume 3 (1929-30)*
(Tampa Red) [Document DOCD-5075] 1991

'Streamline Train'
(Cripple Clarence Lofton)

CD: *Cripple Clarence Lofton – Vol. 1 (1935-36)* [Blues Document BDCD-6006] 1991

'Suitcase Blues'
(Sippie Wallace)

CD: *Sippie Wallace – Volume 2 (1925-45)* [Document DOCD-5400] 1995

'Ticket Agent Blues'
(Noah Lewis)

2-CD: *Sleepy John Estes – Gus Cannon (1928-30)* [J.S.P. JSP-3406] 2002

'The Train Is Coming'
(Roosevelt Sykes)

CD: *Roosevelt Sykes – Volume 5 (1937-39)* [Document DOCD-5120] 1992

Train whistle
[Side 2, Track 6, second part]

LP: *Whistling Through Dixie* [Argo Transacord DA-23] 1960
This LP is now hard to find, but readers may be able to pick up a copy via one of the many Internet auction sites. Try Robert Humm & Co. (**www.roberthumm.co.uk**) in the first instance. They specialize in worldwide railroadiana which includes recordings — this is the source of my own copy. To the best of my knowledge, this album has not been reissued on CD.

'Traveling Blues'
(Ma Rainey)

CD: *Ma Rainey – Volume 5 (1928)* [Document DOCD-5156] 1993

'Waitin' For The Evenin' Mail'
(Clara Smith)

CD: *Clara Smith – Volume 1 (1923-24)* [Document DOCD-5364] 1995

'Wartime Blues'
(Blind Lemon Jefferson)

4-CD: *Blind Lemon Jefferson – All The Classic Sides* [J.S.P. JSP-7706] 2003

I carried water for the elephant

'Carried Water For The Elephant' – Leroy Carr (1930)

CHAPTER 8

CIRCUSES, CARNIVALS, EXCURSIONS, ETC. AND ORAL TRANSMISSION

While running down to the station to *'catch the fastest train I see'* was an absolute symbol of freedom as viewed by countless black citizens in the 1920s and '30s, reality entered the picture when a 'travelin' man/woman' got hungry. Some source of money had to be found while still feeling 'free'. One answer was the travelling show, which started with the circus and later included the carnival. Many blues singers cut their teeth working in these phenomena, as well as in minstrel and medicine shows. Generally speaking, these modes of entertainment travelled by railroad, certainly from the 1880s until the early 1930s.

What is more, these types of travelling shows proved to be ideal vehicles for the oral transmission process in both the early and proto-blues forms. While the minstrelsy era is usually dated from circa 1830 and the appearance of Thomas Rice (a white songwriter/minstrel performer) and his hit 'Jump Jim Crow'[*], both the circus and the medicine show predated

---

[*] According to Harrison & Klotter: 'In 1828, comedian Thomas D. Rice was appearing at Drake's Theatre in Louisville when he chanced to see an elderly, crippled black man, who worked at Crow's livery stable, singing an improvised song. Each verse ended with *'Jump Jim Crow'* and a comic dance step.' The authors go on to say: 'Rice's role in *The Rifle* was that of a "Kentucky Cornfield Negro" and he added a song and dance called 'Jump Jim Crow' that stopped the show for encore after encore. Soon a nationally popular song, at the time it had nothing to do with segregation.'[1]

minstrelsy by several decades. The carnival, a relative newcomer, did not take off in a big way until after 1900. As minstrel and medicine shows have already been extensively covered by writers of the blues — Sam Charters, Paul Oliver, Harold Courlander and Sandra Lieb among them — I intend to concentrate on the circus and the carnival.

This oral transmission process or tradition was to owe much to the contribution by the Native Americans who started the medicine shows in the late Eighteenth Century. Within forty years, 'over 80 Indian brands were on the market, 1840-1920, and the white 'Indian' or herb doctor was a familiar figure to most Americans in that period... An Indian or someone dressed as an Indian played the drum, danced, appeared in colorful costume and performed feats to illustrate his health and strength. At first based on Indian performance alone, the shows later added other popular entertainments.' [2] The latter, of course, included African Americans and the blues singers. They were to largely replace the Indian drummer/dancer in attracting a crowd, to whom the 'doctor' would attempt to sell his wares. The role of the blues singer as an 'advertiser' would be mirrored in the circus and carnival, as we shall see.

Charles Wilson relates that 'the first recorded appearance of the circus in America was in 1791. Early circuses were city shows, and the predominantly rural South had less exposure than the North to circuses in the antebellum era, although circuses did appear along the lower Mississippi River in the 1820s.' [3] Indeed, in the next decade, freedman and barber William Johnson of Natchez, Miss. noted in his diaries (1835-51) an increasing popularity of the circuses in his home town. Amongst several references the most interesting (from a musical perspective) is one made by him on 21 December 1835. This was five days after his first mention of a circus in Natchez, which the editors think 'probably referred to Brown & Company's New Orleans Circus.' [4]

Just four days before Christmas, William Johnson and his closest friend, Robert McCary ('Mc'), 'went to the Circus to hear the song of Billy Barlow.' [5] McCary was 'a free mulatto' and a fellow barbershop owner in Natchez. An advertisement for 'De Kickapoo Whoop' by a blackface artist — one 'Santaclaus' — lists other popular songs of the day (ie circa 1840) on each side of the main ad. These included a well-known sea shanty, 'Shin Bone Alley', and a song entitled 'Billy Barlow' — although the latter, according to Johnson, had already been popular some five years earlier. Of course, this popularity might have been only in the South at that time, and spread northwards (and across the Atlantic?) later on. But Johnson's reference does highlight the importance of the circus in the South as a broadcaster of a kind-of early Nineteenth Century 'Hot 100', where both black and white citizens could go and hear the latest popular tunes. As Towsen observes: 'Before the age of radio and the phonograph, it was the circus clown who popularized such standard tunes as 'Root Hog Or Die',

'Turkey In The Straw', 'Whoa Emma', 'The Man On The Flying Trapeze' and 'Down In A Coal Mine'. Many of the best clown vocalists achieved national fame on the basis of their skills.' [6] At least two of these titles — 'Turkey In The Straw' and 'Root Hog Or Die' — reappeared in the blues under various guises, including Peg Leg Howell's 'Turkey Buzzard Blues' [Columbia 14382-D], Stovepipe No. 1's 'Turkey In The Straw' [Columbia 201-D] and the Harlem Hamfats' 'Root Hog Or Die' [Decca 7439].

Without any further evidence in the early Twenty-First Century, we can only surmise that 'Billy Barlow' was probably cast in a minstrelsy mould and could well have been sung, in 1835, by a white performer in blackface[*]. 'For most of the Nineteenth Century, the circus and minstrel show strongly influenced and enriched one another. Black entertainers had performed in public well before the Revolutionary War, and white entertainers wearing black make-up date back at least to 1769.' [9] Indeed, from the 1840s until the end of the Civil War, 'the minstrel show *[as]* a variety entertainment... rivaled the circus in popularity.' [10]

Theatre ad, c.early 1840s.

---

[*] Certainly, a performance of 'Billy Barlow' by white singer Don Gait in Clifton, Ark. in 1967 would suggest this early minstrelsy scenario. It appears that the song also travelled to the UK and Australia. Many versions exist from the later Nineteenth Century, and the ones I have seen written down would place Billy Barlow in a 'poor man's hero' setting, with some of the seeming invincibility of the black 'travelin' man' who appears a little later in this chapter.

Partridge gives a definition of 'Billy Barlow', describing him as 'a street clown, a mountebank: from ca. 1840. Ex an actual character, the hero of a slang song. Such a clown is also called a Jim Crow.' [7] According to an earlier dictionary, the name derives from an actual character from the Nineteenth Century who was 'well known in the East of London, and died in Whitechapel workhouse.' Apparently he was 'a street droll, a merry Andrew, a half-idiot *[and]* some of his sayings were really witty, and some of his attitudes really droll.' [8]

241

We have already noted that, on 6 December 1836, William Johnson had made reference to 'Brown's Circus' in his diary. On 23 November 1837, he describes the coming of another circus to Natchez: 'Today the Grand Carravan of Animals arrived in town, the Musicians was on the back of the Elephant as they past through the Streets' *[sic]*, while a footnote tells us that 'the Waring, Raymond & Company Circus carried a museum as well as a menagerie.' [11] There is again no intimation as to what music might have been played, or indeed whether the musicians were black or white. But it does illustrate the fact that music and song were an integral part of circuses and travelling shows, even in the early Nineteenth Century.

The celebrated blues singer/pianist, Leroy Carr recalled the menagerie, circus and the elephant over ninety years later on his 'Carried Water For The Elephant' [Vocalion 1593], where he relates how he visits the circus that's just arrived in town but cannot afford a ticket for the show. He eventually gets to see the menagerie after carrying out the task mentioned in the title, and goes on to list several animals, which are given 'jokey' imitations (presumably by his long-time accompanist, Scrapper Blackwell).

Although Towsen claims that 'menageries featuring exotic animals' did not become 'part of the circus until the 1840s', William Johnson's diary entry in 1837 indicates an earlier vintage: 'By 1800 the circus was fairly well established in American cities *[and]* with the introduction of the canvas tent in the 1820s, the opening of new roads, and the eventual possibility of travel by rail or steamboat, the circus soon began to reach out into more remote areas.' [12] The coming of the railroads speeded up the oral transmission process from city to country and back again. As early as 1853, 'experiments were carried on with railroads *[and circuses]*... but Dan Costello's Circus & Menagerie became the first railroad circus to make a transcontinental tour in 1868.' [13] In the 1850s, in the state of North Carolina, 'historians of Raleigh, Salisbury and Charlotte noted the arrival of ready-made clothing, expensive furniture, Parisian fashions, fancy groceries, and other consumer goods in the wake of the railroad. Raleigh soon boasted a soda fountain, as well as the visit of a travelling circus and menagerie.' [14] Raleigh's early circus might well have been Spalding & Rogers' Circus, which had been travelling by rail as far back as 1855.

By 1841, circuses were regularly arriving in Natchez in the spring. William Johnson makes reference to them on 3 April. He also mentions them later in the year, on 27 September, and 4 and 5 October. Even the ongoing effects of the financial 'panic' of 1837 could not put the brakes on this entertainment phenomenon's popularity. On 4 October Johnson confirms 'the Circus is agoing On in full blast, they are having Good Houses not withstanding money is so scarce.' [15] *[sic]* On the following day, the crowd included three of Johnson's slaves, to whom he had issued passes. So, slaves and freedmen were exposed to a variety of songs and music from other regions of the South (and North) as early as 1835, long before the advent of the phonograph and the first blues record — even in the heart of Mississippi, which is often acknowledged as the cradle of the blues. Johnson also mentions circus visits (including that of 'Spalding') in November 1847, and twice in December 1850 — shortly before his murder by a white assassin over a land-border dispute the following year.

Around this time, Spalding & Rogers were also packing them in down in Alabama: 'When Spalding & Rogers' Circus performed in Mobile in 1850, the *Mobile Tribune* estimated that more people attended than on any other like occasion.' [16] Some two years later, the Mobile & Ohio Railroad had 33 miles of track operating out of the Alabama seaport, and Spalding & Rogers would utilise this railroad in the ensuing years. Indeed, Gilbert Spalding and Charles Rogers were soon to incorporate the legend *'The Railroad Circus'* as a subtitle for their shows.[17] Mobile, already a rich receptacle for the oral transmission process (or, as Hugill referred to it, and the Gulf Ports generally, 'a shanty mart or work-song exchange' [18]) would be further enhanced in this role with the expansion of roads such as the M&O, L&N and the Southern.

During the Civil War (1861-65), circuses obviously became seriously curtailed in their movements or else didn't travel at all. After the war, however, 'musical interaction remained important... in railroad crews, in coal camps, and traveling circuses and medicine shows.'[19] The earliest reference to a specific circus train that I know of, relates to an accident in North Carolina — although this was only a minor company which would have hired a small number of cars (probably two) attached to a passenger train — on the North Carolina RR in this instance: 'Special trains were sources of danger. In October 1868, prior to the November election, a special train *[which]* had just distributed details of soldiers to polling places in the Charlotte area collided head-on with a passenger train carrying Maginley & Carrol's Circus.' [20]

However, the following references to Kentucky in 1864 may refer to an even earlier circus train. While escorting 'refugees' (otherwise contraband or freedmen) from Lexington to Camp Nelson, some eight miles south of Nicholasville, Ky., black soldiers in the US Army found much time on their hands. Apart from opportunities offered by the military camp 'to improve their minds, bodies, and occasionally their pocketbooks', apparently 'soldiers could also make extra money in their spare time. When passing through Nicholasville, the men... earned a few dollars by guarding a circus.' [21]

The latter may have travelled by a branch of the Bardstown & Louisville Railroad to Nicholasville 'where the tracks ended.' [22] This railroad had already been acquired by the L&N (the 'Old Reliable') some four years earlier. Around this time, a General Palmer 'had been attending a circus in Louisville' [23], which was probably the same outfit. Indeed, there is a distinct

Chapter 8 — I carried water for the elephant

Teets Bros Car No. 5.
The legend on the side reads: 'OLD RELIABLE – ORGANIZED 1835'.

possibility that the latter was part of the Teets Bros.' Palmetto Shows running on L&N lines, 'a trick that played crossroads and junction towns in Kentucky and Tennessee for nearly fifty years (but not sixty-five[*]).' [24]

A 'crossroads' was generally little more than a country store at a road junction. 'Junction towns' were those settlements where a branch of a particular railroad met the main line. For example, in her 'Leavin' Gal Blues' [Paramount 12697], Bertha Henderson sings:

> Get my ticket at the junction an' flag the 'fore day train[**]. *(x2)*
> I'm goin' [to] leave this country before I go insane.[25]

In the closing verse, Henderson adds that her epitaph should read that she died *'of the leaving **here** blues'* which, considering the racist conditions of the South in the 1920s, is probably the song's correct title.

But the spread of songs across the South at this time did not rely

---

[*] The bracketed text alludes to the fact that the authors were not convinced that this one-car outfit had been going as long as since 1835. Although the photograph was taken around 1900, the circus was probably around as early as 1850, when the L&N was first inaugurated. The 'Palmetto' part of the title is a nickname for the state of South Carolina, which might be an indication of its base and/or origins.

[**] Some small towns were deemed not to warrant the privilege of a train service unless the depot agent requested the train to stop by waving a flag at the approaching train, whose engineer would blow the whistle to announce its imminent arrival — hence a 'flag stop' or 'whistle stop'.

wholly upon singers travelling the 'lonesome rail'. It must be borne in mind that early individual roads were not built with an overview of a later 'joined-up system'. For, even though thousands of miles had been built by the end of the Civil War, as Stover noted: 'the existing rail network in 1865 was certainly not integrated or really very efficient. The lack of physical rail connections in several cities and the absence of bridges at wide rivers kept the system from being a complete network. The diversity of gauge, especially in the South, also made impossible the cross-country shipment of freight without break of bulk. Manual braking and coupling of the cars made railroad operations both dangerous and slow.' [26] With the spread of automatic braking (air brakes), the adoption of 4'8½" as standard gauge, and the streamlining of the myriad of local 'sun times' into the current five time zones[*], the 1880s became the real period of expansion for Southern railroads. Stover points out that 'in the Eighties, Southern states built *[railroads]* much more rapidly than the nation as a whole.' [27]

It would appear, however, that circuses took to the rails in earnest somewhat earlier than this — certainly by 1872.[**] This was also the case with the 'first' blues singers, and a little later on, the female vaudeville performers from around the beginning of the Twentieth Century, who came to dominate the first five years of recorded blues (1920-25). These early singers played an important part in the oral transmission process via the circus and other travelling shows.

Although a popular 'floating verse' in the blues runs:

When a woman gets the blues, she hangs her head and cry. *(x2)*
When a man gets the blues, he flags a train and ride.

this did not apply to many of the vaudeville women. Apart from being featured on the TOBA[***] circuit, they also appeared in numerous tent shows as an adjunct to the circus proper. Most of the time, these shows travelled by rail — certainly in the first three decades of the Twentieth Century. Probably the most common were the two-car shows, which also carried the tent or 'big top'. 'The two-car format was so popular that printers of stock advertising materials offered showmen such art as this' *(see over)*.

This promotional artwork 'could also be used... by such other two-car

---

[*] Strictly speaking, there were only four in the 1880s: Eastern, Central, Mountain and Pacific. The fifth, Alaska time, only appeared in 1959 when that state became the 49th to join the Union.

[**] See *Trains Of The Circus (1872-1956)* by Fred Dahlinger Jr. (Iconografix. Hudson, Wis., 2000), especially *Introduction* (p.6). Some photos from this work have been included in this book, which must stand as the definitive pictorial history of the circus train in the USA.

[***] The initials stood for 'Theater Owner's Booking Association', which ran shows all over the Southern states. Because of the often grim and spartan travelling/living conditions resulting from racial discrimination in hotels/rooming houses, and irregularity of wages on occasion, this company was generally referred to as 'Tough On Black Asses' by the blues singers.

enterprises as Uncle Tom's Cabin shows, minstrel shows *[and]* tent theatres.' [28] The authors also note that the cars are 'luckily numbered'. This refers to the '7' and '11' adorning the sides of the two cars shown. In the world of the blues, a popular gambling game using dice known as 'crap(s)' counted 7 and 11 as the best winning scores.*

Also, many of these women travelled by train to reach the Northern recording studios of Paramount, Columbia, etc. One of these was Clara Smith, born circa 1894 in Spartanburg, S.C., who already had extensive travelling/tent show experience behind her belt prior to her Columbia recording debut in 1923. As one of the 'big four' vaudeville-blues divas (along with Ma Rainey, Ida Cox and Bessie Smith (no relation)), Clara Smith featured railroads in her songs more than most of her contemporaries: 'Freight Train Blues' [Columbia 14041-D], Death Letter Blues' [Columbia 14045-D], 'San Francisco Blues' [Columbia 14049-D], 'The L&N Blues' [Columbia 14073-D] and 'My John Blues' [Columbia 14077-D] in 1924 and 1925, for example. On her 'Steel Drivin' Sam' [Columbia 14053-D], she boasts about her lover who is a lusty railroad man from *'Bam'* (otherwise Alabama), working for the Southern Railway:

---

* Players of crap(s) were usually known as 'crapshooters'. Waring observes that 'it is interesting to discover that the term 'crap shooting' actually developed from the French. Apparently, small boys wishing to play dice but discouraged from doing so by their parents, would crouch out of sight in the attitude of toads and their activity was given the name 'crapaud', the French word for toad. In America the term was shortened to 'crap'.[29]

He's six feet tall, an' he's big an' 'e's broad,
But 'e's just like a lamb 'round his mama, Lord.

Refrain: Steel-drivin' Sam, steel-drivin' man o' mine.
   He works on the railroad, makin' that railroad time.

There ain't nobody that lives in 'Bam
Who can make a hammer ring like my man Sam.

Refrain: Steel-drivin' Sam, steel-drivin' man o' mine.
   He works on the railroad, makin' them white folks' time.

Having taken a swipe at the fact that all the railroad companies were white-owned, Ms. Smith then pokes gentle fun at her saxophonist, Ernest Elliott, who she obviously thinks has a soft time of it as a horn-blower, compared to her 'steel-drivin' man'... or perhaps she was simply chastising him for not playing a 'harder', more blues-oriented accompaniment:

He swings a mean hammer, just as sure as you are born,
'Cos he can't drive steel with a doggone horn.

Refrain: Steel-drivin' Sam, steel-drivin' man o' mine.
   He works on the railroad on that old Southern line.

Although illiterate, like many rural blacks in the 1920s, Sam nevertheless seems to give Clara satisfaction:

He wouldn't know his name printed on a wall,
An' box car letters that's as long as he is tall.

Refrain: But steel-drivin' Sam, steel-drivin' man o' mine.
   He works on the railroad. Still, I'm feelin' fine.
   Steel-drivin' Sam, steel-drivin' man of mine.[30]

On 'The L&N Blues' however, she adopts the black (usually male) persona who has 'got the travelin' blues', stating:

If I ain't ridin', I ain't satisfied.[31]

Until the year prior to this recording, 1924, the railroad she would have travelled on back to Spartanburg would have been the Charleston, Cincinnati & Chicago. However, after another merger, this became the Clinchfield Railroad 'on January 1, 1925 *[and]* was leased jointly to the Louisville & Nashville and the Atlantic Coast Line'. So, Clara Smith was bang up to date with her 'L&N Blues'. Hubbard informs us that the Clinchfield Railroad was a line 'running north and south for 277 miles in five states between Elkhorn City, Ky. and Spartanburg, S.C.'. [32]

In her recorded legacy (1923-32), Ms. Smith makes at least two references to exotic animals which might indicate an actual experience with the circus, as well as the tent shows. For instance, on 1924's 'Done Sold My Soul To The Devil' [Columbia 14041-D] she includes the following lines:

> I live down in the valley, right by a hornet's nest
> Where lions, bears an' tigers all come an' take their rest.
>
> *Refrain:* I done sold my soul to, sold it to the Devil,
> An' my heart done turned to stone. [33]

thereby evoking a popular folk belief amongst Southern blacks in the 1920s and '30s.

Wild beasts, such as lions, and the travelling circus, seemed to have impressed black singers more than somewhat. For instance, in 1937, Merline Johnson recorded 'He Roars Like A Lion' [Bluebird B-6985], and there is another intriguing title from August 1927, 'They Wanted A Man To Lead The Lions Around' by Joe Evans and Arthur McClain, who sometimes recorded as the Two Poor Boys. This Gennett recording unfortunately remains unissued.

On 12 November 1903 a white rice planter, Elizabeth Allston (under the pen-name of 'Patience Pennington') wrote in her diary about the visit of a circus to her local town of 'Peaceville', S.C.. The latter place name was also most likely a fictitious one, but it represents a location in the Georgetown and Charleston area. The circus apparently 'put up three big tents... right in front of the post office.' [34] Allston lived on her rice plantation with her black employees and their families 'two miles from any white person'! She taught some of the children rudimentary lessons on the plantation, but on this particular November day, only three turned up: 'All the others have gone to hear the lion roar, and to see if they could get a peep at him,' explained one of the trio. All three honestly admitted 'in chorus', that 'we didn't want to come – mamma made us; we wanted to hear the lion roar, too.' [35]

The vociferous 'King of the Jungle' was certainly one of the top attractions of any circus, and Elzadie Robinson employed this powerful motif in her graphic and very moving account of an approaching tornado or 'twister' on her 1927 recording, 'St. Louis Cyclone Blues' [Paramount 12573]:

The wind was howling, the buildings begin to fall.
Mmmmm, the wind was howling, the buildings begin to fall.
I see that mean old twister comin' just like a cannon ball.

World was black as midnight, I never heard such a noise before.
(Spoken) Oh, Lord!
Like a million lions if turned loose they all roar.[36]

Allston goes on to record that, on the following day (the 'grand day'), 'there were two exhibitions, one at 1 o'clock and at 8 pm. The two stores were shut for the day, and business suspended while the village gave itself up to dissipation.'[37] An event such as a circus or medicine show provided welcome relief from the monotony of agricultural life in the rural South of the early Twentieth Century. As Allston observed: 'Altogether for many days joy will reign in the memory of these delights.'[38] And interestingly: 'There were great crowds of darkies coming from miles around and only about thirty white people all together. Yet they had the seats arranged on different sides* so that all were satisfied.'[39] Many of the 'darkies' would have used the railroad at Georgetown, S.C. as part of their journey to 'Peaceville' to see this circus, which is referred to by Allston as 'the Shelby show'. Indeed, the circus itself undoubtedly travelled this road, which most likely would have been the South Carolina RR.

Apart from the roaring lions, the 'Shelby show' also included acrobats and 'a very stout lady' who had a big snake. While the popularity of lions amongst blues singers is not apparently obvious, there is no denying the sexual symbolism of the snake and its familiarity to many Southern blacks. Harrison not only relates that singers such as Alberta Hunter 'washed dishes in a whorehouse when she arrived in Chicago at age twelve *[and]* Lizzie Miles was a barmaid in New Orleans', but that Sippie Wallace 'was a maid for a snakedancer in Texas'[40] — a job also once performed by Clara Smith perhaps. Smith, from South Carolina, sang of the circus and a snake charmer, on her sultry 'Daddy Don't Put That Thing On Me Blues' [Columbia 14398-D] in 1929, possibly recalling a previous experience as a young teenager:

I'm goin' down to the circus to see that snake-charmin' man.
The man that's got that big black thing wrapped around 'is hand.
When I bin in there, I'll deliver this plea:
Mr. Snake-charmin' Papa, have mercy on me.
Here's what I'll say before the undertakers haul me away:

---

* This was a reference to the Jim Crow laws of segregation, then at its height in the South. By quoting the contrasting numbers of the two races present, 'Pennington' may have been wishing to point out the absurdity of racialism, constituting an implied protest.

> *Refrain:* Oh! Daddy, don't you put that thing on me.
> I don't like it very much.
> Daddy, don't you put that thing on me.
> I simply can't stand its touch.
> Don't like the way it looks, especial[ly] its head.
> If you put it on me papa, you will kill me dead.
> You hear me screamin', you know what I'm meanin'.
> Don't put that thing on me.

> I have a big handsome papa, called that 'Snake-charmin' King'.
> A man that loves to show folks that big black thing.
> He's just as nice as any man can be
> But he loves to put that thing on childrens like me.
> Here's what I'll say if I should see him start comin' my way:

> *Refrain:* Oh! Don't you dare to put that thing on me.
> Go ahead an' let me be.
> Now, you know very well I can't stand that thing.
> I don't like the way it looks, especial[ly] its twist.
> Hear me screamin', you know what I'm meanin'.
> Don't you dare to put that thing on me.[41]

Jim Jackson, a man some ten years older than Clara Smith, was veteran of the medicine shows as well as circuses. Along with Frank Stokes, he was one of the most popular blues artists based on Beale Street down in Memphis, Tenn.. On 'Long Gone' [Victor V-38517] he draws on two other songs, 'Travelin' Man' (from oral tradition) and 'Long Gone'*, (published by W.C. Handy with words by black writer Chris Smith), and also incorporates a couple of references to the circus — an escaping lion and a one-legged man:

> One day a circus came to town, with beasts I wanted to see.
> [With] a one-legged man by the name of Jones,
>   we went to see the street parade.
> But just as we went to the circus ground, I heard somebody say:
> 'You better be mighty particular, 'cos the lion's done got away.'
> But then I grabbed my hat, for home I fairly flew,
> But when I got there, my one-legged friend says: 'Jim, I'm right 'ere too!'[42]

The theme of both song segments is the fast-moving black trickster/hero who can outrun his white pursuers — like the well-known 'Travelin' Man' recorded by several singers including Luke Jordan, Virgil Childers, Washboard Sam and Jackson himself. In fact, his version was issued on the

---

* For in-depth discussion of these songs, see *Songsters & Saints* by Paul Oliver (pp. 68-70). Ibid.

Chapter 8 — I carried water for the elephant

The Barnum & Bailey Circus unloading flat cars or 'flats' in Lexington, Ky. in 1908. Some of the onlookers include African Americans hoping to get a temporary job.

reverse of 'Long Gone' in 1928.

Many blues singers and songsters had first-hand experience in circuses. These included the aforementioned Frank Stokes, Memphis Minnie, Bumble Bee Slim and Fiddlin' Joe Martin, who all worked for Ringling Brothers; Jesse Fuller with Hagenback-Wallace (taken over by Ringling in 1930); Ma Rainey and Butterbeans & Susie with Tolliver's Circus; and Cow Cow Davenport with Haeg's. These outfits, as well as Barnum & Bailey's (which ran a joint operation with Ringling) and many others, all travelled by rail. As Baker & Kunz rightly point out: 'The train was the only possible means of transportation for the circus, with its heavy equipment and its animals. How else could it transport the "tallest giraffe in captivity", its huge elephants, its cages of lions and tigers, which had to be loaded on dozens of flatcars?' [43] Parkinson & Fox concur: 'It was inevitable; everything that moved went by rail, and the multifacets of show business were no exception.' [44]

Circuses and railroads were necessarily often 'ploughing the same furrow' in their commercial enterprises — certainly until the 1970s. In at least one instance, the railroad was owned by the circus. Running along the East–West Texas 'border', the Eastland Wichita Falls & Gulf Railroad Co. 'was financed by Richard T. Ringling of circus fame.' This company had been 'chartered on December 12, 1918, to construct a road from May in Brown County to Newcastle in Young County, a distance of about 96

Chapter 8 — I carried water for the elephant

Three Southern Pacific 'helpers' about to shunt a 29-car train of the Al G. Barnes Circus up a winding incline at Weed, Ca. in 1924. Was this the train Barbecue Bob had in mind?

miles.' [45] This road, which was completed in 1920, included connections with both the Katy and the TP. The larger circuses also entered into hire agreements with railroads such as the L&N and the C&NW to use a whole train, which usually reached lengthy proportions. 'Ringling Bros. and Barnum & Bailey Circus often advertised *'100 double length steel railroad cars, crammed and jammed with wonders from all corners of the world.'* [46] One such 100-car train belonging to these circuses was hired from the Missouri Pacific in 1927 and ran from Little Rock to Memphis. This could well be another possible source for the *'longest train I see'* group of songs, along with the seemingly endless string of jimmies on the coal trains operating in Pennsylvania and Georgia *(Chapter 6)*.

It was a Georgia singer, Barbecue Bob, who made a rare mention of these long circus trains on his 'California Blues' [Columbia 14573-D] in 1929. According to Bob, *'the longest train I ever rode was 79 coaches long'.*[*] Mo-Pac also moved the Hagenbeck-Wallace Circus with 35 cars from 'Russelville to Conway, Arkansas' in 1932, while back in 1904 the L&N elected to ship 'John Robinson's 10 Big Shows *[on]* 45 cars... *[from]* Jellico, Tenn. to London, Ky.'.[47] The latter became known as *'The Railroad Show'* and played mainly in the South.

Certainly, the circus was as much a part of the early blues singers' environment as the railroad itself. Texas Alexander refers to 'a circus show'

---

[*] Standard passenger trains in the US consisted of coaches at the time, in contrast to the luxury Pullman cars on the crack expresses like the *Panama Limited*. The term 'carriage', a leftover from the stagecoach era, was used for all passenger vehicles on rails in the UK.

on his 'St. Louis Fair Blues' [OKeh 8688] from 1928, and reveals that he himself was part of a travelling show, while on 'Cocaine Blues' [Victor 21076] another early singer, Luke Jordan from Virginia, recounts how members of a circus got into hot water when trying to satisfy their habit in Lynchburg:

> Now, a Barnum an' Bailey circus came to town.
> They had a elephant, lookin' good an' brown.
> They didn't know it's against the law,
> For the monkeys stopped at a five [and ten cent] drug store.
>
> Just around the corner, just a minute too late;
> Another one standin' at the big back gate.
> I'm simply wild about my good cocaine.[48]

Memphis bluesman Furry Lewis likewise evokes some circus imagery on his 'Cannon-Ball Blues' [Victor 23345]:

> They call me 'high-pockets' because I'm long an' tall[*].
> Call me 'high-pockets' because I'm long an' tall.
> My brown yesterday, left on the *Cannon-Ball*.[49]

and his scintillating bottleneck guitar eases chills down your spine as fellow Beale Street denizen Jim Jackson makes another visit to the circus on 'This Ain't No Place For Me' [Victor V-38003], from 1928:

> I went out to the circus just to pass the time away.
> I bought my ticket an' walked right in just like any other old jay.
> A bear got loose in there, right after me he went.
> The only place I had to hide was in the ladies' circus tent.
>
> *Refrain:* I took one look an' then I said:
>   'This ain't no place for me.'
>   I was runnin' everywhere,
>   But what I saw in there;
>   I'd rather face ten grizzly bears.
>   I took one look an' then I said:
>   'This ain't no place for me.'[50]

Though these lyrics seem almost childishly naïve today, they would have brought a smile to the face of many a black citizen down on 'Fourth an' Beale' in the 1920s.

One of the railroads transporting the circus Jim Jackson was singing

---

[*] 'High-pockets' is a poetic reference to the clown on stilts.

about could well have been the Mobile, Jackson & Kansas City line. Eventually becoming part of the GM&N, it featured in his 'Mobile–Central Blues' [Vocalion 1145] — the latter probably a Jackson invention amalgamating the Illinois Central, which ran through his home town of Hernando, Miss., with the Gulf, Mobile & Northern, which terminated in Mobile, Ala.. Whatever, he was obviously taken with the idea of the 'Mobile–Central' and recorded four versions of the song between 1927 and 1928:

> Have you ever taken a trip on the Mobile–Central line? *(x2)*
> That's the road to ride to ease your trouble in mind.[51]

The highly-popular Jackson probably inspired the rural-sounding Mozelle Alderson, who cut her 'Mobile Central Blues' [Black Patti 8029] in 1927, albeit it was an entirely different song:

> And it's look-a here, daddy, how did you get that way?
> Look-a here, daddy, how did you get that way?
> Makes me feel like goin' to Mobile City to stay.
>
> I got the travelin' blues an' I can't stay here no more.
> I got the travelin' blues, can't stay here no more.
> If the train don't come, pack my grip an' go.
>
> I-IIIII-trains don't run this way. *(x2)*
> I'm tired of lovin', goin' to Mobile to stay.
>
> Now, it seems like every minute goin' to be my last.
> Says, that doggone Mobile Central runs so doggone fast.
> Babe, seems like every minute, daddy, 's goin' to be my last.
> Babe, that Mobile Central runs so doggone fast.
>
> Now, I'm goin away to see what I can find.
> Goin' away, to see what I can find.
> Well, that Mobile Central train, says, kinda changed my mind.
>
> Ah-heyyyy! All trains don't run this way.
> Ah-heyyyy! Trains don't run this way.
> Baby, I'm(?) goin' to Mobile to stay.[52]

Alderson's blues appears to be more personalised and casts her in that rarer role as a female hobo attempting to board a moving train at speed *(Chapter 10)*. Or perhaps the MJ&KC supplied the means of getting to a Southern railroad centre such as Memphis where the circus was due — in other words, the excursion train.

To ensure that it was well-advertised, so as to create a demand for an excursion train in the first place, 'the circus supplied thousands of heralds, or handbills, to ballyhoo the excursions and announce the schedules.' This was not only practised by large outfits such as Barnum & Bailey, but also the myriad of much smaller shows like the 'little Dode Fisk Circus of 1910', which sent a letter ahead to each depot or station agent along the line of all the places they were going to visit. Various sizes of posters and leaflets would be sent, and the agent was expected to put some up in the waiting room at the depot. The sweetener was *'a special free ticket for yourself and lady to our Famous Shows, and also an admission ticket for one boy, who you will please have distribute the bills in your vicinity. We thank you for what you may do in this regard, and trust your station will make a good showing on this excursion'.* These posters and handbills would be put up on the side of barns, in local stores, on telegraph poles, and anywhere it was thought they would attract the attention of the public. Then, farmers and the townspeople generally would go down to the depot and pick up a train ticket which, of course, was sold at a cut price. They could often buy their ticket for the circus at the same time. As in William Johnson's Natchez in the middle of the Nineteenth Century, 'going to the circus was a gala event; friends and neighbors would be on the train, too; and everyone would be in a holiday mood.' [53]

An advance car was often also sent 'carrying the billposters who advertised the show *[and]* moved about two weeks ahead of the circus itself. The lone car moved on passenger trains when possible, freights when necessary.' [54] There was, in fact, a series of such advance cars which proclaimed the arrival of a circus in town. As Wilmeth explains, these were 'special train cars used by the circus in advance work for a circus appearance.

There were four principal cars, each with special functions. Car No. 2 traveled the route thirty days ahead of the circus in order to place posters at prearranged locations. Car No. 3 arrived fourteen days ahead of the circus with lithographs to be placed in storekeeper *[sic]* windows and over or next to the posters previously posted by Car No. 2. Car No. 4 arrived a week in advance and covered the same locations again. Car No. 1, the skirmishing car, had no regular route but carried troubleshooters who handled last-minute problems and possible rerouting.' [55] Any blues singers employed by the circus would have travelled in the latter car. Part of their job, presumably, would have been to drum up an audience, as in the carnival and medicine shows. In circus/carnival parlance this was to 'ballyhoo'.

Wilmeth observes that 'ballyhoo' (or 'bally') is 'one of the most common terms in all of popular entertainment jargon. Used as part of pitchmen's slang in… especially the medicine show, carnival and circus. A bally, ballyhoo, or sometimes bally act, is simply an attraction used to draw a crowd.' [56] The platform used as a form of small stage was also known as a bally. As the famous jazz band leader, Count Basie recalled, when he was in Tulsa, Okl. circa 1928, 'playing the ballyhoo' for the Gonzelle White show out on the sidewalk at the entrance to the Dreamland Theatre, 'there was a drummer and there was a trumpet, and I was playing the upright piano that

Norris & Rowe Car No. 3 attached to a regular passenger train and heading to the next city. Unknown location, c.1908.

was rolled out there from somewhere inside the lobby, and we would play a couple of numbers and the barker would spiel the come-on for the show. Playing for that was what we used to call "ballying" or "playing the ballyhoo". We used to bally before the show, and then sometimes we used to roll the piano back out there again and bally between shows.'[57]

In the role of a prostitute, Memphis Minnie employs the term on 'Down In The Alley' [Vocalion 03612] when being induced by her pimp to start advertising her business down in an alley[*] of the city (which, like alleys all over Southern cities — and Northern ones too — would have been unlit, unpaved and likely the home of blacks on the very bottom of the socio-economic scale: criminals, hobos, bootleggers, prostitutes and drifters):

> I met a man, asked me did I want to bally.
> Yes, baby let's go down in the alley.
>
> *Refrain:* Take me down in the alley *(x3)*
> Where I can get my business fixed all right.

As well as often featuring open sewers rife with diseases, the alleys were fraught with dangers such as potential muggings and killings, which had little

---

[*] See *Woman With Guitar: Memphis Minnie's Blues* by Paul & Beth Garon (Da Capo Press, New York, 1992, pp.123-4) for further discussion and psychological analysis of 'the alley'. Also W.E.B. Dubois' quote in *The Promise Of The New South (Life After Reconstruction)* by Edward L. Ayers (Oxford University Press, 1992, p.76).

A ballyhoo string band c.1925: Howard Armstrong (fiddle, age 16), Roland Armstrong (bass, age 12), L.C. Armstrong (guitar, age 8) and P.L. Armstrong (mandolin, age 6). The brothers collectively billed as 'Louie Bluie' (see *Blues & Gospel Records* under 'Tennessee Chocolate Drops' with Carl Martin and Roland Martin).

chance of being reduced, due to a small or sometimes non-existent police presence. After sorting out one rough customer, Minnie comments during an instrumental break:

> *(Spoken)* Oh! It's so dark. Can't see no light.
> [If] I can feel my way out of this alley
> I'm sure gonna stop workin' at night.

At the end of her song, she reiterates to her accompanists.

> *(Spoken)* Boys, I'm sure gonna stop workin' an' walkin' late at night.
> 'Cos it's so dangerous,
>   'specially when you got to go down the alley.[58]

In addition to the four advance cars, once they had set up their tents and heavy equipment, a circus would also continue to ballyhoo in the town centre using a 'downtown wagon', described as 'a platform show carried on a circus train which could be exhibited in the town area during the day, thus attracting patrons to the main show. It also refers to a show ticket wagon stationed on streets in the downtown area.' [59]

Georgia bottleneck guitar ace Kokomo Arnold uses the term 'ballyhoo' on at least two of his five recorded versions of 'Milk Cow Blues' (Nos. 2 and 5 remain unheard by me). This is on 'Milk Cow Blues No. 3 [Decca 7116] and 'Milk Cow Blues No. 4' [Decca 7163], both made at the same session on 11 September 1935. He later also employed a variation of his 'ballyhoo' verse on 'Sister Jane Across The Hall' [Decca 7275], which celebrates an attractive female resident living opposite in the same tenement, who appears to be unattached:

> Says, old Sister Jane, right across the hall,
> She's got good stuff but no mule in her stall.
>
> *Refrain:* Old Sister Jane, right across the hall,
> Oh, she drinks some liquor an' she sure, God, has a ball.
>
> She smokes cigars an' cigarettes too.
> She don't do nothin' but ballyhoo.
>
> *Refrain:* Old Sister Jane, etc.
>
> She got a kitchenette, an apartment, too.
> She don't do nothin' but ballyhoo.
>
> *Refrain:* Old Sister Jane, etc.[60]

'Sister' Jane sports a hedonistic life-style with no visible means of financial support. Her choosing to frequently *'ballyhoo'* is a clear reference to being a successful prostitute.

In 1936, Arnold employed another piece of circus slang, 'beef', on his 'Coffin Blues' [Decca 7242]. Here, he expresses a fear that the lady he *'really love'* might suddenly grow tired of him and not want him any more, and he confides how he would feel if such an emotionally traumatic event came to pass:

> Now, I'm goin' out on Lake Michigan,
> I'm gon' kneel down an' say my prayers.
> Says, I'm goin' out on Lake Michigan,
> I'm gon' kneel down an' say my prayers.
> Now, if the blues overtake me, you gon' find me in this lake somewhere.
>
> Now, I bin sittin' here, beefin' to the good Lord way up above.
> Says, I'm just sittin' here, beefin' to the good Lord way up above.
> Says, I done got lucky, found the little girl I really love.[61]

Leroy Carr also used this term in 1934 on his 'You Can't Run My Business No More' [Vocalion 02681].

Wilmeth informs us that 'to beef' is 'carnival slang meaning to bellow or complain over a real or imaginary wrong.'[62] Did Kokomo Arnold spend some time performing blues in a circus? Certainly, his origins, along with his use of these slang references, suggest this may be true.

He was born in Lovejoy, Ga. (referred to by Calt & co. as 'Lovejoys Station' and described as 'a tiny railroad town in the southeast part of Clayton County, about twenty-five miles from Atlanta.'[63]) This would have been on the East Tennessee, Virginia & Georgia Railroad, whose south-eastern line 'branched off at Cleveland, Tenn. to Dalton, Rome, Atlanta, Macon and Brunswick.'[64] In 1894, the East Tennessee was absorbed into the newly-organised Southern Railway which, not surprisingly, featured prominently in Arnold's 'Lonesome Southern Blues' [Decca, unissued] and 'Southern Railroad Blues' [Decca 7139], both recorded in 1935. The latter title reflects a possible harrowing experience of a girlfriend leaving him at the station *(Chapter 7)* at some point during his later teenage years:

> Says, my gal she caught the Southern, an' the fireman he rang the bell. *(x2)*
> An' the engineer he left the station, just like a bat that's out o' hell.
>
> An' I waved my hand, she didn't even look around.
> Says, I waved my hand, she didn't even look around.
> Says, an' I felt like droppin' right down to the ground.

Could *this* be why he left Lovejoy in 1918?

> So, now I got a notion to leave this lonesome town. *(x2)*
> Says, my gal she caught the Southern, an' I know she done put me down.[65]

As a railroad town, Lovejoy — now so insignificant it is omitted from some maps — would have boasted at least one point where the line cut across the highway. According to Wilmeth, it was at such crossings that circus trains halted: 'Normally, this word refers to a railroad show that is loaded or unloaded.'[66] In the case of Lovejoy, might have been the well-known John Robinson Circus or the Walter L. Main Circus. The latter, for instance, travelled hundreds of miles to many small towns in Mississippi and Arkansas. Sometimes the circus might use the crossing (which also usually included the depot) as its showground, as well as for loading/unloading — the Walter L. Main outfit, for example, using railroads like the M&O, the Gulf, Mobile & Northern, the IC, the Frisco and the Columbus & Greenville. The last of these ran west to east across Mississippi from Greenville in the Delta to meet the Frisco at Columbus on its way northwards to St. Louis *(see Walter L. Main ad on next page)*.

Special excursion trains organised by the circuses were laid on to bring in customers from outside the town or city they were playing. People

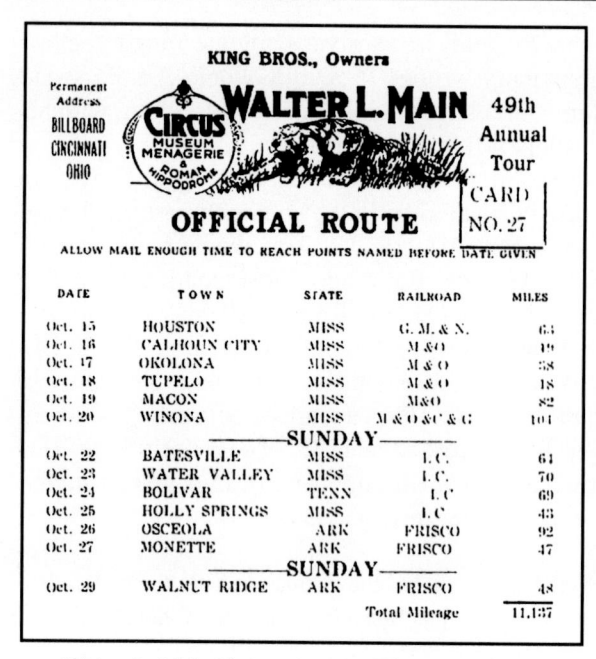

KING BROS., Owners				
Permanent Address: BILLBOARD CINCINNATI OHIO	WALTER L. MAIN CIRCUS MUSEUM MENAGERIE ROMAN HIPPODROME		49th Annual Tour CARD NO. 27	
OFFICIAL ROUTE				
ALLOW MAIL ENOUGH TIME TO REACH POINTS NAMED BEFORE DATE GIVEN				
DATE	TOWN	STATE	RAILROAD	MILES
Oct. 15	HOUSTON	MISS	G. M. & N.	63
Oct. 16	CALHOUN CITY	MISS	M & O	19
Oct. 17	OKOLONA	MISS	M & O	38
Oct. 18	TUPELO	MISS	M & O	18
Oct. 19	MACON	MISS	M&O	82
Oct. 20	WINONA	MISS	M & O & C & G	101
——SUNDAY——				
Oct. 22	BATESVILLE	MISS	I. C.	61
Oct. 23	WATER VALLEY	MISS	I. C.	70
Oct. 24	BOLIVAR	TENN	I. C	69
Oct. 25	HOLLY SPRINGS	MISS	I. C	43
Oct. 26	OSCEOLA	ARK	FRISCO	92
Oct. 27	MONETTE	ARK	FRISCO	47
——SUNDAY——				
Oct. 29	WALNUT RIDGE	ARK	FRISCO	48
			Total Mileage	11,137

Walter L. Main Circus ad. – an official route in the South. Probably late 1920s/early '30s.

would be picked up from anywhere up to forty miles down the line, from every direction, to maximise takings. The excursion ticket would be a one-off fare which 'usually included a ticket to the circus.' [67] Ever since Emancipation and the end of the Civil War, black citizens had loved to travel — especially on the excursion trains, which became more popular in the last two decades of the Nineteenth Century. Atlanta would have fallen within this forty-mile catchment area if a circus pitched at Lovejoy. And, of course, Atlanta itself often played host to the larger circuses. John White observed that in the US 'just about everyone, even those from fairly small towns, would at some time see the circus train unload. It was a fairly ordinary event between 1880 and 1950.' [68]

As Kokomo Arnold spent roughly the first eighteen years of his life in and around Lovejoy, he would have had ample opportunity to absorb the atmosphere and excitement of the travelling circus, either in his home town or in Atlanta (to say nothing of the opportunity to make some comparatively easy money by singing and playing the blues on such a show, or being part of the ballyhoo act which preceded it).

The excursion trains virtually took over the railroad timetable when shows appeared in one of the larger Southern cities: 'These special passenger trains began arriving in town just after the show trains, and they were likely to continue until parade time.' [69] Meanwhile, all other passenger services were shunted to the back of the queue or temporarily abandoned — as Leroy Carr found to his exasperation on 'Memphis Town' [Vocalion 1527], when he wanted to see *'that gal of mine'*, and discovered that all trains were only running to Memphis that day, on account of the circus or *'jubilee'*:

> I said: 'Conductor, where's the trains all gwine?
> I want to see that gal o' mine.'
> He answered me with a railroad frown:
> 'All trains gwine to Memphis Town.'

> *Refrain:* Memphis Town, Memphis Town,
> All trains goin' to Memphis Town.
> Shovel in the coal, see the wheels go round.
> Lord! Everybody's goin' down to Memphis Town.

> I said: 'What's goin' down old Memphis way?
> The trains all goin' there today.'
> The trainman said: 'There's a jubilee,
> And Memphis Town is the only place for me.'

> *Refrain:* Memphis Town, etc.

In his frustration, he injects some humour and a rare reference of a physical threat to a white man, the *'station man'*:

> I said to the station man: 'Where's my train?'
> He said: 'I never know you owned the train.'
> I said: 'You better answer, I'll smack you down.'
> He said: 'All trains goin' to Memphis Town.' [70]

Once the circus was set up and the excursion trains had brought everybody into town, the next step was the 'grand free street parade' which usually set off between 11:00 and 11:30 in the morning from the depot. A massive display of what a particular circus had to offer, it often included elephants linked trunk-to-tail, lions and tigers in cages, show horses, clowns, bands, cowboys and 'Indians', and many other attractions. This was, of course, a last-ditch attempt to persuade as many of the local populace as possible to pay their admission fee at the showground. There was also a final clarion call to those who lived near the town who had not boarded an excursion train. 'The traditional finale to the circus parade was the Pied Piper of the circus, the steam calliope: 32 steam whistles, keyboard operated, powered by coal fire and boiler, hissing steam and smoke, and blasting out such favorites as 'Go Tell Aunt Rhodie' and 'The Sidewalks of New York'. Under steam pressure of from 80 to 100 pounds per square inch, its tones carried four miles against a breeze.' [71]

Circuses normally put on two shows each day they were in town, and in the late evening when it was time to leave, everything was dismantled and packed up. 'The wagons and teams followed flares to the train, where they rolled onto flatcars to disappear into the night.' [71]

During this period in the 19-teens and through the 1920s, the railroad was THE way to travel: 'It was the era of multitudinous passenger service on the railroads. People were accustomed to coming into the nearest city by train, doing their business, and going home via a local [service] later in the day.' [72] And so too it was with circuses. In the 'golden age' of the American circus (1871-1917), such outfits as 'Sells Brothers Great European Seven Elephant Railroad Show [and] the Walter L. Main Show' [73] were immensely popular and travelled the length and breadth of the US. Wilmeth concurs: 'The 1890s and early years of the [Twentieth] Century saw many small railroad circuses traveling around the country, usually on two or three cars, sometimes on a single long car.' [74]

A 'show' car purchased by Bessie Smith in 1925, being 78 feet long, is a classic example. Featuring a corridor that ran along its entire length and was 'long enough to transport the tent's centre pole', this vehicle included a kitchen, bathroom, hot and cold running water, and seven 'staterooms'. It was long enough to 'carry the entire show'. Maud Smith, one of the performers, who had just joined the show, later explained what a difference it made not having to rough it on tour when Jim Crow laws often barred them from hotels and boarding houses: 'Some of the towns we hit didn't have hotels for us, so we used to have to spread out, one staying here, another one there. Now, we could just live on the train.' [75]

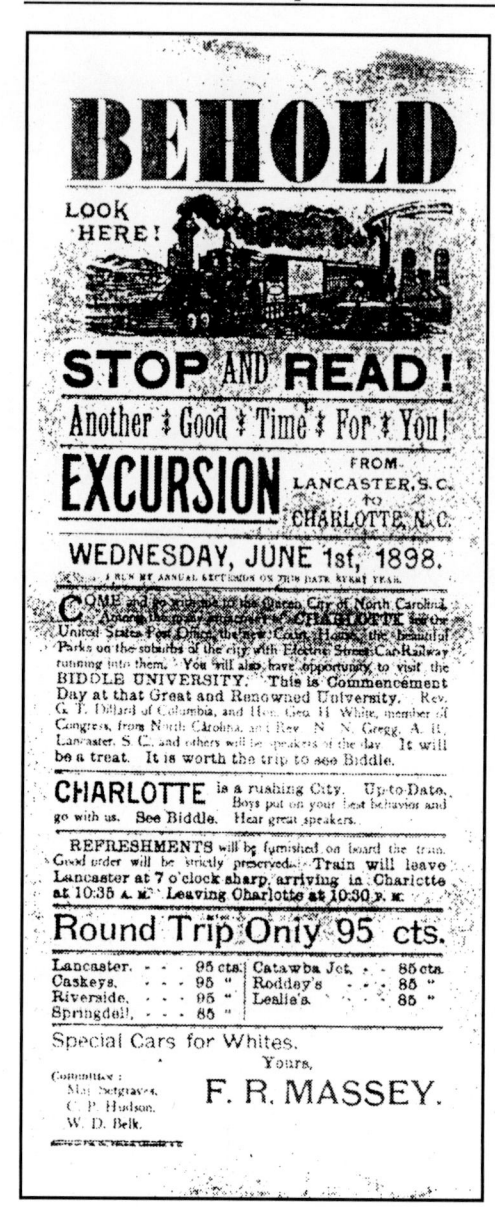

Southern Railway excursion ticket for visit to opening of Biddle University, Charlotte, N.C., in 1898. Note Jim Crow arrangement of 'Special cars for whites'.

The oral transmission process via the circus/tent shows and the

Chapter 8 — I carried water for the elephant

Hagenbeck & Wallace Circus parade in Birmingham, Ala., 1929.
Co-owner B.E. Wallace claimed that Birmingham was 'the best circus town in the South'.

railroads is self-evident in Daphne Duval Harrison's defence of the TOBA, which of course featured so many earlier blues singers — Bessie Smith among them. Harrison claims (rightly, I feel) that TOBA added greatly to the growth and advancement of black entertainment generally. The black community 'reaped economical and cultural benefits when the train uncoupled the show railcar at the local siding. The traditional parade that followed not only brought folks to the show, it brought business to the little shops, cafés, and "joints" as people crowded in to mingle with the show people.'* Echoing Patience Pennington's words from 1903, she adds that 'high spirits remained for weeks after the train was gone.' [77]

As circuses, carnivals and railroads were so intertwined, it is hardly surprising that workers from all three often shared the same colloquialisms and slang expressions in their everyday speech. Much of this speech surfaced quite naturally in the lyrics of the blues — for, it should be remembered, the blues singer sang as he/she spoke: terms such as 'highball', 'gandy dancer', 'rattler' and 'getaway' for instance. The latter expression crops up in a fine recording by Robert Wilkins in 1930 called 'Get Away Blues' [Brunswick 7158]. An unusual slant on the 'leaving at the station' theme *(Chapter 7)*, Wilkins' blues contains an invitation to a (presumably) married woman to run away with him, or otherwise elope!

---

* An American writer observed that, during the mid-1930s, 'traveling carnivals attracted crowds of black and white rural people'. The crowds were probably swelled because of the Jim Crow segregation laws which made a major competitor, the movies, 'still difficult to get to'.[76]

Told 'er: 'Come on woman, let us board this train. *(x2)*
Ride here while we get away from your man.' [78]

A 'getaway day' is defined as 'the last day of a circus engagement'.[79] The related 'get away stake' is a 'medicine show expression for having the means to move from one place to another.' [80] 'Get away' may be found in compositions by Frank Stokes and Jim Jackson — both popular medicine show performers — and others. Wilkins is also known to have worked in medicine shows before his religious conversion and indeed, he offers his 'stake' to his lover, consisting of *'silver, paper an' gold'*.

One of the main icons of the circus, the clown, lends itself particularly well to the language of the blues. To 'clown' means to fool around, get drunk, sleep around and make a general public spectacle of yourself. The word is used in this context by such diverse singers as Robert Johnson, Gus Cannon, Peetie Wheatstraw and Bo Carter, for example, while Blind Willie McTell instils some blues poetry into his 'Your Time To Worry' [Decca 7117]:

> You drink your whisky, run around,
> Get out in the street an' act like a fan-foot clown.
>
> *Refrain:* Your time to worry, my time to be alone.
> Your reckless disposition done drove
> your good man away from home.[81]

— the expression 'fan-foot' graphically describing the outsize footwear worn by clowns, who would often stand heel-to-heel with their feet at right angles to their bodies as part of a comic routine. The obvious sexual connotations of a woman lying in the 'missionary position' for intercourse, also led to this term being applied to prostitutes. A combination of these definitions appeared on a 1933 Curly Weaver recording, 'You Was Born To Die' [A.R.C., unissued], on which McTell also featured, and some four years earlier on Jim Jackson's 'Ain't You Sorry Mama? (Part 2)' [Vocalion 1413]. That same year Blind Blake also recorded a 'Fan Foot Woman' for Paramount, which remains unissued, while Irene Scruggs included McTell's phrase on her first version of 'My Back To The Wall' [Gennett 7296] in 1930.

In 1936, the clown appeared in a blues by Georgia White named after another circus term, 'Little Red Wagon' [Decca 7287]:

> If you wanna be foolish, an' act like a clown,
> Be a laughin' stock all over town.
>
> *Refrain:* That's your red wagon.
> That's your red wagon.
> That's your red wagon, keep on rollin' along.[82]

A less impressive singer, Willie Mae McKenzie, also recorded 'Little Red Wagon' [Vocalion 03562] in March 1937 with a similar line-up and the addition of an unidentified trumpet player.

Wilmeth reveals that the 'red wagon' in question was 'the circus box-office wagon and main office of the circus, also known as the "money wagon" — so called because it was formerly painted red, although the name stuck no matter what color was used.' [83] In all probability, this wagon was, in earlier days at least, the caboose found at the tail-end of Southern trains. These were generally painted red (as celebrated by Henry Thomas on his 'The Little Red Caboose' [Vocalion 1138] in 1927). The theme of White's song, therefore, is that, if her man wants to fool around, get drunk, etc, he'll pay for it sooner or later. In other words: 'You've got to reap what you sow.'

As I have said, circuses and railroads permeated the experience of the early blues singers. So, it is not surprising to find these phenomena appearing in their everyday speech, which is the language of the blues. The same applies to the carnival and medicine show. While in transit, both the carnival and circus presented a similar picture, carried on much the same rolling stock, but of course presented two different scenarios when they hit town and 'detrained'.

One of the most well-known carnival terms (to blues collectors/fans) is the word 'hokum'. It lent itself to a whole new, more urbanised form of the blues, first appearing in a record title in December 1928, when Texas string band leader Coley Jones laid down 'Hokum Blues' [Columbia 14410-D]. Seemingly endless raunchy titles such as 'Touch It Up A Little' [A.R.C., unissued] by James De Berry & His Memphis Playboys, 'Somebody's Been Using That Thing' [Paramount 12796] and 'I'm Gonna Get It' [Vocalion 03232] by the Hokum Boys, 'Shove It Up In There' [Columbia 14641-D] by James McCravy, 'Wipe It Off' [OKeh 8762] by Lonnie Johnson, and the notorious 'It's Tight Like That' [Vocalion 1216] by Tampa Red & Georgia Tom, were issued by the record companies and bought in their thousands by blacks in the ghettos of Northern cities like Chicago, Detroit and New York.

Precursors of this aspect of the blues from pre-hokum days are Papa Charlie Jackson (often seen as the 'father' of the genre — 'Shake That Thing' [Paramount 12281], etc) and some early vaudeville-blues titles such as 'It's Right Here For You (If You Don't Get It – 'Taint No Fault O' Mine)' [OKeh 4169] by Mamie Smith, 'Spread Yo' Stuff' [Gennett 4712] by Daisy Martin and 'Just A Little Bit More' [Black Swan, unissued] by Trixie Smith — recorded in 1920, 1921 and 1922 respectively. Although they use a more 'New Orleans' style of jazz accompaniment, these titles nevertheless contain the spirit of hokum blues.

During a discussion on hokum blues (which lasted on record for about thirteen years from Jackson's debut in 1924 to the Hokum Boys' last session in 1937), the pre-eminent blues historian, Paul Oliver, noted that, in the vaudeville theatre, 'hokum' meant 'the use of acts, jokes or routines that were guaranteed to produce a laugh or an audience response'. He added that it

The famous Silas Green From New Orleans as a single-car show. Unknown date/location.

eventually 'became synonymous with successful "corn" and was used with this meaning in the travelling circus.' [84] A dozen years later, Oliver repeated his 'guaranteed audience' quote and noted that 'con men' also used the term: 'Hokum for them meant the "come on" patter and deceit that attracted a crowd or encouraged a sucker to fall for their line of jive.' [85]

Wilmeth confirms Oliver's 'guaranteed response' explanation, as well as adding a second: 'Cheap, sugary candy, useless and inexpensive souvenirs and the like, sold at carnival booths... time-worn gag, speech, situation, piece of business, line and such, that is foolproof and can be relied upon to produce a predictable response, usually applause or tears, from any audience. Also called gonk or hoke.' [86]

So, it would appear that the term 'hokum' as applied in the blues originated from the travelling carnival, rather than the circus. Oliver's definition of 'con men' is more aptly described by the term 'ballyhoo', which did come from the circus (as discussed elsewhere in this chapter with reference to recordings by Memphis Minnie and Kokomo Arnold).

II

Many blues artists featured the language of the circus, carnival and other travelling shows in their recordings, and it is therefore hardly surprising to discover that these singers were reflecting their past (or present) experiences. As we have seen, these included Memphis Minnie, Ma Rainey, Bumble Bee Slim, and Fiddlin' Joe Martin, who had spent time with a circus in their younger days. Other very popular singers, such as Leroy Carr and Frank Stokes, can also be added to this list. Robert Wilkins spent some time on the medicine shows, as did Furry Lewis, Charley Patton, Curly Weaver and Blind Willie McTell — amongst hundreds of others — while Irene Scruggs and Clara Smith spent some time in the world of minstrelsy and tent shows, like many of their blues-singing sisters.

Two-car Rabbit Foot Minstrels show in 1934.

It would seem quite justifiable to presume that Kokomo Arnold did 'time' in the circus when he was starting out in Lovejoy, simply by the inclusion of circus slang in some of his blues such as 'Sister Jane Across The Hall' and 'Coffin Blues'. A similar case could be made for Blind Blake, who, while deservedly famous for his awesome guitar prowess, nevertheless remains a biographical enigma. The 'rum dum' of his 'Bootleg Rum Dum Blues' [Paramount 12695] from 1928 is 'principally a carnival word and some circus use for no-account, shiftless, or intoxicated.' [87] An unissued side, 'Blue Getaway', likewise indicates a circus link *(see also 'Get Away Blues' by Robert Wilkins, page 263)*, as does his 'Fan Foot Woman', likewise unissued.

Blake employed another minstrelsy/vaudeville term — 'chump' — on his 'Chump Man Blues' [Paramount 12904] in 1929, which also crops up on Barbecue Bob's 'It Just Won't Quit' [Columbia 14614-D] from the same year and Lonnie Johnson's 'Not The Chump I Use To Be' [OKeh 8916] from 1931. Johnson worked on the TOBA circuit and Bob sometimes went out with medicine shows. Wilmeth states that 'chump' is a commonly-used expression 'among most outdoor amusement workers and burlesque personnel, meaning one who is easily duped or deluded. By extension, it is used to identify a paying customer or patron.' [88] So, 'chump', by definition, would also have been used by carnival workers. Such references in Blind Blake's repertoire indicate that he travelled around extensively after leaving Jacksonville, Fla. (that is to say, on carnival and circus trains) before eventually moving north to Chicago.

By the same token, some small detail about an even more obscure blues singer, 'Hi' Henry Brown, might be gleaned from his recording soubriquet. Don Kent suggests Pace, Miss. as a place of origin, although Brown had already teamed up with St. Louis-based Charley Jordan by the time their beautiful twin-guitar sound was captured by Vocalion Records in 1932.

One of the many shows travelling the South at the turn of the Twentieth Century was *Hi Henry's Minstrels*, and was reportedly 'active in 1903' [89], along with many others. Of course, many blues singers including Ma Rainey, Charley Patton, Bessie Smith, Jaybird Coleman and Sleepy John Estes worked these and other 'funny little shows' (as Blind Willie McTell called them) in their earlier days. Kent comments that 'Brown sounds to be older' [90], and indeed he probably was. If he was a contemporary of Gus Cannon and Frank Stokes (who were born in 1883 and c.1888 respectively), Henry Brown was old enough to have toured with the *Hi Henry Minstrels* when he was a teenager, though this must all remain pure conjecture. It is also interesting to note that a 'Hi Henry' was also a 'theatrical term for a tall silk hat.' [91]

It is readily apparent that travelling shows, the railroads and the blues were inextricably intertwined, and this combination proved an extraordinary and very important part of the oral transmission in the blues from the turn of the century up to 1920 and the first blues record (that we know of) by Mamie Smith.

Notes to Chapter 8

1	Harrison, L.H., & J.C. Klotter	p.162
2	Sturtevant, W.C. (Gen. Ed.)	p.601
3	Wilson & Ferris	Ibid, p.1247
4	Hogan, W.B., & E.A. Davis	Ibid, p.84
5	Ibid.	p.86
6	Towsen, J.H.	p.126
7	Partridge, E.	*Penguin Dictionary of Historical Slang*, ibid, p.70
8	Brewer, E.C.	www.bartleby.com
9	Towsen	Ibid, pp.119-120
10	Ibid.	p.120

11	Hogan & Davis	Ibid, p.203
12	Towsen	Ibid, p.109
13	Matlaw, M. (Ed.)	p.178
14	Trelease, A.W.	Ibid, p.331
15	Hogan & Davis	Ibid, p.350
16	Summersell, C.G.	Ibid, p.36
17	Matlaw	Ibid, p.179
18	Hugill, S.	p.15
19	Conway, C., & S. Odell	p.2
20	Trelease	Ibid, p.238
21	Lucas, M.B.	p.169
22	Ibid.	p.174
23	Ibid.	p.184
24	Parkinson, T., & C.P. Fox.	p.?
25	'Leavin' Gal Blues'	Bertha Henderson - vocal; Blind Blake - guitar (c.May 1928, Chicago, Ill.)
26	Stover, J.	*Railroads of the South*, p.149
27	Ibid.	p.148
28	Parkinson & Fox	Ibid, p.286
29	Waring, P.	pp.75-6
30	'Steel Drivin' Sam'	Clara Smith - vocal; Ernest Elliott - alto sax; Porter Grainger - piano; unk. woodblock (16 December 1924, New York City)
31	'The L&N Blues'	Clara Smith - vocal; Lemuel Fowler - piano (27 March 1925, New York City)
32	Hubbard, F.	Ibid, p.74
33	'Done Sold My Soul To The Devil'	Clara Smith - vocal; Don Redmon - clarinet; Porter Grainger - piano (30 September 1924, New York City)
34	Pennington, P.	p.46
35	Ibid.	p.5
36	'St. Louis Cyclone Blues'	Elzadie Robinson - vocal, speech; Bob Call - piano (c.November 1927, Chicago, Ill.)
37	Pennington	Ibid, p.46
38	Ibid.	p.47
39	Ibid.	p.48
40	Harrison, D.D.	Ibid, p.68
41	'Daddy Don't Put That Thing On Me Blues'	Clara Smith - vocal; Charlie Green - trombone; poss. Porter Grainger - piano (26 January 1929, New York City)
42	'Long Gone'	Jim Jackson - vocal, guitar (7 September 1928, Memphis, Tenn.)
43	Baker, S.L., & V.B. Kunz	p.22
44	Parkinson & Fox	Ibid, p.323
45	Reed	Ibid, p.449

46	Baker & Kunz	Ibid, p.23
47	Parkinson & Fox	Ibid, p.43
48	'Cocaine Blues'	Luke Jordan - vocal, guitar (16 August 1927, Charlotte, N.C.)
49	'Cannon Ball Blues'	Furry Lewis - vocal, guitar (28 August 1928, Memphis, Tenn.)
50	'This Ain't No Place For Me'	Jim Jackson - vocal, guitar (28 August 1928, Memphis, Tenn.)
51	'Mobile Central Blues' [Take 4]	Jim Jackson - vocal, guitar (2 February 1928, Memphis, Tenn.)
52	'Mobile Central Blues'	Mozelle Alderson - vocal; poss. Blind James Beck - piano (c.April/May 1927, Chicago, Ill.)
53	Parkinson & Fox	Ibid, p.235
54	Ibid.	p.78
55	Wilmeth, D.B.	pp.5-6
56	Wilmeth	Ibid, p.15
57	Basie, C.	p.18
58	'Down In The Alley'	Memphis Minnie - vocal, guitar, speech; Blind John Davis - piano; Fred Williams - drums (17 June 1937, Chicago, Ill.)
59	Wilmeth	Ibid, p.78
60	'Sister Jane Across The Hall'	Kokomo Arnold - vocal, guitar (12 January 1937, Chicago, Ill.)
61	'Coffin Blues'	Kokomo Arnold - vocal, guitar; Peetie Wheatstraw - piano; unk. bass (24 October 1936, Chicago, Ill.)
62	Wilmeth	Ibid, p.19
63	Calt, S., & J. Miller.	Notes to Yazoo L-1049 (LP)
64	Lambie, J.T.	p.111
65	'Southern Railroad Blues'	Kokomo Arnold - vocal, guitar (18 April 1935, Chicago, Ill.)
66	Wilmeth	Ibid, p.67
67	Ibid.	p.86
68	White, J.H.	*The American Railroad Freight Car*, ibid, p.392
69	Parkinson & Fox	Ibid, p.235
70	'Memphis Town'	Leroy Carr - vocal, piano; Scrapper Blackwell - guitar (2 January 1930, Chicago, Ill.)
71	*Encyclopædia Britannica*	p.4
72	Parkinson & Fox	Ibid.
73	Matlaw	Ibid, p.180
74	Wilmeth	Ibid, p.178
75	Albertson, C.	Ibid, p.79
76	Kirby, J.T.	p.301

77	Harrison	Ibid, p.34
78	'Get Away Blues'	Robert Wilkins - vocal, guitar (c.21 February 1930, Memphis, Tenn.)
79	Wilmeth	Ibid, p.110
80	Ibid.	p.109
81	'Your Time To Worry'	Blind Willie McTell - vocal, guitar (25 April 1935, Chicago, Ill.)
82	'Little Red Wagon'	Georgia White - vocal; Les Paul - guitar; Richard M. Jones - piano; John Lindsay - bass (7 December 1936, Chicago, Ill.)
83	Wilmeth	Ibid, p.218
84	Oliver, P.	Notes to Matchbox MSE-217 (LP)
85	Oliver, P.	Notes to Matchbox MSE-1014 (LP)
86	Wilmeth	Ibid, p.132
87	Ibid.	p.229
88	Ibid.	p.531
89	Parkinson & Fox	Ibid, p.324
90	Kent, D.	Notes to Belzona L-1003 (LP)
91	Wilmeth	Ibid, p.129
92	Ibid.	p.84

Discography – Chapter 8

'Cannon-Ball Blues' (Furry Lewis)
4-CD: *Masters Of Memphis Blues (1927-39)* [J.S.P. JSP-7725] *2004*

'Cocaine Blues' (Luke Jordan)
3-CD: *Never Let The Same Bee Sting You Twice (1927-38)* [Document DOCD-5678] 2005

'Coffin Blues' (Kokomo Arnold)
CD: *Kokomo Arnold – Volume 3 (1936-37)* [Document DOCD-5039] 1991

'Daddy Don't Put That Thing On Me Blues' (Clara Smith)
CD: *Clara Smith – Volume 5 (1927-29)* [Document DOCD-5368] 1995

'Done Sold My Soul To The Devil' (Clara Smith)
CD: *Clara Smith – Volume 2 (1924)* [Document DOCD-5365] 1995

'Down In The Alley' (Memphis Minnie)
5-CD: *Memphis Minnie (1929-37)* [J.S.P. JSP-7716] 2003

'Get Away Blues' (Robert Wilkins)
4-CD: *Masters Of Memphis Blues (1927-39)* [J.S.P. JSP-7725] 2004

'The L&N Blues' (Clara Smith)
CD: *Clara Smith – Volume 3 (1925)* [Document DOCD-5366] 1995

'Leavin' Gal Blues' (Bertha Henderson)	5-CD: *Blind Blake* [J.S.P. JSP-7714] 2003
'Little Red Wagon' (Georgia White)	CD: *Georgia White – Volume 2 (1936-37)* [Document DOCD-5302] 1994
'Long Gone' (Jim Jackson)	CD: *Jim Jackson – Volume 2 (1928-30)* [Document DOCD-5115] 1992
'Memphis Town' (Leroy Carr)	2-CD: *Leroy Carr – Sloppy Drunk* [Catfish KATCD-108] 1998
'Mobile Central Blues' (Mozelle Alderson)	CD: *Blue Girls – Volume 2 (1925-30)* [Document DOCD-5504] 1996
'My Mobile Central Blues' [Take 4] (Jim Jackson)	CD: *Jim Jackson – Volume 1 (1927-28)* [Document DOCD-5114] 1991
'St. Louis Cyclone Blues' (Elzadie Robinson)	CD: *Elzadie Robinson – Volume 1 (1926-28)* [Document DOCD-5248] 1994
'Sister Jane Across The Hall' (Kokomo Arnold)	CD: *Kokomo Arnold – Volume 3 (1936-37)* [Document DOCD-5039] 1991
'Southern Railroad Blues' (Kokomo Arnold)	CD: *Kokomo Arnold – Volume 2 (1935-36)* [Document DOCD-5038] 1991
'Steel Drivin' Sam' (Clara Smith)	CD: *Clara Smith – Volume 2 (1924)* [Document DOCD-5365] 1995
'This Ain't No Place For Me' (Jim Jackson)	CD: *Jim Jackson – Volume 2 (1928-30)* [Document DOCD-5115] 1992
'Your Time To Worry' (Blind Willie McTell)	4-CD: *Blind Willie McTell (1927-40)* [J.S.P. JSP-7711] 2003

Gonna leave a Pullman, an' ride the L&N

'The L&N Blues' – Clara Smith (1925)

CHAPTER 9

CROSS-FERTILISATION OF RURAL AND VAUDEVILLE BLUES VIA THE RAILROAD

The travelling circus, carnival and medicine show were the background of many of the earliest recorded blues exponents, who, as noted in the previous chapter, were predominantly women. While professional black writers supplied a lot of material for many of these early singers, some also composed their own lyrics. As with country/rural blues singers — male and female — influences were often drawn from contemporaries, as well as from earlier traditions. This was a two-way process, although it is not generally recognised that the flow from vaudeville to country blues was almost as prevalent as the reverse. The railroads played a pivotal role in this process.

Most of the early female blues singers were born in the 1880s and 1890s, whereas the majority of rural singers came into the world within the first two decades of the Twentieth Century. These vaudeville-blues singers — and black women in general — were an important part of the oral transmission process, and often had a close connection with the railroads, either as trackside workers, platform vendors, or show singers who travelled nearly everywhere by train.

Even before the Civil War, younger women were increasingly rejecting the arduous work in the fields — picking cotton, pulling corn, etc — and turned to easier and more lucrative alternatives in Southern cities. Reidy reports that 'quasi-independent slaves at times developed entreprenurial *[sic]* skills. Slave women sold fruit and baked goods in the vicinity of railway depots.'[1] Moreover, Licht notes that 'an article in the *American Engineer* in July of 1857... indicates that black women in the South were commonly employed on southern railroads. "There is a colored woman on every passenger train," the report noted, "to carry water and wait on ladies, and who sells [sic] to such as choose to buy. Without further information it can only be assumed that these women were either hired or purchased slaves[*]."'[2]

Indeed, Blind Boy Fuller might well have been evoking the scene described by the *American Engineer* on his 1940 recording, 'Passenger Train Woman' [OKeh 06231]:

> Little girl, little girl, little girl. Just as sweet as you can be.
> Little girl, little girl, little girl. You just as sweet as you can be.
> An' I begin to wonder, do you ever think of me?
>
> Then she left me this mornin', clock was strikin' four.
> Then she left me this mornin', an' that clock was strikin' four.
> An' when she walked out, yes, them blues stepped in my door.
>
> Well, the time I need you, baby, that's the time you gone.
> Well, the time I need you, mama, Lord, that's the time you gone.
> I believe you got ways like a passenger train:
>   when one gittin' off, the other one gittin' on.
>
> Now, my left eye jump, mama, my flesh begin to crawl.
> Says, my left eye jump, baby, an' my flesh begin to crawl.
> Says, that's a mighty true sign [that] some man kickin' in my stall.
>
> Don't mind you goin' out, mama, if you don't stay both night an' day.
> I don't mind you goin' out, sugar, if you don't stay out both night an' day.
> Says, that's a mighty true sign, baby, that you givin' my lovin' away.[3]

---

[*] In the years leading up to the Civil War, railroad companies found it increasingly necessary to hire or buy their own slaves, due to growing resistance from plantation owners to release their hands, for a variety of reasons. The 'ladies' mentioned in the article would have been white women of the plantation-owner class — the so-called Southern 'aristocracy'.

Perhaps Fuller's partner is absent so often because of her time-consuming job selling her wares on Southern trains, although the only railroad reference is the *'passenger train woman'* rendered as poetic symbolism for sexual infidelity. Even so, this blues could be another link between railroads and this very popular East Coast bluesman, along with references to the M&O discussed in *Chapter 3 (see pages 99-101)*. Interestingly, Fuller had adapted a 1937 Lee Brown recording, 'Little Girl, Little Girl' [Decca 7054] for his blues, although the latter makes no mention of a passenger train.

Blind Boy Fuller, c.1935.

The lyrics of 'Funny Feeling Blues' [Vocalion 04237] meanwhile suggest that Fuller's partner may have sold vegetables as well as fruit:

> Ah, you string your string beans, mama, whilst I shell my peas.
> You string your string beans, mama, whilst I shell my peas.
> Goin' to my rider, you can stay with who you please.

But he bemoans the fact that she spends so much time selling her produce on the trains, or at the depot:

> I wish to the Lord, my baby would stay home.
> Said, I wish to the Lord, my baby would stay home.
> So in the midnight hours I can be lyin' in my good gal's arms.
>
> She left me this mornin', an' that clock was strikin' four.
> When she walked out, them blues walked in my door.[4]

Fuller obviously enjoys being kept by his *'passenger train woman'*, but doesn't like the time she spends away from home. And he hints at his girlfriend misusing this situation to *'stay with who she please'*. He now appreciates his *'rider'*, or regular woman, whom he has temporarily abandoned: the latter might not bring home so much money, but she is there in *'the midnight hours'*.

Two young vendors at what appears to be a depot in 1900. Unknown location.

Another Fuller recording made in the same year of 1938, 'Painful Hearted Man' [Vocalion 04175], perpetuates the theme of desolation caused by his woman's long working hours, which cause him to go down to the depot in the hope that she will arrive on that *'evenin' train'* — from whichever direction:

> Says, I was standin' at the station, waitin' on that evenin' train.
> I was standin' at the station, waitin' on that evenin' train.
> Says, my head hangin' low, mama, my heart was growing in vain.
>
> Please hurry down sunshine, see what that morrow bring.
> Ey-hey! See what that morrow bring.
> May bring down my woman, ridin' on that southbound train.
>
> Mmmmmmm-mmm-mm-mmm.
> Ey-hey! Mmm-mm-mmm.
> May bring down the woman I'm lovin', ridin' on that eastbound train.
>
> Yeah! Went to the station, I sure didn't see no train.
> Says, I went to the station, mama I didn't see no train.
> Says, I didn't see the woman I was lovin', no one to call her name.[5]

It could be that Fuller had cause to dwell on his past life at the time he recorded these two blues in 1938, and the 'sighted' references allude to the period before he started going blind around 1927. Does this infer that Fuller once worked on a railroad prior to losing his sight? It might still not be too late for some researcher to find out.

Male and female platform vendors on the C&O.

It seems that, after the Civil War, black women continued to sell produce at the depots as well as on the trains: 'At one time food could... be bought through the car windows from station platform vendors. It is impossible to say how common this practice was, but it is documented in an engraving from a volume of American pictures in 1872 *(above)*. The scene, reminiscent of India or Guatemala, shows a crowded platform at Gordonsville, Va., where African American women are selling coffee, hot cakes and chicken from trays, some of which are balanced on their bandanna-covered heads.' [6] A table giving average hourly rates of pay for 33 industries in Virginia during 1928 shows that the presence of black women in the railroad industry was still firmly established almost half a century later. Under the heading 'Railroad Activities', their pay for 1928 is listed as 39 cents per hour, compared with 46 cents for black male workers and 60 cents for white males. It is worth noting this is the only industry (apart from Fertilizer & Guano) where black women workers are included, but not their white female counterparts.[7]

Indeed, several titles recorded by female singers in the 1920s and '30s indicate just how widespread the use of black female labour on the railroads was. In 1924, Maggie Jones did 'Anybody Here Want To Try My Cabbage?' [Columbia 14063-D] — a song with obvious sexual connotations. This was duly 'covered' by Mildred Austin in 1928 [Champion 15530], using the same title, and the raunchy Lil Johnson remade it as 'Anybody Want To Buy My Cabbage?' in 1935 [Champion 50002]. In 1925 meanwhile, Lucille Hegamin celebrated the 'virtues' of 'Hot Tamale Molly' [Cameo 723]. And, judging by the lyrics of his 'Every Day In The Week Blues' [Columbia 14400-D], East Coast bluesman Pink Anderson — like Blind Boy Fuller — also appears to have had a relationship with a *'passenger train woman'*:

Chapter 9 — Gonna leave a Pullman, an' ride the L&N

> If you ride the Seaboard, I'll ride the L&N.
> *(Spoken)* What?
> Mama, that's the train [that] will sure carry you in the wind.
> Low-down, mean old fireman, a cruel old engineer
> Took my good girl an' left me standin' here.

Anderson finishes his song, brilliantly enhanced by the driving twin guitars played by himself and Simmie Dooley, with an instruction for his *'brownie'* to sell blackberries (presumably on the Seaboard Air Line) if she can't get apples:

> You must get your basket, brownie, an' make it into the woods.
> If you don't find old apple, you must make blackberry good.[8]

On 1929's 'Travelin' Blues' [Columbia 14484-D], Blind Willie McTell (recording as 'Blind Sammie' — Samuel was his middle name) recalls a lighter side of hoboing on the railroads, and obviously admiring some of the women he encountered along the way... which would doubtless have included platform vendors as well as passengers:

> *(Spoken)* I heard old bell ring kinda like this (...).
> I went on down, I heard old whistle blow.
> I heard it sing.
>
> *(Vocal)* Look-a-yonder (...), look-a-yonder (...).
> At the women (...), at the women (...).[9]

(...) = guitar 'sings'

A remarkably 'sighted' lyric for a blind singer to use, this begs the question as to whether McTell was totally blind, much the same way as Blind Lemon Jefferson. In a 1930 recording, again under the pseudonym 'Blind Sammie', McTell makes what may be another indirect reference to platform vendors on 'Talkin' To Myself' [Columbia 14551-D]:

> I even went down to the depot with my suitcase in my hand.
> Crowd of women run, crying: 'Mr. Samuel, won't you be my man?'[10]

The custom of selling produce and food on the depot platforms had become prevalent during the Nineteenth Century, as 'early eating houses along the railroad were privately operated. They were filthy and the food was terrible. Often their owners were in cahoots with train crews. The charge was four bits, in advance. No sooner had the customer paid and started to eat, than the bell rang, the whistle blew and the passenger had to dash back aboard his train, most of his meal uneaten. The beanery then paid off the train crew at a dime a passenger and waited for the next victim.'

Around 1875, Scottish-born Frederick Harvey, who had first-hand experience of these horrendous conditions, approached the superintendent of the Santa Fe Railway with a view to operating a series of restaurants serving good-quality food at the railroad's major stops. The superintendent, Charles F. Morse, liked the idea and Harvey opened his first establishment, 'a small eating place... in the old Topeka depot and office building.' [11] (The full title of the Santa Fe railroad is 'Atchison, Topeka & Santa Fe'. Topeka is in the state of Kansas.) This quickly escalated to a whole chain of highly successful 'Harvey Houses', staffed by the famous (all white) 'Harvey girls', on railroads all over the US, and must at least partly explain the lack of more damning reports like the one of 1872 since that time. Fred Harvey's restaurants made platform vendors largely redundant — except for those catering for black passengers, who were usually barred from them in the South. Recalling the conditions in Georgia in 1917, retired Pullman employee James T. Steele explained to his interviewer: 'During those days, when you stop in the towns, people would make all kinda sandwiches and things and sell it to ya through the windows. But you couldn't go in no dining room. Didn't allow you in there.' [12]

If McTell wasn't *'looking at the women'* selling food at the depot, he may have been referring to female trackside workers. Indeed, as a hobo on 'Travelin' Blues', he would more likely have been gazing at the latter, as he would have boarded the train at some point after it had left the depot. Reidy reports that 'former slave Hanna Fambro from Monroe County recalled having "worked on de gradin' 'long with de other people of de plantation"... Although some women were hired as cooks and shovel hands, men predominated' [13] — Monroe County being in McTell's home state of Georgia.

The 'gradin'' is a reference to the railway embankment built to maintain the stability of the railroad bed upon which the tracks were laid. As well as cutting down trees for land clearance and picking cotton, female slaves or 'bonded women' also performed the heaviest of tasks alongside the men. White reports: 'They hauled logs by leather straps attached to their shoulders. They plowed using mule and ox teams, and hoed — sometimes with the heaviest implements available. They dug ditches, spread manure

'Look-a-yonder...'
Black women digging with long Southern hoes in the fields. Marlboro, S.C.,1928.

fertilizer, and piled coarse fodder with their bare hands.' And, significantly, they 'helped construct Southern railroads.' [14]

Despite being an older singer, Martha Copeland (sometimes billed as 'Everybody's Mammy') nevertheless possessed a fine voice, and on 'Police Blues' [Columbia 14237-D] saw a job on the railroad as a way of getting quick money to bail out her man... even though she had asked the police to put him jail for beating her up in the first place!

> I would get a job workin' on the railroad track.
> 'Til I make myself some money so to get him back.[15]

Although the number of female trackside workers greatly reduced after 1865, a great many women remained employed in agriculture: 'White landlords, and many black husbands, expected black women to work regularly in the fields as well as to perform whatever domestic labor they had time left for; black women did "a man's share in the field, and a woman's part at home". In 1900, over half of all black households in the Cotton Belt had at least one daughter sixteen or younger working in the fields as a laborer.' [16] However, it would appear that, upon reaching the age of sixteen, these young female field hands could and did leave the land in droves. A little known singer, Henry L. Castle (*aka* 'Too Tight Henry') alluded to this scenario in 1930, injecting some humour into his sexual-based 'The Way I Do' [Brunswick 7189]:

> I never did lie, neither robbin' nor steal,
> But I stole a little mama from the cotton field.
>
> *Refrain*: It ain't none of me, she says, it's the way I do.[17]

It may have been these teenage girls that caused McTell to sing *'look-a-yonder, at the women'*, although in 'Scarey Day Blues' [OKeh 8936], he seems to have become involved with a *'hot-shot mama'* who was a platform vendor:

> I wants to wait round here, baby, until your fried pies get done. *(x2)*
> Because I think I got a nickel, I wants to buy me one.[18]

Many black women — whether food vendors at the depots or on the trains, trackside labourers, domestic servants or field hands — would sing as they carried out their tasks. David Evans observes that 'Johann Tonsor, writing on black singing from Louisville, Ky., in 1892... noted... as did John Lomax some years later, that women would sing while working. He stated: "It is quite a common thing for the negro women to improvise words and music while they are at work, a sort of Wagnerian 'melos', or endless melody, as it were. I have often heard them drone softly thus all through the live-long, bright summer day." Tonsor must have been hearing the kind of singing which, within a few years, would be transformed into the blues.' [19]

On the basis of an interview with Ma Rainey by musicologist and researcher John W. Work Jr. in the late 1930s, Evans reiterates: 'In 1902, a woman in a small town in Missouri sang a blues for Gertrude 'Ma' Rainey, a singer whose traveling show was passing through. Rainey liked the song and incorporated it into her act, calling it simply "the blues".' [20] Via their time spent on the travelling shows, vaudeville-blues singers became a catalyst in the perpetuation and evolution of the oral black tradition in the blues.

Contrary to the popular concept that the vaudeville-blues singers drew on the material of country/rural blues performers in the majority of cases is not to present a true picture. It was much more of a two-way street, as I hope to demonstrate. By way of illustration, I will cite several examples of songs originally recorded by vaudeville-blues singers (predominantly female), whose lyrics, or part thereof, reappeared in later recorded blues by rural singers (predominantly male). I shall also explore to what extent all of these songs were drawn from an oral tradition that existed before 1920 (when blues was first recorded), or were in fact composed by at least some of these women singers.

One notable exception to the popular view *has* been given some publicity, and that is Ma Rainey's 'Booze And Blues' [Paramount 12242], recorded in 1924 with her Georgia Jazz Band. The melody and the theme of Rainey's blues quite obviously inspired Delta blues master Charley Patton's 1929 recording, 'Tom Rushen Blues' [Paramount 12877)], as well as a remake titled 'High Sheriff Blues' [Vocalion 02680] some five years later.*

Another equally obvious 'vaudeville-to-country blues' influence is Clara Smith's superb 'Awful Moanin' Blues' [Columbia A-4000] from 1923, which was later recorded by several other vaudeville-blues singers including Rosa Henderson and Mattie Hite:

> I feel bad, always sad.
> Trouble, trouble, driving me mad.
> Good old days of long ago, all are gone to come no more.
> That is why you always hear me moan.
>
> Mmmmmmmmmmmmmm.
> Mmmmmmmmmmmmmm.
> Mmmmmm-mmmm.
> How my heart aches.
> Soon it will break, I'm almost through.
> What can I do, just to cure these 'Awful Moanin' Blues'? [22]

In 1926, the obscure Bo Weavil Jackson cut a rural blues version of the song as 'Why Do You Moan?' [Paramount 12423], featuring some archaic-sounding, albeit intricate guitar-work. However, he made no attempt to change the vocal approach, emulating Ms. Smith's 'moaning style' using the extended hum; while forgetting some of the words and omitting the title. This vocal ornamentation was only used by Jackson on one other of his thirteen recorded sides, and this was 'Some Scream High Yellow', on the reverse of Paramount 12423 — perhaps in an attempt to match the mood of the other side. A commercial flop, Jackson appeared and disappeared after his two sessions in the summer of 1926 (one for Paramount, the other for Vocalion as 'Sam Butler').

Other examples of vaudeville-to-country blues transmissions that may be cited include Lucille Bogan's 'Kind Stella Blues' [Paramount 12504] from 1927, which resurfaced the following year as 'Gamblin' Charley' [Columbia 14420] by Charley Lincoln; and Sippie Wallace's 1925 recording, 'The Man I Love' [OKeh 8251], which was remade as 'Married Man Blues' [Vocalion 03454] and 'Dallas Woman Blues' [Vocalion, unissued], in 1936 and 1937 respectively, by the fine Texas pianist Black Boy Shine (Harold Holiday).

Bessie Smith's 1924 record, 'Mountain Top Blues' [Columbia 14031-D] contained the *'Got myself a hammock, placed it underneath the tree'* verse later employed by Charley Patton on Paramount 12298, which the company incorrectly titled 'Hammer Blues'. That same year, she recorded

---

* This was noted by Calt & Wardlow in 1988 — see *King Of The Delta Blues* (Rock Chapel Press).[21]

'Work House Blues' [Columbia 14032-D], from which another great Delta bluesman, Son House, appropriated the *'I wish I had a heaven of my own'* verse for his powerful 'Preachin' The Blues (Part 1)' [Paramount 13013] — albeit sung from a different viewpoint. In 1931, Sam Collins (another 'first generation' bluesman like Patton, born a little earlier, in 1887) borrowed the following verse from Smith's 'Work House Blues':

> 'Cos I'm goin' to the Nation*, goin' to the Territor'.
> Say, I'm bound for the Nation, bound for the Territor'.
> I got to leave here, I got to catch the next train [that] goes.[23]

for his beautiful 'I'm Still Sitting On Top Of The World' [Banner 32395] — which itself partly influenced Robert Johnson's 'Come On In My Kitchen' [ARC 7-07-57] some five years later. Collins' high, eerie vocal delivers a variation of the Bessie Smith verse:

> Went to the Nation, new Territor'.
> Gonna catch me the first train, I got to go.[24]

Similarly, in 1926 East Coast guitar supremo Blind Blake borrowed a verse from Texas singer/pianist Sippie Wallace's 1924 recording, 'Stranger's Blues' [OKeh 8159] for his 'Stonewall Street Blues' [Paramount 12431]. On this, Wallace sang of the ever-present urge (shared with many other working-class blacks) to travel on the rails, no matter where those twin steel lines may lead to, in the hope that her situation will improve:

> I'm gonna catch that train, don't care where it stops. *(x2)*
> 'Cos I ain't gonna stay here, be made no stumblin' block.[25]

It has already been noted by other writers that 'You Don't Know My Mind Blues' [OKeh 8115], recorded by Virginia Liston in 1923, influenced many other later versions. One of these was a rural blues styling by Barbecue Bob (Robert Hicks) called 'Honey You Don't Know My Mind' [Columbia 14246-D] from 1927, while his older brother Charlie (as 'Charley Lincoln') inaugurated his recording career that same year with 'Jealous Hearted Blues' [Columbia 14305-D] — a song originally recorded three years earlier by Ma Rainey [Paramount 12252]. And the famous 1923 Ida Cox waxing, 'Graveyard Dream Blues' [Paramount 12044], was given an inspired twin-guitar treatment by Willie Harris and an unidentified partner in 1930 as 'Lonesome Midnight Dream' [Brunswick 7149]. There are many other such examples, with lines, verses and even complete songs recorded prior to the 'male blues breakthrough' in 1926 reappearing in the repertoires of Peg Leg Howell, Frank Stokes, Skip James and Robert Johnson, to name but a few.

---

* This is a reference to the Indian Territory or 'Nation'. See footnote on page 315 for fuller explanation.

While the influence on the above-mentioned male blues singers was mainly via recordings, it is to the oral tradition that we must turn for the sources that were drawn on by the early blues women — both rural and vaudeville. Lucille Bogan (who started out recording in the latter style in 1923, had by 1927 developed into a tough and uncompromising country blues singer), Sippie Wallace, Ida Cox, Ma Rainey and other female blues performers often composed their own material, and had to draw on existing oral traditions in the absence of a recorded rural blues legacy. For instance, Barbecue Bob's *'So glad I'm brownskin, chocolate to the bone'* chorus on his 'Chocolate To The Bone' [Columbia 14331-D] from 1928 first appeared on 'Kitchen Mechanic Blues' [OKeh 4481], an acappella item recorded in 1922 by the male Excelsior Quartette, whose roots probably stretched back to an earlier age. It is more than likely that, even without recordings, Bob could have drawn on his famous chorus from the oral traditions back in the closing years of the Nineteenth Century.

Those traditions encompassed not only acappella groups, itinerant male blues guitarists/fiddlers, pianists, banjo and harmonica players, but also the women who sang as they worked, 'droning softly' — the field hands, platform vendors, 'passenger train women', etc.

Recorded in 1923, Ethel Ridley's 'Alabama Bound Blues' [Columbia A-3965] could easily have originated from one of the latter:

> *No. 7's in the station, No. 11 in the yard.*
> *No. 7 in the station, No. 11 in the yard.*
> *Gonna leave this town if I have to ride the rods.*[26]

The highly-popular Leroy Carr (who was admittedly more urban than rural in style) later used a variation of this theme for his 'Mean Old Train Blues' [Vocalion 1214] in 1928:

> *No. 1's in the station, No. 2's out on the road. (x2)*
> *Then I begin to wonder where did my baby go?* [27]

while Dora Carr (no relation) is quite possibly the first woman to have recorded a traditionally 'male' blues verse on her 'Cow Cow Blues' [OKeh 8250] in 1925. Here, she discovers that her man has left by train from the Union Station, apparently either on the Seaboard Air Line or the Western & Atlantic (albeit the Central of Georgia had long since taken over the once state-owned W&A):

> *Some say he left on that Seaboard, some say it was the W&A.*
> *I don't care which train it was, it carried my man away.*
> *Starch up my jumper, iron up my over-hall.*
> *I'm gonna ride that train, I mean that Cannonball.*[28]

A 'cannonball' stove in a yardmaster's shack on the SP.

On this, the first version of the great Cow Cow Davenport's 'signature tune', where the pianist plays his own rolling boogie accompaniment, Carr declares: *'I had the railroad blues, I just too mean to cry.'* [28]

The *'Cannonball'* mentioned in the song originally referred to the *Wabash Cannonball*, which headed for St. Louis from Detroit on the Wabash Railway, but it soon became a colloquialism for a fast train on any railroad. However, it also has another meaning, which has sometimes confused blues

Blind Willie McTell *aka* Blind Sammie, c.1927.

writers where singers have used the term to describe the physical charms of their partner (as in *'He/she's long and tall like a cannonball'*).

The earliest recording to feature a version of the line quoted above was 1923's 'I Love My Man Better Than I Love Myself' [Paramount 12056] by Ida Cox. Here, the reference is not to a fast train, but to the 'cannonball' stove that was a feature of most rural homes in the South by the 1900s, as well as in the shacks of the freight yard superintendents or 'yard-masters' on railroads all over the US. Not only that, this functional piece of hardware had also been used to provide heating on passenger trains since the 1880s — the beginning of 'the age of the cannon-ball stove in the cars themselves' [29], as Beebe & Clegg put it. So, access to using this ubiquitous appliance for poetic imagery was open to both male rural and female vaudeville-blues singers from the latter part of the Nineteenth Century onwards. Most importantly perhaps, the cannonball stove was a familiar object to the people who listened to (and later on bought records of) the blues: working-class blacks, and some poor whites too.

In the case of Blind Willie McTell's 'Statesboro Blues' [Victor V-38001], recorded in 1928, its inspirational source was more complex. In fact, McTell drew on several songs — all by vaudeville-blues women. As he so disarmingly says on the introduction of his final version of 'The Dyin' Crapshooter's Blues' [LP *Last Session* (Bluesville BVLP-1040) 1962], recorded in 1956: *'See, I had to steal music from every which-a way to get it, to get it, get it fixed. But I-I messed it up anyway, somehow.'* [30] Although these comments were applied to 'Crapshooter' in particular (which I have traced back ultimately to Dublin, Ireland in 1760), McTell obviously used this method — as many other singers did — to create what in his case are other masterpieces of the rural blues.

The acclaimed 'Statesboro Blues' is a case in point. Here, McTell drew on at least five other songs, dating from 1923 to 1927, for inspiration.

From Sippie Wallace's first recording, 'Up The Country Blues' [OKeh 8106] from 1923, he borrowed the first and last verses:

> Eh-hey, mama,
> Run tell your papa.
> Go tell your sister.
> Run tell your auntie.
> That I'm goin' up the country, don't you wanna go?
> I need another half-a-dozen to take them on my ragtime Joe[*].
>
> My mama's got 'em.
> My papa's got 'em.
>
> My sister's got 'em.
> Might-a had 'em when I woke up this mornin'.
> Papa [I] had up-the-country blues.
> When I looked over in the corner, my grandma had 'em too.[33]

He was also clearly inspired by Bessie Smith's 'Reckless Blues' [Columbia 14056-D] from 1925, which, although a completely different song, alluded to the format of Wallace's 'Up The Country Blues' in the following lines:

> My mama says I'm reckless, my daddy says I'm wild. *(x2)*
> I ain't good lookin', but I'm somebody's angel child.[34]

Ragtime/jazz pianist Fred Longshaw, who backed Smith on reed-organ on this occasion, is credited with writing 'Reckless Blues' and most likely picked up the *'ain't good-looking'* phrase from the oral tradition. On 'Statesboro Blues' McTell expertly redeploys these lines in a slightly altered form:

> My mother died an' left me reckless,
>   my daddy died an' left me wild, wild, wild.
> Mother died an' left me reckless,
>   daddy died an' left me wild, wild, wild.
> [I] know I'm not good-lookin'
>   but I'm some sweet woman's angel child.[35]

delivering them in an almost-raffish uptempo vein to the accompaniment of his 'worrying', moaning twelve-string guitar.

Some three months after Smith recorded 'Reckless Blues', another vaudeville singer named Marie Grinter used the *'ain't good-lookin' '* verse on

---

[*] From two sources via Partridge: (1) 'rag-time', adj. Merry: coll: from 1901 or 1902.'[31] (2) 'Joe or joe... rather a contracted telescoping 'joke' becoming 'jo', which is folk-etymology'd to 'Joe'.[32] In other words, an exciting adventure or jaunt.

her 'Morning Dove Blues' [Gennett 3004], albeit she omits the phrase entirely. Instead, she sings:

> Some folks don't like me because I'm young an' wild. *(x2)*
> But my lovin' man told me I was his baby child.[36]

Grinter's song was actually a cover of a similarly-titled Sippie Wallace recording [OKeh 8205] made a few months earlier in February 1925 (on which Wallace actually sings *'moanin'* dove'). The latter did not feature the *'ain't good lookin''* verse either, but it begs the question where Ms. Grinter got her verse from. There are several possibilities: she may have drawn on the oral tradition, seen a live performance by Smith or McTell or she may have picked it up from Smith's record.

Interestingly, in December of that same year (1925), Dora Carr included another variant on her 'Cow Cow Blues':

> Mama says I'm crazy, I say they know I'm wild;
> Everybody tells Cow Cow [is] mama's baby child.[37]

Elements of both these songs can be clearly identified in 'Statesboro Blues'.

Finally, McTell also adapted a verse from another unrelated song, 'Cincinnati Southern Blues' [Paramount 12472], recorded some eighteen months earlier in April 1927, by Ivy Smith. This singer appears to have been based in Birmingham, Ala., though her song about the Cincinnati Southern train that will carry her back home to Birmingham is very much in the 'rural' tradition, with a smoking vocal that had a razor-sharp edge to it:

> She leaves Cincinnati at five o'clock. *(x2)*
> You oughta see the fireman getting' his boiler hot.[38]

The Cincinnati Southern ran from Cincinnati, Oh. to Chattanooga, Tenn. and was leased by 'a syndicate led by Baron Emile Erlanger of Frankfort and London *[which]* ambitiously set out in 1881 to create a railroad system in the heart of the South, with the Alabama Great Southern line, from Meridian by Birmingham to Chattanooga, as a nucleus.' [39] Following other mergers/takeovers, this system became known as the 'Queen & Crescent' route. It was leased by the East Tennessee, Virginia and Georgia RR, which in turn was totally absorbed by the Southern Railway in 1898 — yet Smith and her pianist, Cow Cow Davenport, still saw the railroad as the 'Cincinnati Southern' almost thirty years later!

It was Ivy Smith's last line which appealed to Willie McTell and now, together with some of his own, he was ready to commit to wax one of the finest blues in the genre.

Wake up, mama, turn your lamp down low. *(x2)*
Have you got the nerve to drive Papa McTell from your door?

Big 80 left Savannah, Lord, an' did not stop.
You ought to saw that colored fireman when he got them boiler hot.
You can reach over in the corner, mama, an' hand me my travelin' shoes.
You know by that I've got them 'Statesboro Blues'.[40]

This blues achieved greater recognition in the 1970s when the globetrotting Taj Mahal cut an updated version with a small group featuring himself on slide guitar. Just in case some of his international audience were not sure of where Blind Willie was singing about, Taj interjects at one point: *'Statesboro, Georgia, that is!'*

II

Blind Willie McTell was very aware of the US music scene in the 1920s and '30s (he was his own agent and promoter!) and must have been familiar with the aforementioned recordings by Sippie Wallace, Bessie Smith Marie Grinter, Dora Carr, and Ivy Smith, or may even have heard the songs performed live by these artists. Indeed, in many ways McTell fits the popular concept of a rural bluesman: an itinerant guitarist hoboing his way on various freight trains, or playing in medicine and carnival shows. However, the question remains, where did these women get their songs from? The answer is quite straightforward: many, such as the field hands, platform vendors and passenger train women had ample opportunity to hear early blues in the closing decades of the Nineteenth Century, and the chances to hear, exchange and reshape blues ballads and 'blues proper' were countless.

As has already been noted, both rural and vaudeville-blues often drew on an existing oral tradition within the Southern black community. A classic example is the blues ballad, 'Careless Love'. Recorded by several singers in the pre-war era including Bessie Smith, Lulu Jackson and Lonnie Johnson, it was a request by white folkologist Frederic Ramsey Jr. in 1948 to Leadbelly, who was then recording one of his last sessions, just over a year before he died 'in New York on December 6, 1949.'[41] In response to a question by Ramsey as to whether it was an old song when he first heard it, Leadbelly replied: 'Well, it's-yeah-somethin' like that. Yes, pretty old then... Somethin' like barrelhouse. You know, people make up words around the barrelhouse, you know. Thing like that.'

Also referring to it as 'an old-time song', Leadbelly recalled singing 'Careless Love' in Dallas, Tex. with Blind Lemon Jefferson in 1904: 'Now, to my ideas, which I think is true, Blind Lemon *[was]* the first man to put out that record of 'Careless Love'. But since then it had bin a lot o' records, you know, made since that, you know. But he's the first one that did record *[it]*... Him an' I used to sing it in Dallas, Texas, an' I was around *[there]* in 1904, you know.' [42]

Leadbelly, however, appears to have confused the song with a Blind Lemon number from 1926 called 'Corinna Blues' [Paramount 12367], for Jefferson in fact never recorded 'Careless Love'. The opening verse of the former song includes the line: *'See see rider, just see what you have done'*, which made its first appearance on record in 1924, on Ma Rainey's 'See See Rider Blues' [Paramount 2252]. But the song 'Careless Love' itself is much older than that, and it is entirely possible that Leadbelly could have sung a variant of it with Blind Lemon early on in the Twentieth Century.

Certainly, these songs can be seen as 'musical cousins' or otherwise related to each other. 'Careless Love' was actually first recorded in January 1922 by Katherine Handy (W.C. Handy's second daughter) as 'Loveless Love' [Paramount 12011], accompanied by Handy's Memphis Blues Orchestra. In his autobiography, Handy says that 'Careless Love' (Katherine actually sang *'careless'*) was his arrangement of an old folk song.[43] By Leadbelly's reckoning, 'Careless Love'/'Corinna Blues'/'See See Rider Blues' was already an old song in 1904. This puts it back into the Nineteenth Century, and firmly into the oral tradition that sustained so many early rural and vaudeville-blues singers, as well as composers/bandleaders like Handy himself. Indeed, 'Careless Love' could just as easily have been written by an early urban female worker as an itinerant rural male troubadour — a singer like Ma Rainey or Clara Smith perhaps.

Finally, let us consider the case of Mae Glover, who is thought to have also recorded as 'May Armstrong' and 'Side Wheel Sally Duffie' (aural evidence seems very much in favour of this theory). Armstrong and Glover's similar forenames and the latter's use of 'Sally Sad' on one of her recordings, would seem to support this theory. Further to this, 'Duffie' and Glover both recorded a 'Plantation Blues' in 1927 and 1931 [Paramount 12545 and Champion 16408 respectively]. Unfortunately, the latter version remains undiscovered, thereby thwarting any comparison. While Mae Glover recorded three sessions, in 1929 and 1931, 'Armstrong' and 'Duffie' only cut one each, both in 1927.

Glover possessed an attractive vibrato which had deepened by the time she cut her 1929 session. Although she was sometimes given a 'vaudeville-blues' accompaniment (trumpet, violin and piano) on her records, Glover's singing displays a rawness that has more in common with rural blues — especially on those sides featuring the twelve-string guitarist, John Byrd, or barrelhouse pianist Will Ezell. A case in point is 'Kid Man Blues' [Paramount 12581], which she originally recorded as 'Sally Duffie' in 1927, and subsequently remade under her own name as 'I Ain't Givin' Nobody None' [Gennett 6948] in 1929.

On Wednesday, 27 April 1927, Glover cut 'Lonesome Atlanta Blues' for Brunswick as 'May Armstrong'. Unissued at the time, this was accompanied by violin and piano, which lent an urban atmosphere to proceedings. However, seven months or so later Bobby Grant covered it (almost word for word) as a lowdown rural blues complete with staggered phrasing and exquisite slide guitar [Paramount 12595].

At the same session, Armstrong had also recorded 'Woodchopping Blues' — likewise unissued at the time — with the violin replaced by a mandolin, heading back to a more country blues sound:

'May Armstrong' ad, *Chicago Defender*, 1927.

> I'm goin' up on the mountain, gonna root just like a hog. *(x2)*
> These old men round here treat a good woman like a dog.
>
> If you get one man, better get you five or six.
> I said, if you get one man, better get you five or six.
> So if that one should quit you, it wouldn't leave you in an awful fix.
>
> You treated me mean, when I tried to do the best I could. *(x2)*
> But tell me, since I've gone, who in the world's gonna chop your wood? [44]

In the same month of April 1927, a great blues guitar-man by the name of Walter Hawkins, thought to be from Blytheville, Ark., cut a session for Paramount. Recording as Buddy Boy Hawkins, he took 'Armstrong's' opening lines and incorporated them into his 'Shaggy Dog Blues' [Paramount 12489]. At his next session in September that year, Hawkins used the other two 'Armstrong' verses quoted above, also drawing on one of them for a title, 'Awful Fix Blues' [Paramount 12539]:

> If you get one old woman, boys, you better get you five or —
> You better get you five or — I mean — six.
> If you get one woman, you better get you five or six.
> So if that one happen to quit you, it won't leave you in a awful fix.
>
> When I had you, pretty mama,
> > you know I was tryin' to do the best I, I mean could
> Said it was no lie.
> I said when I had you, little black woman, I tryin' to do the best I could.
> Now, your little daddy's gone,
> > now who's you gonna get to chop your wood? [45]

As both the Armstrong sides, 'Lonesome Atlanta Blues' and 'Woodchopping Blues', remained unissued until 1993, when they appeared on the CD *Mae Glover (1927-31)* [Document DOCD-5185], this begs the question how they came to be re-recorded by two different country blues singers in the 1920s. The only answer seems to be that all three singers heard these songs in live performance.* This would be more convincing if there were one or more common factors to indicate this could have actually happened, and — for our purposes — if this also involved the railroad.

Once again, we have to look to the recordings themselves. For example, Mae Glover's two 1931 sessions included a vaudeville-blues, 'Two Timin' Mamma' [Champion 16244], and an offering that owed more to hokum (*à la* Butterbeans & Susie, etc.) than to rural blues, 'Grasshopper Papa' [Champion 16351]. Since hokum derived from the carnival and circus *(see pages 265-6)*, it is not surprising to find such a connection here.

'Grasshopper Papa' is a duet between the throaty Glover and trumpet-player James Parker, who is being given his marching orders or *'the boot'*:

> You just an old banana that's been peeled.
> So go on an' sleep out in some old field.
> For your lovin' mama, she just can't use you now.

In case her man hasn't got the message, she closes with these words:

> So be on the hop, grasshopper papa, 'cos I'm through with you.
> I mean, I'm just too through with you. [46]

Meanwhile, in her superb 'I Ain't Givin' Nobody None' [Gennett 6948], Glover invokes the sexual coffee-grinder imagery previously employed by Lucille Bogan on 'Coffee Grindin' Blues' [Brunswick 7083] and Jaybird

---

* Hawkins may have seen May Armstrong in Chicago during April 1927, as both recorded there for Brunswick and Paramount respectively in that month.

Coleman on 'Coffee Grinder Blues' [Columbia 14534-D]:

> I drink so much coffee, the grounds are in my sleep. *(x2)*
> I don't care how I do, you so doggone hard to please.[47]

Once again, we turn to Wilmeth for a definition of a 'coffee-grinder'. He writes: 'A type of classic act in striptease involving a particular strenous *[sic]* type of grind.'[48] A grind — like a 'bump' — is an erotic, sensual movement emanating from the pelvic region.

On her last recorded side, 'Good Hearted Woman' [Champion 16244], Ms. Glover includes a unique verse:

> There's a blues on the wire, blues everywhere I go.
> Blues on the wire, blues everywhere I go.
> They are even on the golf course, when they holler 'Fore!'[49]

If this refers to the 'high-wire' in a circus tightrope act, then this would appear to provide fairly conclusive evidence that Glover spent some time singing or performing in a circus/carnival. In passing, it is interesting to note that, as golf courses in Georgia were generally barred to blacks in the 1920s, Glover's reference could be interpreted as an implied protest against Jim Crow segregation laws. On the strength of Buddy Boy Hawkins' ventriloquist act on his 'Voice Throwin' Blues' [Paramount 12802] and his possibly-autobiographical 'Workin' On The Railroad' [Paramount 12558], it can be assumed that he too spent some time in travelling shows and on the railroad itself.

This leaves Bobby Grant. Apart from his two sides for Paramount in 1927 (which included the version of 'Lonesome Atlanta Blues' discussed above), and the accompaniment he provided on two others for an equally obscure singer, Ruby Paul, on the same day, this guitarist is a biographical blank. Although he has in the past been deemed to be a Delta man because of his performance on record, he could almost as easily fit into the Georgia blues styles exemplified by the likes of Barbecue Bob, Kokomo Arnold and George Carter. It might well be significant that Grant singled out 'Atlanta' from Mae Glover's fairly extensive repertoire when cutting his only 78 rpm release.

As Glover is also something of a shadowy figure, it is to her recordings that we must look for any possible clues. In 1931, she recorded three sides about prison. The unissued Champion title, 'Prison Bound Blues', could well be a straight cover of the very popular 1929 Leroy Carr hit [Vocalion 1241], recorded in December 1928. However, her 'County Farm Blues' [Champion 16268] and 'Hoboken Prison Blues' on the flip side, may reflect personal experience *(see also page 189)*.

A state-by-state search of US maps covering a hundred year period reveals four places called Hoboken. These are (or were) situated in

Pennsylvania and New Jersey in the North, and in the Southern states of Alabama and Georgia. The last of these, on the Atlantic Coast Line RR, lies some twenty miles almost due east of Waycross, Ga., in the south-eastern part of that state. One of the busiest railroad crossings in the first half of the Twentieth Century, Waycross was celebrated by Barbecue Bob in 1928 on his 'Waycross Georgia Blues' [Columbia 14331-D] after a visit to the city, and another Georgia twelve-string guitarist, Willie Baker, may also have been there around this time. Home to a turpentine distillery plant, and a major source of black employment, this Hoboken doubtless also included a jailhouse and appears to be the most likely subject of Mae Glover's blues.

The Hoboken in Alabama (not on any modern map) was situated in Marengo County about fifty miles north-east of State Line, Miss. and was apparently not served by a railroad. Although an ad in the *Chicago Defender* claimed that May Armstrong (Mae Glover) was 'from Alabama', she employs what I call the 'singing falsetto cry' — a technique used by singers like Blind Willie McTell, Barbecue Bob and Curley Weaver, which seems to be almost totally confined within the Georgia tradition. She uses it on 'I Ain't Givin' Nobody None' (though not on the earlier version, 'Kid Man Blues', from the 1927 'Duffie' session). This was with John Byrd on twelve-string guitar. She sounds at her most confident (and arguably her best) on the four sides with this bluesman, who reputedly hailed from southern Mississippi. As one writer put it, 'the genuine rapport on their duets is fuel for a theory that their relationship was more than just professional.'[50] One indication of this perhaps is her inclusion of two new verses — both sexual — on 'I Ain't Givin' Nobody None' [Gennett 6948], one containing the *'coffee grinder'* lines already quoted, the other pledging total commitment to her man, combined with an air of domesticity:

> I wash your clothes in the mornin', cook jelly roll at night.
> I wash your clothes in the mornin', bake jelly roll at night.
> When you come home, [I'll] try to be so doggone tight.[51]

If Romanowski's theory is correct, it would help explain John Byrd's adoption of the twelve-string guitar, which is generally absent in Mississippi players but very prevalent in Georgia ('the Atlanta twelve-string school', including Barbecue Bob *et al*), especially if Byrd had moved to Glover's home for the duration (she infers having lived in Hoboken, Ga. for a while and may herself have been a native of that state, if not from that city itself — yet another avenue of research!)

As an artist in a travelling show, Glover may well have encountered Bobby Grant while he was going down *'that dirty old dirt road'* to Decatur Street in Atlanta, way back in 1927. Or, like Buddy Boy Hawkins, as a hobo he would catch a train where possible. It could have been at one of these shows that these three singers, Hawkins, Grant and Glover, exchanged ideas of repertoire in their individual acts such as 'Awful Fix Blues', 'Lonesome Atlanta Blues' and 'Woodchopping Blues'.

A final example of a likely candidate for a vaudeville-to-rural blues influence is Trixie Smith, born in Atlanta, Ga. in 1895. She was unusual in that she 'attended university before going on the road as a singer' [52] Ms. Smith wrote some of her own material, including 1924's 'Freight Train Blues' [Paramount 12211], which she re-cut in 1938 [Decca 7489]. Blind Boy Fuller used one of its verses for his 'Big Bed Blues' [ARC 6-11-71] in 1936, substituting *'that M&O whistle'* for *'freight train'*:

Trixie Smith ad, *Chicago Defender*, 1924.

> I hate to hear that M&O whistle blow, boo-hoo.[53]

Smith also recorded other rail-oriented blues including 'Choo Choo Blues' [Paramount 12245] in 1924 and 'Railroad Blues' [Paramount 12262] in 1925. Although born in Georgia, she had attended 'Selma University, Alabama, as a youth' [54] Maybe that's why she sings *'I'm Alabama bound'* on the latter:

> Now, the train went by with my papa on the inside.
> I say, the train went by with my papa on the inside.
> Lord, I couldn't do nothin' but hang my head an' cry.
>
> Did you ever take a trip on the Seaboard & Air Line? *(x2)*
> 'Cos if you ride that train, it'll satisfy your mind.
>
> I got the railroad blues, I wanna see my home town. *(x2)*
> An' if the Seaboard don't wreck, I'm Alabama bound.[55]

With an unusually 'hard' vocal attack, backed by some scintillating cornet from Louis Armstrong and 'dirty' trombone from Charlie Green, this song has the feel of lowdown country blues about it, and is a fitting end to this chapter. It can clearly be seen that the two-way flow between vaudeville and country blues was much more evenly divided than has previously been acknowledged, and one of the main routes of this exchange was the railroads, via the various types of travelling shows, as well as the platform vendors and the 'passenger train women'.

Notes to Chapter 9

1. Reidy, J.P. — Ibid, p.105
2. Licht, W. — Ibid, p.215
3. 'Passenger Train Woman' — Blind Boy Fuller - vocal, guitar (5 March 1940, New York City)
4. 'Funny Feeling Blues' — Blind Boy Fuller - vocal, guitar (5 April 1938, New York City)
5. 'Painful Hearted Man' — Blind Boy Fuller - vocal, guitar (5 April 1938, New York City)
6. White, J.H. — *The American Railroad Passenger Car*, Ibid, p.312
7. Risher, H. — Ibid, p.173
8. 'Every Day In The Week Blues' — Pink Anderson - vocal, guitar; Simmie Dooley - vocal, guitar, speech (14 April 1928, Atlanta, Ga.)
9. 'Travelin' Blues' — Blind Willie McTell (as 'Blind Sammie') - vocal, guitar, speech (30 October 1929, Atlanta, Ga.)
10. 'Talkin' To Myself' — Blind Willie McTell (as 'Blind Sammie') - vocal, guitar, speech (17 April 1930, Atlanta, Ga.)
11. Marshall, J. — p.98
12. Perata, D. — p.75
13. Reidy — Ibid, p.103
14. White, D.G. — pp.120-2
15. 'Police Blues' — Martha Copeland - vocal; Porter Grainger - piano; unk. whistle (22 July 1927, New York City)
16. Ayers, E. — Ibid, pp.204-5
17. 'The Way I Do' — Too Tight Henry - vocal, prob.guitar; prob. Jed Davenport - harmonica; unk. piano (c.2 October 1930, Chicago, Ill.)

18	'Scarey Day Blues'	Blind Willie McTell - vocal, guitar, speech (23 October 1931, Atlanta, Ga.)
19	Evans, D.	p.42
20	Ibid.	
21	Calt, S., & G. Wardlow	Ibid, p.240
22	'Awful Moanin' Blues'	Clara Smith - vocal, humming; Fletcher Henderson - piano (13 September 1923, New York City)
23	'Work House Blues'	Bessie Smith - vocal; Charlie Green - trombone; Fletcher Henderson - piano (23 July 1924, New York City)
24	'I'm Still Sitting On Top Of The World'	Sam Collins - vocal, guitar (8 October 1931, New York City)
25	'Stranger's Blues'	Sippie Wallace - vocal; Clarence Williams - piano (c.29 May 1924, New York City)
26	'Alabama Bound Blues'	Ethel Ridley - vocal; Leroy Tibbs - piano (23 June 1923, New York City)
27	'Mean Old Train Blues'	Leroy Carr - vocal, piano; Scrapper Blackwell - guitar; unk. sound effects. (14 August 1928, Chicago, Ill.)
28	'Cow Cow Blues'	Dora Carr - vocal; Cow Cow Davenport - piano (1 October 1925, New York City)
29	Beebe, L., & C. Clegg.	*The Central Pacific & Southern Pacific*, p?
30	'Dyin' Crapshooter's Blues'	Blind Willie McTell - vocal, speech, guitar (1956, Atlanta, Ga.).
31	Partridge, E.	*Penguin Dictionary of Historical Slang*, Ibid, p.750
32	Partridge, E.	*A Dictionary of the Underworld*, ibid, p.367
33	'Up The Country Blues'	Sippie Wallace - vocal; Eddie Heywood - piano (c.26 October 1923, Chicago, Ill.)
34	'Reckless Blues'	Bessie Smith - vocal; Louis Armstrong - cornet; Fred Longshaw - reed organ (14 January 1925, New York City)
35	'Statesboro Blues'	Blind Willie McTell - vocal, guitar (17 October 1928, Atlanta, Ga.)
36	'Morning Dove Blues'	Marie Grinter vocal; unknown clarinet, alto sax, violin, piano (6 April 1925)
37	'Cow Cow Blues'	Dora Carr vocal; Cow Cow Davenport piano (1 October 1925)
38	'Cincinnati Southern Blues'	Ivy Smith - vocal, speech; Cow Cow Davenport - piano, speech; unk. sound effects (c.April 1927, Chicago, Ill.)
39	Doster, J.F.	Ibid, pp.46-7
40	'Statesboro Blues'	Ibid.
41	Asman, J.	Notes to Melodisc MLP-12-113 (LP)

42	Ramsey Jr, Frederic	Interview with Huddie Ledbetter (Leadbelly) Notes to Melodisc MLP-12-113 (LP)
43	Handy, W.C.	Ibid, p.306
44	'Woodchopping Blues'	May Armstrong (prob. Mae Glover) - vocal; unk. mandolin, piano (27 April 1927, Chicago or St. Louis)
45	'Awful Fix Blues'	Buddy Boy Hawkins - vocal, guitar, speech (c.September 1927, Chicago, Ill.)
46	'Grasshopper Papa'	Mae Glover - vocal, speech; James Parker - vocal, speech; Charles O'Neil - piano (23 February 1931, Richmond, Ind.)
47	'Coffee Grinder Blues'	Jaybird Coleman - vocal, harmonica; unk. piano (22 April 1930, Atlanta, Ga.)
48	Wilmeth, D.B.	Ibid.
49	'Good Hearted Woman'	Mae Glover - vocal; Charles O'Neil - piano (24 February 1931, Richmond, Ind.)
50	Romanowski, K.	Notes to Document DOCD-5185 (CD)
51	'I Ain't Givin' Nobody None'	Mae Glover - vocal, speech; John Byrd - guitar, speech (29 July 1929, Richmond, Ind.)
52	Larkin, C. (Gen. Ed.)	p.315
53	'Big Bed Blues'	Blind Boy Fuller - vocal, guitar (29 April 1936, New York City)
54	Harris, S.	Ibid, p.474
55	'Railroad Blues'	Trixie Smith - vocal; Louis Armstrong - cornet; Charlie Green - trombone; Buster Bailey clarinet; Fletcher Henderson - piano; Charlie Dixon - banjo (March 1925, New York City)

Discography – Chapter 9

'Alabama Bound Blues'
(Ethel Ridley)

CD: *Female Blues – Volume 1 (1922-27)* [Jazz Perspectives JPCD-1526-2] 1997

'Awful Fix Blues'
(Buddy Boy Hawkins)

CD: *William Harris & Buddy Boy Hawkins (1927-29)* [Document DOCD-5035] 1991

'Awful Moanin' Blues'
(Clara Smith)

CD: *Clara Smith – Volume 1 (1923-24)* [Document DOCD-5364] 1995

'Big Bed Blues'
(Blind Boy Fuller)

4-CD: *Blind Boy Fuller (1935-38)* [J.S.P. JSP-7735] 2004

'Cincinnati Southern Blues'
(Ivy Smith)

CD: *Ivy Smith / Cow Cow Davenport (1927-30)* [Blues Document BDCD-6039] 1993

'Cow Cow Blues'
(Dora Carr)

CD: *Cow Cow Davenport – Vol. 1 (1925-29)* [Document DOCD-5141] 1993

'Dyin' Crapshooter's Blues'
(Blind Willie McTell)

LP: *Last Session – Blind Willie McTell*
[Bluesville BVLP-1040] 1962
LP: *Last Session – Blind Willie McTell*
[Prestige HBS-8008] 1982

'Every Day In The Week Blues'
(Pink Anderson)

CD: *Sinners And Saints (1926-31)*
[Document DOCD-5106] 1992

'Funny Feeling Blues'
(Blind Boy Fuller)

4-CD: *Blind Boy Fuller (1935-38)*
[J.S.P. JSP-7735] 2004

'Good Hearted Woman'
(Mae Glover)

CD: *Mae Glover (1927-31)*
[Document DOCD-5185] 1993

'Grasshopper Papa'
(Mae Glover)

CD: *Mae Glover (1927-31)*
[Document DOCD-5185] 1993

'I Ain't Givin' Nobody None'
(Mae Glover)

CD: *Mae Glover (1927-31)*
[Document DOCD-5185] 1993

'I'm Still Sitting On Top Of The World'
(Sam Collins)

CD: *Sam Collins (1927-31)*
[Document DOCD-5034] 1991

'Mean Old Train Blues'
(Leroy Carr)

CD: *Leroy Carr – Volume 1 (1928-29)*
[Document DOCD-5134] 1993

'Morning Dove Blues'
(Bessie Smith)

CD: *Female Blues Singers – Vol. 7: G/H (1922-29)* [Document DOCD-5511] 1997

'Painful Hearted Man'
(Blind Boy Fuller)

4-CD: *Blind Boy Fuller (1935-38)*
[J.S.P. JSP-7735] 2004

'Passenger Train Woman'
(Blind Boy Fuller)

4-CD: *Blind Boy Fuller (1935-38)*
[J.S.P. JSP-7735] 2004

'Police Blues'
(Martha Copeland)

CD: *Martha Copeland – Volume 1 (1923-27)*
[Document DOCD-5372] 1995

'Railroad Blues'
(Trixie Smith)

CD: *Trixie Smith – Volume 2 (1925-39)*
[Document DOCD-5333] 1995

'Reckless Blues'
(Bessie Smith)

8-CD: *Bessie Smith: The Complete Recordings – Volume 3* [Frog DGF-42] 2002

'Scarey Day Blues'
(Georgia Bill [Blind Willie McTell])

5-CD: *Blind Willie McTell – The Classic Years (1927-40)* [J.S.P. JSP-7711] 2003

'Statesboro Blues'
(Blind Willie McTell)

5-CD: *Blind Willie McTell – The Classic Years (1927-40)* [J.S.P. JSP-7711] 2003

'Stranger's Blues'
(Sippie Wallace)

CD: *Sippie Wallace – Volume 1 (1923-25)*
[Document DOCD-5399] 1995

'Talkin' To Myself'
(Blind Sammie [Blind Willie McTell])

5-CD: *Blind Willie McTell – The Classic Years (1927-40)* [J.S.P. JSP-7711] 2003

'Travelin' Blues'
(Blind Sammie [Blind Willie McTell])

5-CD: *Blind Willie McTell – The Classic Years (1927-40)* [J.S.P. JSP-7711] 2003

'Up The Country Blues'
(Sippie Wallace)

CD: *Sippie Wallace – Volume 1 (1923-25)* [Document DOCD-5399] 1995

'The Way I Do'
(Too Tight Henry)

CD: *Rare Country Blues – Volume 3 (1928-36)* [Document DOCD-5642] 1999

'Woodchopping Blues'
(May Armstrong [Mae Glover])

CD: *Mae Glover (1927-31)* [Document DOCD-5185] 1993

'Work House Blues'
(Bessie Smith)

8-CD: *Bessie Smith: The Complete Recordings – Volume 3* [Frog DGF-42] 2002 The Bessie Smith volumes referred to throughout the book are part of this 8-CD series, and can be bought as a complete set or individually. However the full set is essential to lovers of the 'Empress of the Blues' and is in impeccable sound quality.

Lined out smokin', look like it takin' to scat

'Charleston Contest (Part 1)' – Too Tight Henry (1928)

CHAPTER 10

HOBOS AND RAILROADS

For the itinerant blues singer of the 1920s and '30s hoboing was one of the main attractions of the railroad — the ride was always free. This depended, of course, on whether a tramp (the term generally used before the 1900s) was discovered in his chosen hiding place on the train, or not. While railroad companies took great exception to the hobo because of wanton damage to freight trains and potential loss of revenue on passenger trains, some conductors and engineers did exercise a degree of leniency. Some might trade a short ride for a couple of songs if the hobo was a musician, or for some farm produce that had earlier been begged, borrowed or stolen. The railroad police ('bulls', 'special agents', shack bullies', etc.), on the other hand, were often little better than thugs and were usually very brutal towards the 'free rider'. Even if they didn't get you, then the two most prevalent modes of travelling on a train, 'riding the blinds' and 'riding the rods', could result in serious injury or even death to the hobo. While tens of thousands of whites rode the trains for two or three years following the arrival of the Great Depression in 1930, for black citizens it was a way of life from the 1900s into the late 1930s. This made for some very tough individuals, who often gave as good as they got when discovered. If they didn't retaliate physically — which they certainly did on occasion — they harboured dire wishes to kill the engine crew. So, whereas Trixie Smith hoped in 'Railroad Blues' [Paramount 12262] to make it to Alabama *'if the Seaboard don't wreck'*, 'Mean Conductor Blues' [Paramount 12546] found Ed Bell praying to God that the Southern will do exactly that — and with fatal consequences to the

Chapter 10 — Lined out smokin', look like it takin' to scat

Steel rungs situated between connecting corridor and unknown figure, who was presumably an employee of the St. Louis Southwestern.

locomotive crew for good measure:

> I pray [to] the Lord, that Southern train would wreck. *(x2)*
> So's it kill that fireman, break that engineer's neck.[1]

Smith, and indeed Dora Carr *(see Chapter 9)*, sang their blues from the standpoint of a fare-paying passenger, but Bell was trying to hobo his way to his destination. He refers to 'riding the blinds' and 'blinding it' as far as Hagerstown. Unusual in blues in that it is a sequential narrative, Bell's 'Mean Conductor Blues' [Paramount 12546] graphically describes how his woman (his *'soulie'*) is leaving, like Glover and Carr, on a passenger train. Being broke or *'cold in hand'*, the singer attempts to get a free ride, *'riding the blinds'* as far as Hagerstown:

> The same train, same engineer. *(x2)*
> Took my woman away, Lord, left me standin' here.
>
> My soulie caught the passenger, I caught the mamlish* blind. *(x2)*
> Eey, you can't quit me, it ain't no need of tryin'.
>
> Hey! Mr. Conductor, [can a] broke man ride your blinds? *(x2)*
> 'You better buy your ticket, [you] know this train ain't mine.'

---

* This word, of unknown origin, still lacks a definition. It was used by blues singers as a substitute swear-word (or 'emotional intensifier', as one writer put it!).

I just want to blind it far as Hagerstown.
Yeah, I just want to blind it far as Hagerstown.
When she blows for the crossin', I'm gonna ease it down.

The phrase 'riding the blinds' appears to have two definitions. One describes a position at the end of the baggage or mail car coupled to the tender of the locomotive ('blind' because there is no end door and therefore no access to the hobo from inside the train). The main method of getting rid of a free-rider from here was for the fireman (often black on Southern trains, certainly in the 1920s) to throw lumps of coal at him in an effort to knock him off. The other refers to a far more preferable — but still dangerous — way of travelling as a hobo, which was to ask permission of the (white) conductor or engineer (as Bell does on 'Mean Conductor Blues') to cling to a series of steel rungs (usually three or four) situated at the end of the passenger cars on either side of the concertina-type connecting corridors ('the blinds'). These rungs formed a crude ladder which was usually about two feet wide and led to the roof of the car. They were also 'blind', as such a traveller would not generally have been visible (except on some long sweeping curves) from the interior of the train. In Bell's case, he is spotted clambering aboard, without permission, by the conductor (who in general were sometimes sympathetic) but, conscious of the value of his job with the railroad company, advises Bell to buy a ticket.

Often, the extent of a conductor's or engineer's sympathy could be influenced by what the hobo was able offer them by way of unofficial payment. This could be cash (which would have gone straight into the conductor's/engineer's pocket), but was more often some sort of agricultural produce that the hobo had procured prior to boarding the train. Musicians who had their instruments with them could also offer to sing/play requests. The usual practice was to let hobos travel to a point where a 'division' ended — these being sections of the railroad, usually about 100 miles in length, where the conductor might be going off duty or the crew might need to change engines, for example. Hubbard describes the practice of 'rustling the bums' which entailed the train crew 'searching a freight train for hobos. In bygone days, [they] often collected money from freight-riding tramps at a rate of a dollar a division.' [2]

In the above scenario, the hapless Bell cannot supply any of these inducements, so he is made to get off the train which is about to leave, carrying away the woman he loves — forever! He makes a final, desperate attempt to change the conductor's mind by pleading that he only wants to go as far as Hagerstown and will jump off when the engineer sounds the locomotive whistle as the train slows for the crossing— but to no avail. And so, Bell's emotional state turns to illogical hatred, not merely towards the conductor, but the locomotive crew up front, as we have seen. Having just recorded a song about a train that broke his heart *'when it left the yard'*, presumably with his lover on board ('Frisco Whistle Blues', the flip of Paramount 12546), Bell maintains the continuity on his next song, 'Mean Conductor Blues', injecting some humour into his opening lines: *'The same train, same engineer.'*

He watches the rapidly disappearing train with a heavy heart, his anger overtaken by almost unbearable sadness. Yet, even in the depths of despair, the positive side of the blues reduces this feeling to one of mere resignation:

> I sat here lookin' up at the risin' sun. *(x2)*
> That train don't run, gwine be some walkin' done.[3]

On his 'Kentucky Blues' [OKeh 8815], another guitarist, Little Hat Jones from East Texas, also appears to be referring to the 'blinds' between the passenger cars — this time on the Santa Fe:

> Well, here come the Santa Fe just puffin' an' flyin'.
> Oughta see me when I reach up an' really caught them blinds.[4]

In this blues, Jones adopts the mystical persona of 'Lost John' or 'Fleetin' John', a traditional figure in black folklore akin to the 'travelin' man' who outwitted the white authorities by virtue of his supernatural speed. 'John' appeared in many blues including titles by Papa Charlie Jackson, Charlie Turner and Sonny Terry.

While 'riding the blinds' had its dangers and discomforts for the hobo, it was positively luxurious compared to 'riding the rods'. George Milburn, a chronicler of the L&N, includes a description of this hair-raising method of rail travel in the course of contemplating the origin of the railroad hobo: 'It is not known when the first hobo made his initial appearance upon an American railroad, but it must have been well before 1874, which is the year when steel or iron was first used in the underframes of freight cars. Such construction signified the beginning of the end of the practice of 'riding the rods' — *ie* the steel rods which were placed beneath the cars to strengthen the wooden underframing. When steel underframing was used, there was no place for the hobo to rest his weary head beneath the car.'[5] Another account has described how hobos rode the rods — or rather the rod — on the earlier four-wheeled passenger cars: 'Between the cross-section and the axle of the oblong four-wheel truck is a slender rod, little more than a yard long, parallel to the partition and the axle. On this, the tramp once fitted the groove of his "ticket", a board as broad as a man's hand and about six inches long. Crowded in this small space on the forward truck... the passenger stiff rides, a feat requiring skill and courage.' It was on this rod that the 'stiff' or hobo laid for the duration of his journey, watching the rails and ties (sleepers) flash by

Rare shot of a hobo riding the rods, c.1930s.

in a frightening blur! But, with the advent of the bogie truck and longer wheel-based rolling stock, the hobo took to lying on the steel trusses or gunnels running 'lengthwise beneath a freight or passenger car, and *[which]* on freights are comparatively easy to ride.' [6]

On his 'Loving Talking Blues' [Victor V-38032] from 1928, Blind Willie McTell imbued a seemingly unique verse with more than a taste of irony when relating a desperate search for his *'lil' Mary'*:

> Don't want no sleeper, don't want no Pullman car.
> Don't want no sleeper, don't even want no Pullman car.
> I'm gon' find lil' Mary [if I] have to ride the box car rods.[7]

while on 'Mr. Brakes-Man (Let Me Ride Your Train)' [Columbia 14227-D] Martha Copeland milked this scary mode of transport for laughs, more than hinting at a romantic liaison between herself and a *'certain brakes-man'* (who would almost certainly have been white), who is going to get her back to Alabama:

> I'll get by the station guard, standing at the gate,
> If you let me ride the rods on that Southern freight.

> There's a certain brakes-man who runs to Birmingham,
> An' I know he's willing to take me back to 'Bam.
>
> *Refrain:* Mr. Brakes-man, let me ride your train.[8]

In complete antithesis to the vaudeville atmosphere of this recording with its 'gas-pipe' clarinet accompaniment, the tough pianist Jesse James employs an almost-vicious vocal/instrumental attack as he gruffly tells it like it is on his original 'Southern Casey Jones' [Decca 7213] from 1936:

> Now, Casey Jones say before he die
> He'd fix the road so a bum could ride.
> An' if he ride, he'd have to ride the rods,
> Rest his heart in the hand of God.
> Hand o' God.
> In the hand o' God.
> Had to rest his heart in the hand of God.[9]

The hobo often had to *'rest his heart in the hand of God'* or otherwise Providence, as the dangers he encountered were always close at hand. Notwithstanding the rather disparaging remarks made by Milburn in 1930, that 'few tramps nowadays know how to locate the rods, much less dare ride them' [10], this frightening form of hoboing was still quite prevalent in the period in which Milburn was writing; judging by the number of references to it in the early blues. A freight train was usually boarded while it was in motion, but moving slowly — either at a crossing, on a long gradient, on a sweeping bend or 'curve', or when a train was making its laborious exit from a freight yard. Although the speed of these trains in the earlier part of the Twentieth Century averaged only about ten miles per hour (including stops), 'grabbing a freight' was still a very risky business. Many a poor hobo found this to his cost and suffered loss of limbs and other serious injuries — even death — because of an ill-judged attempt to ride the blinds or jump aboard, with a momentary lapse of concentration.

A particularly gruesome example[*] is recounted by Oliver Jensen: 'William Davies, a Welshman bumming around North America at the turn of the *[Twentieth]* Century, told of trying to hop aboard a freight: "My foot came short of the step, and I fell, and, still clinging to the handle-bar, was dragged several yards before I relinquished my hold. And there I lay for several

---

[*] From *'Autobiography Of A Supertramp'* by W.H. Davies (Oxford University Press, 1980, *(reprinted)*). And see especially *Hard Travellin' (The Hobo and His History)* by Kenneth Allsopp (Pimlico, 1993 *(reprinted)*). The latter includes much on hobos, albeit from the perspective of white tramps. It features the blues only marginally, but is still a recommended read.

minutes, feeling a little shaken, whilst the train passed swiftly on into the darkness." At length Davies attempted to climb to his feet, and only then did he discover that his right foot had been cut off just above the ankle.' [11]

Nearly thirty years later, on his 'No. 29', [Paramount 12958] the excellent blues/boogie pianist, Wesley Wallace, described how he almost had a serious accident while trying to get to Troy, Ill.. He attempted to check how fast the train was going by placing one foot on the ground, but misjudged its speed and *'my heel like knock my brains out... an' I fell off.'* [12] His right hand describes on the piano how he rolled some distance before picking himself up and waving the disappearing train goodbye, heading on into East St. Louis, Ill., as Troy now lay far behind him.

II

But there was also danger from other quarters — the railroad police. By the 1920s, because of lack of employment, poor housing and education, and daily racial discrimination, many black males left their homes in the South in search of better prospects for themselves and their families. The number of black hobos alone increased dramatically at this time.*

When riding in the comparative luxury of the box car, hobos would smash open the boxes and crates stored there in search of food, drink and often any items that could be converted into cash. The railroads quite understandably grew tired of this damage and the financial loss it caused. So, special employees were hired to combat the hobo — 'combat' being the operative word. Known variously as 'railroad bulls', 'shack bullies' (the box car is sometimes called a 'shack' in railroad parlance) or 'special agents', these men (who were invariably white) were often little more than thugs. For instance, one story survives about how a shack bully would take a long piece of rope and attach an iron bar to one end. He would then slip this device between the gaps in the floorboards of the box car and ease it down to the side of the rods that the hobo was clinging to for dear life. The shack bully would then start to swing the iron bar back and forth in pendulum fashion along the rods until the bar made connection with the hapless hobo's already freezing fingers and hands He would repeat this movement until the hobo was forced

---

* The most famous black hobos were a group of young teenagers — the 'Scottsboro Boys' — who were accused of raping two white girls (also hobos) in 1931 near Lookout Mountain in Tennessee on the Southern Railway. They were taken off at Paint Rock, Ala. just south-west of Stevenson, Ala. In fear of their lives from an angry white mob, the boys were removed to the County seat in Jackson County: Scottsboro, Ala.. The case dragged on for nearly thirty years and drew worldwide protests at the initial death sentences, which were later rescinded. Despite one of the two plaintiffs retracting her charge of rape — of either girl — by 1933, the last of the accused was not freed until 1950. *Scottsboro Boy*, as told by two of the group, Haywood Patterson and Earl Conrad, makes gripping if harsh reading and is highly recommended (published in the UK by Panther, 1966 *(reprint)*; first published 1950).

to release his grip and drop to an almost certain vicious and usually anonymous death.

On 'Freight Train Blues' [Brunswick 7133], Eddie Miller, after announcing his intention to *'catch me a freight train an' ride it around the bend'*, states starkly that:

> I'm goin' leave here walkin', takin' chances I might ride.
> I'm gon' leave here walkin', take chances I might ride.
> If I get killed, no-one knows the death I died.[13]

On 'Special Agent (Railroad Police Blues)' [Decca 7491], Sleepy John Estes from Ripley, Tenn. gives a unique account of the special agent whom he hears *'tippin' over the top'* of the box car he has chosen to ride in while he and either Charlie Pickett or Son Bonds conjure up a vision of the smoking freight train with the pounding rhythm of their twin guitars:

> Now, when I left ol' Ripley, the weather was kinda cool. *(x2)*
> Say, boys you-all be careful, buddies, you might catch the 'flu.
>
> Now, I swung that manifest*, I went down in the free rail box (?)
> Now, I hung that manifest, I went down in free rail box.
> Now, I could hear the special agent when 'e come tippin' over the top.
>
> Now, some special agents up the country, sure is hard on a man.
> Now, some special agents up the country, they sure is hard on a man.
> Now, they will put 'im off when he hongry,
>   an' won't even let 'im ride no train.
>
> Now I was settin' down in Centralia, an' I sure was feelin' bad. *(x2)*
> Now they wouldn't let me ride no fast train,
>   they put me off on the doggone grass(?).
>
> Now special agent, special agent, put me off close to some town.
> Special agent, special agent, put me off close to some town.
> Now I got to do some recordin', I oughta be recordin' right now.[14]

— Estes, who had earlier worked as a track-caller, injecting some humour into his closing lines.

---

* A 'manifest' is US railroad jargon for a train of cars — freight or passenger — 'made up' and ready to leave, or already in transit.

III

The hobo is part of a mobile hierarchy that seems to have been peculiar to the USA in the Nineteenth and early Twentieth Centuries. To paraphrase one anonymous definition: a *hobo* travels in search of work; a *tramp* travels to see what is at the next stopping place and begs; while the *bum* just hangs around the town he is in. Of course, these terms became interchangeable as far as the railroad police and, indeed, the general public were concerned. As Stilgoe stated: 'Wanderlust and repeated financial panics sent thousands of American men adrift on the railroads, some in search of adventure, most in search of work or escape from responsibility. Railroad hoboing began at the end of the Civil War, but not until the panic of 1893 forced thousands of job seekers onto freight trains did the public learn to fear the ragged drifters it identified as tramps or hobos. Respectable folk saw hobos staring from empty box cars, crouching on express train baggage cars, and trudging along railroad tracks.' [15]

But such comments were usually applied to a large influx of white hobos as a result of any economic depression or panic. Their black counterparts had probably been riding the rods long before 1865, and for other reasons in addition to those referred to above. The main one was to escape the appalling Jim Crow conditions in the South which only exacerbated the difficulty of finding work, whether there was a panic or not. As a Lonnie Johnson title starkly pointed out in 1937, 'Hard Times Ain't Gone Nowhere' [Decca 7388].

The hobo could play rough, too! A drawing from 1888.

Of course, African Americans bore the brunt of the depression in 1893, as they did in any other national economic crisis. From the beginnings of the 1890s, and especially in 1893, 'communities in Virginia, the Carolinas and Georgia watched as huge crowds of local blacks gathered at railroad stations to await transportation to the Mississippi Delta, the Louisiana rice or sugar fields, or the turpentine camps of the piney woods.' As an observer noted in

January 1890: 'The negro exodus now amounts to a stampede.' [16]

It was not only the hope of a job that goaded these black Southerners into a 'stampede', for the 'white backlash' was also at its peak in these post-Reconstruction years. Lynchings, whippings, burnings, rapes and other atrocities, as well as the destruction of black-owned property, marked a nadir in the life of the African American in the South — often surpassing even the brutal conditions of the antebellum period, as many historians and hundreds of ex-slaves' statements (collected in the 1930s) have testified. This puts into stark context why black people might have been in such a desperate hurry to board a train bound for the Louisiana rice fields, which were almost as unhealthy and dangerous to work in as the ones they were fleeing from in Georgia and South Carolina, or why they appeared keen to embrace the even more dangerous turpentine farms in east Texas and northern Florida, or the harsh regime in the Mississippi Delta cotton fields. At the same time, Southern whites (mainly plantation owners) complained that 'our young Negro men are becoming tramps, and moving about over the country in gangs to get the most remunerative work.' [17]

Paul Oliver has noted that, during the period from 1910 to 1941, nearly three million blacks migrated from the South to Northern cities, and also that 'large numbers moved to the West, where hitherto they had been few in number.'[18] Many of these would have hoboed their way by simply following the twin silver-steel ribbons that seemed to stretch into eternity. If no train was handy, the hobo would simply start walking between the railway lines, safe at least in the knowledge that they would eventually lead him somewhere else, somewhere different, somewhere that was hopefully better. But he, or she, would gradually realise that an almost-surreal sense of isolation could set in as they walked the countless ties, as Charlie McCoy, a bluesman from Jackson, Miss. graphically related in 'That Lonesome Train Took My Baby Away' [OKeh 8863] — his superb retitled rendition of Cow Cow Davenport's 'Cow Cow Blues' [Vocalion 1198] — here played brilliantly on banjo-mandolin:

> I walked down the track, when the stars refused to shine.
> Looked like every minute I was goin' to lose my mind.
> Now, my knees was weak, my footsteps was all I heard.
> Looked like every minute I was steppin' in another world.[19]

Pioneer blues writer Sam Charters described McCoy's performance in typically enthusiastic, disarming fashion: 'The piece would have gotten everybody out on a dance floor for a noisy minute of loose-legged movement. The song had some of the feeling of a delta *[sic]* blues in the text, even though the music was closer to country ragtime.' [20]

IV

Possibly the earliest reference we have on a record of the word 'hobo' (albeit in a shortened form) is contained in the title of an acappella performance by the Standard Quartette, 'Say Bo, Give Me Them Two Bits' [Columbia, not numbered], recorded between February and March, 1894. Sadly, the precise subject-matter of the song is unknown, as this cylinder has so far not been recovered.

One of the most likely origins of the term 'hobo' is given in Partridge's *Dictionary Of The Underworld*, abstracted from *A Dictionary of American English 1936-42*. According to Partridge 'the *DAE* thinks the most likely origin to be 'Ho! Beau!' in address to, or among tramps: that is my opinion too.' [21] Of course, this phrase (which loosely translates in this context as 'Hello, my beauty') was quickly corrupted to 'bo' — as the title by the Standard Quartette probably indicates. It also gave Charlie McCoy's back-up guitarist, Armenter Chatmon, his pseudonym, Bo Carter; ditto the obscure Texas singer, Bo Jones; and no doubt there were many others on and off the record scene in the 1920s and '30s.

Although thousands of black and white hobos travelled in search of work during these decades (and earlier), Charlie McCoy had other reasons for *'steppin' in another world'*. It should be remembered that the blues singer often stood apart from, and on the edge of black mainstream society. Not every African American in the 1920s was a blues performer or part of the blues audience. Black lawyers, teachers or physicians did not form any part of the blues genre. Indeed, the black middle-classes shunned the blues singers generally speaking, and looked down on them as inferior riff-raff. It is important to remember that, in this earlier period, the blues was a genre performed by working-class singers (unlike the majority of their hillbilly counterparts) for a working-class audience. Yet 'ordinary' work such as farming, etc. was often scorned by the blues singer, who would sometimes refer to conventional workers as a 'monkey man' or 'monkey woman'. Many blues singers were bootleggers, pimps, prostitutes, gamblers, gangsters, itinerant wanderers, beggars and drifters. When circumstances demanded they do some 'proper' work, they turned to the only jobs open to them, such as domestic service, various unskilled railroad occupations, or labouring as janitors, washer women, draymen, roustabouts, loggers or coal miners. But in the main, for many, their real work was *being* a blues singer.

Not only that, the black religious community, who often employed black middle-class people to run their establishments and preach the gospel, viewed the blues and all stringed instruments, as the Devil's work and his tools. As is widely known today, the blues is still sometimes called 'the Devil's music'. The black churches also thought that the blues was evil, and the practice of hoodoo (very prevalent at this time and believed by a vast majority of Southern blacks and nearly half the whites) only confirmed this 'fact'. (Like the railroads and sexuality, hoodoo, a 'modern' version of West African voodoo acquired via Haiti, etc, is another central theme in the early blues.)

Indeed, many of the working class blacks who remained in farming after the Civil War and were, in effect, trapped in agricultural slavery, did not necessarily participate in the blues. A classic example is Alabama's Ned Cobb, whose story of grinding poverty and ceaseless toil as a sharecropper (and later as a tenant farmer) is retold in his autobiography[*], and no mention of music of any kind features in over 550 pages. Similarly, in the first two volumes of his groundbreaking work in the South, *Children Of Crisis*, which covers nearly one thousand pages, the white American physician and psychologist Robert Coles makes only one reference to the blues, and it's the popular, lop-sided one at that: 'Sharecroppers grow up into an increasingly sad life — they see gloom all about them and speak out (in the blues, for instance) the heaviness of their hearts.' [22]

The only other entry in his writings concerning music *per se* comes from a black sharecropper's twelve-year old son (circa early 1960s), who told Coles that 'the older people do a lot of singing. I'm no good at singing — not like them. They'll go out and pick the crops, even my grandmother does, and they'll have their songs and they go from one song to another. I'm learning some now, because I'm old enough to leave school and be all grown up... and my daddy's uncle told me I was big now, big enough to come and learn from him how to play the banjo. He said he'd teach me how to sing, and then I'd know the songs. I'm afraid I'll forget the words, but he says no, I'm big enough, I'm grown enough. I guess I am.' [23] But these songs would most likely have been either worksongs or spirituals and other religious songs which could also be used to help pick cotton and do other tasks[**]. As Blind Willie McTell told John Lomax in 1940, his mother and father would go to work in the fields and sing 'them old time fashioned hymns' like 'Just As Well Get Ready, You Got To Die' and 'I'm Climbing High Mountains, Trying To Get Home', so that they could make some of "that old country money".'[24]

V

But the blues singer often regarded his/her singing and playing as their work, and had no desire to be on a farm stuck behind a plough 'smellin' mule farts'. Mississippi's David 'Honeyboy' Edwards is a typical example of a working bluesman: 'He was hustling and made a lot of nickels, dimes and

---

[*] See *All God's Dangers – The Life Of Nate Shaw* as told to Theodore Rosengarten (Alfred A. Knopf, New York, 1975 *(reprinted)*, first published 1974). 'Nate Shaw' was a necessary pseudonym for Ned Cobb at the time.

[**] See Chapter 1, *The Quest For Certainty: Slave Spirituals* (especially pages 30-31) in the essential work, *Black Culture and Black Consciousness* by Lawrence Levine (Oxford University Press, 1978 *(reprinted)*, first published 1977).

A Rock Island train storming through RI freight yards, c.1935.

quarters. He was a traveling musician trying to make it, hoboing around, catching freight trains, and laying around in town till the next train came through.' [25] Totally eschewing the Protestant 'work ethic' and the social mores of the white ruling classes, as well as those of the black bourgeoisie and religious community, many singers would hobo for personal reasons as much as for independence and freedom. As Lonnie Coleman, an older singer with an archaic-sounding banjo accompaniment, sang in 1929 on his 'Old Rock Island Blues' [Columbia 14440-D]:

> I've got a free transportation, lookin' for the freedom ride. *(x2)*
> I need to ride the Rock Island [to] get perfectly satisfied.

The song alludes to his origins possibly being further north or west, as the Rock Island (otherwise the Chicago, Rock Island & Pacific) did not run down to Atlanta where he was recording, or even enter the state of Georgia. It was one of many railroads out of Chicago heading across the Mississippi River down to St. Louis, Mo. and via Oklahoma, Arkansas and Texas, eventually reaching the Gulf of Mexico. Maybe Coleman had been part of a minstrel outfit or other travelling show, as he 'signs off' his personal blues with the wandering musician's traditional attempt to establish their 'immortality' in song:

> An' if anyone should ask you who composed this song. *(x2)*
> Just tell 'em Lonnie Coleman done bin to your town an' gone.[26]

Gene Campbell also reflects this essentially transient, independent hobo existence on 'Western Plain Blues' [Brunswick 7154], when he declares that he is going to *'catch me [an] armful of train'*:

> An' I don't know when I'll stop my wandering ways.
> I don't know when I'll stop my wandering ways.
> But I may change my mind an' wander back here some day.[27]

Tampa Red, on the other hand, claims on 'IC Moan Blues' [Vocalion 1538] that the Illinois Central is the only railroad he would choose to ride. Rather than conform to the 'normal' attitude to work in Chicago, where conditions were sometimes a little easier for blacks, he prefers the 'free' life of the hobo and going *'a-beggin' '* back down South:

> Nobody knows that IC like I do. *(x2)*
> Now, the reason I know it, I've rode it through an' through.
>
> That IC Special is the only train I choose. *(x2)*
> That's the train I ride when I get these IC blues.
>
> The IC Engineer make the whistle moan.
> The IC Engineer makes that whistle moan.
> I got the IC blues' an' I just can't help but groan.
>
> Goodbye Chicago, hello Southern town. *(x2)*
> I'd rather go there a-beggin' than to be a boss around [this town].
>
> I got the IC blues an' box cars on my mind. *(x2)*
> I'd rather pack my grip an' beat it on down the line.[28]

Here, Red adopts the persona of a hobo and employs some delicious bottleneck guitar to imitate the train whistle.

In the case of Henry Thomas, however, it would seem he did indeed ride many railroads *'through an' through'*. Thought to represent the oldest style of blues or 'pre-blues' on a record, Thomas (sometimes as 'Ragtime Texas') accompanied himself on guitar with a set of pan-pipes on a harness round his neck. Although McCormick allows this is a possibility, he favours an alternative: the pan-pipes, he says were 'more probably held in a box attached to the side of the guitar.'[29] But this seems a cumbersome arrangement at best and would entail Thomas lifting his guitar up to the level of his face any time he wanted to play his quills. Since 'harmonica holders' had been available from as early as 1895 in the Montgomery Ward mail order catalogue at a cost of only 50 cents *(see illustration)*, it is entirely possible that he employed one (suitably modified) for easy access to his second instrument — the rarely recorded pan-pipes — while simultaneously playing his guitar. This gadget was, of course, also utilized by harp players.

Chapter 10 — Lined out smokin', look like it takin' to scat

Harmonica Holders.

25635 Excelsior Harmonica Holders (see cut) are constructed on an entirely new principle, and are giving excellent satisfaction. They consist of a wood breastplate, to which are attached heavy spring wire shoulder pieces. Harmonica of any size is held firmly in proper position for playing by two springs, thus leaving the hands free to play accompaniment on any other instrument. They are quickly and easily adjusted. Price, each $0.50. Weight, 8 ounces.
25636 Harmonica Holder, consists of heavy metal tube, painted and varnished, with opening at top for either Richter or Concert harmonicas; also opening at one end, and is used to regulate the tone and produce "tremolo" vibrations.
Each....$0.10 Per dozen...$1.00 Weight, 6 ounces.

Ad from Montgomery Ward catalogue No. 57 (Spring & Summer, 1895).

Henry Thomas was born in 1874 in or near Big Sandy, Upshur County in Texas, right down there in the piney woods. His song, 'Railroadin' Some' [Vocalion 1443], which inspired the title of this book, encapsulates the independence and limitless travel potential of the 'professional' hobo. *'I'm on my way, but I don't know where'* he says at one point, which really must have summed up the whole concept of freedom for many black US citizens. His rhythms also convey this feeling, having virtually little or no musical structure, as he tells of 'changing cars' on various railroads on a convoluted journey from Fort Worth in Texas via Arkansas, Oklahoma, Kansas and Missouri to Chicago:

> *(Spoken)* I leave Fort Worth, Texas, and go to Texarkana,
> An' double back to Fort Worth.
> Come on down to Dallas.
> Change cars on the Katy.
> Comin' through the Territor' to Kansas City.

Thomas then gets back on the M-K-T or 'Katy' to make his way to the north Texas border and on into Oklahoma, noting South McCalester and Muskogee (which he pronounces *'Muskoga'*) before crossing the bridge over the Arkansas River at Three Forks (so called as that is the point where the Neosho and Verdigris Rivers join the Arkansas). From Muskogee, the Katy, with Henry Thomas on board, heads up through Wagoner, Okl. and then onward to St. Louis, where the singer switches to the C&A or IC bound for Chicago:

> *(Spoken)* Parsons, Kan.! [*]
> Kansas City!
> Sedalia!
> And I change cars an' jump in Soo rail!

---

[*] The M-K-T (or MK&T as it was then) had built its next destination, Parsons, Kansas, some nine months before completing the bridge at Three Forks in late 1871. At that time, Three Forks was still in the Cherokee Nation. Together with other tribal designated areas — Creek, Seminole, etc. — this made up the 'Indian Territory' or 'Nation'. Forming part of Oklahoma, which received statehood in 1907, the 'Territor'' figured in blues by Robert Johnson, Charley Patton, A. & J. Baxter, Jesse James, Mooch Richardson and many others.

Chapter 10 — Lined out smokin', look like it takin' to scat

The IC depot at Springfield, Ill. c.1890s. Henry Thomas might have just gone by! Also note drayman and dray in the foreground.

Although Thomas sings *'Soo rail'* [30], it could well be a mistake in speech, or he may have seen a manifest of Soo Line box cars leaving St. Louis (see *Introduction* re freight exchange agreement). This railroad, whose full title was the Minneapolis, St. Paul & Sault Ste. Marie Railway, did not serve St. Louis, and Thomas could not have used this road on the way to Chicago from East Texas. Nor does another road, the Minneapolis & St. Louis fit into his long and devious journey. The M&St.L (later the Chicago & North Western) 'was called the Louie, though it did not go near St. Louis.' [31] While the Soo Line was controlled in the Nineteenth Century and early Twentieth by the Canadian Pacific from the Twin Cities to Sault Ste. Marie in Ontario, Canada. [32] Thomas probably meant to say 'St. Louis', as shortly afterwards he enters the state of Illinois (*'Hello, Springfield'*, he says). This is a main station on the C&A heading for the Windy City. Likewise, Bloomington and Joliet (both also in Illinois) are stops on this railroad. After running on through the latter with its infamous state pen, Thomas declares triumphantly: *'Chicago!'* [33] having probably just described for the listener how he travelled to what was to be his final recording session. As McCormick observes: 'Henry Thomas has done a remarkable thing here. The material is as skeletal as a railway timetable and yet the thrust of it takes the listener sweeping along with him, grabbing one train and then another, the stations flashing past, the clacking of unwelded rails and the long whistle blasts for crossings all wrapped into one of the most evocative entries in that rich category of music… dedicated to railroadin'.' [34]

Although some blues singers appeared to hobo with the intent of looking for work — for example Charley Jordan on 'Tough Times Blues' [Vocalion 15681] and his close friend Peetie Wheatstraw on 'Jungle Man Blues' [Vocalion 03231] — they seem to have been the exception rather than the rule. For instance, on 'Mistreated Boy' [A.R.C. 6-02-63] Georgia's Buddy Moss cites a most unusual reason for wishing to leave: an estranged father who beats him up regularly. In desperation, he decides to contact his mother:

> I'm gonna write to my mama just to send me my railroad fare.
> I'm gonna write to my mama to send me my railroad fare.
> An' if she don't send it, I'm gon' walk the railroad there.[35]

Charley Jordan meanwhile takes a different tack on 'Lost Ship Blues' [Vocalion 1657], laying the blame for his becoming a hobo squarely at the feet of his partner/wife, who caused him *'to be drifting just like a lost ship up on the sea'*:

> Well, I love you so hard baby, 'til I could not settle down.
> I say, I love you so hard babe, until I could not settle down.
> So I caught me a fast freight train an' I begin to run around.
>
> Hard rocks was my pillow an' the cold ground was my bed. *(x2)*
> Well, you called me a hobo an' you say you wish that I was dead.[36]

But, for many blues singers and black wanderers generally, the hobo lifestyle became an icon of ultimate freedom — as both Henry Thomas and Lonnie Coleman have illustrated. Within their own social sphere, the professional hobo/blues singer was regarded on a par with a doctor or preacher or steamboat captain. Indeed, many would place the itinerant musicians above these more 'normal' occupations, especially if they dropped off *'close to some town'* (in Sleepy John Estes' words) to do the odd recording session now and again. Although the Alabama Sheiks also explain — like Jordan — that women are the cause for them to ride the rails on 'Travelin' Railroad Man Blues' [Victor 23265], the singer's vocal (probably fiddler Eddie West) is charged with a degree of pride and self-esteem:

> Love you, woman, don't throw me down, hey babe.
> Love you woman, honey, but I believe it's all in vain.
> Some of these mornin's, I'll catch a lonesome train.
>
> I'm a travelin' man, oh Lord, travel most everywhere.
> Pretty mama, travelin' man, travel most everywhere.
> Don't believe I'm travelin', you just count those days,
>   you just count those days I'll be gone.

> Oh! You can go to Nacogdoches, or you don't find me there.
> Pretty mama, go to Memphis, you don't find me there.
> [You catch the] first thing smokin', find me on the road,
>   find me on the road somewhere.[37]

This duo, about whom virtually nothing is known, sound to be from the first generation of blues singers, along with Charley Patton, Frank Stokes, Sam Collins, Papa Harvey Hull, etc. The 'sing-songy' atmosphere, filled out with a beautifully rough and 'resin-less' fiddle sound (akin to Henry Sims, who recorded with Patton) gives this performance an oddly haunting feel.

The place names referred to in the song would have taken the Sheiks far from home — if indeed they were from Alabama. Travelling from the latter state (if the duo were intending to go to Nacogdoches), they could have used either the L&N or the Southern, and changed cars in New Orleans, heading towards Texas on the Southern Pacific's 'Sunset Route'. Then, by making a quick switch at Beaumont to the Kansas City Southern, they could have stopped off at Nacogdoches (which the vocalist pronounces *'Nacogdooches'*) as the train wended its way to Kansas City, Mo. via Shreveport, La. This was also the route of the KCS's named train, *The Flying Crow*, which was featured in a number of songs, as related in *Chapter 7*.

This romantic image of the totally 'free' and independent traveller was soon to be extended by the blues singer when the image of the black hobo acquired an aura of 'evil', simultaneously making him even more of an anti-establishment (and, indirectly, anti-white) figure.

Reflecting a more urban style of blues at his second session in 1935, yet retaining a beautifully warm rural 'feel', 'Casey Bill' Weldon's steel guitar, augmented by (probably) Black Bob's sympathetic piano and Bill Settles' throbbing double bass lend a suitably 'devil-may-care' atmosphere to 'My Stove Won't Work' [Bluebird B-6243]:

> Well, well, I'm just a traveller, mama, I travel all around,
> An' all I do's mama, is travel from town to town.
> Anybody ask you my name an' ask where I bin,
> Tell 'em I'm the Devil — whooooh! — I mean from the lion den.
> Well, well, my chief occupation — whooooh! — is takin' women
>   from their men.[38]

The *'Devil'* verse had actually appeared as early as 1924 on 'Do Right Blues' [Vocalion 14770] by Rosa Henderson, and was also the source of a Sam Collins title, 'Devil In The Lion's Den' [Gennett 6181], from 1927.

To help ensure their state of freedom, hobos dressed themselves in a cloak of unassailable anonymity by adopting all sorts of nicknames: 'The names — Hypo Gann, Lefty Moran, Little Punk Klein, K.C. Jack, Mobile Mac, Spokane Slim, Chi Red — and hundreds more emphasise the essential rootlessness of the drifters.'[39] Many other early blues singers can be added to this list: 'Buddy Boy' Hawkins, Bo Carter, Henry 'Ragtime Texas' Thomas, 'Too Tight Henry', 'Tampa Kid', George 'Bullet' Williams and 'Hot Shot Willie' — names that surely denoted a hobo's identity as well as that of a blues performer. A 'hotshot' for example, is an alternative name for a 'red ball' or fast freight train of the type Charley Jordan refers to on his 'Lost Ship Blues', while Henry Lee Castle, a Georgia twelve-string guitarist, relates how he got his musical start in life by hoboing his way on the railroad. He recorded six sides between 1928 and 1930 (usually as 'Too Tight Henry'), sometimes in the company of Beale Street's Jed Davenport on harp and a couple of unidentified musicians on piano and second guitar. His first studio outing, in 1928, the remarkable two-part 'Charleston Contest' [Columbia 14374-D] was a solo performance. Here, he conducts a conversation with himself, as 'Too Tight' and 'Chappie', while demonstrating his prowess on his chosen instrument. Having invited Chappie to pull up a chair, 'Too Tight' begins to tell his story:

> Too Tight: 'But you know one thing, Chappie, when I was a hobo an' first started out playing music, an' tried to travel from town to town; an' I didn't have any money.'
>
> Chappie: 'What did you do, Too Tight?'

He then describes going on down to the freight yard and seeing a train ready to leave:

> Too Tight: 'An' the first thing I saw lined out smokin', look like it takin' to scat. Boy, you oughta see me mount that door!'

He brags to his imaginary friend that he could control both the engineer (the 'hog man') and the locomotive ('the hog') by playing some red-hot twelve-string guitar:

> Too Tight: 'I want you to hear how I made that hog man bring that old hog he got, down [here] in Georgia.'

— then kicks in with some impressive and frenetic playing.

Chapter 10 — Lined out smokin', look like it takin' to scat

Chappie: 'Hey boy, if you do that again, I'm gon' have you run out of town!'

Too Tight: 'Yeah, that's what they told me at the mill, but I kept on playin' guitar.'

Having promised Chappie they would *'get it fixed'* at the Charleston Contest by getting a *'couple of gals full of sass'*, Too Tight reminisces how it might be if he had one of his girlfriends on the train with him, when it got on one of those 'long old lonesome grades' and had to slow down to reach the top:

Too Tight: 'I just could imagine if I had one of my old browns of mine there to shake that thing with me, how we could keep time with that old locomotive engine singin' songs with this twelve-string guitar.' [40]

In a eulogy to her hero, 'Hobo Bill' [Columbia 14248-D], Martha Copeland adds two further monikers to the list, 'Sawyer Sam' and 'Bad Man Pugh':

> Hobo Bill standin' at the tank,
> Waitin' on the train that they call *Nancy Hanks**.
>
> *Refrain:* Ride on. Ride on, Hobo Bill.
>
> Hobo Bill, he got so bad,
> He took everything that the fireman had.
>
> *Refrain* Ride on, etc.
>
> Old Sawyer Sam, Bad Man Pugh,
> Wasn't nothing to them when Bill got through.
>
> *Refrain:* Ride on, etc.
>
> Hobo Bill always on a hop,
> Hungry, dirty, an' raggedy as a mop.
>
> *Refrain:* Ride on, etc.
>
> Hobo Bill [got] nothing on his mind,
> He's at home when he's riding on the blinds.
>
> *Refrain:* Ride on, etc.

---

* In 1893, the Central of Georgia inaugurated what is said to have been the country's first 'name' train, the *Nancy Hanks* (after a famous racehorse and also Abraham Lincoln's mother).[41] This was 'the fastest train in the South at the time.'[42] The faster (and therefore more difficult and dangerous) a particular train was to board, the more prestigious the hobo riding it appeared in the eyes of his fellows.

> Hobo Bill never takes a bluff,
> He rode every freight train from Chicago to the Gulf.
>
> *Refrain:* Ride on, etc. [43]

A travelling man through and through, Bill tells his buddy that before he died he wanted to hobo *'an airplane an' a submarine'*.

Hobo Bill and Sawyer Sam would have landed in the city of their destination and spent the night in a 'hobo jungle'. These 'jungles' were derelict areas near the railroad yards and encroaching into the yards as well, where the switchmen made up the next freight train scheduled to leave the city. The hobos would make a fire out of scrap wood and paper, and cook any provisions they had to hand in pots and pans that might be hanging around, abandoned by those who had been there before them. A loose sort of 'community' would often exist in the jungles, and, while many a homeless man 'claimed a city of origin, most knew only the right-of-way *[the railroad track itself]* as home, and the jungle as a sort of city.' [44]

In 1937, Sleepy John Estes referred to spending all night in the jungle in Chicago Heights, a suburb of the Windy City, in his 'Hobo Jungle Blues' [Decca 7354]. Although it shares the same title as Peetie Wheatstraw's record *(see page 317)*, Papa Charlie Jackson's 'Jungle Man Blues' [Paramount 12721] is an entirely different song containing comic imagery of a *real* jungle, with references to a tiger, gorilla, etc. But one verse adds another layer of meaning, by referring to the *hobo* jungle and alluding to the superhuman — if not quite evil — powers of the hobo:

> I'll make a tsetse catch a freight train, make a flea grab the mail.
> I'll make a tsetse catch a freight train, I'll make a flea grab the mail.
> I'll make a Jumbo elephant grab an airplane an' sail. [45]

The *'tsetse'* (here pronounced 'see-see') is a highly poisonous African fly and the *'mail'* is of course the fast mail. Although Jackson injects some humour into his song, the underlying theme is the hobo's ability to control any living thing, projecting a similar aura as Casey Bill's *'Devil in the lion den'*. And when Jackson boasts *'There ain't nothin' in the jungle that's any badder than me'*, he is implicitly also claiming superiority over the white man — a detail that would have been much appreciated by his black listeners.

VI

Of all the major US cities, Chicago was the kingpin of the US railroad system. It was the place that Papa Charlie Jackson, Big Bill, Tampa Red, Memphis Minnie, Washboard Sam, Jazz Gillum and countless other blues singers headed for in the first three decades of the Twentieth Century, followed by Muddy Waters, Little Walter, Jimmy Rogers and others in the 1940s. Invariably, they would ride the rails on the Illinois Central, C&A, CB&Q, the Big Four, the Monon, or one of the other 34 railroads running into the city from all points of the compass in the US. As Anderson observed in 1923: 'Chicago is the greatest railway center in the United States. No-one knows these facts *[sic]* better than the hobo... Twenty-five through package cars leave Chicago every day for 18,000 shipping points in 44 states.' [46] Twenty-three years later, Holbrook described the city as the hobo's 'Mecca of Meccas', adding: 'Chicago is the great railroad hub of the United States, a city with some 3,000 miles of tracks within its corporate limits, a city from which fan out the lines of forty railroads.' [47]

Memphis Minnie, 'Queen of the Coutry Blues', 1940.

Another name given to a freight train — usually the slower variety — was the 'rattler', so designated in both railroad and circus slang. It appears on record in connection with that rarer phenomenon, the female hobo, as referred to in Mozelle Alderson's 'Mobile Central Blues' *(Chapter 8)*. On 'Roll And Rattler' *[sic]* [Banner 32904], one of the finest of all women blues singers, Lucille Bogan (who is known to have been married to a railroad man for a time) describes attending her man's funeral. After paying him a final, sad farewell, she is minded to hit the railroad yard to catch a long old freight train which is slowly easing out of the yard across a myriad of switches and scissor crossings to meet the main line, for parts unknown:

> I slowly followed him to the burying ground.
> Say, I slowly followed him to the burying ground.
> *(Spoken interjection – Sonny Scott)* 'You were right, then!'
> Then I'll catch a rollin' rattler an' I'll leave this town. [48]

An equally superb singer, Geeshie Wiley, who also played guitar, reputedly came from northern Mississippi. She recorded a pitifully small number of sides in 1930 including the awesome 'Last Kind Words Blues' [Paramount 12951], which contained the prospective hobo's declaration that, if no train arrives at the depot, there's *'gonna be some walkin' done'*.

Another of the handful of female guitarists recorded in the pre-war era was Memphis Minnie, who was as famous as Geeshie Wiley was obscure. From 1929 to 1953, Minnie (born Lizzie 'Kid' Douglas) recorded prolifically for various labels*. On 'Nothing In Rambling' [OKeh 05670] from 1940, she reveals that she left home to hobo in her late teens, in 1917. That she still did so on occasion is indicated by some of the lyrics on 'Chickasaw Train Blues (Low Down Dirty Thing)' [Decca 7019], recorded six years earlier.

The song is ostensibly about an express on the IC, *The Chickasaw*, which was named after one of the 'Five Civilised Tribes' of the Southwest, but she likens it to a female rival for her man's love and affection, as this train barred female hobos from riding the blinds:

I'm-a tell everybody what that *Chickensaw [sic]* have done, done for me. *(x2)*
She done stole my man away an' blowed that doggone smoke on me.

Refrain: She's a low-down dirty dog.

There ain't no woman like to ride that *Chickensaw*.
Ain't no woman like to ride that *Chickensaw*.
Because everywhere she stops, she's stealing some woman's good man off.

Refrain: She's a low-down dirty dog.

I walked the railroad track, that *Chickensaw*
                  even won't let me ride the blinds.

I walked down the railroad track, that *Chickensaw*
                  wouldn't even let me ride the blinds.
An' she stop, pickin' up men all up an' down the line.

Refrain: She's a low-down dirty dog.

Mmmmmmm-mmmmmmm, *Chickensaw* don't pay no woman no mind.
Mmmmmm-mmmmmmm, that *Chickensaw* don't pay no woman no mind.
And she stop, pickin' up men all up an' down this line.[49]

Pearl Dickson, who has been noted as a precursor of Minnie's lowdown, acrid vocal style, was not known to have played a musical

---

* For the definitive work on Memphis Minnie, see *Woman With Guitar: Memphis Minnie's Blues* by Paul & Beth Garon (ibid.).

Chapter 10 — *Lined out smokin', look like it takin' to scat*

Anti-Hoover drawing featuring a black hobo (with a guitar at his feet!) outside Columbus, Oh. in the 1930s. Note the graffitti on the left wall of the bridge.

instrument, and certainly did not do so on her handful of recorded sides. Possibly a native of Mississippi, she admirably illustrates the freedom of the hobo, when choosing her destination across the river in Arkansas on her 'Little Rock Blues' [Columbia 14286-D]:

> I started to Helena, but I changed my mind. *(x2)*
> Well, I'm goin' to Little Rock where I can have better times.[50]

while Mattie Delaney, also thought to be a Mississippian, declares to her own guitar accompaniment on 'Down The Big Road Blues' [Vocalion 1480]:

> I'm a travelin' woman, I got a travelin' mind.

She sings what would have been deemed an essentially 'female' verse at the time, and openly admits to the powerful urge to travel, despite having no real reason to leave her family home:

> My mother said six months before I was born. *(x2)*
> She was gonna have a girl-child wouldn't never stay at home.
>
> I feel like cryin', ain't got no tears to spare. *(x2)*
> I 'ad a happy home an' I wouldn't stay there.[51]

Although the percentage of female hobos was small — one source puts the figure at less than 2% — the actual numbers would still have been considerable. Even at the end of the Nineteenth Century 'there were as many as 75,000 out-and-out bums' [52] in the USA. But, by the beginning of the 1930s, as the Great Depression deepened, more and more families — women and children included — took to wandering the rails and the highways. The jungles became larger, sprawling 'cities' as the number of hobos swelled to unprecedented proportions. President Herbert Hoover, along with his political advisers, refused to accept the urgency of the problem of rising poverty spreading across the nation, and misplaced their faith in the self-regulatory powers of the 'free market place'. The people on the sharp end of this policy dubbed the hobo jungles 'Hoovervilles', as Joe Stone (probably a pseudonym for J.D./Jaydee Short) related in 'It's Hard Time' [Bluebird B-5169] after being laid off from his job:

> I went down to the factory where I worked three years or more.
> I went down to the factory, worked three years or more.
> An' the bossman told me, man, that 'I ain't hirin' here no more.'
>
> Now, we have a little city, that they call down in Hooverville.
> An' we have a little city call[ed] down in Hooverville.
> Times have got so hard, people ain't got no place to live.[53]

Many of the jobs in cities such as St. Louis (where Short lived most of his life) were less dangerous and unhealthy in comparison with some of those in the Lower South. Yet the unequal pay (compared to white workers), the unbearably crowded and filthy housing conditions in the ghettoes, and the prospect of an eternally hopeless future must have caused more than one employed black male to think: 'What is the point?' Rejecting the endless drudgery of his job, Washboard Sam was asking for his 'cards' or 'racking them back' on his 1938 rendition of 'Rack 'Em Back' [Bluebird B-8044], and returning to the life of a hobo, travelling on the *'double track'*:

> I went down on my job, but I didn't go to work,
> Just to see the time-keeper an' the money clerk.
>
> *Refrain:*   So, I believe, I believe I will rack 'em back.
>   I'm cuttin' out this mornin', goin' back to that double track.
>
> I called the station, about a train southbound.
> The agent say he will hold one if I run on down.
>
> *Refrain:*   So I believe, etc.

Chapter 10 — Lined out smokin', look like it takin' to scat.

C&A train *No.4* heading north through Alton, Ill., 1932.

So I quit my job, an' I quit my baby too.
I did all here I intend to do.

Refrain: So I believe, etc.

If I make it over, I'll get all you people [to] know.
So goodbye, people, I have to go.

Refrain: 'Cos I believe, etc.[54]

Although Sam was travelling as a paying passenger in this instance (after all, he had just collected his paycheck), he was not averse to hoboing back to the 'sunny South', as he makes clear on 1936's 'Nashville, Tennessee' [Bluebird B-6765]:

Ohh! This old box car rock me like a rockin' chair. *(x2)*
So I'm just goin' to keep on rockin', till this old train get me there.[55]

For the black hobo as well as the itinerant blues singer, the railroad was the preferred way to travel in the 1920s and '30s, and in the South often still remained the only real choice. David 'Honeyboy' Edwards, but one example of a railroading bluesman, recalled that 'there wasn't too many cars or trucks going a long ways then. You had to ride a freight train to get around.' His close contemporary, 'Big'/'Poor' Joe Williams, did the same: 'Joe Williams would catch trains. Joe wasn't nothing but a hobo! He couldn't write his name! But he had a lot of sense, mother wit sense. He go to any town, get off at a corner and look around… he knowed them spots that he went by.'[56]

It is true that many poor whites also felt compelled to ride the rails —

at the height of the Great Depression, for example. As Edwards notes, around 1936 'there were a gang of men and boys hoboing then, white and black. Times was tough and nobody could find a job. So many people on the trains, the cops quit bothering them.' [57]

But, for some working-class blacks, hoboing was an almost-permanent way of life during the first three decades of the Twentieth Century. As well as blues performers, this also included earlier black musicians from around the end of the Nineteenth. For example, in 1894, the *Leavenworth Herald*, a black newspaper in northern Kansas, reported: 'There are a great many Kansas City[*] tramps called piano players in town' [59] — reflecting the low esteem in which the black bourgeoisie held such performers, who were described elsewhere as 'piano thumpers'. These would have been barrelhouse pianists and the early precursors of ragtime performers who usually worked in brothels and cheap liquor saloons. Intriguingly, 'rag' itself appears to have derived from an earlier black string-band tradition — possibly from this area — and included the highly popular 'Forty Drops', an early recording of which [Victor V-38002] was made in 1928 by Andrew & Jim Baxter, a black father-and-son duo from northern Georgia who played fiddle and guitar.[**]

VII

The black hobo's day-to-day existence is brilliantly portrayed in a performance already quoted *(see Chapter 9)*, 'Travelin' Blues' [Columbia 14484-D] by 'Blind Sammie' *aka* Blind Willie McTell. McTell was a giant of the Georgia blues scene every bit as much as Charley Patton in Mississippi or Blind Lemon Jefferson in Texas. Here, he paints a fascinating picture in words and music of the hobo 'from the inside', just as surely as if the listener had been transported back through time to an autumnal afternoon in 1929, possibly in Hampton, Ga.. This town, some twenty miles south-east of Atlanta, had been a onetime home to barrelhouse pianist Speckled Red (Rufus Perryman), and McTell was to record there with this artist's brother, Piano Red (Willie Perryman), in 1936. His reference to Americus, Ga. possibly indicated a planned journey in a north-easterly direction on the Central of Georgia Railway heading for Macon, then north-west towards Hampton on the way to Atlanta. A major railroad crossing at Americus, where the Seaboard Air Line crossed the Central, made it an important base for many a hobo. Major cities such as Montgomery and Birmingham in Alabama, Jacksonville in Florida, as well as Atlanta and Savannah in McTell's home state, were readily accessible via these railroads:

---

[*] The reference here is Kansas City, Kansas, not the more famous blues and jazz centre of Kansas City, Missouri (once referred to, in 1909, 'as cities divided merely by an imaginary state line'[58] — that 'line' of course being the Missouri River).

[**] For interested readers, the complete article in *78 Quarterly* No. 10 (pages 121-143) is recommended.

> *(Spoken)* I was travelin' through south Americus.
> Walked up to a lady's house.
> Called 'er 'Grandma'.
> Didn't know 'er name.
> She give me somethin' to eat.
> Walked on down the road,
> I heard a old train getting' off like this. (...)

His guitar pounds out the rhythm of the wheels — and then:

> *(Spoken)* I heard old bell ringin' kinda like this. (...)

(...) = guitar 'sings'

After walking a little further alongside the track and *'lookin' at the women'* *(Chapter 9)*, McTell tries his luck, much as Ed Bell had approached his 'Mean Conductor' *(pages 301-2)* :

> *(Spoken)* I went on, then I begin to sing to the engineer:

> *(Vocal)* 'Mr. Engineer, let a man ride the blinds.
> Mr. Engineer, let a poor man ride the blinds.'
> Says: 'I wouldn't mind it, feller,
> but you know this train ain't mine.' [60]

McTell displays an intimate knowledge of railroad practice as he hears the locomotive's coded whistle give one long blast and three short ones which indicate that the 'flagman *[will]* protect the rear of *[the]* train.' [61] In other words, where a train makes an unscheduled stop, this crew member has to stand some distance behind it, to warn any other approaching train of the obstruction. This, of course, is an ideal moment for the hobo to approach the engineer:

> *(Spoken)* I begin to hear the old feller blow long, sh-shorts.
> Get away blowin'...
> Then I begin to sing to 'im one more time:

> *(Vocal)* 'You is a cruel fireman, low-down engineer. *(x2)*
> I'm tryin' to hobo my way an' you leave me standin' here.'

> *(Spoken)* Then I go along farther an' begin to sing 'Poor Boy' to 'im.

McTell's exquisite bottleneck guitar duly 'sings' an excerpt from 'Poor Boy, Long Way From Home' — one of the oldest of blues — and the engineer's attitude towards him appears to soften:

(Spoken)	Then 'e begin to smile in my face:
(Vocal)	'Get up feller, an' ride all round the world. *(x2)* Poor boy, you ain't got no girl.'

Though his stupendous slide-playing has not won him a *'free transportation ride'*, McTell — unlike Ed Bell — has one more card to play. Hobos often carried some farm produce — some begged vegetables, or maybe a stolen chicken — with which they could bargain. In this case, it appears that 'Grandma' gave McTell some cheese and eggs, for he now offers these to the engineer — to be cooked, presumably, on the fireman's shovel.

(Spoken)	Then I begin to hear 'im tell me about those cheese an' eggs, how 'e want 'em fixed. I heard 'im say:
(Vocal)	'Scrambled down... Scrambled do-own... Scrambled down...'
(Spoken)	Then I begin to hear 'im tell me about them cheese an' eggs. I heard 'im say:
(Vocal)	'Cheese... Eggs...'
(Spoken)	'Dinner... Dinner.' [62]

McTell's offer of cheese and eggs invokes one particular Georgia railroad – the Oberlin, Hampton & Eastern. Running from Oberlin in Lorain County, northern Ohio, a direct line ran through Columbus and Cincinnati down to Hampton in Georgia. According to Partridge, this road was referred to by tramps as 'the "Original Ham & Egg Route" since circa 1910.' [63] As an example of this nickname's origins, he notes: 'the initials OH&E with reference to vanished gastronomic blisses.' [64] Interestingly, the only secular title recorded by the Bessemer Sunset Four, an acappella group, was 'Ham And Eggs' [Vocalion 1260], recorded in November 1928[*]. The group, who hailed from Alabama, sing of *'goin' back to Georgia'*, and the number is described by Ray Funk as a 'humorous folk song'.[66] It sentimentalises sarcastically about the states of both Georgia and Alabama, which were responsible for some of the harsher conditions in the South for blacks:

---

[*] In 1938, Blind Boy Fuller, who was probably a hobo before he lost his sight *(Chapter 9)*, used *'ham and eggs'* in a sensual context on 'Meat Shakin' Woman' [Vocalion 04137] (*'Says, for my dinner, I want ham an' eggs / Heyyy-hey! I want ham an' eggs / An' for my supper, woman, I wants to feel your legs'* [65]), while Leadbelly recorded a different song by the same title four times between 1940 and 1941.

> Oh, good old Georgia,
> Happy land.
> I am going back to Georgia, if I can.
>
> In good old Georgia,
> Happy land.
> Let me live an' die in Georgia land.

As well as that old trash favourite, greasy greens, the group pay tribute to ham an' eggs:

> Got good old ham an' eggs.
> I mean got good old ham an' eggs.
> First thing you do, put 'em in the pan,
> Then you shove 'em out to the Man.

'The Man' was/is one of several expressions used by blacks when referring to the white man. Although the song does not contain any specific references to railroads, it may have alluded to the engineer, who on Southern trains in the 1920s were nearly always white.

The advice for cooking those *'good old greasy greens'* meanwhile concludes with the lines:

> Shove up the fire an' get the water hot.[67]

This instruction may have been directed at the fireman (often black in those days), who is also mentioned by Blind Willie McTell.

The only pre-war black performances that equalled McTell's railroad epic were by Mississippi's Bukka White[*] who cut his 'Panama Limited' [Victor 23295] and 'Special Stream Line' [Vocalion 05526] in 1930 and 1940 respectively. However, *Mississippi Blues* [Takoma B-1001], the first album he recorded in 1963 after his 'rediscovery', included 'The Atlanta Special', an impressive 'dialogue' between singer and guitar — all the more so considering it 'was composed on the spot during the recording session'.[68]

White begins his story in Mississippi in 1924, *'when I was a little boy, I was fifteen years old'*, and recalls the day he was on his way to plough a field for his grandfather and heard *'that 8.45 was hittin' that rail'*. Gripped by wanderlust, he stops his mule and heads straight for the railroad tracks, saying: *'I believe I'll try the world.'* After hoboing *'all down the Gulf of Mexico and everywhere else'*, he decides to visit his grandmother in Atlanta.

At this point, some confusion creeps into the narrative (one of the hazards of making up songs on the spot!), and while he is there he is apparently mistaken for Blind Willie McTell by an old lady called Miss

---

[*] See also *Appendix III*.

Esther, who says: *'I had one of your records 'bout Atlanta, Georgia. Can you play it now?'* He acquiesces, and readily adapts his 'Atlanta Special' to include what is, in part, a version of McTell's 'Travelin' Blues'[*], but soon falls back into his 1930 'Panama Limited', with its moaning, hummed choruses, and variations of his earlier monologues from both 'Panama' and the later 'Special Stream Line'. When he finishes playing, a grateful Miss Esther offers him a meal:

> *(Spoken)* I was sittin', lookin' out toward the railroad tracks, I never will forget it. She brought me ham an' egg an' toasted cheese, an' hot cup of coffee.

The absolute brilliance of McTell's 'Travelin' Blues', made over thirty years earlier, appears not to have just influenced White but invaded his very psyche! For the first minute or so of 'Atlanta Special', he gives the 'feel' of McTell's earlier recording; especially in his guitar accompaniment; like McTell, he includes an encounter with an old lady in his song; and like McTell's engineer, who gets a hot meal of cheese and eggs, White's repast consists of ham, egg and cheese, and a warm drink besides.

Halfway through his meal, however, he hears *'that Stream Line'* slowing down for a *'fifteen mile curve'*. Commencing with a startlingly unique phrase, he continues:

> *(Spoken)* I dropped my head an' I dropped my food.
> I said: 'I got to ride the *Stream [Line]* back.
> Well now, Aunt Esther,' I said, 'Bukka got to go.' [69]

Unlike White, the *'lowdown engineer'* on Willie McTell's song gets to finish his cheese and eggs, and this seems to mellow him. Now, with his belly full, he starts thinking of the woman he loves:

> I love you Emry.
> I love you true.
> Love you, Emry.
> Tell the world I do.
> Emry... [70]

McTell's shimmering steel notes melting into the still-humid autumn air, just like the spiralling black column belching from the smokestack of the disappearing train as it eases on round a Georgia bend — leaving Hampton far behind...

---

[*] It's unclear whether White's memory is rusty (he didn't make any records until 1930, and McTell only commenced recording in 1927), or whether he is describing more recent events.

Chapter 10 — Lined out smokin', look like it takin' to scat

Notes to Chapter 10

1	'Mean Conductor Blues'	Ed Bell - vocal, guitar (c.September 1927, Chicago, Ill.)
2	Hubbard, F.	Ibid, p.194
3	'Mean Conductor Blues'	Ibid.
4	'Kentucky Blues'	Little Hat Jones - vocal, guitar (14 June 1930, San Antonio, Tex.)
5	Herr, K.A.	Ibid, p.182
6	Milburn, G.	pp. xviii and xix
7	'Loving Talking Blues'	Blind Willie McTell - vocal, guitar, speech (17 October 1928, Atlanta, Ga.)
8	'Mr. Brakes-Man (Let Me Ride Your Train)'	Martha Copeland - vocal; Ernest Elliott - clarinet; Bob Fuller - clarinet; Porter Grainger - piano; unk. sound effects (5 May 1927, New York City)
9	'Southern Casey Jones'	Jesse James - vocal, piano (3 June 1936, Chicago, Ill.)
10	Milburn	Ibid, p.xix
11	Jensen, O.	p.235
12	'No. 29'	Wesley Wallace - speech, piano (c.November 1929, Grafton, Wis.)
13	'Freight Train Blues'	Eddie Miller - vocal, piano (19 October 1929, Chicago, Ill.)
14	'Special Agent'	Sleepy John Estes - vocal, guitar; Son Bonds or Charlie Pickett - guitar (22 April 1938, New York City)
15	Stilgoe, J.R.	Ibid, p.147
16	Ayers, E.	Ibid, p.22
17	Ibid.	
18	Oliver, P.	*Blues Fell This Morning*, ibid, p.43
19	'That Lonesome Train Took My Baby Away'	Charlie McCoy - vocal, banjo-mandolin; prob. Bo Carter - guitar (15 December 1930, Jackson, Miss.)
20	Charters, S.	Notes to R.B.F. RBF-14 (LP), p.5
21	Partridge, E.	*A Dictionary of the Underworld*, ibid, p.336
22	Coles, R.	p.266
23	Ibid.	pp.532-3
24	Lomax, John A.	Interview with Blind Willie McTell
25	Edwards	Ibid, p.34
26	'Old Rock Island Blues'	Lonnie Coleman - vocal, banjo; unk guitar (12 April 1929, Atlanta, Ga.)
27	'Western Plain Blues'	Gene Campbell - vocal, guitar (c.May 1930 Chicago, Ill.)
28	'IC Moan Blues'	Tampa Red - vocal, guitar; Georgia Tom - piano (c.mid-June 1930, Chicago, Ill.)

29	McCormick, M.	Ibid.
30	Garon, P., & G. Tomko.	pp.113-4
31	Saunders Jr, R.	p.137
32	Ibid.	p.14
33	'Railroadin' Some'	Henry Thomas - speech, guitar, reed pipes (c.7 October 1929, Chicago, Ill.)
34	McCormick	Ibid.
35	'Mistreated Boy'	Buddy Moss - vocal, guitar; Joshua White - guitar (28 August 1935, New York City)
36	'Lost Ship Blues'	Charley Jordan - vocal, guitar; Peetie Wheatstraw - piano (4 November 1930, Chicago, Ill.)
37	'Travelin' Railroad Man Blues'	Alabama Sheiks: Eddie West - violin, prob. vocal; Ad Fox - guitar (20 January 1931, Camden, N.J.)
38	'My Stove Won't Work'	Casey Bill - vocal, steel guitar; prob. Black Bob - piano; prob. Bill Settles - bass (31 October 1935, Chicago Ill.)
39	Stilgoe	Ibid, p.150
40	'Charleston Contest (Part 1)'	Too Tight Henry - speech, guitar (27 October 1928, Atlanta, Ga.)
41	Hubbard	Ibid, p.157
42	Wheaton, M. (Ed.)	Ibid, p.8
43	'Hobo Bill'	Martha Copeland - vocal; Porter Grainger - piano; Buddy Christian - banjo; unk. sound effects (9 August 1927, New York City)
44	Stilgoe	Ibid, p.127
45	'Jungle Man Blues'	Papa Charlie Jackson - vocal, banjo (c.December 1928, Chicago, Ill.)
46	Anderson, N.	p.12
47	Holbrook, S.H.	Ibid, p.397
48	'Roll And Rattler'	Lucille Bogan (as 'Bessie Jackson') - vocal; Walter Roland - piano; prob. Sonny Scott - speech (19 July 1933, New York City)
49	'Chickasaw Train Blues'	Memphis Minnie - vocal, guitar, speech (24 August 1934, Chicago, Ill.)
50	'Little Rock Blues'	Pearl Dickson - vocal, speech; 'Pet' and 'Can' (Maylon and Richard Harney) - guitars (12 December 1927, Memphis, Tenn.)
51	'Down The Big Road Blues'	Mattie Delaney - vocal, guitar (c.21 February 1930, Memphis, Tenn.)
52	Carmichael, B.	Notes to Document DOCD-5665 (CD)
53	'It's Hard Time'	Joe Stone (prob. Jaydee Short) - vocal, guitar or poss. unk. guitar (2 August 1933, Chicago, Ill.)

54	'Rack 'Em Back'	Washboard Sam - vocal, washboard.; Big Bill - guitar; prob. Joshua Altheimer - piano; prob. Bill Settles - bass (16 December 1938, Aurora, Ill.)
55	'Nashville, Tennessee'	Washboard Sam - vocal, washboard, speech; Black Bob - piano; Big Bill - guitar; unk. bass (21 December 1936, Chicago, Ill.)
56	Edwards	Ibid, p.41
57	Ibid.	p.70
58	Seroff, D., & L. Abbott	p.123
59	Williams W.	p.249
60	'Travelin Blues'	Ibid.
61	Unknown author	p.11
62	'Travelin' Blues'	Ibid.
63	Partridge	Ibid, p.486
64	Ibid.	pp.486-7
65	'Meat Shakin' Woman'	Blind Boy Fuller - vocal, guitar (6 April 1938, New York City)
66	Funk, R.	Notes to Document DOCD-5379 (CD)
67	'Ham And Eggs'	Bessemer Sunset Four: Dave Brown - vocal (lead); Sam Riley - vocal (tenor); Wash Ivey - vocal (baritone); Pat Gaines - vocal (bass); unacc. (12 Nov. 1928, Birmingham, Ala.)
68	Fahey, J.	Notes to Takoma B-1001 (LP)
69	'The Atlanta Special'	Bukka White - vocal, speech, guitar (1963, Memphis, Tenn.)
70	'Travelin''Blues'	Ibid.

Discography – Chapter 10

'The Atlanta Special'
(Bukka White)
CD: *Mississippi Blues – Vol. 1: Bukka White*
[Takoma CDTAK-1001] 1998
Reissue of 1963 Takoma LP + 3 extra tracks.

'Charleston Contest (Part 1)'
(Too Tight Henry)
CD: *Rare Country Blues – Vol. 3 (1928-36)*
[Document DOCD-5642] 1999

'Chickasaw Train Blues'
(Memphis Minnie)
5-CD: *Memphis Minnie (1929-37)*
[J.S.P. JSP-7716] 2003

'Down The Big Road Blues'
(Mattie Delaney)
CD: *Mississippi Blues – Volume 1 (1928-37)*
[Document DOCD-5157] 1993

'Freight Train Blues'
(Eddie Miller)
CD: *Chicago Piano (1929-36)*
[Document DOCD-5191] 1993

'Ham And Eggs'
(Bessemer Sunset Four)
CD: *Bessemer Sunset Four (1928-30)*
[Document DOCD-5379] 1995

'Hobo Bill' (Martha Copeland)	CD: *Martha Copeland – Volume 1 (1923-27)* [Document DOCD-5372] 1995
'IC Moan Blues' (Tampa Red)	CD: *Tampa Red – Volume 3 (1929-30)* [Document DOCD-5075] 1991
'It's Hard Time' (Joe Stone [J.D. Short?])	CD: *St. Louis Country Blues (1929-37)* [Document DOCD-5147] 1993
'Jungle Man Blues' (Papa Charlie Jackson)	CD: *Papa Charlie Jackson – Vol. 3 (1928-34)* [Document DOCD-5087] 1992
'Kentucky Blues' (Little Hat Jones)	4-CD: *Texas Blues (1927-40)* [J.S.P. JSP-7730] 2004
'Little Rock Blues' (Pearl Dickson)	CD: *Memphis Blues (1927-38)* [Document DOCD-5159] 1993
'Lost Ship Blues' (Charley Jordan)	CD: *Charley Jordan – Volume 1 (1930-31)* [Document DOCD-5097] 1992
'Loving Talking Blues' (Blind Willie McTell)	5-CD: *Blind Willie McTell – The Classic Years (1927-40)* [J.S.P. JSP-7711] 2003
'Mean Conductor Blues' (Ed Bell)	CD: *Ed Bell (1927-30)* [Document DOCD-5090] 1992
'Meat Shakin' Woman' (Blind Boy Fuller)	4-CD: *Blind Boy Fuller (1935-38)* [J.S.P. JSP-7735] 2004
'Mr. Brakes-Man (Let Me Ride Your Train)' (Martha Copeland)	CD: *Martha Copeland – Volume 1 (1923-27)* [Document DOCD-5372] 1995
'Mistreated Boy' (Buddy Moss)	CD: *Buddy Moss – Volume 3 (1935-41)* [Document DOCD-5125] 1992
'My Stove Won't Work' (Casey Bill Weldon)	CD: *Casey Bill Weldon – Volume 1 (1935-38)* [Document DOCD-5217] 1993
'Nashville, Tennessee' (Washboard Sam)	CD: *Washboard Sam – Volume 1 (1935-36)* [Document DOCD-5171] 1993
'No. 29' (Wesley Wallace)	CD: *St. Louis Barrelhouse Piano (1929-34)* [Document DOCD-5104] 1992
'Old Rock Island Line Blues' (Lonnie Coleman)	CD: *Sinners And Saints (1926-31)* [Document DOCD-5106] 1993
'Rack 'Em Back' (Washboard Sam)	CD: *Washboard Sam – Volume 3 (1938)* [Document DOCD-5173] 1993
'Railroadin' Some' (Henry Thomas)	CD: *Henry Thomas (1927-29)* [Document DOCD-5665] 2000

'Roll And Rattler'
(Bessie Jackson [Lucille Bogan])

CD: *Lucille Bogan – Volume 2 (March 1930-20 July 1933)* [Blues Document BDCD-6037] 1993

'Southern Casey Jones'
(Jesse James)

2-CD: *Cincinnati Blues* [Catfish KATCD-186] 2001

'Special Agent'
(Sleepy John Estes)

CD: *Sleepy John Estes – Volume 2 (1937-41)* [Document DOCD-5016] 1990

'That Lonesome Train Took My Baby Away'
(Charlie McCoy)

CD: *Charlie McCoy (1928-32)* [Blues Document BDCD-6018] 1992

'Travelin' Blues'
(Blind Sammie [Blind Willie McTell])

5-CD: *Blind Willie McTell – The Classic Years (1927-40)* [J.S.P. JSP-7711] 2003

'Travelin' Railroad Man Blues'
(Alabama Sheiks)

CD: *Violin Sing The Blues For Me (1926-49)* [Old Hat CD-1002] 1999

'Western Plain Blues'
(Gene Campbell)

CD: *Gene Campbell (1929-31)* [Document DOCD-5151] 1993

Epilogue

By the 1960s, blacks, as with the US population generally, took more and more to the automobile — some of them living in one in preference to a brownstone tenement on Chicago's South Side or Harlem in New York City — and the railroad companies finally abandoned the passenger train. It was not until the following decade that a semi-national railway system was set up: Amtrak. This network returned people to rail travel and is now gradually extending from the Northern states both south- and westwards. Also, major US cities including St. Louis 'have built new light rail lines, many of them as part of systems that are still expanding geographically, and is scheduling to meet the demand engendered by their success.' [1]

In 1980, there was even an 'Amtrak Blues' [LP *Amtrak Blues*, Columbia JC-36430] by one of the earliest vaudeville-blues singers to record, commencing in 1921 for the Black Swan label. Alberta Hunter, from Memphis, Tenn., was just 85 years old at the time! Her voice was by now more gritty and infinitely more bluesy than in 1921, as she moaned her own personal blues about her wayward man:

> I know he's ornery, triflin'. He's the type of man that just don't care.
> Oooh! Lord, he's ornery, he's selfish. He's the type of man that just don't care.
> *(Spoken)* Oh! Help me! Help me, somebody!
> Ah! He pawned the *Holy Bible* just to get his Amtrak railroad fare.
> *(Spoken)* Oh, Lord! The dirty dog! [2]

With a sheer *joie de vivre*, Hunter injects her vocals with a power and conviction that has her sounding thirty years younger!

As well as light railways, their opposite number 'heavy rail' or commuter trains, all but abandoned since the 1960s, saw a resurgence of life at the beginning of the 1990s. At the time of writing there are there are more companies expanding across the US — including systems based in Chicago, New York, New Jersey, Los Angeles, San Diego, Boston, Baltimore, Philadelphia, San Francisco and other cities. These often include freight as well as passenger services. As with Amtrak, these rail networks are partly subsidised by regional bodies such as the Metropolitan Transportation Authority of New York and the Metra system of the Chicago Regional Transportation Authority.[3] The latter owns/leases track of the old IC and Rock Island Line and other roads.

Amtrak has even penetrated to the 'deepest' South: a promotional six-car passenger train organised by Amtrak and the Florida East Coast RR running from Jacksonville, Fla. to West Palm Beach over FEC lines on 18-19 June 2001 proved 'nothing short of a smashing success'. This resulted in 'unequivocal state support for the new service, with two trains daily proposed to operate on the route by sometime late in 2004, although construction and infrastructure improvements could delay the service up to two years.' [4] Bramson says: 'Currently, Daytona Beach is the largest US city without rail passenger service, and these trains would remedy that deficiency. If Amtrak is able to convince Congress that passenger service is a necessary and an important part of the overall transportation picture... I am certain we will see passenger trains again operating on the FEC after an absence dating back from July 30, 1968.' [5] Often working with Amtrak, the current US railroad system(s) is looking forward to a continuing renaissance in its increasing expansion in the Twenty-First Century..

One of the most enduring of US railroads, the FEC and its predecessors go back over 130 years. It is celebrated, almost uniquely, in Lizzie Washington's 'East Coast Blues' [Gennett 6134], from April 1927:

> You hear them all screamin' about the Florida East Coast blues.
> You hear them all screamin' about the Florida East Coast train.
> That's the train that brought me from the sunshine into the rain. [6]

Although allocated a place of origin in St. Louis, Ms. Washington is a shadowy figure about whom little is known. The location of this recording session is given in *Blues & Gospel Records* as either Chicago, Ill. or Richmond, Ind.. As the FEC had no service running to St. Louis, it seems reasonable to assume the singer travelled *'into the rain'* in one of these Northern cities. This is supported by the fact that the *Havana Special*, *Palmetto Limited* and *Florida Special* ran through Richmond on their way to New York City, while the *Dixie Limited* and *Dixie Flyer* headed for Chicago from Miami via Jacksonville. All these 'name' trains were operated by the Florida East Coast in conjunction with other railroads (once over the Florida state line) at the time, and were the only FEC trains that could have *'brought'* Lizzie Washington to either Chicago or Richmond — a possible pointer to her being one of that rare breed, a pre-war recorded Floridian blues singer.

As for railroads in the blues, the genre has never been more popular universally than it is today, and many contemporary singers/ musicians (of all races and nationalities) bring a new look/attitude to the blues that reflects their own experiences. The early blues (1890-1943) considered in this book were a zenith in the genre, which was not rivalled until the late 1940s and into the 1950s with the electric Chicago blues of Muddy Waters, Howlin' Wolf, etc. Both of these pinnacles of African American cultural/musical talent were achieved by *working-class* black singers for their working-class audience spread across the Southern states and later some Northern and Western cities like Chicago, Detroit, New York, Los Angeles and San Francisco. Some of the most horrendous reasons for singing the blues in these eras have mercifully disappeared from US society — the convict-lease system, sharecropping, lynchings and other atrocities, for example. Black society has gradually merged more and more with the mainstream. Although the ghetto and its attendant racism still spawns a marginalized black population, the sexual boast of having a woman/man 'for every day in the week' is not as well received — or understood — by the blues audience of today (who are predominantly white and middle-class), as it was in the 1920s in the black community, any more than riding the 'blinds' or the 'rods' on the railroad.

Here in the early Twenty-First Century, the hobo is an icon from a bygone age. Although there is quite a cult following for hoboing today, and it is still has its risks and dangers, these 'bindle stiffs' are usually reasonably well-off middle-class whites looking for kicks, rather than desperate and hungry working-class blacks looking for a decent job or escaping violence and institutionalised discrimination in the South. And it is certain that hardly anybody would attempt to ride the rods (the 'blinds' having virtually disappeared with the advent of new passenger rolling stock introduced by Amtrak, Conrail and other railroad companies). Moreover, the diesel locomotive, from the mid-1930s to the present, has not inspired the blues singer in the same way as its steam predecessor. A few post-war blues referred to the *Super Chief* or *El Capitan* on the Santa Fe via Memphis Slim and others, but these seem the exception rather than the rule. But then, almost miraculously, an Alberta Hunter resurfaces:

> I got a mind to ramble, oooh! never work no more;
> *(Spoken)* Have mercy!
> Yes, I got a mind to ramble never work no more.
> *(Spoken)* Talk to me.
> I-I got a mind to take a chance an' gamble everywhere I go.
>
> Yes! Just as sure as Amtrak — oooh! — leaves that Pennsy yard.[*]
> *(Spoken)* Hallelujah!
> Yes, I said sure as Amtrak leee-aves that Pennsy yard — oh!
> I'm goin' back to Memphis (if) I have to ride the rods.[8]

While some of Hunter's words might seem an anachronism — even back in 1980 — it transpires the reason she's *'got a mind to ramble'* is bad treatment from the man she loves. Indeed, the blues will always reflect the human condition in societies across the world. If your man/woman leaves

---

[*] 'In May 1971, the new Amtrak took over from Pennsylvania Central.'[7] The latter was a merger of the two Eastern railroad giants of the earlier Twentieth Century, the New York Central and the Pennsylvania RR. However, Ms. Hunter still refers to the *'Pennsy'*.

you, your landlord evicts you, or your boss gives you the push, or you suddenly lose a loved one to the Grim Reaper (or 'Old Father Time' as Blind Willie McTell once said [9]), you still got the blues. Yes! Even when your train is an hour or two late. And more and more people on the planet are waking up to the fact that listening to and/or singing the blues will fix that 'hole in your soul'. Let Alberta the blues singer have the last word:

> I'm havin' a fiesta while I'm livin',
> 'Cos tomorrow I may die.
> *(Spoken)* Yeah!
>
> For if I make my rugged road rough
> That's the price that *I've* got to pay.
> *(Spoken)* Not you!
> I-I'm havin' a good time, livin' my life today![10]

Notes to Epilogue

1	Chant, C.	p.355
2	'Amtrak Blues'	Alberta Hunter - vocal, speech; acc. Billy Butler - guitar; Vic Dickenson - trombone; Frank Wess - tenor sax/flute; Norris Turney - tenor sax; Gerald Cook - piano; Aaron Bell - brass bass; Jackie Williams - drums (8 January 1980, New York City)*
3	Chant	Ibid, pp.367-373
4	Bramson, S.H.	p.199
5	Ibid.	p.200
6	'East Coast Blues'	Lizzie Washington - vocal; Henry Johnson - violin; James Johnson - piano (19 April 1927, Chicago or Richmond, Ind.)
7	Chant	Ibid, p.402
8	'I've Got A Mind To Ramble'	Alberta Hunter - vocal, speech; acc. Billy Butler - guitar; Vic Dickenson - trombone; Frank Wess - tenor sax/flute; Norris Turney - tenor sax; Gerald Cook - piano; Aaron Bell - brass bass; Jackie Williams - drums (8 January 1980, New York City)
9	'Death Cell Blues'	Blind Willie McTell - vocal, guitar; Curly Weaver - guitar (19 Sept. 1933, New York City)

---

* Additional data from *Alberta: A Celebration In Blues* by Frank C. Taylor with Gerald Cook (see *Bibliography*).

[10] 'I'm Having A Good Time' Alberta Hunter - vocal, speech; acc. Billy Butler - guitar; Vic Dickenson - trombone; Frank Wess - tenor sax/flute; Norris Turney - tenor sax; Gerald Cook - piano; Aaron Bell - brass bass; Jackie Williams - drums (8 January 1980, New York City)

Discography – Epilogue

'Amtrak Blues' (Alberta Hunter)
LP: *Alberta Hunter – Amtrak Blues* [Columbia JC-36430] 1980
CD: *Alberta Hunter – Amtrak Blues* [Sony Collectors Classics 36430] 1990

'Death Cell Blues' (Blind Willie McTell)
5-CD: *Blind Willie McTell – The Classic Years (1927-40)* [J.S.P. JSP-7711] 2003

'East Coast Blues' (Lizzie Washington)
CD: *St. Louis Girls (1927-34)* [Document DOCD-5182] 1993

Epilogue

Appendix I

When discussing signs for liquor saloons in the 1880s, Duis noted that some places 'employed a simple red light, which in Chicago could indicate a respectable saloon instead of a brothel.' [1] It seems that, in New Orleans and Chicago at least, during the 1880s the brothel and the red light were not synonymous. But, interestingly, the origins of this association appear to have come from more than a decade earlier. In the admittedly rather coy reporting of Beebe & Clegg: 'In the early days of Great Plains railroading after the tracks of the Kansas Pacific & Santa Fe had been laid across the long tangents of Kansas, the young and lusty train crews of the day added the phrase "red light" to the American lexicon. In the tough frontier cowtowns of Abilene, Dodge City, Hays, Wichita and Newton, when a trainman with time on his hands between runs went on an errand of relaxation to a bagnio *[brothel]*, it was conventional for him to hang his switchman's red lantern outside to facilitate the callboy on his rounds in the event the trainmaster wanted a train made up. The portions of the cowtowns devoted to love-stores was shortly known as the red-light district from the multiplicity of lanterns proclaiming the presence within of brakemen, conductors and members of the head-end crew.' [2] The latter were the fireman and the engineer. Derived from the US term 'red light district', in Britain 'red lamp' referred to 'a brothel' [3] around the turn of the Twentieth Century.

Notes to Appendix I

[1] Duis, P.P. — p.23
[2] Beebe & Clegg — Ibid, p?
[3] Partridge — Ibid. p.759 (*Historical Slang*)

Appendix II

In his unique book, *Long Steel Rail*, Norm Cohen devotes some twenty-six pages to an in-depth discussion of the 'In The Pines'/'The Longest Train'. He draws heavily from the study of this song group by Judith McCulloh[1] in which she 'examined 160 separate versions of 'In The Pines'/'The Longest Train' or other closely related folk songs from printed, recorded and manuscript sources dating from 1917 to 1969'[2], based on 'four important identifying elements, one musical and three textual.'[3] One of the textual elements was 'a group of verses describing briefly an accident in which someone is beheaded (presumably by a train).'[4]

The 'accident stanzas' as I term them, relate to the 'The Longest Train' part of this song group or cluster, which first appeared on a record in 1925 by Bertie May Moses[5] in North Carolina. McCulloh actually investigated 157 songs, in which the accident stanzas 'occurred in forty versions'.[6] Cohen summarises his own survey thus: 'Of the history and development of this song — or group of songs — prior to the turn of the *[Twentieth]* century then, we can say nothing.'[7]

However, the discovery of a manuscript originally written in 1896 which had lain dormant in an American university's archives for almost a hundred years was published in book form in 1994, edited by James A. Ward, and goes some way towards filling Cohen's historical gap from the Nineteenth Century. Entitled *Southern Railroad Man: Conductor N.J. Bell's Recollections of the Civil War Era*, it covers the period 1857-95, when Bell worked in various jobs on a number of Southern railroads. His longest stay (as a conductor) was one of nearly twenty years on the East Tennessee, Virginia & Georgia RR, which later became part of the new Southern Railway in 1894.

Bell recalled some accidents which had occurred in the early 1880s (circa 1884), on trains he worked on with the ETV&G — including one he refers to as 'another sickening sight'. Apart from the grisly nature of this accident, Bell reflects a deep resentment at the fact it was not his train that was involved: 'I had to make out a written statement of the facts, instead of the man who ought to have done so.' His narrative runs: 'I met a train one night, and the engineer of this train told me to look out at a certain place along the *[rail]*road, where he had run over something, and said he was afraid it was a woman, as he had found some long hair on the pilot of his engine, but he did not stop to see what it was that he had run over. When I got near the place (on Bell's own train) where I was told to look out, I put a man on the front of the engine to keep a lookout, so we would not run over it again, should it be a man or a woman… When we found the object it proved to be a woman, with her head cut off and her body mangled. The agent whom I had taken along, in case it should be a human body, stayed and aroused the nearest citizens and had an inquest held, and the mangled pieces were picked up and buried by the roadside… The place where this happened soon became haunted, or at least that was the rumour among some of the boys on the road. Some of them saw a ghost once in a while on moonlight nights. One said he saw a woman one night standing by the roadside dressed in white, and that she had no head. It was said that he just ran for life through the sleepers and coaches, scared nearly to death.' [8]

The above grim detail is surely the factual basis for at least one part of the 'In The Pines'/'The Longest Train' song cluster, although it is the head that was missing rather than the body. Unfortunately, Bell does not give a location. However, he and his family lived in north Georgia — in Dalton — and later moved to Acworth, 'a nice little town on the Western & Atlantic Railroad, thirty-five miles out from Atlanta.' [9] His trains took him through Tennessee, Georgia and Alabama. On the ETV&G, he mainly travelled between Knoxville and Chattanooga in Tennessee, and Dalton; and sometimes through Dade County, Georgia. Bell had also spent some seven years on the Alabama & Chattanooga RR (also later to be absorbed by the Southern). This was over two periods (1868-71 and 1872-76), prior to his joining the ETV&G, on which road Bell says this accident happened.

The A&C ran from Wauhatchie just over the state line in Tennessee through Trenton and Rising Fawn. Both stops were in Dade County, which is where Joe Brown's coal mine was situated — the only coal deposit in Georgia. Although it is possible that the scene of this accident could have been any one of three (Tennessee, Alabama or Georgia), Georgia seems to be the most likely. With Judith McCulloh's reference to Joe Brown's coal mines in Dade County operating 'as early as the 1870s', she was on the right track when she hypothesized that 'The Longest Train' had 'originated in the South — whether specifically in Georgia is unclear — as early as the Reconstruction years.' [10] The latter era officially ended in 1877 with the Hayes Compromise, some seven years before Conductor N.J. Bell related the gruesome accident on the ETV&G Railroad.

Notes to Appendix II

1	McCulloh, Judith	*In The Pines: The Melodic-Textual Identity of an American Lyric Folksong Cluster* (Unpublished PhD dissertation, Indiana University, 1970)
2	Cohen	Ibid, p.492
3	Ibid.	
4	Ibid.	p.493
5	See Cohen	Ibid, p.496
6	Ibid.	p.493
7	Ibid.	p.508
8	Ward, J.A. (Ed.)	p.124
9	Ibid.	pp.44-5
10	Cohen	Ibid, p.495

Appendix II

Appendix III

Just after completion of this book I came across another black railroad performance (recorded by Library of Congress) which comes very close to the superb standard set by Blind Willie McTell and Bukka White.

In 1941 at Hampton, Va., a singer known only as 'Big Boy' recorded a title listed simply as 'Blues' under his entry in *Blues & Gospel Records*.[1] Displaying some exquisite slide guitar playing to rival McTell's, he was obviously aware of the earlier commercial recording of 'Travelin' Blues' and, interestingly, one of his verses repeats the line *'I'm Georgia-raised, but I'm Alabama bound'* three times. Big Boy commences his piece — as did McTell — with a spoken introduction:

>   *(Spoken)* I traveled the South a few years ago, on a hobo trip. Go by freight. Come up to the yard. You oughta tone the bell in the yard. (…)
>
>   *(Spoken)* Gettin' near a crossin'. I mean, you-all look at these hobos when the whistle [*blow*], which is two long, two short. (…).[2]

(…) = guitar 'sings'

Like McTell, he describes the blues he *'sang to the brakeman'*.[2] Although Tony Russell says this is 'probably the piece filed by the Library of Congress which acquired the Hampton material, as 'Train Song' ' [3], it is far more likely to be 'The Hobo Song' which is also listed in *Blues & Gospel Records* under the heading 'Late Additions'.[4]

Notes to Appendix III

[1] Dixon, Godrich & Rye — Ibid p.69
[2] 'Blues' — 'Big Boy'- vocal, speech, guitar (Library of Congress recording, 1941, Hampton, Va.)
[3] Russell, Tony — Notes to Document DOCD-5575 (CD)
[4] Dixon, Godrich & Rye — Ibid, p.1071

Discography

'Blues'
(Big Boy)

CD: *Field Recordings – Volume 1: Virginia (1936-41)* [Document DOCD-5575] 1997

BIBLIOGRAPHY

Adams, James Truslow - *Dictionary Of American History (Volume V)*
    (Charles Scribner's Sons, New York) 1940
Adams, Ramon F. - *The Language Of The Railroader*
    (University of Oklahoma Press, Norman, Okl.) 1977
Albertson, Chris - *Bessie: Empress Of The Blues*
    (Abacus, London) 1975, reprinted. First published 1973.
Ambrose, Stephen E. - *Nothing Like It In The World:*
    The Men Who Built The Transcontinental Railroad 1863-69
    (Simon & Schuster, New York/London) 2000
Anderson, Nels - *The Hobo*
    (University of Chicago Press, Chicago) 1927, reprinted.
    First published 1923.
Asman, James - Notes to LP *Leadbelly's Last Sessions (Volume 1)*
    (Melodisc MLP-12-113) 1959
Armes, Ethel - *The Story Of Coal And Iron In Alabama*
    (Arno Press, New York/Birmingham, Ala.) 1973, reprinted.
    First published 1910.
Ayers, Edward L. - *The Promise Of The New South*
    (Oxford University Press, New York/Oxford) 1992
Bagby, G.W - *Picturesque America* (Centennial Edition – 2 volumes)
    (Lyle Stuart Inc, N.J.) 1974
Baker, Stanley L., & Virginia Brainard Kunz - *The Collector's Book Of Railroadiana*
    (Castle Books, Secaucus, N.J.) 1979, reprinted. First published 1976.
Ballagh, James Curtis - *The South In The Building Of The Nation*
    (The History Of The Southern States) Volume 3 [12 vols.]
    (Pelican Publishing, Gretna, La.) 2002, reprinted. First published 1909.
Basie, William 'Count' (as told to Albert Murray) -
    Good Morning Blues: The Autobiography Of Count Basie
    (Paladin, London/Glasgow) 1987, reprinted. First published 1986.
Beebe, Lucius - *The Central Pacific & The Southern Pacific Railroads*
    (Howell-North, Berkeley, Ca.) 1963
Beebe, Lucius, & Charles Clegg - *The Age Of Steam*
    (Rhinehart & Co. Inc, New York) 1957
Beebe, Lucius, & Charles Clegg - *The Trains We Rode*
    (Promontory Press, New York) 1990 reprinted.
    First published in 2 volumes, 1965 & 1966
Bolles, Albert S. - *Industrial History Of The United States* (3rd edition)
    (August M. Kelley, New York) 1966, reprinted. First published 1888.
Botkin, B.A. (Ed.) - *A Treasury Of Southern Folklore*
    (Crown Publishers, New York) 1953, reprinted. First published 1949.
Botkin, B.A., & Alvin Harlow - *A Treasury Of Railroad Folklore*
    (Crown Publishers Inc, New York) 1956, reprinted. First published 1953.

Bowman, Hank W. - *Pioneer Railroads*
    (Arco Publishing Co. Inc, New York) 1954
Bramson, Seth H. - *Speedway To Sunshine:*
        The Story Of The Florida East Coast Railway
    (Boston Mills Press, Erin, Ontario) 2003
Brandfon, Robert L. - *Cotton Kingdom of the New South*
    (Harvard University Press, Cambridge, Mass.) 1967
Brewer, Cobham E. - *Dictionary Of Phrase And Fable*
    (Unknown publisher) 1898
Briegar, James - *Hometown Mississippi*
    (Historical & Genealogical Association of Mississippi, Jackson, Miss.) 1980
Broven, John - *A Rap With Johnny Otis*
    (*Blues Unlimited* No. 100) April 1973
Bunce, O.B. - *Picturesque America (Centennial Edition)* [2 vols.].
    William Cullen Bryant (Ed.) (Lyle Stuart Inc., New Jersey) 1974
Calt, Stephen, & John Miller - Notes to LP *Mama Let Me Lay It On You*
    (Yazoo L-1040) c. 1973
Calt, Stephen, & John Miller - Notes to LP *Bottleneck Guitar Trendsetters Of The 1930s*
    (Yazoo L-1049) mid-1970s
Calt, Stephen, & Gayle Dean Wardlow - *The Buying And Selling of Paramounts (Part 3)*
    (*78 Quarterly* Volume 1, No. 5) 1990
Calt, Stephen, & Gayle Wardlow -
    King Of The Delta Blues: The Life & Music Of Charley Patton
    (Rock Chapel Press, Newton, N.J.) 1988
Campbell, Rev. John P. - *Southern Business Directory And General*
        Commercial Advertiser (Volume 1, Part 1)
    (Unknown publisher, Charleston, S.C.) 1854
    On microfilm supplied by University Microfilms Inc, Ann Arbor, Michigan via the British Lending Library.
Carmichael, Bill - *Tramp Art*
    (Quoted in notes to LP *Henry Thomas: Ragtime Texas* (Herwin 209) c. 1974
Carter, Betty - *Mules In The Delta*
    (*Mules & Mississippi*, Mississippi Department of Archives & History) 1981
Catton, Bruce - *American Heritage: New History Of The Civil War*
    Edited, with Introduction by James M. McPherson
    (Viking Penguin, New York) 1996, reprinted. First published 1960.
Chant, Christopher -
    The World's Railways: The History & Development Of Rail Transport
    (S. Webb & Son, Isle of Anglesey) 2002, reprint.
    First published 2001.
Charters, Samuel B. - *The Country Blues*
    (Da Capo, New York) 1977, revised edition. First published 1959.
Charters, Samuel B. - Notes to LP *Blues Roots Mississippi*
    (R.B.F. RBF-14) 1966
Charters, Samuel B. - *The Bluesmen*
    (Oak Publications, New York) 1967
Clark, Thomas D. - *A Pioneer Southern Railroad From New Orleans To Cairo*
    (University of North Carolina Press, Chapel Hill, N.C.) 1936

Clarke, Victor S. - *History Of Manufactures In The United States (Volume II: 1860-93)*
    (Peter Smith, New York) 1949, reprinted. First published 1929.
Cline, Wayne - *Alabama Railroads*
    (University of Alabama, Tuscaloosa & London) 1997
Cobb, James C. - *The Most Southern Place On Earth*
    (Oxford University Press, London) 1994, reprinted. First published 1992.
Cohen, Norm - *Long Steel Rail*
    (University of Illinois Press, Urbana/Chicago) 1981
Cohn, Lawrence (Ed.) - *Nothing But The Blues*
    (Abbeville Press, New York / London / Paris) 1993
Coles, Robert - *Migrants, Sharecroppers, Mountaineers* (*Volume II* of *Children In Crisis*)
    (Atlantic Monthly Press, Boston/Toronto) 1969, reprinted.
    First published 1967.
Conway, Cecilia, & Scott Odell - Notes to CD *Black Banjo Songsters*
                                          Of North Carolina & Virginia
    (Smithsonian Folkways SFCD-40079) 1998
Corliss, Carlton J. - *Main Line Of Mid-America: The Story of the Illinois Central*
    (Creative Age Press, New York) 1950
Coulter, E. Merton - *The South During Reconstruction 1865-77*
    (Louisiana State University Press, Baton Rouge, La. / The Littlefield Fund
    For Southern History of the University of Texas, Austin, Tex.) 1962, repr.
    First published 1947.
Cowley, John H. - Notes to CD *Ida Cox: Volume 3 (1925-27)*
    (Document DOCD-5324) 1994
Creckmore, Betsey Beeler - *Knoxville*
    (University of Tennessee Press, Knoxville) 1979, reprinted.
    First published 1958.
Cronon, William - *Nature's Metropolis: Chicago And The Great West*
    (W.W. Norton & Co, New York/London) 1992
Curtin, Mary Ellen - *Black Prisoners & Their World: Alabama 1865-1900*
    (University Press of Virginia, Charlottesville, Va. and London) 2000
Dance, Helen Oakley - *Stormy Monday* [T-Bone Walker autobiography]
    (Da Capo, New York) 1987
Daniels, Douglas Henry - *Pioneer Urbanites:*
                                A Social Cultural History Of Black San Francisco
    (Temple University University Press, Philadelphia, Pa.) 1980
Davis, Burke - *The Southern Railway: Road Of The Innovators*
    (University of North Carolina Press, Chapel Hill, N.C./London) 1985
De Bow, J.D.B. - *The Industrial Resources, etc.*
                              Of The Southern And Western States (Vol. I)
    (Office of De Bow's *Review*, Merchant's Exchange, New Orleans) 1852
    University Microfilms Inc. Ibid.
DeCell, Harriet, & Joanne Prichard - *Yazoo: Its Legends and Legacies*
    (Yazoo Delta Press, Yazoo City, Miss.) 1977, reprinted.
    First published 1976.
De Voe, Thomas Farrington - *The Market Book (Volume 1)*
    (Unknown publisher, New York) 1862
    University Microfilms Inc. Ibid.

Dixon, Robert M.W., J. Godrich & Howard W. Rye -
>*Blues & Gospel Records 1890-1943* (4th edition)
>(Clarendon Press, Oxford) 1997

Dixon, Willie (as told to Don Snowden) - *I Am The Blues*
>(Quartet Books, London/New York) 1995

Doster, James F. - *Railroads In Alabama Politics, 1875-1914*
>(*University of Alabama Studies* No. 12) July 1957

Doyle, Don H. - *New Men, New Cities, New South*
>(University of North Carolina Press, Chapel Hill, N.C.) 1990

Drobney Jeffrey A. - *Lumbermen And Log Sawyers [Labor, And Culture In The North Florida Timber Industry, 1830-1930]*
>(Mercer University Press, Macon, Ga.) 1997

Droege, John A. - *Freight Terminals And Trains* (2nd edition)
>(McGraw-Hill, New York /London) 1925, reprinted. First published 1912.

Dubin, Arthur D. - *Some Classic Trains*
>(Kalmbach Publication, Milwaukee) 1973, reprinted. First published 1964.

Duis, Perry R. - *The Saloon (Public Drinking In Chicago & Boston 1880-1920)*
>(University of Illinois Press, Urbana/Chicago) 1983

Eavenson, Howard N. - *The First Century And A Quarter Of The American Coal Industry*
>(Privately published, Pittsburg, Pa.) 1942

Edwards, David 'Honeyboy' - *The World Don't Owe Me A Living*
>(Chicago Review Press, Chicago) 1997

Emmet, Boris – *Catalogue No. 57. Montgomery Ward & Co. 1895*
>(Dover Publications Inc. New York) 1969, reprinted with a new introduction by Boris Emmet.

Evans, David - *Big Road Blues*
>(University of California Press, Berkeley, Ca.) 1982

Fair, James R. - *The Louisiana & Arkansas Railway – The Story Of A Regional Line*
>(Northern Illinois University Press, DeKalb, Ill.) 1997

Farrington, S. Kip - *Railroads Of Today* (Coward-McCann Inc, New York) 1949

Fahey, John - Notes to Bukka White LP *Mississippi Blues (Volume 1)*
>(Takoma B-1001) 1963

Froget, Peter Marl - *Roget's Thesaurus Of Synonyms & Antonyms* (Revised ed.)
>(Tophi Books, London) 1988

Funk, Ray - Notes to CD *Bessemer Sunset Four (1928-30)*
>(Document DOCD-5379) 1995

Garon, Paul & Beth - *Woman With Guitar: Memphis Minnie's Blues*
>(Da Capo, New York) 1992

Garon, Paul & Gene Tomko - *Black Hoboes And Their Songs (What's the Use of Walking If There's a Freight Train Going Your Way)*
>(Charles H. Kerr Publishing Co.) 2006

Gates, Paul Wallace - *The Illinois Central Railroad And Its Colonisation Work*
>(Harvard University Press, Cambridge, Mass.) 1934

Glendinning, Gene V. - *The Chicago & Alton Railroad: The Only Way*
>(Northern Illinois University Press, DeKalb, Ill.) 2002

Handy, William C. - *Father Of The Blues*
>(Sidgwick & Jackson, London) 1957

Harlow, Alvin F. - *Old Post Bags*
    (D. Appleton & Co, New York/London) 1928

Harlow, Alvin F. - *The Road Of The Century: The Story of the New York Central*
    (Creative Age Press Inc, New York) 1947

Harris, Michael W. - *The Rise Of Gospel Blues*
    (Oxford University Press, Oxford) 1992

Harris, Rex - *Jazz* (3rd edition)
    (Penguin, Harmondsworth, Middlesex) 1954, reprinted.
    First published 1952.

Harris, Sheldon - *Blues Who's Who*
    (Da Capo, New York) 1989, reprinted. First published 1979.

Harrison, Daphne Duval - *Black Pearls: Blues Queens of The 1920s*
    (Rutgers University Press, New Brunswick/London) 1990

Harrison Lowell H. & James C. Klotter. – *A New History Of Kentucky*
    (University of Kentucky, Lexington, Ky.) 1997

Herr, Kincaid A. - *The Louisville & Nashville Railroad 1850-1942*
    (*L&N Magazine*, Louisville, Ky.) August 1943, reprinted.
    First published April 1943.

Hickman, Nollie -
    Mississippi Harvest: Lumbering In The Longleaf Pine Belt 1840-1915
    (University of Mississippi, University, Miss.) 1962

Hogan, William Ransom, & Edwin Adams Davis -
    William Johnson's Natchez (The Ante-Bellum Diary Of A Free Negro)
    (Louisiana State University Press, Baton Rouge/London) 1993, reprinted.
    First published 1951.

Holbrook, Stewart H. - *The Story Of American Railroads*
    (Crown Publishers, New York) 1947

Hubbard, Freeman - *Encyclopaedia Of North American Railroading*
    (McGraw-Hill, New York) 1981

Hugill, Stan - *Shanties From The Seven Seas*
    (Routledge & Kegan Paul, London) 1984, reprinted. First published 1961.

Hungerford, Edward - *Men And Iron: The History of New York Central*
    (Thomas Y. Cromwell, New York) 1938

Hyatt, Harry Middleton - *Hoodoo – Conjuration – Witchcraft – Rootwork (Vol. 1)*
    (Alma Egan Hyatt Foundation, Hannibal, Mo.) 1970, reprinted.
    First published 1935.

Jameson, Raymond D. -
    Funk & Wagnalls Standard Dictionary Of Folklore, Mythology & Legend
    (New English Library, Times/Mirror) 1975, reprinted.
    First published 1949.

Jensen, Oliver - *The American Heritage History Of Railroads In America*
    (American Heritage Publishing, New York) 1975

Kent, Don - *First And Last Days In Lynchburg*
    (*78 Quarterly* No. 7, Key West, Fla.) 1992

Kent, Don - Notes to LP *St. Louis Town (1927-32)*
    (Belzona L-1003) c. 1965

Kirby, Jack Temple - *Rural Worlds Lost: The American South 1920-60*
    (Louisiana State University Press, Baton Rouge, La.) 1987

Kirkland, Frazier - *Cyclopedia of Commercial and Business Anecdotes (Volume 1)*
    (D. Appleton & Co, New York/London) 1864
Lambie, Joseph T. - *From Mine To Market: The History Of Coal*
        Transportation On The Norfolk & Western Railway
    (New York University Press, New York) 1954
Lansden, John M. - *A History Of The City Of Cairo*
    (R.R. Donnelley & Sons, Chicago, Ill.) 1910
Larkin, Colin (Gen. Ed.) - *The Guinness Who's Who Of Blues*
    (Guinness Publishing, London) 1993
LaVere, Steve - Notes to Bukka White LP *Big Daddy* (Biograph BLP-12049) 1974
Leadbitter, Mike (Ed.) - *Nothing But The Blues* (Hanover Books, London) 1971
Leadbitter, Mike, & Neil Slaven - *Blues Records 1943-70 (Volume 1: A-K)*
    (Record Information Services, London) 1987
Leadbitter, Mike, Leslie Fancourt & Paul Pelletier - *Blues Records 1943-70 (Vol. 2: L-Z)*
    (Record Information Services, London) 1994
Lemly, James Hutton - *Gulf, Mobile & Ohio*
    (Richard D. Irwin Inc, Homewood, Ill.) 1953
Lewis, Ronald L. - *Coal, Iron And Slaves:*
        Industrial Slavery in Maryland, Virginia, 1715-1865
    (Greenwood Press, Westport, Ct.) 1979
Licht, Walter - *Working For The Railroad:*
        Organisation Of Work In The Nineteenth Century
    (Princeton University Press, N.J.) 1983
Lieb, Sandra R. - *Mother Of The Blues: A Study Of Ma Rainey*
    (University of Massachussetts Press, Amherst, Mass.) 1981
Linklater, Andro - *Measuring America: How The US Was Shaped By The*
        Greatest Land Sale In History
    (Harper Collins, New York/Toronto/Scarborough, Ontario) 2002
Litwack, Leon E. - *Been In The Storm So Long: The Aftermath Of Slavery*
    (Athlone Press, London) 1980
Lomax, Alan - *The Land Where The Blues Began*
    (Methuen, London) 1994, reprinted. First published 1993.
Lomax, Alan - Notes to LP *Murderer's Home*
    (Pye Nixa NJL-11) 1957
Long, Bryant Alden, with William Jefferson Dennis - *Mail By Rail*
    (Simmons-Boardman, New York) 1951
Loree, L.F. - *Railroad Freight Transportation*
    (D. Appleton & Co, New York/London) 1922
Lucas, Marion B. - *A History Of Blacks In Kentucky:*
        (Volume 1: From Slavery To Segregation)
    (Kentucky Historical Society, Frankfort, Ky.) 1992
Marshall, James - *Santa Fe: Railroad That Built An Empire*
    (Random House, New York) 1948
Martin, Albro - *Railroads Triumphant*
    (Oxford University Press, Oxford/New York) 1992
Matlaw, Myron (Ed.) - *American Popular Entertainment*
    from *Circuses & Side Shows* by Marcello Truzzi
    (Greenwood Press, Westport, Ct.) 1979

Maxwell, Robert S. - *Whistle In The Piney Woods*
    Introduction by Archie P. McDonald
    (East Texas Historical Association & University of North Texas Press, Denton, Tex.) 1998, reprinted. First published 1963.
McCormick, Mack - Notes to LP *Henry Thomas: Ragtime Texas*
    (Herwin 209) c. 1974
McCormick, Mack - Notes to LP *Robert Shaw: Texas Barrelhouse Piano*
    (Arhoolie F-1010) c. 1964
McIlwaine, Shields - *Memphis Down In Dixie*
    (Colonial Press, Boalsburg, Pa.) 1948
McMillan, Malcolm C. - *Yesterday's Birmingham*
    (E.A. Seeman Publishing Inc, Miami, Fla.) 1975
Meier, August, & Elliott Rudwick - *From Plantation To Ghetto* (3rd edition)
    (Hill & Wang, New York) 1976. First published 1966.
Milburn, George - *The Hobo's Hornbook* (Ives Washburn, New York) 1930
Moore, Jeremy - from website of Gulf, Mobile & Ohio Historical Society,
    P.O. Box 2457 Joliet, Ill. 60434-2457
Mosley, Donald C. - *The Labor Union Movement*
    from *A History Of Mississippi (Volume 2)*
    (University & College Press of Mississippi, Jackson, Miss.) 1973
Oliver, James, & Lois E. Horton. (Consultant Eds.) -
    History Of The African American People
    (Salamander, London) 1995
Oliver, Paul - *Blues Fell This Morning* (2nd edition, revised)
    (Cambridge University Press, Cambridge) 1990
Oliver, Paul - *Conversations With The Blues*
    (Jazz Book Club by arrangement with Cassell & Co. Ltd, London) 1967
Oliver, Paul - *Songsters & Saints*
    (Cambridge University Press, Cambridge) 1984
Oliver, Paul - Notes to LP *Bessie Tucker & Ida Mae Mack: The Texas Moaners*
    (Magpie PY-1815) 1979
Oliver, Paul - Notes to LP *Famous Hokum Boys (1930-31)*
    (Matchbox MSE-1014) 1989
Oliver, Paul - Notes to LP *Piano Blues (Volume 11: Texas Santa Fe, 1934-37)*
    (Magpie PY-4411) 1979
Oliver, Paul - Notes to LP *Robert Wilkins (1928-35)*
    (Wolf WSE-111) c. 1985
Oliver, Paul - Notes to LP *Rufus & Ben Quillian (1929-31)*
    (Matchbox MSE-217) c. 1977
Oshinsky, David – *Worse Than Slavery:*
    Parchman Farm and The Ordeal of Jim Crow Justice
    (Free Press Paperbacks, New York) 1997, reprinted.
Owen, Thomas McAdory - *History Of Alabama (Volumes 1 & 2)*
    (S.J. Clarke Publishing Co, Chicago) 1921
Parkinson, Tom, & Charles Philip Fox - *The Circus Moves By Rail*
    (Pruett, Boulder, Co.) 1978
Partridge, Eric - *A Dictionary Of The Underworld*
    (Wordsworth Editions, Ware, Herts) 1989, reprinted. First published 1950.

Partridge, Eric - *The Penguin Dictionary Of Historical Slang*
       Abridged by Jacqueline Simpson
       (Penguin Books, Harmondsworth, Middx) 1986, reprinted.
       First published 1937.
Pennington, Patience - *A Woman Rice Planter*
       (Belknap Press, Cambridge, Mass.) 1961
Perata, David D. - *Those Pullman Blues: An Oral History Of The African American Railroad Attendant*
       (Twayne Publishers, New York/Prentice Hall, London etc.) 1996
Porter, Horace - *Railway Passenger Travel 1825-80*
       (Chandler Press, Maynard, Mass.) 1987, reprinted.
       First published by Scribner's in 1888.
Powell, J.C. – *The American Siberia (or FourteenYears Experience In A Southern Convict Camp)*
       (Patterson Smith, Montclair, New Jersey) 1970, reprinted.
       First published 1891.
Prince, Richard E. - *Atlantic Coast Line Railroad*
       (Indiana University Press, Bloomington/Indianapolis) 2000, reprinted.
       First published 1966.
Prince, Richard E. - *Nashville, Chattanooga & St, Louis Railway*
       (Indiana University Press, Bloomington/Indianapolis) 2001, reprinted.
       First published 1967.
Prince, Richard E. – *Seaboard Airline Railway*
       Indiana University Press, Bloomington/Indianapolis) 2000, reprinted.
       First published 1966.
Ramsey Jr, Frederic - Interview with Huddie Ledbetter [Leadbelly], Sept. 1948
       (LP *Leadbelly's Last Sessions (Volume 1)* (Melodisc MLP-12-113)) 1959
Reed, S.G. - *A History Of Texas Railroads*
       (Arno Press, New York) 1981, reprinted. First published 1941.
Reidy, Joseph P. - *From Slavery To Agrarian Capitalism: In the Cotton Plantation, Central Georgia 1800-80*
       (University of North Carolina Press, Chapel Hill/London) 1992
Rice, Lawrence D. - *The Negro In Texas (1874-1900)*
       (Louisiana State University Press, Baton Rouge, La.) 1971
Riley, Franklin L. (Ed.) - *Mississippi Historical Society (Volume XIII)*
       (University of Mississippi Press, University, Miss.) 1913
Risher, Howard W. - *The Negro In The Railroad Industry (Report No. 16)*
       (University of Pennsylvania Press, Philadelphia, Pa.) 1971
Romanowski, Ken - Notes to CD *Mae Glover (1927-31)*
       (Document DOCD-5185) 1993
Rowland, Dunbar - *History Of Mississippi: The Heart Of The South (Volume II)*
       (S.J. Clarke Publishing Co, Chicago/Jackson, Miss.) 1925
Rowe, Mike - *Joe Dean From Bowling Green*
       (*Blues Unlimited* No. 127) Nov/Dec 1977
Rowe, Mike - Notes to CD *Sippie Wallace (Volume 1: 1923-25)*
       (Document DOCD-5399) 1995
Russell, Tony - *Blacks, Whites And Blues*
       (Studio Vista, London) 1970

Russell, Tony -
> Notes to CD *Field Recordings (Volume 4: Mississippi & Alabama 1934-42)*
> (Document DOCD-5578) 1997

Rye, Howard - Notes to CD *Mississippi Field Recordings (Volume 3: 1936-42)*
> (Document DOCD-5577) 1997

Saunders Jr., Richard – *Merging Lines: American Railroads 1900-70*
> (Northern Illinois University Press, DeKalb, Ill.) 2001

Scharf, J. Thomas - *History Of Saint Louis City & County* (2 volumes)
> (Louis H. Everts & Co, Philadelphia, Pa.) 1883
> *From microfilm in British Library. St. Pancras, London*

Schoener, Allen (Ed.) - *Harlem On My Mind*
> (Delta, New York) 1979, reprinted. First published 1969.

Seroff, Doug, & Lynn Abbott - *The Origins Of Ragtime* (*78 Quarterly* No. 10) 1999

Silvester, Peter - *A Left Hand Like God*
> (Omnibus Press, London) 1990, reprinted. First published 1988.

Spero, Sterling D., & Abram L. Harris -
> *The Black Worker: The Negro And The Labor Movement*
> (Atheneum, New York) 1974, reprinted. First published 1931.

Spottswood, Dick - Notes to LP *Rev. Robert Wilkins*
> (Piedmont PLP-13162) c. 1965

Stevers, Martin D. - *Steel Trails*
> (Putnam & Co. Ltd, London) 1933

Stilgoe, John R. - *Metropolitan Corridor*
> (Yale University Press, New Haven, Ct./London) 1983

Stover, John F. - *American Railroads*
> (University of Chicago Press, Chicago) 1962

Stover, John F. - *History Of The Illinois Central Railroad*
> (MacMillan Publishing Co. Inc, New York/London) 1975

Stover, John F. -
> *The Railroads Of The South 1865-1900: A Study In Finance And Control*
> (University of North Carolina Press, Chapel Hill, N.C.) 1955

Sturtevant, William C. (Gen.Ed.) - *Handbook of North American Indians*
> *(Volume 4: History of Indian-White Relations)*
> Wilcomb E. Washburn (Vol. Ed.)
> (Smithsonian Institute, Washington, DC) 1988

Sullivan, Mark - *Our Times: The United States 1900-25*
> (Charles Scribner's Sons, New York/London) 1927

Summersell, Charles Grayson - *Mobile: History Of A Seaport Town*
> (University of Alabama Press, University, Ala.) 1949

Sweet, Bradley - Notes to LP *Mississippi Blues 1927-41*
> (Belzona L-1001) c. 1965

Taylor, Frank with Gerald Cook – *Alberta: A Celebration In Blues*
> (McGraw-Hill Book Company, New York) 1987

Taylor, Joe Gray - *Civil War & Reconstruction in Louisiana*
> From *Louisiana: A History*, Bennett H. Wall (Ed.) (2nd edition)
> (Forum Press Inc, Arlington Heights, Ill.) 1990. First published 1984.

Thigpen, S.G. - *Pearl River*
> (Kingsport Press Inc, Kingsport, Tenn.) 1965

Tindall, George Brown - *South Carolina Negroes 1877-1900*
    (University of South Carolina Press, Columbia, S.C.) 1970, reprinted.
    First published 1952.
Todes, Charlotte - *Labor And Lumber*
    (International Publishers, New York) 1931
Townsend, Henry (as told to Bill Greensmith) - *A Blues Life*
    (University of Illinois Press, Urbana/Chicago) 1999
Towsen, John H. - *Clowns* (Hawthorn Books, New York) 1976
Trelease, Allen W. - *The North Carolina Railroad 1849-71*
    (University of North Carolina Press, Chapel Hill, N.C./London) 1991
Trotter Jr, J.W. - *Coal, Class and Color: Blacks in Southern West Virginia 1915-32*
    (University of Illinois Press, Urbana/Chicago) 1990
Trynka, Paul - *Portraits Of The Blues*
    Foreword by John Lee Hooker
    (Hamlyn, London) 1996
van Rijn, Guido - 'Lonesome Woman Blues – The Story of Alice Moore'
    (*Blues & Rhythm* No. 208) April 2006
van Rijn, Guido, & Hans Vergeer -
    Notes to Scrapper Blackwell LP *Blues That Make Me Cry*
    (Agram AB-2008) 1980
van Rijn, Guido, Cor van Sliedregt and Hans Vergeer -
    Notes to Joe Pullum LP *Black Gal*
    (Agram AB-2012) 1986
Various - *Encyclopædia Britannica* (Encyclopædia Britannica Inc.) 2000
Wall, Bennett H. (Ed.) - *Louisiana: A History* (2nd edition)
    (Forum Press Inc, Arlington Heights, Ill.) 1990, repr. First published 1984.
Wallenstein, Peter - *From Slave South To New South:*
    Public Policy In Nineteenth Century Georgia
    (University of North Carolina, Chapel Hill, N.C./London) 1987
Ward, James A. - *Southern Railroad Man*
    (Conductor N.J. Bell's Recollections Of The Civil War Era)
    (Northern Illinois University Press, DeKalb, Ill.) 1994
Wardlow, Gayle Dean - *Chasin' That Devil Music (Searching for the Blues)*
    (Miller Freeman Books, San Francisco) 1998
Waring, Philippa - *A Dictionary Of Omens & Superstitions*
    (Souvenir Press, London) 1997 (reprinted). First published 1978..
Webster, Gordon - email, 27 March 1994
Welty, Eudora – *Selected Stories Of Eudora Welty*
    Introduction (1941) by Katherine Anne Porter
    (The Modern Library, New York) 1992, reprinted. First published 1936.
Wheaton, Melville (Ed.) - *All Aboard America: Classic American Trains*
    (Smithmark, New York) 1995
Wheeler, Mary - *Steamboatin' Days*
    (Louisiana State University Press, Baton Rouge, La.) 1944
White, Deborah Gray - *Ar'n't I A Woman?*
    (W.W. Norton & Co, New York/London) 1985

White Jr, John H. - *The American Railroad Freight Car:*
From The Wood-Car Era To The Coming Of Steel
(John Hopkins University Press, Baltimore/London) 1995, reprinted.
First published 1993.

White Jr, John H. - *The Great Yellow Fleet:*
A History Of American Railroad Refrigerator Cars
(Golden West Books, San Marino, Ca.) 1986

White Jr, John H. - *The American Railroad Passenger Car*
(John Hopkins University Press, Baltimore/London) 1978

White Jr, John H. - *American Locomotives: An Engineering History 1830-80*
(John Hopkins University Press, Baltimore/London) 1997, revised edition.
First published 1968.

Wiener, Jonathan M. - *Social Origins Of The New South: Alabama 1860-85*
(Louisiana State University Press, Baton Rouge/London) 1978

Wilmeth, Dan B. - *The Language Of American Popular Entertainment*
(Greenwood Press, Westport, Ct.) 1981

Wilson, Charles Reagan, & William Ferris (Co-Eds.) - *Encyclopedia of Southern Culture*
(University of North Carolina Press, Chapel Hill, N.C.) 1989

Wilson, J.B. - *Handbook Of Yazoo County, Miss.* (Oxford, Miss.) 1884
Manuscript in the Mississippi Collection at the University of Mississippi

Withun, William - *Rails Across America* (Salamander, London) 1993

Woodward, Vann C. - *Origins Of The New South (1877-1913)*
(Louisiana State University Press, Baton Rouge, La.) 1962, reprinted.
First published 1951.

WPA Writers Project - *Mississippi: The WPA GuideTo The Magnolia State*
(University Press of Mississippi, Jackson/London) 1988, reprinted.
First published 1938.

Wyatt, Marshall - Notes to CD *Folks, He Sure Do Pull Some Bow:*
Vintage Fiddle Music (1927-35)
(Old Hat CD-1003) 2001

Yetman, Norman R. - *Life Under The Peculiar Institution*
(Selection from the Slave Narratives Collection)
(Holt, Rinehart & Winston, University of Kansas, Lawrence, Kan.) 1970

Zur Heide, Karl Gert - *Deep South Piano* (Studio Vista, London) 1970

INTERVIEW SOURCES

Dorsey, Thomas A. ('Georgia Tom')
– Harris, Michael W. - *The Rise Of Gospel Blues*

Huddie Ledbetter ('Leadbelly')
– Ramsey Jr, Frederic - LP *Leadbelly's Last Sessions (Volume 1)*

Perryman, Rufus ('Speckled Red')
– Oliver, Paul - *Conversations With The Blues*

Pickens, Edwin 'Buster'
– Oliver, Paul - *Conversations With The Blues*

Rachell, James 'Yank'
— Trynka, Paul - *Portraits Of The Blues*
White, Bukka
— Cobb, James C. - *The Most Southern Place On Earth*
Williams Walter
— Ballagh, James Curtis - *The South In The Building Of The Nation*
Young, Litt
— Yetman, Norman R. - *Life Under The Peculiar Institution*

GLOSSARY OF RAILROAD ABBREVIATIONS & NICKNAMES

A&C	Alabama & Chattanooga
A&V	Alabama & Vicksburg
ACL	Atlantic Coast Line
B&O	Baltimore & Ohio
Big Four	Cleveland, Cincinnati, Chicago & St. Louis
C&A	Chicago & Alton
C&G	Columbus & Greenville
C&NW	Chicago & North Western
C&O	Chesapeake & Ohio
Cairo Short Line	St. Louis, Alton & Terre Haute
Carrier Railroad	Sardis & Delta
CB&Q	Chicago, Burlington & Quincy
CI&L ('Monon')	Chicago, Indianapolis & Louisville
C. of G.	Central of Georgia
Cotton Belt Route	St. Louis & Southwestern
ETV&G	East Tennessee, Virginia & Georgia
FC&G	Fernwood, Columbia & Gulf
FEC	Florida East Coast
Frisco	St. Louis & San Francisco
FW&DC	Forth Worth & Denver City
G&A	Greenwood & Augusta
G&SI	Gulfport & Ship Island
GM&N	Gulf, Mobile & Northern
GM&O	Gulf, Mobile & Ohio
HE&WT	Houston, East & West Texas
I&GN	International & Great Northern
IC	Illinois Central
Katy	Missouri–Kansas–Texas
KCS	Kansas City Southern
L&N ('Old Reliable')	Louisville & Nashville
LNO&T	Louisiana, New Orleans & Texas
M&O	Mobile & Ohio
MJ&KC	Mobile, Jackson & Kansas City
M-K-T ('Katy')	Missouri–Kansas–Texas
Monon	Chicago, Indianapolis & Louisville
Mo-Pac	Missouri–Pacific
NC&St.L	Nashville, Chattanooga & St. Louis
NO&NE	New Orleans & North Eastern
NOJ&GN	New Orlcans, Jackson & Great Northern
OH&E	Oberlin, Hampton & Eastern
Old Reliable	Louisville & Nashville
R&G	Raleigh & Gaston
Rock Island Line	Chicago, Rock Island & Pacific
S&D ('The Carrier Railroad')	Sardis & Delta
SAL	Seaboard Air Line

St.LIM&S	St. Louis, Iron Mountain & Southern
T&NO	Texas & New Orleans
T&P	Texas & Pacific
TCI&RR	Tennessee Coal, Iron & Railroad Co.
W&A	Western & Atlantic
YD	Yazoo Delta
Y&MV ('Yazoo Delta Line')	Yazoo & Mississippi Valley
Yellow Dog	Yazoo & Mississippi Valley

INDEX OF ARTISTS' NAMES

'22' 185
Alabama Sheiks 317-8
Alderson, Mozelle 254, 322
Alexander, Texas (Alger Alexander)
 51, 52, 61, 189, 252-3
Anderson, Pink 277
Andrews, Ed 225
Armstrong, Louis 296
Armstrong, May (Mae Glover) 290-2, 294
 See also Glover, Mae
Arnold, Kokomo (James Arnold)
 20, 154, 156, 258-9, 260, 266, 267, 293
Austin, Mildred 277
Bailey, Buster 89
Bailey, Kid 191
Baker, James 'Iron Head' 212, 213, 214
Baker, Willie 294
Barbecue Bob (Robert Hicks)
 19, 20, 153, 232, 252, 267, 283, 284, 293, 294
Barnes, Faye (Fae Barnes) 123-4
 See also Jones, Maggie
Barnes, George 126
Basie, Count 255
Baxter, Andrew 18, 327
Baxter, Jim 327
B.B. 190
Becky, Son (Leon Calhoun) 80
Bell, Ed 180, 301-4, 328, 329
Bennett, Will 180
Bessemer Sunset Four 329
Big Bill - *See* Broonzy, Big Bill
Big Boy 349
Bigeou, Esther 39
Big Maceo (Major Merriweather) 229
Birmingham Jug Band 135
Black Bob 154, 318
Black Boy Shine (Harold Holiday) 282
Black Ivory King (Dave Alexander) 222
Blackwell, Scrapper (Francis Blackwell)
 19, 74, 98, 157-8, 242
Blake, Blind (Arthur Blake)
 144, 210, 264, 267, 283
Blind Sammie (Willie McTell) 278, 327
 See also McTell, Blind Willie
Blythe, James 123

Bogan, Lucille 31, 42, 43-4, 71-2, 75,
 115-6, 145-6, 150, 153,
 156, 166, 282, 284, 292,
 322
 See also Jackson, Bessie
Bonds, Son 308
Boy, Andy 80, 229
Bracey, Ishmon 27
Brooks, Shelton 151
Broonzy, Big Bill 29, 32, 68, 115, 129,
 137, 153-4, 156, 321
Brown, Ada 40
Brown, Henry 114
Brown, Hi Henry 268
Brown, Lee 20-1, 275
Brown, William 112
Brown, Willie 38, 100, 114, 191
Bull City Red (George Washington) 164
Bumble Bee Slim (Amos Easton)
 98, 112, 115, 214, 251, 266
Burks, Pinetop (Conish Burks) 80
Butler, Sam 282
 See also Jackson, Bo Weavil
Butterbeans & Susie 251, 292
Byrd, John (Rev. George Jones)
 201, 203, 205-6, 207, 290, 294
Calicott, Joe 27
Campbell, Bob 116
Campbell, Gene 314
Cannon, Gus 229, 264, 268
Carr, Dora 20, 72, 73, 284-5, 288, 289, 302
Carr, Leroy 33, 74, 157, 210, 214, 221,
 231, 232, 242, 258, 260-1,
 266, 284, 293
Carson, Fiddlin' John 202
Carter, Bo (Armenter Chatmon)
 122, 135, 137-9, 264, 311, 319
Carter, George 293
Casey Bill (Will Weldon) 318, 321
Childers, Virgil 250
Clayton, Doctor (Peter Clayton) 32
Cleveland, Big Boy 229
Clifton, Kaiser 217
Coleman, Jaybird (Burl C. Coleman)
 180, 268, 293
Coleman, Lonnie 313, 317
Collins, Kokomo (Chasey Collins) 187

Collins, Sam 34-5, 152-3, 154, 156, 176, 187, 191, 215, 283, 318
Cooper, Rob 74, 80
Copeland, Martha 280, 305, 320
Cox, Ida 89, 90, 91, 210, 212, 213, 214, 246, 283, 284, 286
Crosby, Bing 72
Crump, Jesse 212, 213
Dailey, Dusky 222
Daniels, Julius 171, 173
Davenport, Cow Cow (Charles Davenport) 72, 133, 135, 180, 251, 288, 310
Davenport, Jed 319
Davis, Walter 20, 35, 75, 114, 115, 207, 217-8, 232
Dean, Joe 18, 21-2, 74
DeBerry, James 265
Delaney, Mattie 324
Delaney, Tom 169-70, 171
Desdume, Mamie 72
Dickson, Pearl 323-4
Dixon, Mary 89
Dixon, Willie 139
Donegan, Lonnie 127
Dooley, Simmie 278
Dorsey, Thomas - *See* Georgia Tom
Duffie, Side Wheel Sallie (Mae Glover) 290
   See also Armstrong, May
           Glover, Mae
Dupree, Champion Jack 115
Edwards, David 'Honeyboy' 17, 22, 27, 132, 312-3
Edwards, Piano Kid 64
Elliott, Ernest 247
Estes, Sleepy John 19, 44, 101, 105-6, 106-7, 153, 268, 308, 317, 321
Evans, Joe 248
Excelsior Quartette 284
Ezell, Will 30, 64, 290
Flyin' Lindburg (Milton Sparks) 169
   See also Sparks, Milton
Foster, Eugene 126
Fuller, Blind Boy (Fulton Allen) 98, 115, 214, 274-7, 295, 329
Fuller, Jesse 251
Gait, Don 241
Georgia Bill (Willie McTell) 127
   See also McTell, Blind Willie
Georgia Tom (Thomas Dorsey) 74, 115, 134-5, 265
Gibson, Clifford 231
Gillum, Jazz (Bill Gillum) 126, 321
Glaze, Ruby 26

Glover, Mae 189, 290-5
   See also Armstrong, May
           Duffie, Side Wheel Sallie
Gorham, Georgia 70
Grand Central Red Cap Quartet 30
Grant, Bobby 291, 293-5
Grant, Coot (*née* Leola B. Grant) 89, 91
   See also Wilson, Leola B.
Green, Charlie 89, 296
Green, Lee (Leothus Green) 74, 75-6, 168-9
Grinter, Marie 287-8, 289
Gross, Helen 213
Handy, Katherine 290
Handy, W.C. 68, 143, 145, 147, 151, 152, 154, 156, 158, 250, 290
Harlem Hamfats 241
Harris, Blind Jesse 180
Harris, Willie 283
Harris Jr, Willie 139
Hawkins, Buddy Boy (Walter Hawkins) 291, 293, 294-5, 319
Hegamin, Lucille 131, 209, 277
Hemphill, Sid 154, 156, 157
Henderson, Bertha 244
Henderson, Fletcher 89, 131, 151, 216
Henderson, Rosa 131, 133, 216, 225, 282, 318
Hicks, Edna 131, 133
Hill, Bertha 'Chippie' 40, 179
Hill, King Solomon (Joe Holmes) 34, 187
Hite, Mattie 282
Hokum Boys 265
Hooker, John Lee 20
Hopkins, Lightnin' 20, 214
Hot Shot Willie (Willie McTell) 127, 319
   See also McTell, Blind Willie
House, Son (Eddie James House Jr) 35, 100, 283
Howard, Frank 38
Howell, Peg Leg (Joshua Barnes Howell) 19, 176, 241, 283
Howling Wolf - *See* Smith, J.T.
Howlin' Wolf (Chester Burnett) 38, 338
Hull, Papa Harvey 203, 318
Hunter, Alberta 216, 249, 337, 339
Hurt, Mississippi John 101
Hyde, Hattie 42, 44
IC Glee Club 40, 182
Jackson, Bessie (Lucille Bogan) 42, 115-6
   See also Bogan, Lucille
Jackson, Bo Weavil (James Jackson) 282
   See also Butler, Sam
Jackson, Jim 250-1, 253, 264

Index of Artists' Names

Jackson, Lulu 289
Jackson, Mike 70
Jackson, New Orleans Willie 172-3
Jackson, Papa Charlie 129, 132, 133, 210, 265, 304, 321
James, Elmore 20, 207
James, Frank 'Springback' 50, 75
James, Jesse 101, 306
James, Skip (Nehemiah James) 64, 90, 283
Jefferson, Blind Lemon 17, 37, 44, 73, 86, 89, 166, 211-4, 221, 229, 230, 232, 278, 289-90, 327
Johnson, Alec 37
Johnson, Blanche 44
Johnson, Bunk 80
Johnson, Edith North 114
Johnson, Elnora 30
Johnson, Henry, & His Boys 30
Johnson, Hot Box (Hobson Johnson) 126
Johnson, James P. 65
Johnson, James 'Stump' 219
Johnson, Lil 218, 277
Johnson, Lonnie 51, 231, 265, 267, 289, 309
Johnson, Mary 32, 114
Johnson, Merline 248
Johnson, Robert 32, 90, 100, 132, 187, 188, 189, 190-1, 192, 215, 217, 218, 221, 222, 230, 232, 264, 283
Johnson, T.C. 27
Johnson, Tommy 187
Jones, Bo 311
Jones, Coley 265
Jones, Curtis 126
Jones, Jab 153
Jones, Little Hat (Dennis Jones) 304
Jones, Maggie (Fae Barnes) 32, 123-4, 277
    See also Barnes, Faye
Jones, Richard M. 66
Jordan, Charley 268, 317, 319
Jordan, Louis, & The Tympany Five 69
Jordan, Luke 35-6, 250, 253
Kansas Joe (Joe McCoy) 137
Kelly, Jack 101
Kelly, Willie (Roosevelt Sykes) 74
    See also Sykes, Roosevelt
Kid Sox/Socks - *See* Wilson, Wesley
Kid Spoons 93
Kid Stormy Weather 64
King, B.B. 128
Kirkman, Lillie Mae 126

Lacy, Rube (Reubin Lacy) 121-2, 144, 230
Lawlars, Ernest - *See* Little Son Joe
Leadbelly (Huddie Ledbetter) 64-5, 68, 127, 191, 212, 213-4, 289, 329
Leavy, Calvin 190
Lee, Bertha 104, 105
Lewis, Furry (Walter Lewis) 101, 127, 156, 253, 266
Lewis, Ham 227
Lewis, Meade Lux 65
Lewis, Noah 204, 227
Lewis, Walter 69
Lincoln, Charley (Charlie Hicks) 67-8, 176, 178, 282, 283
Liston, Virginia 283
Little Son Joe (Ernest Lawlars) 93
Little Walter 101, 322
Lofton, Cripple Clarence 129, 226
Longshaw, Fred 169, 287
Mac & Bob 202
Mack, Ida May 35, 67
Macon, Uncle Dave 202
Mahal, Taj 289
Martin, Daisy 265
Martin, Fiddlin' Joe 251, 266
Martin, Ollis 180
Maxey, Hogman 187
McCabee, Palmer 204
McClain, Arthur 248
McClennan, Tommy 101, 115
McClintock, Harriet 97-8
McCoy, Charlie 20, 310, 311
McCravy, James 265
McKenzie, Willie Mae 265
McMullen, Fred 183
McPhail, Black Bottom 98-9
McShann, Jay 50
McTell, Blind Willie 20, 26, 89-90, 91, 112, 115, 126, 127, 166, 214, 264, 266, 268, 278, 279, 281, 286-9, 294, 305, 312, 327-9, 330, 331, 340, 349
    See also Blind Sammie
        Georgia Bill
        Hot Shot Willie
Memphis Jug Band 222
Memphis Minnie (*née* Lizzie Douglas) 122, 136-7, 251, 256, 266, 321, 323
Memphis Slim 339
Miles, Lizzie (*née* Elizabeth Landreaux) 98, 151, 152, 153, 156, 158, 249
Miller, Al 216
Miller, Booker 'Mr. Pink' 35
Miller, Eddie 308

Miller, Lillian 124
Miller, Luella 112, 216
Miller, Sodarisa 191
Mississippi Jook Band 187
Mississippi Matilda (Matilda Powell) 139
Mississippi Sheiks 137, 228
Mitchell, William 98
Montgomery, Little Brother (Eurreal Montgomery) 63, 74, 187
Moore, Little Alice 114, 189
Moore, Whistlin' Alex 61
Morris, Thomas, & His Seven Hot Babies 70
Morton, Jelly Roll (Ferdinand Lamothe) 71-2
Mosely, Andy 187
Moses, Bertie May 345
Moss, Buddy 98, 183, 317
Muddy Waters 222, 322, 338
Nelson, Sonny Boy (Eugene Powell) 138-9
Nelson, Tom 'Blue Coat' 27, 29
Nix, Rev. A.W. 175
Nixon, Hammie 106
Noble, George 18
Nonpareil Trio 152, 156
Oak Cliff T-Bone - *See* Walker, T-Bone
Old Man 126
Otis, Johnny 32
Overstreet, Benton 30
Pace, Kelly 127
Palmer, Sylvester 114
Parker, James 292
Patton, Charley 15, 33-4, 35, 38, 40, 44, 63, 73, 100, 104, 145, 147, 156, 166, 191, 225, 266, 268, 282, 283, 318, 327
Paul, Ruby 293
Peg Leg Will 213
Piano Red (Willie Perryman) 327
Pickens, Edwin 'Buster' 73
Pickett, Charlie 308
Platt, Mose 'Clear Rock' 213
Porkchop 27
Pullman Porters Quartette 30
Pullum, Joe 74, 225
Rachell, Yank (James Rachell) 68-9, 101, 153, 156-7, 227
Ragtime Texas (Henry Thomas) 314, 319
  See also Thomas, Henry
Rainey, Ma (*née* Gertrude Pridgett) 33, 57-8, 60, 189, 225, 227-8, 232, 246, 251, 266, 268, 281-2, 283, 284, 289, 290
Rainey, Pa (Will Rainey) 57

Ranger, Jack 26, 27
Red Nelson (Nelson Wilborn) 226, 232
Rice, Thomas 239
Ridley, Ethel 35, 384
Robinson, Elzadie 30, 44, 248
Rodgers, Jimmie (hillbilly singer) 94
Rogers, Jimmy 321
Roland, Walter 42, 64, 75, 116
Rolling Stones 222
Rose, Bayless 144
Ross, Bertha 31
Ross, Dr. 101
St. Louis Bessie (Bessie Mae Smith) 95
Sane, Dan 192
Santaclaus 240
Scruggs, Irene 264, 266
Settles, Bill 318
Shaw, Allen 156
Shaw, Robert 74, 213
Short, Jaydee/J.D. 114, 325
  See also Stone, Joe
Simpson, Coletha 216
Sims, Henry 33, 318
Sing, Dan 192
Smith, Bessie 29, 33, 42, 57, 143, 151, 156, 189, 246, 262, 263, 268, 282, 283, 287, 288, 289
Smith, Chris 250
Smith, Clara 189, 208, 213, 216, 246-8, 249-50, 266, 282, 290
Smith, Faber 112
Smith, Ivy 135, 288, 289
Smith, J.T. 'Funny Paper' 44
Smith, Mamie 17, 35, 265, 268
Smith, Maud 262
Smith, Spark Plug 206
Smith, Trixie 50, 265, 295-6, 301-2
Smith, William 73
Sparks, Milton 169, 204
Spaulding, Henry 109
Speckled Red (Rufus Perryman) 73, 74, 80, 327
Standard Quartette 311
Stavin' Chain 66
Stokes, Frank 27, 191-2, 250, 251, 264, 266, 268, 283, 318
Stone, Joe (J.D. Short) 325
  See also Short, Jaydee/J.D.
Stovepipe No.1 241
Sykes, Roosevelt 64, 74, 75, 114, 115, 217, 223, 230
  See also Kelly, Willie
Sylvester, Hannah 216

Index of Artists' Names

Tallahassee Tight (Louis Washington) 214
Tampa Kid 319
Tampa Red (Hudson Woodbridge)
   74, 134-5, 217, 265, 314, 321
Taylor, Charley 64, 74
Taylor, Eva (Irene Gibbons) 130-1
Taylor, Walter 50
TCI Sacred Singers 182
TCI Section Crew 182
TCI Women's Four 182
Temple, Johnnie 112
Terry, Sonny (Sanford Terrell) 304
Texas Tommy 189
Theard, Sam 122, 133-4, 135
Thomas, Henry 19, 78, 113, 180, 187,
               265, 314-6, 317, 319
               See also Ragtime Texas
Thomas, Ramblin' (Willard Thomas)
   165-6
Thompson, Edward 29
Tomlin, Kingfish Bill 126
Too Tight Henry (Henry Lee Castle)
   281, 319
Torey, George 31, 156
Townsend, Henry 110-1, 114, 217
Truvillion, Henry 191
Tucker, Bessie
   60-1, 79-80, 104, 189-90, 217
Turner, Charlie 304
Two Poor Boys 248
Vaughn, Cooney 187
Vinson, Walter 137, 227
Walker, T-Bone (Aaron Thibeaux Walker)
   22, 128, 132
Wallace, Sippie 19, 210-11, 213, 222,
             232, 249, 282, 283, 284,
             287, 288, 289
Wallace, Wesley 205, 307
Warner, Bud, & His Red Caps 30
Washboard Sam (Robert Brown)
   222, 250, 321, 325-6
Washington, Lizzie 338
Watson's Pullman Porters 30
Weaver, Curley 98, 183, 264, 266, 294
Weaver, Sylvester 30
Welch, Guitar 187
Weldon, Will - *See* Casey Bill
Wells, Junior 101
West, Eddie 317
Wheatstraw, Peetie (William Bunch)
   20, 32, 78, 113, 137, 232, 264, 317
White, Bukka (Booker Washington White)
   40, 69, 86, 99-100, 114-5, 166-7, 232,
   321, 330-1, 349

White, Georgia 31, 264-5
White, Gonzelle 255
White, Washington - *See* White, Bukka
Wiley, Geeshie 323
Wilkins, Robert 29, 93-4, 222, 232,
             263-4, 266, 267
Williams, Big/Po' Joe
   50, 51, 95, 96, 98, 114, 326
Williams, Clarence 29, 30, 70, 73, 131
Williams, George 'Bullet'
   18, 99, 100, 180, 204, 319
Williams, Jabo 64, 75, 179, 180, 219-20
Williams, John 203
Williams, Willie 176
Williamson, Sonny Boy
   (John Lee Williamson) 23, 101, 207
Williamson, Sonny Boy
   (Aleck 'Rice' Miller) 23
Wilson, Lena 216
Wilson, Leola B. 26
   See also Grant, Coot
Wilson, Wesley ('Kid Sox/Socks') 26, 91
Wingfield, B.T. 72

INDEX OF SONG TITLES

BOLD = full or part transcription

A&V Blues 139
Aberdeen Mississippi Blues 99
Ain't You Sorry Mama 264
Alabama Bound Blues 35, **284**
Alberta Let Your Bangs Grow Long 187
Alberta Let Your Bangs Hang Down 187
Alberta Let Your Bangs Hang Low 187
Amtrak Blues **337, 339-40**
Another Man Done Gone 95
Ants In My Pants 137
Anybody Here Want To Try My Cabbage 277
Anybody Want To Buy My Cabbage 277
Armour Ave. Struggle 123
Atlanta Special, The **330-1**
Auction Day Blues 94
Awful Fix Blues **291-2**, 295
Awful Moanin' Blues **282**
Baby Please Don't Go 95
Banana In Your Fruit Basket **135**, 137
Banana Man 137
Banana Man Blues **136-7**
Barbara Allen 213
Barrel House Blues **225**
Barrel House Flat Blues 32
Beefsteak When I'm Hongry 28
Biddle Street Blues 109
Big Bed Blues 115, **295**
Big 80 Blues 214
Big Four Blues 232
Big Mama 75
Big Railroad Blues 229
Billy Barlow 240-1
Billy Goat Blues (Byrd) **201-2**, **203**, 204, 205-6, 207
Billy Goat Blues (Smith) 206
Black Bottom Blues, The 98
Black Diamond Express To Hell 175
Black Dog Blues 144
Black Horse Blues **230-1**
Black Train Blues 99
Bluebird Blues 101
Blue Getaway 267
Blues 349
Blues In The Night 209

Bonnie Barbara Allen 213
Booster Blues **211**
Bootleg Rum Dum Blues 267
Boots And Shoes 98
Booze And Blues 189, 281-2
Broke Down Engine Blues **20**
Bull-Doze Blues 113
Bye Bye Baby Blues 115
Cairo Blues **109-10**
California Blues 252
C and A Blues 232
Cannon-Ball Blues **253**
Careless Love 289-90
Carried Water For The Elephant 242
Carrier Railroad, The **154-5**
Chain Gang Trouble 176, **178**
Charleston Contest **319-20**
Charmin' Betsy 78
Chicago Blues (Miller) 216, **217**
Chicago Blues (Smith) 216
Chicago Gouge, The 123
Chickasaw Train Blues **323**
Chocolate To The Bone 284
Choo Choo Blues 295
Chump Man Blues 267
Cincinnati Southern Blues **288**
Clinton, The 80
Coal Camp Blues 50
Coast Line Blues **214-5**
Cocaine Blues **253**
Coffee Grinder Blues 293
Coffee Grindin' Blues 292
Coffin Blues **258**, 267
Cold Iron Walls 189
Come On In My Kitchen **90**, 283
Corinna Blues 290
Cottonfield Blues **113**
Country Breakdown **67-8**
Country Spaces 67
County Farm Blues 189, 293
Cow Cow Blues 20, 72, 73, **284-5**, **288**, 310
Cows, The 74
Cows, See That Train Comin' 74, 225
Crazy About My Rider 218

Index of Song Titles

Crazy Blues 17
Cross Road Blues 100
Cummins Prison 190
Daddy Don't Put That Thing On Me
   249-50
Dallas Woman Blues 282
Death Letter Blues 213, 246
De Kalb Chain Gang **183**
De Kickapoo Whoop 240
Devil Got My Woman 90
Devil In The Lion's Den 318
Ding Dong Ring 191
Dirty Dozen(s), The 73
Dog Train Blues 145
Done Sold My Soul To The Devil **248**
Don't Go Down In Black Bottom 99
Don't You Leave Me Here 95
Do Right Blues 318
Down By The M&O **21**
Down In A Coal Mine 241
Down In Black Bottom 98
Down In The Alley **256-7**
Down South Blues **157, 216**
Down The Big Road Blues **324**
Drayman Blues **231**
Dry Southern Blues **221**
Dummy, The **60-1**
Dusky Stevedore 89
Dyin' Crapshooter's Blues 286
East Coast Blues **338**
East St. Louis Blues 112
Easy Rider Don't You Deny My Name
   153
Elder Green Blues 95
Erie Train Blues 204
Every Day In The Week Blues **277-8**
Fan Foot Woman 264, 267
Fare Thee Honey Blues 35
Fast Mail, The 206
Fast Mail Rambler 214
Fat Mama Blues **75**
Fives, The 73, 80
Floating Bridge 19, 105, **106**, 107
Florida Bound **29**
Florida Bound Blues **29-30**
Flying Crow, The 222
Flying Crow Blues 222
Fort Worth & Denver Blues 217
Forty Drops 327
44's, The 80
4, 5 and 9 64
Freight Train Blues (Miller) **308**
Freight Train Blues (Clara Smith) 246
Freight Train Blues (Trixie Smith) 295

Frisco Leaving Birmingham 18, **100**
Frisco Whistle Blues 304
From Four Until Late **187**
Funny Feeling Blues 275
Galveston Blues **44**
Gamblin' Charley 282
G. Burns Is Gonna Rise Again 27
Georgia Stockade Blues **169-70**
Get Away Blues **263-4**, 267
Gibson Hill **99-100**
Giving It Away 135
Givin' It Away 133, 134
Goat, The 203
Goin' Away To Leave You Blues 229
Goin' Where The Monon
   Crosses The Yellow Dog 19, **157**
Gone Dead On You Blues
   211-2, 213, 214, 217
Goodbye Rider 35
Good Hearted Woman **293**
Good Time Flat Blues 32
Go Tell Aunt Rhodie 261
Got The Blues 231
Gouge Of Armour Avenue, The 123
Grasshopper Papa **292**
Graveyard Dream Blues 283
Green River Blues **147**
Gulf Is A Long Railroad, The 184
Ham And Eggs **329-30**
Hammer Blues 282
Hammond Blues 124
Hard Times Ain't Gone Nowhere 309
Harvest Moon Blues 229
He Roars Like A Lion 248
Hey! Lawdy Mama – The France Blues
   203
High Sheriff Blues 148, 282
Highway No. 61 Blues 101
Hobo Bill **320-1**
Hobo Jungle Blues 321
Hoboken Prison Blues 189, 293
Hobo Song, The 349
Hokum Blues 265
Honey Blues **44**
Honey You Don't Know My Mind 283
Hot Box **126**
Hot Tamale Molly 277
How Long Daddy, How Long **209-10**
How Long – How Long Blues 210, 214
Hurry Down Sunshine **231**
I Ain't Givin' Nobody None
   290, **292-3**, 294
I Been Pickin' And Shovellin' **163**
I Can Tell By The Way You Smell 75

Index of Song Titles

IC Moan Blues **314**
IC Train Blues 169
If I Got What You Want **129-30**
If You Don't Give Me What I Want **131**
If You Lose Your Good Gal,
    Don't Mess With Mine 18
I Got A Home In That Rock 182
I Got The Blues 229
I Hate That Train Called The M&O **115-6**
I Love My Man
    Better Than I Love Myself 286
I'm Climbing High Mountains,
    Trying To Get Home 312
I'm Going Home On The Chicasaw Train 182
I'm Gonna Get It 265
I'm Gonna Shave You Dry 75
I'm Having A Good Time **340**
I'm So Glad
    I'm Twenty-One Years Old Today 21
I'm Still Sitting On Top Of The World **283**
In The Mornin' 27
In The Pines 176, 215, 345-6
I Packed My Suitcase,
    Started To The Train 222
It Just Won't Quit 267
It Makes A Long Time Man Feel Bad **184-5**, 187, 213
It's A Low Down Dirty Shame 126
It's Hard Time **325**
It's Right Here For You 265
It's Tight Like That 135, 265
I've Been Blue
    Ever Since You Went Away 20
I've Got A Mind To Ramble **339**
I've Got The Yes!
    We Have No Banana Blues 130
I Wonder Where My Easy Rider's Gone 151
Jackson Blues **101**
Jail Break Blues 189
Jail-House Blues 189
Jealous Hearted Blues 283
Joe Brown's Coal Mine **173-4**
Jump Jim Crow 239
Jungle Man Blues (Jackson) **321**
Jungle Man Blues (Wheatstraw) 317
Just A Little Bit More 265
Just As Well Get Ready,
    You Got To Die 312
Katy Blues **79**
Katy Lee Blues 101
Katy Left Memphis 155

KC Railroad Blues 18
Kelly's Special **74**
Kentucky Blues **304**
Key To The Bushes Blues **189-90**
Kid Man Blues 290, 294
Kind Stella Blues 282
Kitchen Mechanic Blues 284
L&N Blues, The 246, **247**
Last Fair Deal Gone Down
    187, **188**, **190**, **192**
Last Kind Words Blues 323
Leavin' Gal Blues **244**
Levee Camp Moan Blues **51-2**
Little Girl, Little Girl 275
Little Red Caboose, The 265
Little Red Wagon **264-5**
Little Rock Blues **324**
Log Camp Blues **57-8**
Lonesome Atlanta Blues
    291, 292, 293, 295
Lonesome Man Blues **31**
Lonesome Midnight Dream 283
Lonesome Road Blues 176
Lonesome Southern Blues 259
Long And Tall **154**
Long Distance Blues **212**, 214
Long Distance Moan 212
Longest Train - *See* In The Pines
Long Gone (Handy/Smith) 251
Long Gone (Jackson) **250**, 251
Long Time Men **172-3**
Lost Man Blues **31**
Lost Ship Blues **317**, 319
Love In Vain Blues **221**, 223
Loveless Love 290
Loving Talking Blues 305
Ma Grinder, The 73, 74, 80
Mail Train Blues, The **210-11**
Mama, Let Me Scoop For You **26**, 127
M&O Blues (Brown) **100**
M&O Blues (Davis) 35, **115**
M&O Blues No. 3 115
Man I Love, The 282
Man On The Flying Trapeze, The 241
Married Man Blues 282
Match Box Blues 231
Maxwell Street Blues 129
Mean Black Moan 33-4, 35
Mean Conductor Blues **301-4**, 328
Mean Old Train Blues 284
Meat Shakin' Woman 329
Meet Me Around The Corner **98**
Meet Me In The Bottom
    (Hey Lawdy Mama) 98, 99

Index of Song Titles

Memphis Town **260-1**
Mexico Bound Blues 21
Midnight Blues 42
Midnight Special 191
Midnight Special Blues 191
Milk Cow Blues 258
Milk Cow Blues No. 3 258
Milk Cow Blues No. 4 258
Mind Reader Blues **104-5**
Mining Camp Blues 50
Mississippi Boweavil Blues 16
Mississippi Jail House Groan 121
Miss Meal Cramp Blues 37
Mr. Brakes-Man
  (Let Me Ride Your Train) **305-6**
Mistreated Boy **317**
Mobile Central Blues (Alderson) **254**, 322
Mobile Central Blues (Jackson) **254**
Moon Going Down **37-8**, **63**
Moore Girl, The 18
Morning Dove Blues **288**
Mountain Top Blues 282
My Baby **137**
My Baby's Gone 115, 116
My Back To The Wall 264
My Best Gal Gonna Leave Me 115
My Girl's Done Quit Me **35**, **36**
My John Blues 246
My Pullman Porter Man 30
My Stove Won't Work **318**
Nashville, Tennessee **326**
New Big 80 Blues 214
New Cow Cow Blues 72
New Stock Yard Blues **93-4**
Ninety-Nine Year Blues **171**
No Job Blues 165-6
Nothing In Rambling 323
Not The Chump I Use To Be 267
Now She Gives It Away 135
No.29 205, 307
O'Grady's Goat 205
Oh! Lawdy Mama 98
Oh! Lawdy Mama No. 2 98
Oh Lordy Mama 98
Old Alabama **190**
Old Rock Island Blues **313**
Out O' Line Blues 229
Painful Hearted Man **276**
Panama Limited, The **40-1**, 99, 330, 331
Panama Limited Blues 39
Panama To Chi 40, 182
Papa's Billy Goat 202, 204, 205
Passenger Train Woman **274-5**
Pay Roll Blues **145-6**, 150, 153

Pea Vine Blues 145
Peel Your Banana 139
Penitentiary Moan Blues **189**
Pick And Shovel Blues 164
Pick And Shovel Captain 164
Pick On Me Blues 61
Plantation Blues 290
Police Blues **280**
Polock Blues **219-20**
Pony Blues 225
Poor Boy, Long Way From Home 328
Poor Coal Loader 50
Poor Little Johnny **97**
Pratt City Blues 179
Preachin' The Blues 283
Prison Blues 189
Prison Bound Blues 293
Prodigal Son, The 222
Pullman Passenger Train 30
Rabbit Foot Blues **37**
Rack 'Em Back **325-6**
Railroad Bill 180
Railroad Blues **295-6**, 301
Railroadin' Some 114, **315**
Railroad Man Blues 207, **217-8**, 232
Railroad Porter Blues 30
Railroad Wreck 176
Rambler Blues **229**
Ramblin' On My Mind **215**, 217
Ram Rod Daddy 138
Reckless Blues **287**
Red Ball 126
Red Ball Turning Over 126
Red Cap Porter 31
Red Cap Porter Blues 30
Red River Blues 187
Reuben 176
Riding On The Seminol 182
River Bottom Blues **227**
Rock Island Blues 127
Rock Island Line 127
Rock Pile Blues 189
Roll And Rattler **322**
Roll And Tumble Blues 80
Rolling Mill Blues **176**
Rolling Stone **222-3**
Root Hog Or Die 240, 241
Root Man Blues 75
Rosenthal's Goat 202
Run Mollie Run 78
St. Louis Cyclone Blues **248-9**
St. Louis Fair Blues 253
San Francisco Blues 246
Santa Fe Blues 113

Index of Song Titles

Saturday Night Fish Fry 69
Say Bo, Give Me Them Two Bits 311
Scarey Day Blues **126-7**, **281**
Scoop It 26
Screw Worm 75
Section Gang Song 182
See See Rider Blues 289
Seminole Blues, The 18
Send Me To The 'Lectric Chair 189
Serving Time Blues 189
Shaggy Dog Blues 291
Shake That Thing 265
Shave 'Em Dry 72, 75
She's Givin' It Away **133-4**
She's Gone Blues **232**
She's Your Cook But She Burns
   My Bread Sometimes 138
Shin Bone Alley 240
Shootin' Craps And Gamblin' **164**
Shorty George **212-3**, 214
Shorty George Blues 213
Shove It Up In There 265
Sidewalks Of New York, The 261
Sister Jane Across The Hall **258**, 267
Sitting On Top Of The World 137
Snake Hip Blues 75
Snitcher's Blues, The 219
Somebody's Been Using That Thing 265
Some Scream High Yellow 282
Southern Blues (Broonzy) **153-4**
Southern Blues (Green) **168-9**
Southern Casey Jones **306**
Southern Railroad Blues 259
Special Agent (Railroad Police Blues) **308**
Special Stream Line 41, 330, 331
Spread Yo' Stuff 265
Statesboro Blues 214, **286-9**
Station Time Blues 217
Steel Drivin' Sam **246-7**
Stevedore Blues 89
Stevedore Man **89**, 91
Stole Rider Blues **89-90**
Stomp That Thing **191-2**
Stonewall Street Blues **283**
Stranger's Blues **283**
Streamline Train **226-7**
Suitcase Blues **222**
Sunnyland (James) 207
Sunny Land (Williamson) 207
Sweetheart Land 126
Sweet Home Chicago 21
Sweet Mama 153
Tale Of A Shirt, The 202
Talkin' To Myself 278

T&NO Blues **42-3**, 44
Terraplane Blues 32
That Great Day 182
That Lonesome Train
   Took My Baby Away **310**
That's No Way To Get Along 222
These Bones Are Gonna Rise Again 27
They Wanted A Man
   To Lead The Lions Around 248
Think You Need A Shot 75
Third Street's Going Down 113
31st Street Blues 216
This Ain't No Place For Me **253**
Ticket Agent Blues **227**
TN&O Blues 42
Tom Rushen Blues 282
Touch It Up A Little 265
Tough Times Blues 317
TP Window Blues **26**
Track Linin' 182
Train Is Coming, The **223-4**
Train Song 349
Travelin' Blues (McTell) **278**, 279, **327-9**, **331**, 349
Traveling Blues (Rainey) **227-8**
Travelin' Man 250
Travelin' Railroad Man Blues **317-8**
Trinity River Blues 128
Turkey Buzzard Blues 241
Turkey In The Straw 241
Two Timin' Mamma 292
Up The Country Blues **287**
Voice Throwin' Blues 293
Waitin' For The Evenin' Mail **208-9**
Wartime Blues **229**
Waycross Georgia Blues 294
Way I Do, The **281**
West Dallas Drag No. 2 74
Western Plain Blues **314**
Whatcha Doin' **44**
When Can I Change My Clothes **166-7**
When I Die 203
When The Sun Goes Down 221
Whip It Up And Down 75
Whoa Emma 241
Who's Dat Knockin'
   On De Old Ding Dong 191
Why Do You Moan 282
Wichita Falls Blues 128
Winin' Boy Blues 71
Wipe It Off 265
Wires All Down 214
Woodchopping Blues **291**, 292, 295
Work House Blues **283**

Workin' On The Railroad 293
Worried Mama Blues 89, 91
Yellow Dog Blues (Collins) **152-3**, 156
Yellow Dog Blues (Miles, Smith *et al*)
    143, 151, 152
Yellow Dog Gal Blues 152
Yellow Dog Rag, The 143, **151**, 156
Yes! We Have No Bananas 130
You Can't Run My Business
    No More 258
You Don't Know My Mind Blues 283
Your Time To Worry **264**
You Was Born To Die 264

GENERAL INDEX

Aberdeen, Miss. 99, 100
Advance cars 255-7
Africa - *See* West Africa
Alabama   19, 20, 36, 49, 60, 73, 85, 86,
    87, 91, 92, 93, 96, 97, 99, 100,
    104, 132, 133, 146, 162, 167,
    169, 175, 179, 180, 181, 182,
    203, 204, 220, 243, 246, 294,
    295, 305, 312, 327, 346, 349
Alabama & Vicksburg RR   93, 94, 139
Alabama Great Southern RR   288
Alabama Steel & Wire Company
    of Birmingham   176
Algiers, La.   107
Alleys   256-7
American Engineer   274
American Railway Times   203
Americus, Ga.   327, 328
Amputations - *See* One-legged man
Amtrak   229, 337, 338, 339
Angola State Penitentiary   187
A.R.C. (record company)   75, 129
Arkansas   62, 104, 185, 190, 204, 209,
    259, 313, 315
Arkansas River   315
Armour, Philip D. (meat/fruit packer)   123
Armour Refrigerator Line   124
Artesia, Miss.   95, 96, 99, 116
Atchison, Topeka & Santa Fe RR
    ('Santa Fe')   19, 21, 42, 76, 77, 78, 79,
    80, 113, 125, 126, 127, 128, 206, 214,
    279, 339, 343
Atlanta, Ga.   18, 33, 69, 81, 126, 163,
    171, 176, 191, 207, 232,
    260, 294, 295, 313, 327,
    331, 346
    - Terminal   232
Atlanta Special (train)   330, 331
Atlanta twelve-string school   294
Atlantic Coast Line (ACL)
    33, 99, 124, 134, 201, 214, 247, 294
Atlantic Coast Line
    Fast Mail Passenger Route   214
Atmore, Ala.   181
Augusta, Ga.   62
Bagby, G.W. (author/artist)   167

Baggage cars   41
Ballantine, Miss.   154
Ballyhoo   255-8
Baltimore, Md.   337
Baltimore & Ohio (B&O)   20, 25, 111, 124
Bananas - See Fruit (bananas)
Banana specials   126, 129, 132-3, 139
Bangs, George S.
    (General Superintendent of the RMS)   200
Barbershop quartets   203
Bardstown & Louisville RR   243
Barlow, Billy   241
Barnum & Bailey's Circus
    251, 252, 253, 255
Barrelhouse flats - *See* Good time flats
Barrelhouse piano
    30, 63-4, 66, 70, 73-4, 76
Barrelhouses   49, 54, 59, 61-3, 66, 73, 76,
    80, 95, 99, 112, 147, 289
Baton Rouge, La.   69
Beale Street, Memphis   156, 192, 250, 253
Beaumont, Tex.   42, 77, 318
Beaver Meadow, Ala.   91, 92
Beaver Meadow RR   152
Belmont, Mo.   104
Belzoni, Miss.   148
Big 80 (train)   214, 215, 289
Big Four - *See* Cleveland Cincinnati,
    Chicago & St. Louis RR
Biggety Ben (train)   145
Big Kate Adams (steamboat)   104, 155
Big Sandy, Tex.   315
Binghampton, N.Y.   204
Birmingham, Ala.
    31, 69, 81, 91, 115, 116, 133, 134,
    135, 179, 180, 181, 185, 207, 220,
    232, 288, 306, 327
    - Union Station   134, 207, 232
Birmingham Mineral Railroad   181
Birmingham Southern   181
Black Diamond (train)   175
Black Dog (train)   144, 145
Blackface   241
Bloomington, Ill.   316
Bluebird (record label)   126, 139
Blue coat   27, 28

Blue Goose Saloon 53
Blytheville, Ark. 291
Boogie piano 18, 54, 61, 64-5, 70, 72, 76
Booneville, Miss. 100
Bootleggers 63, 135, 154, 256, 311
Boston, Mass. 337
Bowling Green, Ky. 21, 146
Box cars 21, 41, 54, 59, 61, 66, 76, 88, 128, 144, 146, 181, 307, 326
Brake(s)men 305-6
Brazos Bottoms 214
Br'er Rabbit 201
Bristow, Ky. 146
Broadway Limited (train) 28
Brothels - *See* Prostitutes
Brotherhood of Sleeping Car Porters 32, 150, 157
Brown, Joseph E.
  (Civil War governor of Georgia) 173
Brown, Joseph M.
  (Son of Joseph E. Brown. Mine and railroad owner, and later governor of Georgia) 173, 174-6, 346
Brown & Company's New Orleans Circus 240, 242
Brunswick (record label) 133, 291
Brunswick, Ga. 259
Bryson City (orig. Charleston), N.C. 168
Buffalo, N.Y. 175
Buffet flats - *See* Good time flats
Caboose 176, 221, 265
Caddo County, Tex. 65
Cairo, Ga. 178
Cairo, Ill. 87, 104, 108, 109, 110
Cairo Short Line 111
Calhoun, Ga. 18
California 252
Calliopes 261
Camden & Amboy RR 199
Camp Nelson, Ky. 243
Cannonball (as any express train) 285
Cannonball (as IC named train) 101-3
Cannonball (as wood/coke-burning stove) 154, 285-6
Car floats - *See* Float bridges
Carnivals 240, 263, 265, 266, 267, 273, 289, 292, 293
Carrier Railroad - *See* Sardis & Delta RR
Carter-Kelly Lumber Co. 78
Cass County, Tex. 128
Catfish (reissue label) 22
Cayce, Ky. 101, 104, 107
Central (telephone exchange) 212
Centralia, Ill. 308

Central Of Georgia Rly.
  39, 41, 99, 126, 127, 175, 176, 284, 320, 327
Central Tracks (Dallas) 212, 213, 214
Chain gang - *See* Railroads
Charleston, S.C. 88, 247, 248
Charleston, Cincinnati & Chicago RR 247
Charlotte, N.C. 171, 242, 243, 262
Charters, Samuel (blues author/historian) 51, 240, 310
Chattanooga, Tenn. 18, 163, 175, 288, 346
Checkerboard crews 88
Cherokee County, N.C. 167
Chesapeake & Ohio (C&O) 167, 184, 277
Chicago, Ill. 18, 19, 20, 23, 32, 33, 34, 35, 36, 38, 39, 40, 58, 59, 65, 81, 85, 87, 109, 110, 114, 123, 126, 129, 130, 157, 200, 201, 204, 216, 230, 249, 314, 315, 316, 321, 322, 343
  - South Side 33, 133, 134, 337, 339
  - Union Station 224, 225, 226
Chicago & Alton (C&A)
  20, 34, 58, 86, 111, 114, 315, 316
Chicago & North Western (C&NW)
  200, 201, 252, 261, 316
Chicago, Burlington & Quincy (CB&Q)
  16, 58, 201, 206, 218
Chicago Heights, Ill. 321
Chicago, Indianapolis & Louisville Rly.
  (Monon) 20, 157
Chicago, Rock Island & Pacific
  (Rock Island) 127, 201, 313, 337
Chickasaw (train) 41, 323
Chickasaw County, Miss. 99
Chief, The (train) 206
Churches 22, 182, 219, 311
Cincinnati, Oh. 20, 81, 232, 288, 329
  - Terminal 232
Cincinnati Southern RR 288
Circuses 22, 91, 239-41, 242, 245, 248-50, 253-6, 260, 262
  - circus trains 242-6, 249, 251-4, 260, 262, 268
  - slang 241, 256-8, 263-6, 322
  - parades 242, 261, 263
Citronelle, Ala. 92
Civil War 15, 17, 19, 21, 25, 26, 39, 49, 55, 66, 67, 71, 123, 125, 162, 165, 173, 175, 241, 245, 260, 277, 309, 312, 345
Clarke County, Miss. 92

General Index

Clayton County, Ga. 259
Cleveland, Tenn. 259
Cleveland, Cincinnati, Chicago &
 St. Louis RR ('Big Four') 322
Clinchfield RR 248
Clowns 240, 241, 264
Coahoma County, Miss 104
Coal/mining camps 50, 53, 243
Coal trains 174, 175
Coast Line Florida Mail (train) 215, 215
Cobb, Ned (sharecropper/tenant farmer)
 312
Cobden, Ill. 123
Cole City, Ga. 175
Coles Robert (US psychiatrist/writer) 312
Columbia (record label) 30, 246
Columbus, Ga. 57
Columbus, Ky. 87, 91, 104, 107
Columbus, Miss. 96, 99, 259
Columbus, Oh. 324, 329
Columbus & Greenville RR 168, 169, 259
Combination cars - *See* Baggage cars
Commissary 50
Conductors 28, 260, 303, 304
Conrail 339
Convict lease 66, 161-3, 165, 167, 170-3,
 175, 176, 177-92
Conway, Ark. 252
Copiah County, Miss. 186
Corinth, Miss. 100
Corn 273
Corsicana, Tex. 114
Cotton - fields 273, 279, 280-1, 310
 - mills 151
 - workers 134, 312
Cotton Belt 77, 78, 114
Cottondale, Miss. 191
Country picnics/frolics 67, 68
Courlander, Harold (blues author/historian)
 240
Crawford, Miss. 95
Crossings (railroad) 259, 303, 349
Crossroads 244
Crystal Springs, Miss. 187
Cummins State Farm, Ark. (state pen)
 185, 190
Dade Coal Company 173, 174
Dade County, Ga. 175, 346
Dallas, Tex.
 44, 60, 61, 79, 114, 128, 212, 289, 290
Dalton, Ga. 259, 345
Dan Costello's Circus & Menagerie 242
Daniels, George H. (19th Century
 publicist for New York Central RR) 29

Darien, Ga. 203
Decatur, Ala. 104
Decatur Street, Atlanta 69, 294
Decca (record label) 154
Delaware & Hudson RR 228
Delta - *See* Mississippi Delta
Denison, Tex. 79, 114
Detroit, Mich.
 32, 33, 35, 169, 218, 230, 339
DeVoe, Thomas (butcher/historian) 162
Ding dong 191, 192, 199
Dixie Flyer (train) 41, 338
Dixie Limited (train) 338
Dockery's plantation 147
Document (reissue label) 22
Doddsville, Miss. 191
Dode Fisk Circus 255
Donaldsonville, La. 66
Draymen 231, 311, 316
Dreamland Theater, Tulsa, Okl. 255
Drew, Miss. 191
Drummer (salesman) 122, 133
Duke/Peacock (record company) 43
Dummy lines/roads 49, 53, 59, 63, 70
Dummy train 60, 145
Dyersburg, Tenn. 20
Eads Bridge 87, 112, 114
Earle, Parker (fruit packer) 123
East Cairo, Ky. 87, 104, 109
East Coast blues (Piedmont blues) 147, 171
Eastland Wichita Falls & Gulf RR 251
Eastman-Gardiner Lumber Co. 63
East St. Louis, Ill. 81, 85, 87, 110, 111,
 112, 113, 114, 205,
 307
East St. Louis & Carondelet Rly. 111
East Tennessee, Virginia & Georgia RR
 259, 288, 345, 346
East Texas 25, 42, 49, 52, 60, 64, 73, 76,
 77, 80, 89, 128, 188, 304
Eatonton, Ga. 176
Edgefield & Trenton Branch RR 172
18th Street, Birmingham 134
Electric Mills, Miss. 95
Elkhorn City, Ky. 248
Elmira, N.Y. 204
Emancipation 28, 70, 260
Empire State Express (train) 39
English Music Hall 130, 131, 132
Ennis, Tex. 79
Ensley, Ala. 181
Ensley, Enoch (mining engineer/speculator)
 181
Erie Railroad Company 204

378

Evans, David (university professor, author, blues singer/guitarist) 281
Evening Mail - *See* Fast mail
Excursion trains - *See* Railroads
Fairfield & Macon RR 116
Fannin Street, Shreveport 65
Farmers/farm work
   51, 55, 70, 203, 311, 312, 322
Fast freight lines 139
   - Blue Line 125
   - Green Line 125
   - Red Ball Service 125, 126
   - Red Line 125
   - White Line 125
Fast mail 37, 199, 201, 202, 204, 205, 206, 207, 210, 211, 214, 215, 218, 232
   - Evening Mail 208-9, 232
   - Fast Mail (as named train) 199-201, 205-7, 232
   - Lightning Express 205
Federal Trade Commission 123
Fernwood, Columbia & Gulf RR 20, 21
Ferry boats - *See* Float bridges
Field hollers 180
Fife and drum bands 154
Firemen (black)
   17, 26, 31, 103, 116, 289, 303, 330
Fish fries 69
Five Civilised Tribes 323
Flag stop 244
Flat cars 17, 88, 108, 261
Float bridges 19, 104-7, 109-10
Flomaton, Ala. 181
Florida 33, 62, 73, 181, 188, 214, 338
Florida East Coast RR 338
Flying Crow (train) 222, 318
Fort Worth, Tex. 42, 114, 315
Fort Worth & Denver City Rly. 77
Friar's Point, Miss. 104
Frog (reissue label) 22
Frolics - See Country picnics
Fruit - apples 122
   - bananas 121-2, 124, 126-7, 130-3, 136-9, 292
   - citrus fruit 123
   - limes 122
   - oranges 122, 129
   - strawberries 123
Fruit Growers Express (FGE) 124
Gallatin, Miss. 218
Galveston, Tex. 44, 79, 126, 127, 128, 214
Galveston Bay 42
Galveston, Houston & Henderson RR 128

Galveston Wharf Company 127, 128
Gandy dancers 219, 263
Gandy Tool Company of Chicago 219
Gellert, Lawrence (folk song collector) 163, 168, 173, 191
Gennett (record label) 248
Georgetown, S.C. 248, 249
Georgia 18, 19, 49, 58, 60, 73, 80, 99, 112, 154, 162, 163, 169, 175, 176, 183, 203, 214, 215, 252, 258, 279, 282, 293, 294, 295, 309, 310, 313, 319, 327, 329, 330, 331, 346, 349
Gibson, Miss. 99, 100, 115
Good time flats 32
Gordonsville, Va. 277
Goshen Pass, Va. 167
Gospel music 23
Gougers 124
Grand River - *See* Neosho River
Greater Birmingham 179, 181
Great Lakes 55, 87, 104
Greene County, Miss. 81
Greensboro, N.C. 151
Greenville, Miss. 51
Greenville, Tex. 79, 80
Greenwood, Miss. 35, 148
Greenwood & Augusta RR 172
Guatemala 277
Gulf & Ship Island RR
   80, 81, 182, 183, 184, 185, 186, 187, 188, 189, 190, 192, 199
Gulf Coast Special (train) 86, 87
Gulf, Mobile & Northern
   85, 93, 186, 254, 259
Gulf, Mobile & Ohio 85, 86
Gulf of Mexico 85, 87, 183, 313
Gulfport, Miss. 183, 184, 185, 186, 187
Haeg's Circus 251
Hagenback-Wallace Circus 251, 252, 263
Hamlin & Northwestern Railway Co. 79
Hammond, Ind. 123, 204
Hammond, La. 124
Hammond, George H. (meat/fruit packer) 123
Hampton, Ga. 327, 331
Hampton, Va. 349
Hannibal & St. Joseph RR 200
Harlem, N.Y. 33
Harp (harmonica) players
   18, 204, 227, 284, 314, 315, 319
Harrison County, Miss. 184
Harvey, Frederick
   (restauranteur/entrepeneur) 279

General Index

Harvey Houses 279
Hattiesburg, Miss. 185, 186, 190
Hausa 201
Havana 86
Havana Limited (train) 86
Havana Special (train) 338
Hazlehurst, Miss. 186, 187, 218
Helena, Ark. 27
Hernando, Miss. 154, 254
Hickman, Ky. 107
Highball 19, 37, 125
Hi Henry Minstrels 268
Hillbilly music 101, 176, 201, 202, 311
Hoboken, Ala. 294
Hoboken, Ga. 294
Hoboken, N.J. 294
Hoboken, Pa. 294
Hobos 20-2, 37, 41, 113, 207, 294, 301-31, 339, 349
 - female 305-7, 322-5
 - hobo jungles 317, 321, 325
 - nicknames 318-21
Hodges Park, Ill. 110
Hokum blues 130, 134, 265, 266, 292
Hollandale, Miss. 138, 139
Hollers 51, 180
Honky tonk - *See* Barrelhouse
Hoover, Herbert (politician/US President) 325
Hoovervilles 325
Hot box 126
Hot shot 126-7, 319
House rent parties 32
Houston, Miss. 99
Houston, Tex.
 42, 44, 78, 88, 113, 127, 128
Houston & Great Northern RR 78
Houston & Texas Central RR 213
Houston, East & West Texas Rly. 77
Hoxie, Ark. 209
Hudson River 204
Huntsville, Ala. 104
Huntsville, Tex. 78
Illinois 110, 112, 204, 316
Illinois Central RR
 16-20, 23, 34, 39, 40, 42, 58, 62, 80,
 81, 85, 86, 93, 101, 102, 103, 108,
 109, 110, 111, 114, 129, 132, 133,
 139, 147, 148, 150, 154, 157, 182,
 186, 201, 205, 219, 254, 259, 314,
 315, 316, 323, 337
India 277
Indiana 23, 157, 204
Indianapolis, Ind. 81, 157

International & Great Northern RR 76, 78, 113
International Railway 78
Interurbans 23
Jackson, Miss. 34, 147, 148, 152, 156, 186, 190, 201, 310, 327
Jackson, Tenn. 101, 115, 156
Jacksonville, Fla. 91, 207, 214, 268, 338
James, Samuel L. (railroad/mine owner) 176, 177
Jazz 66, 69, 131
 - band leaders 70, 80, 89, 131
 - New Orleans style 265
Jefferson - *See* Pullman cars
Jefferson County, Miss. 201
Jeffersonville, Ind. 171
Jellico, Tenn. 252
Jersey City, N.J. 204
Jim Crow
 230, 239, 241, 249, 262-3, 293, 309
Jim Crow cars 41
Jimmies (freight cars) 175, 177, 252
John Henry 22
John Robinson Circus 252, 259
Johnson, William (freedman)
 71, 122, 132, 164, 165, 240, 242, 243, 255
Joliet, Ill. 316
Jones, Casey 101-4
Jonesboro, Ark. 209
J.S.P. (reissue label) 22
Juke joint - *See* Barrelhouse
Kansas 279, 315, 327, 343
Kansas City, Kan. 327
Kansas City, Mo. 79, 100, 207, 318
Kansas City–Florida Special (train) 207-9
Kansas City Southern RR 222, 228, 318
Katy - *See* Missouri-Kansas-Texas RR
Kemper County, Miss. 95
Kentucky 71, 85, 87, 91, 101, 175, 204, 231, 243, 244
King Totsie (gangster) 96
Knights of Labor 150, 157
Knocking a Joe - *See* One-legged man
Knoxville, Tenn. 37, 38, 180, 346
Kokomo, Miss. 20, 21, 187
Ku Klux Klan 161
Lake Erie 204
Lake Shore & Michigan Southern RR 201
Land grants 15, 16, 87, 88, 203
Lauderdale County, Miss. 92
Leavenworth, Atchison & Northwestern RR 107
Leavenworth Herald 327

380

General Index

Lee Line 104
Lehigh Valley RR 175
Levee camps 49-53, 62, 65, 66, 76
Lexington, Ky. 243
Library of Congress
   51, 71, 126, 127, 154, 176, 184, 189,
   191, 349
Lieb, Sandra (blues author/historian) 240
Lightning Express - *See* Fast mail
Limited Mail - *See* Fast mail
Little Rock, Ark. 252, 324
Local/sun times 123, 245
Logansport, La. 165
Lomax, Alan (folklorist) 32, 51, 52, 154
Lomax, John (folklorist) 51, 189, 281, 312
London, Ky. 252
Lorain County, Oh. 329
Loree, L.F. (Chairman & President of
   KCS and NYD&H RRs) 222, 228, 229
Los Angeles, Ca. 78, 230, 337, 339
Louisiana 19, 43, 49, 73, 78, 80, 107,
      156, 165, 167, 176, 185, 191,
      204, 310
Louisiana, New Orleans & Texas RR
   148, 150
Louisville, Ky. 157, 205, 239, 243, 281
Louisville & Nashville RR
   62, 85, 99, 104, 113, 127, 133, 134,
   146, 157, 180, 201, 205, 243, 247, 248,
   252, 304, 318
Lovejoy, Ga. 259, 260, 267
Lula, Miss. 104, 105
Lumber 42, 49, 58, 66, 80, 85, 186, 187,
   219
     - black employment in 49, 55,
       57, 59, 63, 66, 76
     - companies 63
     - logging & logging camps 49,
       53-63, 65-6, 70, 73, 76, 78-81,
       147
     - sawmills 54-5, 58, 62, 76, 80,
       85, 186, 187
     - skidders/skids 56, 107, 108
Luxapalila River 96
Lynchburg, Va. 35, 36, 253
Lynchings 310
Macon, Ga. 207, 259, 327
Macon, Miss. 95
Maginley & Carrol's Circus 243
Magnolia, Miss. 187
M&O Bottoms - *See* River bottoms
Marengo County, Ala. 294
Marietta & North Georgia RR 171
Markets 131, 133-4, 136, 137

Markham, Miss. 148
Maryland 17, 165
Mason-Dixon Line 230
Mauch Chunk, Pa. 174-5
Maxwell Street, Chicago 129, 130
McCary, Robert (freedman) 240
McComb, Miss. 34, 35, 152, 156, 186, 187
Meat 125, 134
   - beef 123
   - pork 123
   - shipping of 123
Medicine shows 239, 243, 250, 273, 289
   - slang 264
Memphis, Tenn.
   23, 27, 29, 31, 39, 40, 52, 61, 69, 85,
   94, 102, 122, 154, 207, 209, 232, 252,
   253, 318, 337
   - Union Station 232
Memphis Branch RR 171
Menageries 242
Merchant's Southern Line Packet Co. 107
Meridian, Miss. 20, 93, 94, 95
   - Union Stock Yards 93-4
Mexico 21, 28
Microsoft 123
Midnight Special (train) 41-2, 191
Millport, Ala. 100
Millstadt Junction, Ill. 110
Minstrelsy 239-41, 246
   - slang 268
Mississippi 15, 16, 19, 23, 38, 40, 42, 49,
      50, 55, 57, 58, 59, 60, 62, 80,
      85, 90, 95, 97, 99, 102, 104,
      110, 122, 129, 132, 145, 156,
      157, 164, 166, 167, 168, 169,
      182, 183, 184, 185, 188, 226,
      230, 232, 259, 312, 323, 324,
      327, 330
Mississippi Central RR 186
Mississippi Delta
   23, 25, 27, 34, 35, 38, 51, 52, 76, 100,
   101, 139, 144, 156, 184, 212, 259, 309
Mississippi River 23, 28, 51, 61, 62, 87,
96, 104, 107, 110, 112, 114, 168, 209,
240, 313
Mississippi River Bottoms - *See* River
bottoms
Mississippi Sound 183
Missouri 87, 91, 101, 200, 209, 315
Missouri-Kansas-Texas RR (Katy)
   42, 79, 80, 85, 127
Missouri Pacific (Mo-Pac)
   21, 80, 107, 114, 127, 252

Mobile, Ala. 62, 86, 87, 88, 89, 91, 95, 104, 109, 110, 113, 115, 180, 214, 243, 254
Mobile Bay 88, 109
Mobile County 91
Mobile & Ohio RR
  19, 20, 21, 23, 42, 58, 62, 81, 85-8, 91-116, 121, 132, 133, 134, 164, 203, 243, 259, 275, 295
Mobile, Jackson & Kansas City RR 186, 254
Monroe - *See* Pullman cars
Monroe County, Ga. 279
Montgomery, Ala. 96, 116, 327
Montgomery Ward (mail order company) 314-5
Moorhead, Miss.
  143, 144, 147, 148, 150, 153, 154, 168
Moscow, Ky. 104
Munsen Steamship Line 86
Murphy, N.C. 167, 168
Murphysboro, Ill. 110
Muskogee, Okl. 315
Nacogdoches, Tex. 44, 318
Nancy Hanks (train) 39, 320
Narkeeta, Miss. 97
Nashville, Chattanooga & St. Louis Ry. 18, 104
Natchez, Miss.
  71, 122, 164, 165, 201, 240, 242, 255
National Railways of Mexico 21
National steel (guitar) 31, 100
Neosho River (Grand River) 315
New Jersey 204
New Orleans, La.
  20, 31, 34, 35, 39, 57, 62, 69, 88, 91, 101, 107, 113, 122, 126, 129, 132, 138, 139, 148, 151, 172, 177, 180, 214, 343
New Orleans, Jackson & Great Northern RR
  20, 34, 218, 219
New Orleans, Northeastern RR 186
Newton, Kan. 21, 343
New York, N.Y. 18, 32, 33, 36, 151, 162, 163, 175, 205, 230, 289, 337, 338, 339
New York & Erie RR 204
New York Central RR
  29, 36, 39, 125, 200, 201, 206, 339
New York Historical Society 162
New York, New Haven & Hartford RR 124
New York State 204, 205
New York Times 88

Niagara Falls, N.Y. 175
Nicholasville, Ky. 243
Non-union labour 150-1, 153, 155, 157-8
Norfield, Miss. 186
Norfolk, Va. 180
Norfolk & Western RR 124
North Carolina 18, 98, 99, 115, 168, 242, 243, 345
  - state penitentiary 167
North Carolina RR 243
Northwestern RR 107
Oberlin, Oh. 329
Oberlin, Hampton & Eastern RR 329
Ohio 91, 175
Ohio River 28, 109, 110
OKeh (record label) 182
Oklahoma 313, 315
Old Hat (reissue label) 22
Oliver, Paul (blues author/historian) 73, 76, 106
One-legged man 136
Oral transmission (tradition)
  17, 19, 20, 49, 91, 92, 94, 96, 99, 191, 210, 212, 213, 239-45, 262-3, 281, 284, 289-96
Owego, N.Y. 204
Oxmoor Furnace, near Birmingham 179
Pace, Miss. 268
Paint Rock, N.C. 168
Panama Canal 39
Panama Limited (train) 39, 40, 86
Panola County, Miss. 154
Pan-pipes 314
Paramount (record label)
  31, 32, 112, 129, 282, 291
Parchman Farm, Miss. (state penitentiary) 16, 17, 42
Paris, Tex. 79
Parsons, Kan. 79, 315
Passenger train women - *See* Railroads
Pay-car 146
Payroll trains 146
Pearl River Valley RR 55
Pea vine railroads 145
Peculiar Institution, The 230
Pennsylvania 152, 175, 204, 252, 294
Pennsylvania RR 28, 36, 124, 201, 339
Pensacola, Fla. 62, 181
Peonage 89, 90
Piedmont blues - *See* East Coast blues
Piermont, N.Y. 204
Pigeon River 168
Pig iron 176, 179

Poetry - in blues 37-8, 165-7, 178, 220,
    223, 224, 227-8, 231, 310
  - poetic licence 121, 122
Polock (Polack/Polak) Town 219-20
Pony Express 199-200
Poor whites 184
Pratt, Daniel (mine owner/capitalist) 179
Pratt City - *See* Greater Birmingham
Pratt Coal & Coke Company
  - *See* Pratt Coal & Iron Co.
Pratt Coal & Iron Company 181
Prohibition 192
Prostitutes/brothels
    15, 59, 60-1, 71, 76, 146, 219-20, 256,
    311, 327, 343
Protest (in blues)
    89-90, 165-7, 171, 183, 188-90, 192
Pseudo-private car lines 125, 128
Pullman, Ill. 33
Pullman - cars 33, 36, 86
    - porters 22, 28-33
Putnam County, Ga. 176
Queen & Crescent RR 288
Quills - *See* Pan pipes
Quincy, Ill. 200
Quitman, Miss. 92
Rabbit Foot Minstrels 57
Race records 31
Race riots 111
Railroad Bill (Morris Slater - train robber)
    180-1
Railroad Gazette 200
Railroads
    91, 93, 99
    - as employers 17, 25-6, 29, 62-3, 219
    - camps 66, 184
    - chain gangs on 163
    - charters 42, 78, 251
    - conductors 26, 301-4
    - construction of 25, 59, 62, 229,
        279-80
    - depots/Union Stations
        16, 17, 94, 180, 199, 209,
        215-32, 239, 263-4
    - divisions 303
    - excursions 70, 254-5, 259-62
    - gauges 60, 123, 245
    - maintenance of 34, 229
    - police 60, 301, 307, 308
    - ticket/depot agents 225-7
    - train wrecks 41, 101-3, 146, 229
    - women employed on 273-81, 284, 289
    *See also individual roads by name and
    depots/stations by city*

Railway Labor Act (1926) 153
Railway Mail Service 200
Railway Post Office (RPO) 200, 210
Raleigh, N.C. 164, 242
Raleigh & Gaston RR 164
Ramsey Jr, Frederic (folklorist) 289
Randolph, Philip A. (Pullman Porters'
    Union leader/organiser) 32
Red Ball 125-6, 319
Red Ball Service 125, 126
Red Bud, Ill. 110
Red Cap porters 22, 29, 30-3
Red Lick, Miss. 201
Red wagon 264-5
Reefers - *See following entry*
Refrigerator cars
    121-30, 132-3, 139, 143, 144
Rice 248, 309-10
Rice, Thomas
    (songwriter/minstrelsy performer) 239
Richmond, Va. 176
Richmond & Danville RR 171
Riding the blinds 301-4, 306-7, 320
Riding the rods 301, 304-6, 307-8, 309
Ringling, Richard T. (circus owner) 251
Ringling Bros. Circus 252
Ripley, Tenn. 308
River Bottoms 96-9
Rocky Mount, N.C. 214
Rolling cages - *See* State penitentiary
Rome, Ga. 90, 259,
Roustabouts 28, 83, 147, 311
Ruleville, Miss. 150, 191
Russellville, Ark. 252
Sabine & Galveston Railroad & Lumber Co.
    42
St. Jo. line - *See* Hannibal & St. Joseph RR
St. Joseph, Mo. 200
St. Louis, Mo. 81, 87, 107, 109, 110, 112,
    113, 114, 223, 231, 253,
    313, 316, 325, 337
St. Louis, Alton & Terre Haute RR
    - *See* Cairo Short Line
St. Louis & Cairo RR 110
St. Louis & San Francisco
    77, 78, 114, 134, 217, 218, 259
St. Louis & Southwestern 77-8
St. Louis, Iron Mountain & Southern Ry.
    104, 114
Salisbury, N.C. 242
San Antonio, Tex. 218
Santa Fe group (East Texas pianists) 80
Saratoga & Schenectady RR 199
Sardis & Delta RR (Carrier Railroad) 154-5

General Index

Saucier, Miss. 184
Saunders, Wallace
    (black locomotive cleaner) 102
Savannah, Ga. 88, 214, 327
Sawmills - *See* Lumber
Scottsboro Boys 307
Seaboard Air Line
    20, 33, 99, 164, 284, 327
Sea ports
    62, 88, 89, 99, 109, 113, 127, 186
Sells Brothers Great European Seven
    Elephants Railroad Show 262
Selma University, Ala. 295
Seminole Limited (train) 18, 41, 182
Sexual symbolism/imagery
    73-6, 122, 129-31, 133-9, 249, 275, 277
Shack bullies - *See* Railroad police
Sharecroppers 312
Ship Island 182-3, 190
Shorty George (train) 212-4
Shreveport, La. 42, 44, 318
Shreveport, Houston & Gulf RR 78
Shuqulak, Miss. 96
Silas, Charley (mercy man) 52
Silas Green From New Orleans 57
Skidders/skids - *See* Lumber
Skiffle 127
Slaves/slavery 15, 16, 17, 25, 26, 39, 49,
    55, 66, 67, 71, 122, 162,
    164-5, 166, 169, 188, 191,
    220, 230, 242, 273-4, 279,
    310, 312
Sledge, Miss. 154
South & North Alabama RR 181
South Carolina 184
South Carolina RR 249
South Columbus, Ky. 104, 108
Southern Pacific RR
    43-4, 113, 127, 214, 252, 318
Southern Pine Lumber Co. 78
Southern Pine Operators' Assoc. 151
Southern Railway 134, 150, 168, 169, 171,
    181, 201, 243, 259
Southern Railway & Steamship Co. 173
South McCalester, Okl. 315
South Western Car Co. 171
Spalding & Rogers Circus 243
Spartanburg, S.C. 246, 247, 248
Special agents - *See* Railroad police
Spirituals 23, 163, 312
Springfield, Ill. 316
State Line, Miss. 294
State penitentiary 166, 168-9, 213
Statesboro, Ga. 126, 289

Steamboats - Big Kate Adams 104, 155
    - captain 29, 317
Stevedores 88-9, 91
Stockyards (livestock) 93-4
Streamline trains 226-7
String bands 228
Sugar Land, Tex. (state penitentiary)
    191, 212, 213, 214
Sukey jumps - *See* Country picnics/frolics
Summit, Miss. 186, 187
Sumterville, Ala. 97
Sunflower, Miss. 148
Sunflower County, Miss. 148
Sunnyland (train) 207, 218, 232
Sunset Route (Southern Pacific) 318
Sunshine Special (train) 86, 217
Sun times - *See* Local/sun times
Switch engines 229
Tallahassee, Fla. 214
Tank cars 144
Teets Bros. Palmetto Shows 244
Temple Lumber Co. 78
Tennessee 101, 167, 175
Tennessee, Coal, Iron & Railroad Co.
    179-82
Tennessee River 104
Tent shows 245, 248, 266
Terminals - *See* Railroads (depots)
Texarkana, Ark. 114
Texas 113, 128, 167, 172, 204, 212, 213,
    214, 217, 283, 310
Texas & New Orleans RR 42-4, 77-8
Texas & Pacific Ry
    77, 79, 86, 114, 171, 217, 252
Texas Mexican Ry. Co. 21
Texas Midland RR 79
Texas South-Eastern RR 78
Texas Special (train) 41
Thayer, Mo. 209
Three Forks, Okl. 315
Tioga County, N.Y. 204
Tipples 50
TOBA 245, 263, 267
Toccoa, Ga. 91
Tolliver's Circus 251
Tombigbee River 96
Topeka, Kan. 279
Tram roads - *See* Dummy lines
Transfer boats - *See* Float bridges
Traveling man/black trickster hero
    250, 304
Travelling shows
    239, 266, 268, 281, 293-4, 296
Trenton, Tenn. 101

General Index

Trinity River 128
Trinity Valley Southern RR 78
Troy, Ill. 205
Tryon, N.C. 163
Tupelo, Miss. 100
Turpentine industry
   169, 294
   - camps 170-1, 309-10
Tuscaloosa, Ala. 96, 99, 116
Tutwiler, Miss. 143, 144, 148, 153
Twentieth Century Limited (train) 206
Tylertown, Miss. 186
Uncle Tom's Cabin shows 246
Underground Railroad 26
Uneeda Biscuits 37
Union Station
   - *See* under Railroads (depots)
United States Steel Corp. 179
Upshur County, Tex. 315
US Supreme Court 153
Vagrancy 165
Vanderbilt, William H. (President of New York Central RR) 200
Vaudeville 131
Vaudeville-blues
   35, 39, 132, 169, 172, 213, 216, 245, 246, 265, 273, 281, 282, 286, 290, 292
Vaughan/Vaughn, Miss. 101-3
Verdigris River 315
Vicksburg, Miss. 168, 184, 191
Victor (record label) 152, 171
Virginia 39, 167, 184, 214, 309
Virginia Central RR 167
Vocalion (record label) 114
Wabash Cannonball (train) 285
Wabash Ry. Co. 109, 285
Wagoner, Okl. 315
Wallace, Lovella 190
Walter L. Main Circus 259, 260, 262
Waring, Raymond & Company Circus 242
Warren & Corsicana Pacific Ry. Co. 78
Warrenton Railroad 164
Warrior River 97, 99, 179
Washington, DC 51
Washington County, Ala. 92
Washington County RR 171
Water haul 146
Waycross, Ga. 214, 294
Wayne County, Miss. 81, 92
Waynesboro, Miss. 92
Waynesville, N.C. 168
Webb, Simm T. (fireman) 103

West Africa 201
Western & Atlantic RR 163, 173, 175, 284
Western North Carolina RR 167, 169
Western Railway of Alabama 99
West Point, Miss. 99
West Virginia 50, 175
Wharves 128
Whipping post 162
Whistle stop - *See* Flag stop
Whitehaven, Tenn. 192
Wiergate, Tex. 191
Wilson, Charles (author/historian) 240
Wooden car era 41, 132
Work Jr., John W. (University professor/musicologist) 281
Worksongs
   42, 51, 88, 97, 163, 187, 190, 312
Works Project Administration (WPA) 192, 218
Wortham, Tex. 89
Yazoo (reissue label) 22
Yazoo & Mississippi Valley RR 143-58, 191
Yazoo City, Miss. 148, 149
Yazoo Delta RR 148, 156
Yellow Dog (train) - *See preceding entry*
Yellow dog contracts
   150-1, 153, 154, 157, 158
Yellow pine 186
Yellow Pine, Ala. 92
Yoruba 201

ILLUSTRATIONS & PHOTO CREDITS

Ads: page 53 courtesy *Blues Unlimited*; 54 courtesy *Southern Business Directory & General Commercial Advertiser*; 87 courtesy Everett De Golyer collection; 127 courtesy *Railways Past, Present & Future*, Freeman G. Allen; 145 courtesy *The Bluesmen*, Sam Charters; 205 courtesy *Men & Iron*, Edward Hungerford; 210 courtesy *78 Quarterly*; 260 courtesy Tom Parkinson & Charles C. Phillips collection; 291 courtesy author's collection; 295 courtesy *Black Pearls*, Daphne Duval Harrison; 315 courtesy Montgomery Ward.

Back cover photo: Courtesy author's collection.

Front cover photo: Photo by A.E. Brown, from author's collection.

Label shots on front cover courtesy Paul Swinton and John Tefteller's Rare Records; pages 89, 220, 222 and 279 courtesy John Tefteller's Rare Records; 109, 115, 169, 216, 274 and 319 courtesy Paul Swinton; 223 courtesy Alasdair Blaazer.

Drawings: page 29 courtesy *Railway Passenger Travel*, Horace Porter; 30 courtesy *Railroads Triumphant*, Albro Martin; 33 courtesy *Men & Iron*, Edward Hungerford; 36 courtesy *Pioneer Railroads*, Hank W. Bowman; 125 courtesy *The Great Yellow Fleet*, John H. White Jr; 132 courtesy *The American Railroad Freight Car*, John H. White Jr; 174 by Harry Fenn, courtesy *Picturesque America (Volume 1)*, William Cullen Bryant (Ed); 186 courtesy *Hattiesburg – A Pictorial History*, Kenneth G. McCarty; 246 courtesy Circus World Museum; 257 by Howard Armstrong, courtesy *78 Quarterly*; 277 courtesy *The Trains We Rode*, Lucius Beebe; 309 courtesy *The Story of American Railroads*, Stewart Holbrook; 324 by Ted Rose, courtesy *Rails Across America*, William L. Withun.

Maps: page 77 courtesy Peter Maxwell; 80 courtesy *Whistle In The Piney Woods*, Robert S. Maxwell; 95 courtesy *Railroads In Alabama Politics 1875-1914*, James F. Doster; 108 by Harry C. Long, courtesy *A History Of The City Of Cairo*, John M. Lansden; 111 courtesy William Stanley Hole Special Collections Library; 149 courtesy author's collection.

Photographs: pages 34 and 114 courtesy *The Chicago & Alton Railroad*, Gene V. Glendinning; 38 courtesy *Knoxville*, Betsy Beeler Creckmore; 40 courtesy *The American Railroad Passenger Car*, John H. White Jr; 43L, 43R, 57, 74, 78 and 208 courtesy Paul Oliver; 44 by Philip R. Hastings, courtesy *The Central Pacific & The Southern Pacific*, Lucius Beebe; 56, 91, 113, 124, 128, 131 and 226 courtesy author's collection; 59 courtesy *Logging Roads of Alabama*, Thomas Lawson Jr; 60 courtesy East Texas Research Center; 62 courtesy *The Louisiana & Arkansas Railway*, James R. Fair; 72 courtesy Institute of Jazz Studies; 86, 217, 313 and 316 courtesy Everett De Golyer collection; 92 and 93 courtesy Armistead Mobile Museum photo archives; 102 courtesy Water Valley Casey Jones Railroad Museum; 102 (inset) courtesy *Long Steel Rail*, Norm Cohen; 105 and 177 courtesy *The American Railroad Freight Car*, John H. White Jr; 107 courtesy *Mississippi Harvest*, Nollie Hickman; 112 courtesy William D. Middleton collection; 122 and 129 courtesy *The Great Yellow Fleet*, John H. White Jr; 130 courtesy *Rails Across America*, William L. Withun; 135 and 286 courtesy *Blues Unlimited*; 138 courtesy *Yesterday's Atlanta*, Franklin M. Garrett; 144 by and © Max Haymes; 147 courtesy Dai Thomas; 148 courtesy *Yazoo – Its Legends And Legacies*, Harriett DeCell and Joanne Pritchard; 156 by Louis Saillard, courtesy *Green Diamond*; 164 courtesy Paul Swinton; 166 courtesy North Carolina Archives of History; 168 courtesy *Encyclopedia of Southern Culture*, Charles Wilson & William Ferris; 178 courtesy *Nashville, Chattanooga & St. Louis Railway*, Richard E. Prince; 181 and 263 courtesy *Yesterday's Birmingham*, Malcolm C. McMillan; 185 courtesy Thomas Duke Park Papers, Birmingham Public Library; 201 and 205 courtesy *Men & Iron*, Edward Hungerford; 206 by C.E. Orr, courtesy author's collection; 215 courtesy *Atlantic Coast Line Railroad*, Richard E. Prince; 224 and 225 by Alfred Johnson, courtesy *The Trains We Rode*, Lucius Beebe & Charles Clegg; 244 courtesy Harry Armstrong collection; 251 courtesy Keeneland-Cook collection; 252 by Walker Morris, courtesy Joseph T.

Bradbury collection; 256 by Brown Bros., courtesy Howard C. Tibbals collection; 266, 267T and 267B courtesy Woodcock collection; 276 courtesy Library of Congress; 280 by W.E.B. Dubsois, courtesy *Missionary Review*; 285 by Jim Shaughnessy, courtesy *The Central Pacific & The Southern Pacific*, Lucius Beebe; 302 by Charles Clegg, courtesy *The Central Pacific & The Southern Pacific*, Lucius Beebe; 305 courtesy of Hard Travellin', Kenneth Allsopp; 322 courtesy *Juke Blues*; 326 by Roland E. Collons, courtesy of Arthur D. Dubin.

Sheet music: page 241 courtesy author's collection.

Tickets: page 261 and 262 courtesy Tom Parkinson & Charles C. Phillips collection.

OTHER TITLES FROM MUSIC MENTOR BOOKS

American Rock'n'Roll: The UK Tours 1956-72
Ian Wallis
ISBN 0-9519888-6-7 *(pbk, 424 pages)* **NOW ONLY £19.99**

The first-ever detailed overview of every visit to these shores by American (and Canadian!) rock'n'rollers. It's all here: over 400 pages of tour itineraries, support acts, show reports, TV appearances and other items of interest. Illustrated with dozens of original tour programmes, ads, ticket stubs and great live shots, many rare or previously unpublished.

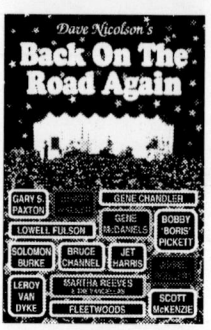

Back On The Road Again
Dave Nicolson
ISBN 0-9547068-2-X *(pbk, 216 pp)* **£12.99**

A third book of interviews by Dave Nicolson in the popular *On The Road* series, this time with more of a Sixties flavour: Solomon Burke, Gene Chandler, Bruce Channel, Lowell Fulson, Jet Harris, Gene McDaniels, Scott McKenzie, Gary S. Paxton, Bobby 'Boris' Pickett, Martha Reeves & The Vandellas, Jimmie Rodgers, Gary Troxel (Fleetwoods), Leroy Van Dyke and Junior Walker.

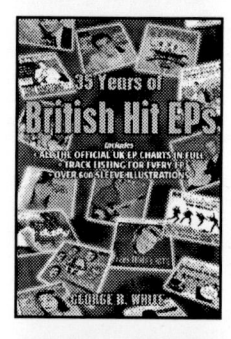

(35 Years of) British Hit EPs
George R. White
ISBN 0-9519888-1-6 *(pbk, 256 pages)* **£16.99**

At last, a chart book dedicated to British hit EPs! Includes a history of the format, an artist-by-artist listing of every 7-inch EP hit from 1955 to 1989 (with full track details for each record), analyses of chart performance, and — for the first time ever — the official UK 1960-67 EP charts reproduced in their entirety. Profusely illustrated with *over 600* sleeve shots. A collector's dream!

Daynce of the Peckerwoods: The Badlands of Texas Music
Michael H. Price
ISBN 0-9547068-5-4 *(pbk, 350 pages)* **£18.99**

From a childhood spent among such key roots-music figures as Bob Wills and Big Joe Turner, and an extended dual career as a musician and journalist, Michael H. Price has forged this frenzied chronicle of life among the denizens of the vanishing borderlands of Texas' indigenous music scene over the past half-century. Contains essays on Billy Briggs, Ornette Coleman, the Light Crust Doughboys, Big Bill Lister, Rudy Ray Moore, Eck Robertson, Ray Sharpe, Robert Shaw, Major Bill Smith, Stevie Ray Vaughan and many more.

Elvis: A Musical Inventory 1939-55
Richard Boussiron
ISBN 0-9519888-7-5 *(pbk, 264 pages)* £17.99

This 'musical inventory' is the product of over 30 years' original research including interviews with Elvis' teacher, church ministers, work colleagues and fellow musicians. Presented like a discography, it is an extraordinarily detailed listing of the King's earliest musical influences, with full historical details shown for each song. The book also includes — for the first time anywhere — complete details of all the legendary Sun sessions, taken directly from the personal files of Marion Keisker. Quite simply a 'must have' for anyone with an interest in early Elvis.

Elvis & Buddy — Linked Lives
Alan Mann
ISBN 0-9519888-5-9 *(pbk, 160 pages)* **NOW ONLY £9.99**

The achievements of Elvis Presley and Buddy Holly have been extensively documented, but until now little if anything has been known about the many ways in which their lives were interconnected. The author examines each artist's early years, comparing their backgrounds and influences, chronicling all their meetings and examining the many amazing parallels in their lives, careers and tragic deaths. Over 50 photographs, including many rare/previously unpublished.

Let The Good Times Rock! — A Fan's Notes On Post-War American Roots Music
Bill Millar
ISBN 0-9519888-8-3 *(pbk, 362 pages)* £18.99

For almost four decades, the name 'Bill Millar' has been synonymous with the very best in British music writing. This fabulous new book collects together 49 of his best pieces — some previously unpublished — in a thematic compilation covering hillbilly, rockabilly, R&B, rock'n'roll, doo-wop, swamp pop and soul. Includes essays on acappella, doo-wop and blue-eyed soul, as well as detailed profiles of some of the most fascinating and influential personalities of each era.

Long Distance Information: Chuck Berry's Recorded Legacy
Fred Rothwell
ISBN 0-9519888-2-4 *(pbk, 352 pages)* £18.99

The lowdown on every recording Chuck Berry has ever made. Includes an overview of his life and career, his influences, the stories behind his most famous compositions, full session details, listings of all his key US/UK vinyl and CD releases (including track details), TV and film appearances, and much, much more. Over 100 illustrations including label shots, vintage ads and previously unpublished photos.

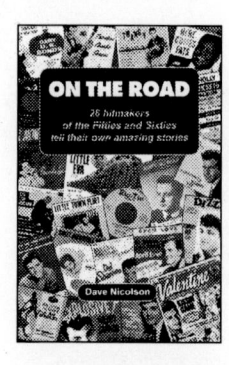

On The Road
Dave Nicolson
ISBN 0-9519888-4-0 *(pbk, 256 pages)* **NOW ONLY £14.99**

Gary 'US' Bonds, Pat Boone, Freddy Cannon, Crickets Jerry Allison, Sonny Curtis and Joe B. Mauldin, Bo Diddley, Dion, Fats Domino, Duane Eddy, Frankie Ford, Charlie Gracie, Brian Hyland, Marv Johnson, Ben E. King, Brenda Lee, Little Eva, Chris Montez, Johnny Moore (Drifters), Gene Pitney, Johnny Preston, Tommy Roe, Del Shannon, Edwin Starr, Johnny Tillotson and Bobby Vee tell their own fascinating stories. Over 150 illustrations including vintage ads, record sleeves, label shots, sheet music covers, etc.

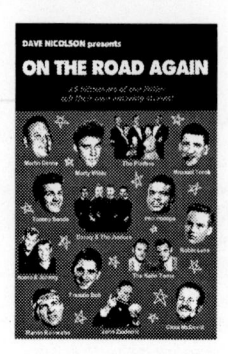

On The Road Again
Dave Nicolson
ISBN 0-9519888-9-1 *(pbk, 206 pp)* **NOW ONLY £12.99**

In this second book of interviews with the stars of pop and rock'n'roll, Dave Nicolson delves deeper into the dazzling and often treacherous world of the music industry, with more revealing and highly personal first-hand accounts from 15 pioneering performers who were at the forefront of the Fifties' music revolution: Freddie Bell, Martin Denny, Johnny Farina (Santo & Johnny), the Kalin Twins, Robin Luke, Chas McDevitt, Phil Phillips, Marvin Rainwater, Herb Reed (Platters), Tommy Sands, Joe Terranova (Danny & The Juniors), Mitchell Torok, Marty Wilde and the 'Cool Ghoul' himself, John Zacherle.

**Music Mentor books
are available from all good bookshops
or by mail order from:**

**Music Mentor Books
69 Station Road
Upper Poppleton
YORK YO26 6PZ
England**

Telephone/Fax: 01904 330308
International Telephone/Fax: +44 1904 330308
Email: music.mentor@lineone.net
Website: http://musicmentor0.tripod.com